BEYOND THE QUMRAN COMMUNITY

BEYOND THE QUMRAN COMMUNITY

The Sectarian Movement of the Dead Sea Scrolls

John J. Collins

WILLIAM B. EERDMANS PUBLISHING COMPANY
GRAND RAPIDS, MICHIGAN / CAMBRIDGE, U.K.

Published 2010 by
Wm. B. Eerdmans Publishing Co.
2140 Oak Industrial Drive N.E., Grand Rapids, Michigan 49505 /
P.O. Box 163, Cambridge CB3 9PU U.K.

Printed in the United States of America

16 15 14 13 12 11 10   7 6 5 4 3 2 1

Library of Congress Cataloging-in-Publication Data

Collins, John Joseph, 1946-
Beyond the Qumran community: the Sectarian Movement of the Dead Sea Scrolls /
John J. Collins.
p.   cm.
Includes bibliographical references and index.
ISBN 978-0-8028-2887-3 (pbk.: alk. paper)
1. Qumran community — History.   2. Essenes — History.
3. Jews — History — 586 B.C.–70 A.D.   4. Dead Sea scrolls.   I. Title.

BM175.Q6C65   2010
296.8′15 — dc22

2009035864

www.eerdmans.com

Contents

Acknowledgments

This book incorporates material from the following articles:

"The Nature and Aims of the Sect Known from the Dead Sea Scrolls." Pages 31-52 in Anthony Hilhorst, Émile Puech, and Eibert Tigchelaar, eds., *Flores Florentino: Dead Sea Scrolls and Other Early Jewish Studies in Honour of Florentino García Martínez*. JSJSup 122. Leiden: Brill, 2007. ISBN 978-90-04-16292-1.

"The *Yaḥad* and 'the Qumran Community.'" Pages 81-96 in Charlotte Hempel and Judith Lieu, eds., *Biblical Traditions in Transmission: Essays in Honour of Michael A. Knibb*. JSJSup 111. Leiden: Brill, 2006. ISBN 978-90-04-13997-8.

"The Time of the Teacher: An Old Debate Renewed." Pages 212-29 in Peter W. Flint, Emanuel Tov, and James C. VanderKam, eds., *Studies in the Hebrew Bible, Qumran, and the Septuagint Presented to Eugene Ulrich*. VTSup 101. Leiden: Brill, 2006. ISBN 978-90-04-13738-7.

"Forms of Community in the Dead Sea Scrolls." Pages 97-111 in S. M. Paul, R. A. Kraft, L. H. Schiffman, and W. W. Fields, eds., *Emanuel: Studies in Hebrew Bible, Septuagint and Dead Sea Scrolls in Honor of Emanuel Tov*. VTSup 94. Leiden: Brill, 2003. ISBN 978-90-04-12679-4.

"Josephus on the Essenes: The Sources of His Information." Forthcoming in Zuleika Rodgers with Margaret Daly-Denton and Anne Fitzpatrick McKinley, eds., *A Wandering Galilean: Essays in Honour of Sean Freyne*. JSJSup 132. Leiden: Brill, 2009.

This material is reused with permission of E. J. Brill, Leiden.

A Note on Translations

Except where otherwise indicated, translations of the Dead Sea Scrolls are from F. García Martínez and E. J. Tigchelaar, *The Dead Sea Scrolls Study Edition* (Leiden: Brill, 1997), with some adaptations.

Translations identified as those of J. Baumgarten are from Joseph M. Baumgarten, with James H. Charlesworth, Lidija Novakovic, and Henry W. M. Rietz, "Damascus Document: 4Q266-273 (4QD a-h)." Pages 1-185 in *Damascus Document II: Some Works of the Torah and Related Documents.* Vol. 3 of *The Dead Sea Scrolls: Hebrew, Aramaic, and Greek Texts with English Translations,* ed. James H. Charlesworth (PTSDSSP; Louisville: Westminster John Knox, 1995), slightly adapted.

Translations identified as those of J. H. Charlesworth are from *Rule of the Community and Related Documents.* Vol. 1 of *The Dead Sea Scrolls: Hebrew, Aramaic, and Greek Texts with English Translations,* ed. James H. Charlesworth (PTSDSSP; Louisville: Westminster John Knox, 1994).

Translations identified as those of M. P. Horgan are from "Habakkuk Pesher (1QpHab)." Pages 157-85 in *Pesharim, Other Commentaries, and Related Documents,* vol. 6B of *The Dead Sea Scrolls: Hebrew, Aramaic, and Greek Texts with English Translations,* ed. James H. Charlesworth (PTSDSSP; Louisville: Westminster John Knox, 2002).

Translations identified as those of J. VanderKam are from James C. VanderKam, *The Book of Jubilees* (Leuven: Peeters, 1989).

Abbreviations

ABD	*Anchor Bible Dictionary*, ed. D. N. Freedman. 6 vols. New York: Doubleday, 1992
ABIG	Arbeiten zur Bibel und ihrer Geschichte
AGJU	Arbeiten zur Geschichte des antiken Judentums und des Urchristentums
ANRW	*Aufstieg und Niedergang der römischen Welt*
ANYAS	Annual of the New York Academy of Sciences
BA	*Biblical Archaeologist*
BAR	*Biblical Archaeology Review*
BASOR	*Bulletin of the American Schools of Oriental Research*
BETL	Bibliotheca ephemeridum theologicarum lovaniensium
BibSem	Biblical Seminar
BJS	Brown Judaic Studies
BZAW	Beihefte zur Zeitschrift für die alttestamentliche Wissenschaft
CBQ	*Catholic Biblical Quarterly*
CJA	Christianity and Judaism in Antiquity
CQS	Companion to the Qumran Scrolls
CRINT	Compendia rerum iudaicarum ad Novum Testamentum
DJD	Discoveries in the Judaean Desert
DSD	*Dead Sea Discoveries*
EBib	Études bibliques
EDSS	*Encyclopedia of the Dead Sea Scrolls*, ed. Lawrence H. Schiffman and James C. VanderKam. 2 vols. New York: Oxford University Press, 2000
ErIsr	*Erets Israel*
HeyJ	*Heythrop Journal*
HTR	*Harvard Theological Review*
HUCA	*Hebrew Union College Annual*
IEJ	*Israel Exploration Journal*

Abbreviations

JAOS	*Journal of the American Oriental Society*
JBL	*Journal of Biblical Literature*
JJS	*Journal of Jewish Studies*
JNES	*Journal of Near Eastern Studies*
JSJ	*Journal for the Study of Judaism*
JSJSup	Journal for the Study of Judaism Supplements
JSOT	*Journal for the Study of the Old Testament*
JSOTSup	Journal for the Study of the Old Testament Supplements
JSPSup	Journal for the Study of the Pseudepigrapha Supplements
JSS	*Journal of Semitic Studies*
LCL	Loeb Classical Library
LHB/OTS	Library of Hebrew Bible/Old Testament Studies
NTOA	Novum Testamentum et Orbis Antiquus
NTOA.SA	Novum Testamentum et Orbis Antiquus, Series Archaeologica
PEQ	*Palestine Exploration Quarterly*
PTSDSSP	Princeton Theological Seminary Dead Sea Scrolls Project
PW	A. F. Pauly, ed., *Realencyclopädie der classischen Altertumswissenschaft,* rev. G. Wissowa. Stuttgart: Metzler, 1893–
PWSup	Supplement to PW
QC	*Qumran Chronicle*
RB	*Revue biblique*
RBL	*Review of Biblical Literature*
RelSoc	Religion and Society (Berlin)
RevQ	*Revue de Qumran*
SAOC	Studies in Ancient Oriental Civilization
SBFLA	*Studii biblici franciscani liber annuus*
SBL	Society of Biblical Literature
SBLAB	SBL Academia biblica
SBLMS	SBL Monograph Series
SBLSCS	SBL Septuagint and Cognate Studies
SBLSymS	SBL Symposium Series
SBT	Studies in Biblical Theology
SDSSRL	Studies in the Dead Sea Scrolls and Related Literature
SFSHJ	South Florida Studies in the History of Judaism
SJLA	Studies in Judaism in Late Antiquity
SNTSMS	Society for New Testament Studies Monograph Series
SPA	*Studia Philonica Annual*
SPB	Studia Post-Biblica
STDJ	Studies on the Texts of the Desert of Judah
SUNT	Studien zur Umwelt des Neuen Testaments
TA	*Tel Aviv*
TLZ	*Theologische Literaturzeitung*

VT	*Vetus Testamentum*
VTSup	Supplements to Vetus Testamentum
WUNT	Wissenschaftliche Untersuchungen zum Neuen Testament

Illustrations

(following page 121)

Historical Chart

168 BCE	Maccabean revolt
161 BCE	Death of Judas Maccabee; Jonathan becomes leader
152 BCE	Jonathan Maccabee becomes high priest
143/142 BCE	Death of Jonathan; Simon becomes high priest
135/134 BCE	Death of Simon
135/134–104 BCE	John Hyrcanus
104–103 BCE	Aristobulus I takes the title King
103–76 BCE	Alexander Jannaeus
76–67 BCE	Salome Alexandra is queen; Hyrcanus II is high priest
67–63 BCE	Aristobulus
63 BCE	Jerusalem captured by Pompey
63–40 BCE	Hyrcanus II restored as high priest
40 BCE	Parthian invasion
40–37 BCE	Antigonus
37–4 BCE	Herod the Great
31 BCE	Battle of Actium; major earthquake in Judea
4 BCE	Disturbances after Herod's death
66–74 CE	Jewish revolt against Rome
132–135 CE	Revolt of Bar Kokhba

Introduction

At some time in late 1946 or early 1947, three Taʿamireh Bedouin discovered several large clay jars in a cave near Qumran. One of these held three bundles wrapped in linen, which contained ancient scrolls, eventually identified as the book of Isaiah (1QIsaᵃ), a commentary or *pesher* on the book of Habakkuk (1QpHab), and a rule, or *serek*, for a religious community (1QS). These scrolls were purchased by the Orthodox Syrian Metropolitan, Mar Samuel, of Saint Mark's Monastery. They were eventually brought to the American Schools of Oriental Research (now the Albright Institute) in Jerusalem, where they were photographed by John Trever. Other scrolls, discovered a few months later, apparently in the same cave, were acquired by Eleazar Sukenik of the Hebrew University. Mar Samuel tried to sell the scrolls he had acquired, plus another one containing the *Genesis Apocryphon,* in the United States for six years. They would eventually be purchased by Sukenik's son, Yigael Yadin, and brought back to Jerusalem in 1955.

In the meantime, excavations at Qumran had brought to light other caves and the ruins of an ancient settlement. In 1952 the Bedouin discovered Cave 4, at the edge of the settlement, with a huge trove of fragmentary texts. Further discoveries in the surrounding area continued to 1956, when Cave 11 was discovered by the Bedouin.[1]

---

1. For an account of the discoveries see W. W. Fields, "Discovery and Purchase," *EDSS* 1.208-12; idem, *The Dead Sea Scrolls: A Short History* (Leiden: Brill, 2006); James VanderKam, *The Dead Sea Scrolls Today* (Grand Rapids: Eerdmans, 1994) 3-8.

A Sect or Monastic Order

The initial press release by the American Schools of Oriental Research, published in the *Times* of London on April 12, 1948, identified one of the scrolls as "a manual of discipline of some comparatively little-known sect or monastic order, possibly the Essenes."[2] From an early point, it was assumed that the scrolls were the library of the community described in this "manual," and that the community had inhabited the settlement at Qumran. Hence the sect came to be referred to as "the Qumran community." We know from Pliny the Elder that there was an Essene settlement near the shore of the Dead Sea, and there are numerous points of similarity between the *Manual of Discipline* and the accounts of the Essenes in the writings of Philo and Josephus.[3] Hence the further identification of "the Qumran community" as Essene. The Essene identification was proposed independently by Sukenik in 1948, and was worked out in detail by André Dupont-Sommer in 1951.[4]

These identifications have commanded a remarkable consensus for six decades. This consensus is still widely held, but all aspects of it have become controversial in recent years. We will return later in this book to the identification with the Essenes and the discussion of the site, but at the outset it is important to realize that references to "the Qumran community" are problematic. The issue here is not just the identification of the site, although that too is disputed, but the fact that the *Manual of Discipline* or *Community Rule*, as it is now called (*Serek ha-Yaḥad,* or 1QS), is quite clearly written with more than one community in mind: "In this way shall they behave in all their places of residence. . . . In every place where there are ten men of the council of the community, there should not be missing among them a priest . . . and in the place in which the ten assemble

2. See VanderKam, *Dead Sea Scrolls Today,* 6. The release was written by Millar Burrows.

3. Pliny, *Nat. Hist.* 5.73; see especially Josephus, *J.W.* 2.119-61; and T. S. Beall, *Josephus' Description of the Essenes Illustrated by the Dead Sea Scrolls* (SNTSMS 58; Cambridge: Cambridge University Press, 1988).

4. E. L. Sukenik, *Megillot Genuzot mi-Tokh Genizah Qedumah she-Nimṣe'ah be-Midbar Yehudah: Seqirah Rishonah* (Jerusalem: Bialik Institute, 1948); VanderKam, *Dead Sea Scrolls Today,* 5; A. Dupont-Sommer, *Observations sur le Manuel de Discipline découvert près de la Mer Morte* (Paris: Maisonneuve, 1951). See also G. Vermes, *The Complete Dead Sea Scrolls in English* (rev. ed.; London: Penguin, 2004) 3.

there should not be missing a man to interpret the law day and night" (1QS 6:1-8).[5] Indeed, if the association described in this rule book is correctly identified as Essene, we should expect that there would have been more than one settlement or community. Philo tells us that the Essenes "live in a number of towns in Judea, and also in many villages and large groups."[6] Josephus says that "they are not in one town only, but in every town several of them form a colony."[7] Different recensions of the *Community Rule* have been found in Qumran Cave 4 (S is the siglum for all these *Serek* texts),[8] and this has raised the problem as to why different, even contradictory, copies should be preserved, if all these texts were intended for a single community. One possible solution, which has only recently begun to receive serious attention, is that the different forms of the text served different communities within the broader association, and that they were only taken to Qumran and hidden there secondarily, in a time of crisis.[9]

Moreover, the *Community Rule* is not the only rule for a community found at Qumran. Two medieval copies of a text describing a sectarian movement had been found in the genizah of the Ben Ezra Synagogue in Old Cairo in 1896, and published by Solomon Schechter as "fragments of a Zadokite work," in 1910.[10] This text subsequently became known as the

5. See my essay, "Forms of Community in the Dead Sea Scrolls," in Shalom M. Paul, Robert A. Kraft, Lawrence H. Schiffman, and Weston W. Fields, eds., *Emanuel: Studies in Hebrew Bible, Septuagint, and Dead Sea Scrolls in Honour of Emanuel Tov* (VTSup 94; Leiden: Brill, 2003) 97-111; and see further chapter 2 below.

6. Philo, *Apologia pro Iudaeis*, quoted by Eusebius, *Praep. ev.* 8.6-7. Translation of G. Vermes and M. Goodman, eds., *The Essenes According to the Classical Sources* (Sheffield: Sheffield Academic Press, 1989) 27.

7. *J.W.* 2.122; Vermes and Goodman, *Essenes*, 39.

8. Philip S. Alexander and Geza Vermes, *Qumran Cave 4*, vol. XIX: *Serekh ha-Yaḥad and Two Related Texts* (DJD 26; Oxford: Clarendon, 1998).

9. Alison Schofield, "Rereading S: A New Model of Textual Development in Light of the Cave 4 Serekh Copies," *DSD* 15 (2008): 96-120. Her book, *From Qumran to the Yaḥad: A New Paradigm of Textual Development for The Community Rule* (STDJ 77; Leiden: Brill, 2009), had not appeared at the time of writing. On the possibility that scrolls were hidden at Qumran on more than one occasion, see Daniel Stökl Ben Ezra, "Old Caves and Young Caves: A Statistical Reevaluation of a Qumran Consensus," *DSD* 14 (2007): 313-33.

10. S. Schechter, *Fragments of a Zadokite work edited from Hebrew manuscripts in the Cairo Genizah collection now in the possession of the University Library, Cambridge and provided with an English translation, introduction and notes* (Cambridge: Cambridge University Press, 1910). Repr., with a prolegomenon by J. A. Fitzmyer, as *Documents of Jewish Sectaries*, vol. 1: *Fragments of a Zadokite Work* (New York: Ktav, 1970).

Damascus Document, or CD (Cairo Damascus), because of several references to Damascus. When the first scrolls from Qumran were published, it
was immediately obvious that the "Zadokite" work was related to them.[11]
Not only were there similarities in the organization of the communities
described in the two rule books, but CD contained several code names that
now reappeared for the first time in the Scrolls. These included "Teacher of
Righteousness," "sons of Zadok," and "man of the lie." The relationship
was subsequently confirmed when fragments of the *Damascus Rule* were
found in Qumran Cave 4 (D is the siglum for CD plus the Qumran fragments of the rule).[12] The fragments found at Qumran preserve the beginning and end of the text. They contain additional passages not found in
CD. Some of these passages indicate further parallels with the *Community
Rule.* For example, the opening passage (4Q266 1 a-b) addresses the "sons
of light," a designation familiar from the *Instruction on the Two Spirits* in
1QS 3–4, but not found in CD.

The modern discovery of the Dead Sea Scrolls was not the first time
writings had been discovered in that area. A letter by the Nestorian patri-
arch of Seleucia, Timotheus I, about 800 CE reports that books had been
found in a cave near Jericho. These books may have included an ancient
copy of the *Damascus Document,* which would then have been copied and
somehow made its way to Cairo. It is quite possible that the medieval
manuscripts preserve an ancient form of the text.

In light of the striking correspondences between the *Damascus Document* and some of the Scrolls, and the fact that fragments of it were found
at Qumran, scholars drew freely on it in their descriptions of "the Qumran
community." It was obvious, however, that there were significant differences between CD and 1QS. CD explicitly provides for women and children, whereas there is no mention of these in 1QS. Also the terminology
for the community and its officers is somewhat different in the two texts.
In CD *'edah,* "congregation," rather than *yaḥad,* "commune or association," is the preferred term. The *maskil,* who has a central role in 1QS, is
only mentioned twice in CD, in passages that deal with the regulations for
the camps (CD 12:21; 13:22). In contrast, the *mebaqqer,* who has a central

11. H. H. Rowley, *The Zadokite Fragments and the Dead Sea Scrolls* (Oxford: Alden,
1952) 31-33.
12. J. M. Baumgarten, on the basis of transcriptions by J. T. Milik, with contributions
by S. Pfann and A. Yardeni, *Qumran Cave 4,* vol. XIII: *The Damascus Document (4Q266-273)*
(DJD 18; Oxford: Clarendon, 1996).

role in CD, appears rarely in 1QS (6:12, 20). CD lacks the multistage admission procedures that are spelled out in 1QS. There are significant differences in the attitude toward the temple in the two rules.

These differences have been accounted for in different ways. The most widely accepted theory holds that D was a rule for "the marrying Essenes," while S was the rule for a celibate community that lived at Qumran.[13] Thus stated, this explanation is certainly too simple. S clearly provides for several small communities, with a quorum of ten, and cannot be regarded as the rule for a single community at Qumran.[14] D, too, envisions more than one form of community, since it contrasts "the men of perfect holiness" with "those who live in camps according to the order of the land and marry and have children," although it seems to be primarily concerned with the latter.[15] The issue, then, is more complicated than a simple contrast between celibate and marrying Essenes would suggest. It remains true, nonetheless, that D is primarily concerned with married people, while S does not acknowledge them at all.

The paleography (study of the handwriting) of the various manuscripts of S and D found at Qumran suggests that both texts were copied throughout the first century BCE, and that some of the D manuscripts were copied in the early first century CE.[16] This evidence suggests that both rules were in use contemporaneously. Nonetheless, it is plausible that one originated before the other. At various times, scholars have proposed a diachronic explanation of the relationship between the two rule books. J. T. Milik argued for the priority of S, and thought that D reflected Pharisaic influences.[17] This position has been defended recently by Eyal Regev,

13. See especially Vermes, *Complete Dead Sea Scrolls,* 26-48.

14. See my essays, "Forms of Community"; and "The *Yaḥad* and 'the Qumran Community,'" in Charlotte Hempel and Judith M. Lieu, eds., *Biblical Traditions in Transmission: Essays in Honour of Michael A. Knibb* (JSJSup 111; Leiden: Brill, 2006) 81-96.

15. CD 7:5-8. See J. M. Baumgarten, "The Qumran-Essene Restraints on Marriage," in L. H. Schiffman, ed., *Archaeology and History in the Dead Sea Scrolls* (JSPSup 8; Sheffield: JSOT Press, 1990) 13-24.

16. For a concise summary of the dates of the 4Q *Serek* manuscripts see F. M. Cross, "Paleographical Dates of the Manuscripts," in J. H. Charlesworth, ed., *The Dead Sea Scrolls: Hebrew, Aramaic, and Greek Texts with English Translations,* vol. 1: *Rule of the Community and Related Documents* (PTSDSSP; Louisville: Westminster John Knox, 1994) 57. For those of the 4Q D manuscripts see C. Hempel, *The Damascus Texts* (CQS 1; Sheffield: Sheffield Academic Press, 2000) 21-23.

17. J. T. Milik, *Ten Years of Discovery in the Wilderness of Judea* (trans. J. Strugnell; SBT

who further argues that D belongs to "an entirely different movement" from the *yaḥad*.[18] The priority of D has enjoyed greater support in recent years. In an influential monograph published in 1983, Philip Davies argued that the *yaḥad* represented by S was an offshoot that broke away from the parent community, which is reflected in CD, although that document is further complicated by an alleged "Qumran recension."[19] Charlotte Hempel, who also defends the priority of D, has also argued that the communal legislation in D "underwent a process of redaction in order to bring it into line with the Community Rule."[20] Since both rules continued to be copied for a century or so, we have to reckon with the possibility that each influenced the other at some points. Nonetheless, I will argue that D preserves the older and more original form of the communal legislation, and that S can be seen to have developed from it at various points.[21] Davies was right that CD should not be assimilated to 1QS, but should be studied first in its own right. We will accordingly begin by analyzing the kind of community envisioned in D, and then examine S, and the relationship between the two. But while the communities envisioned in each rule book are distinct, I will argue that they were not separated by any schism. Rather, they should be seen as complementary branches of a larger movement, one of which aspired to a higher degree of holiness than the other.

1/26; London: SCM, 1963) 83-93. F. M. Cross, *The Ancient Library of Qumran* (3rd ed.; BibSem 30; Sheffield: Sheffield Academic Press, 1995; 1st ed. 1958) 71 n. 2, also seems to assume the priority of S, since he argues that in the development of Essenism the term "camp" replaced *yaḥad* for all but the desert settlement. Cross assumed that *yaḥad* refers to the settlement at Qumran.

18. Eyal Regev, "The *Yaḥad* and the *Damascus Covenant*: Structure, Organization and Relationship," *RevQ* 21 (2003): 233-62, especially 62.

19. Philip R. Davies, *The Damascus Covenant: An Interpretation of the "Damascus Document"* (JSOTSup 25; Sheffield: JSOT Press, 1983). He finds the "Qumranic recension" especially in CD 19:33b–20:34 (pp. 173-97).

20. C. Hempel, *The Laws of the Damascus Document: Sources, Traditions and Redaction* (STDJ 29; Leiden: Brill, 1998) 191.

21. So now also Stephen Hultgren, *From the Damascus Covenant to the Covenant of the Community: Literary, Historical, and Theological Studies in the Dead Sea Scrolls* (STDJ 66; Leiden: Brill, 2007).

Sectarianism

I will follow scholarly convention in referring to this movement, as exemplified in both D and S, as a "sect." I use the term in the Weberian sense of "a religious community founded on voluntary membership achieved through qualification."[22] A sect is first of all a voluntary association, and as such presupposes a deliberate choice and a high level of intentionality on the part of its members. More specifically, it is a voluntary association that is in tension to a greater or lesser degree with the wider society of which it is a part.[23] The sociologists Rodney Stark and William Sims Bainbridge speak of a sect as "a deviant religious organization," understanding "deviance" as tension with the sociocultural environment.[24] The tension can be measured in terms of *difference, antagonism,* and *separation.* In the case of the communities described in the Scrolls, there is clear separation from the rest of Judaism, marked by procedures for admission and expulsion. The antagonism of the members to outsiders, who are regarded as "the sons of the pit," is evident on every page of the sectarian writings. The label "sectarian," then, hardly seems problematic in the context of these communities.[25] Whether other so-called Jewish sects, such as the Pharisees or the Sadducees, qualify as sectarian from a sociological point of view is another question, which does not concern us here.[26]

22. David J. Chalcraft, "The Development of Weber's Sociology of Sects: Encouraging a New Fascination," in idem, ed., *Sectarianism in Early Judaism: Sociological Advances* (London: Equinox, 2007) 27; cf. 33. On the problem of defining a sect see further Jutta Jokiranta, "'Sectarianism' of the Qumran 'Sect': Sociological Notes," *RevQ* 20 (2001): 223-39.

23. The emphasis on tension is associated especially with the work of Rodney Stark and William Sims Bainbridge, *The Future of Religion: Secularization, Revival, and Cult Formation* (Berkeley: University of California Press, 1985); idem, *A Theory of Religion* (Toronto Studies in Religion 2; New York: Lang, 1987); idem, *Religion, Deviance, and Social Control* (New York: Routledge, 1996). See Eyal Regev, *Sectarianism in Qumran: A Cross-Cultural Perspective* (RelSoc 45; Berlin: de Gruyter, 2007) 34-35; Jutta Jokiranta, "Identity on a Continuum: Constructing and Expressing Sectarian Social Identity in Qumran *Serakhim* and *Pesharim*" (diss., Helsinki, 2005) 37-38.

24. Stark and Bainbridge, "Sects: Emergence of Schismatic Religious Movements," in *Theory of Religion,* 121-28.

25. Cecilia Wassen and Jutta Jokiranta, "Groups in Tension: Sectarianism in the Damascus Document and the Community Rule," in Chalcraft, ed., *Sectarianism in Early Judaism,* 205-45, show that the Damascus Rule is just as "sectarian" as the *Serek* or *Community Rule.*

26. See the reflections on this issue by Lester L. Grabbe, "When Is a Sect a Sect — or

Some progress has been made in recent years in bringing the insights of comparative sociology to bear on the study of the Scrolls.[27] Sects are typically "greedy" organizations that allow their members little privacy. They typically make absolute claims to truth and are intolerant of outsiders. While there is much to be learned from such comparisons, they are not my focus here. Rather, I wish to concentrate on a close reading of the Scrolls themselves, to establish as far as possible the primary data. Other sectarian movements may provide interesting comparisons, but we can never infer "facts" about a particular, historical movement such as the *yaḥad* from generalizations based on different data.

Sectarian Origins

From the early days of research on the Scrolls there has been a consensus that the movement developed in the mid-second century BCE, and that its separation from the rest of Jewish society was due in large part to a dispute about the high priestly succession.[28] In part this consensus has rested on a quasi-literalistic interpretation of the figure of 390 years after the Babylonian exile, mentioned in CD 1. Taken literally, this would point to a date of 196 BCE for the beginnings of the movement. Everyone is aware that the number is symbolic, taken from Ezek 4:5, but most take it as approximately correct nonetheless.[29] The attempt to derive chronological information from this passage, however, is clearly invalid. The idea that the sect separated from the rest of Judaism because of a quarrel over the high priesthood derives from references in the biblical commentaries or *pesharim* to a

---

Not? Groups and Movements in the Second Temple Period," in Chalcraft, ed., *Sectarianism in Early Judaism,* 114-32.

27. See especially the groundbreaking study of Regev, *Sectarianism in Qumran,* 269-300, who makes comparisons with the Anabaptists, Mennonites, Hutterites, Amish, Puritans, Quakers, and Shakers.

28. For an overview see James C. VanderKam, "Identity and History of the Community," in Peter W. Flint and James C. VanderKam, eds., *The Dead Sea Scrolls after Fifty Years: A Comprehensive Assessment* (2 vols.; Leiden: Brill, 1998–99) 2.507-23. This theory was first proposed by Geza Vermes, *Les manuscrits du désert de Juda* (2nd ed.; Paris: Desclée, 1954; 1st ed. 1953) 70-104. Compare Vermes, *Complete Dead Sea Scrolls,* 49-66. See also Milik, *Ten Years,* 44-98; Cross, *Ancient Library,* 88-120.

29. So recently Hanan Eshel, *The Dead Sea Scrolls and the Hasmonean State* (SDSSRL; Grand Rapids: Eerdmans, 2008) 30-31.

conflict between the Teacher of Righteousness and a figure called the Wicked Priest. The high priestly succession was disrupted at the time of the Maccabean revolt, and was usurped by the Hasmonean (Maccabean) family, beginning in 152 BCE when Jonathan Maccabee assumed the high priesthood. Scholars accordingly drew the inference that the Wicked Priest was "wicked" because he was illegitimate. The references in the *pesharim* are in code, and are difficult to decipher, but I believe that they do preserve a memory of a historical quarrel. There is no indication, however, that it was this quarrel that led to the rise of the sectarian movement.

Our knowledge of the issues that led to the separation of the sect from the rest of Judaism was transformed by the belated publication of the text known as *Miqṣat Maʿaśe Ha-Torah* (Some of the Works of the Law), or 4QMMT, which was made public only in 1984.[30] This text states explicitly that the reasons for separation concerned the interpretation of religious law *(halakah)* and calendrical differences. There is no mention of any dispute about the high priesthood. Neither is the high priesthood mentioned as an issue in the *Damascus Document,* which discusses several points of dispute that led to the formation of a new covenant.[31] The Wicked Priest is mentioned only in the *pesharim.* Even there, he is never actually said to be illegitimate. I will argue that the dispute between the Teacher and the Wicked Priest is likely to have taken place at a later point in the Teacher's career, in the first century BCE rather than in the second. The sectarian movement had its roots in the late second century BCE, but it did not arise from a dispute about the high priesthood.

---

30. Elisha Qimron and John Strugnell, "An Unpublished Halakhic Letter from Qumran," in J. Amitai, ed., *Biblical Archaeology Today: Proceedings of the International Congress on Biblical Archaeology, Jerusalem, April 1984* (Jerusalem: Israel Exploration Society, 1985) 400-407; idem, *Qumran Cave 4,* vol. V: *Miqṣat Maʿaśe Ha-Torah* (DJD 10; Oxford: Clarendon, 1994).

31. See already my essay, "The Origin of the Qumran Community: A Review of the Evidence," in Maurya P. Horgan and Paul J. Kobelski, eds., *To Touch the Text: Biblical and Related Studies in Honor of Joseph A. Fitzmyer, S.J.* (New York: Crossroad, 1989) 159-78; repr. in my *Seers, Sibyls, and Sages in Hellenistic-Roman Judaism* (JSJSup 54; Leiden: Brill, 1997) 239-60.

The Essenes

I take up the question of the identification of this sect with the Essenes only after I have discussed the evidence of the Scrolls. In my judgment, the reasons for identifying this sect as Essene are still cogent. The *yaḥad*, as described in the *Serek* texts, resembles the Essenes more closely than any other known group. It remains true, however, that there are considerable discrepancies between the Greek and Latin accounts of the Essenes and what we find in the Scrolls. The most controversial item here is the question of celibacy, which is never prescribed explicitly in the Scrolls, although many scholars believe that it is implied. Also the Greek and Latin authors give no indication of the apocalyptic and messianic beliefs of the sect. If the movement described in the Scrolls is indeed to be identified with the Essenes, then the authors of the Greek and Latin accounts wrote as outsiders, who had only a superficial knowledge of the nature and aims of the movement.

Qumran

It is the thesis of this book that the sectarian movement known from the Scrolls cannot be identified simply as "the Qumran community." Qumran was at most one of many settlements of the sect. Nonetheless, the question whether it was in fact a sectarian settlement holds considerable interest. The main arguments in favor of the view that it was a sectarian site are the notice in Pliny that there was an Essene settlement in this region, the fact that the Scrolls were found within a stone's throw of the site, and the extraordinary number of stepped pools, which are most plausibly interpreted as immersion pools or *miqva'ot*. These considerations argue very strongly that Qumran was a sectarian settlement, at least in the last phase of its history, in the first century CE. Whether it was already a sectarian settlement in the Hasmonean period, in the first half of the first century BCE, is more difficult to say.[32] On the one hand, the location of the site, in an area dominated by Hasmonean fortresses, is problematic, at a time when

---

32. See now Robert R. Cargill, *Qumran Through Real Time: A Virtual Reconstruction of Qumran and the Dead Sea Scrolls* (Piscataway, NJ: Gorgias, 2009), which appeared after this book had gone to press.

there was evidently high tension between the sectarians and the Hasmonean rulers. On the other hand, there is no archeological evidence to support the view that the site was occupied by different groups in the different phases of its history. The published archeological record, however, is incomplete, and consequently inconclusive. If multiple stepped pools were part of the complex from the beginning, then it was presumably a sectarian settlement from the start, despite the proximity of the Hasmonean fortresses. But the interpretation of the site is bitterly disputed, and will probably continue to be so.

The Focus of This Book

The focus of this book is on the narrowly defined question of the nature of the communities described in the Scrolls. I do not enter here into discussions of the thought world of the sectarians. I have treated the messianic expectations and the apocalyptic worldview of the sectarian texts at length in previous publications.[33] There is, to be sure, much more to be said on the beliefs and practices of these ancient sectarians, but that will have to wait for another occasion.

33. John J. Collins, *The Scepter and the Star: The Messiahs of the Dead Sea Scrolls and Other Ancient Literature* (New York: Doubleday, 1995); idem, *Apocalypticism in the Dead Sea Scrolls* (London: Routledge, 1997). See also John J. Collins and Robert A. Kugler, eds., *Religion in the Dead Sea Scrolls* (SDSSRL; Grand Rapids: Eerdmans, 2000).

CHAPTER ONE

The New Covenant

When the *Damascus Document* from the Cairo Genizah (CD) was first published in the early twentieth century, it was regarded as the document of "an unknown Jewish sect."[1] When the Dead Sea Scrolls were discovered, it immediately became apparent that this sect was related to the one described in other Scrolls, most notably the *Community Rule* (1QS). Ten copies of the *Damascus Rule* were subsequently found at Qumran.[2]

1. Louis Ginzberg, *An Unknown Jewish Sect* (New York: Ktav, 1976; translation of *Eine unbekannte jüdische Sekte,* published privately in 1922; repr. Hildesheim: Olms, 1972). See Solomon Schechter, *Fragments of a Zadokite Work: Documents of Jewish Sectaries* (Cambridge: Cambridge University Press, 1910; repr. with a "Prolegomenon" by J. A. Fitzmyer, New York: Ktav, 1970). See also Stefan C. Reif, "The Damascus Document from the Cairo Genizah: Its Discovery, Early Study and Historical Significance," in J. M. Baumgarten, E. G. Chazon, and A. Pinnick, eds., *The Damascus Document: A Centennial of Discovery. Proceedings of the Third International Symposium of the Orion Center for the Study of the Dead Sea Scrolls and Associated Literature, 4-8 February, 1998* (STDJ 34; Leiden: Brill, 2000) 109-31.

2. Copies were found in Caves 4, 5, and 6. See Joseph M. Baumgarten with Michael T. Davis, "Cave IV, V, VI Fragments Related to the Damascus Document (4Q266-273 = 4QD^{a-h}, 5Q12 = 5QD, 6Q15=6QD)," in James H. Charlesworth, ed., *The Dead Sea Scrolls: Hebrew, Aramaic, and Greek Texts with English Translations,* vol. 2: *Damascus Document, War Scroll, and Related Documents* (PTSDSSP; Louisville: Westminster John Knox, 1995) 59-79; Baumgarten with James H. Charlesworth, Lidija Novakovic, and Henry W. M. Rietz, "Damascus Document: 4Q266-273 (4QD^{a-h})," in Charlesworth and Rietz, eds., *The Dead Sea Scrolls,* vol. 3: *Damascus Document II, Some Works of the Torah, and Related Documents* (PTSDSSP; Louisville: Westminster John Knox, 2006) 1-185. For the official edition of the Cave 4 fragments see Joseph M. Baumgarten, *Qumran Cave 4,* vol. XIII: *The Damascus Document (4Q266-273)* (DJD 18; Oxford: Clarendon, 1996). See now also Ben Zion

12

The *Damascus Rule,* or D (the comprehensive term for CD plus the 4QD fragments), consists of an Admonition and Laws. In the text from the Cairo Genizah, these are roughly equal in length (Admonition: CD 1–8; 19–20; Laws: CD 15–16; 9–14). When the fragments from Qumran are taken into account, however, the Laws are roughly twice as extensive as the Admonition. Solomon Schechter had the impression "that we are dealing with extracts from a larger work, put together, however, in a haphazard way, with little regard to completeness or order."[3] More recent scholars, however, have regarded it as a more coherent composition, even if it has been assembled from smaller units.[4]

The designation "Damascus Document" is an *ad hoc* label, derived from the mention of Damascus a couple of times in the text. The same was true of Schechter's original designation as "a Zadokite Work." Steven Fraade has suggested that the work might more appropriately be called "The Elaboration of the Laws," *prwš hmšptym,* the phrase used in the conclusion of the work, attested in 4Q266 11 18 (paralleled in 4Q270 7 ii 12): "this is the elaboration of the laws to be followed by them during the entire period [of visitation . . .]."[5] It also appears near the end of the Genizah document, manuscript A, in CD 14:18, just before a reference to the messiahs of Aaron and Israel (so, perhaps, referring to the interpretation of the laws to be followed until the coming of the messiahs). Joseph Baumgarten, in the DJD edition, reconstructs the same phrase in the opening line of 4Q266 1 as a virtual title, but we do not know whether these were in fact the opening words.[6] "The

Wacholder, *The New Damascus Document: The Midrash on the Eschatological Torah of the Dead Sea Scrolls: Reconstruction, Translation and Commentary* (STDJ 56; Leiden: Brill, 2007).

3. Schechter, *Fragments,* X.

4. For example, P. R. Davies, *The Damascus Covenant: An Interpretation of the Damascus Document* (JSOTSup 25; Sheffield: JSOT Press, 1982) 50.

5. Steven D. Fraade, "Law, History, and Narrative in the Damascus Document," in Moshe Bar-Asher and Emanuel Tov, eds., *Meghillot: Studies in the Dead Sea Scrolls V-VI: A Festschrift for Devorah Dimant* (Jerusalem: Bialik Institute, 2007) *35-*55.

6. Baumgarten, DJD 18, 31-32. Hartmut Stegemann, "Towards Physical Reconstructions of the Qumran Damascus Document Scrolls," in Baumgarten et al., eds., *Damascus Document,* 193; and Wacholder, *New Damascus Document,* 110, restore the title in 4Q266 1 as *mdrš htrwh h'hrwn,* which Stegemann takes as "the last Midrash on the Torah," and Wacholder as "the Midrash on the Eschatological Torah." See also Stegemann, *The Library of Qumran: On the Essenes, Qumran, John the Baptist, and Jesus* (Grand Rapids: Eerdmans, 1998) 117.

Elaboration of the Laws" may refer more narrowly to the legal exposition and penal code at the end of the work.[7]

Regardless of whether this was the original title of the work as a whole, Fraade rightly points out that important statements of law and legal scriptural interpretation are central to the Admonition itself, and that the importance of instruction in "the deeds of God" is recognized in the Laws, in the role assigned to the *mebaqqer* in CD 13:7-8. The blend of exhortation and law in any case is typical of Deuteronomy, often thought to be the prototype for CD, and more generally of covenantal texts. The word *berit,* "covenant," occurs some 40 times in CD, including notable references to "the new covenant" (6:19; 19:33; 20:12) or "the new covenant in the land of Damascus" (8:21; cf. 20:12), of which the addressees of the text are members.[8] The text addresses the motivation for making and keeping this covenant, and also provides the stipulations that it entails.

The Laws

The Laws in the *Damascus Document* are of two kinds. Some are intended for "the cities of Israel" (CD 12:19); others are designed for a more elite group who live in "camps" (12:22-23). The end of the document, as preserved in 4Q266 11, says, "This is the elaboration of the laws . . . for all who dwell in their [c]amps and all [who dwell in] their [cities]." Since the laws for "the cities of Israel" (e.g., CD 9:1–12:18) are intended for all Israel, and do not require membership in a more specific association, they are often regarded as a distinct, early stratum that goes back to a

---

7. The beginning of the text is preserved in very fragmentary form in 4Q266, with parallels in 4Q267 and 268. It appears that the opening section in the medieval manuscript was preceded by a passage that exhorts "[the so]ns of light to keep apart from the way[s of wickedness]," and which refers to "the voice of Moses" and to "slander against the commandments of God." The designation "sons of light" is not otherwise used in the D manuscripts, and this raises the possibility that this particular recension of the D Rule may be influenced by S. Compare Davies's "Qumranic recension" in CD 20, but the *yaḥad* should not be simply identified with Qumran. Note, however, the reference to "the lot of light" in CD 13:12, and to the Prince of Lights in 5:18.

8. On the background of the concept of covenant in CD see Stephen Hultgren, *From the Damascus Covenant to the Covenant of the Community* (STDJ 66; Leiden: Brill, 2007) 77-140; Thomas R. Blanton IV, *Constructing a New Covenant: Discursive Strategies in the Damascus Document and Second Corinthians* (WUNT 2/233; Tübingen: Mohr Siebeck, 2007) 24-39.

time before the development of a sectarian organization. In the words of Charlotte Hempel:

> In contrast to the communal legislation in the Laws, this group of texts contains no legislation that is associated with a particular organized group within the larger community of Israel. Inevitably, like every text, it goes back to (a) particular group(s) in the society in which the author(s) were at home. Yet, unlike the material assigned to the communal legislation, these texts lack explicit references to a particular organized community.[9]

In many cases these laws are explicitly based on the interpretation of scriptural texts.

In general, these laws not only exhort people to observe the Torah of Moses, but insist on a stricter interpretation than was prevalent in the society. For example, one fragment envisions the case of a man who "approaches to fornicate with his wife" (4Q270 7 12-13), presumably by having relations with her during menstruation, or during pregnancy, or violating some other rule.[10] The law of the Sabbath in CD 10:14–11:18b specifies all sorts of restrictions that are presumably entailed by the commandment to keep the day holy:

> No one should do work on the sixth day from the moment when the sun's disc is at a distance of its diameter from the gate. . . . On the Sabbath day, no one should say a useless or stupid word. He is not to lend anything to his fellow. He is not to take decisions with regard to riches or gain. He is not to speak about matters of work or of the task to be carried out on the following day. . . . No one should help an animal to give birth on the Sabbath day. And if (it falls) into a well or a pit, he should not take it out on the Sabbath. . . . And any living man who falls into a place of water or into a (reservoir), no one should take him out with a ladder or a rope or a utensil. . . .

The laws of the *Damascus Rule* deal with a wide range of issues. These include such topics as the disqualification of various categories of

---

9. Charlotte Hempel, *The Laws of the Damascus Document: Sources, Tradition, and Redaction* (STDJ 29; Leiden: Brill, 1998) 26.

10. See Cecilia Wassen, *Women in the Damascus Document* (SBLAB 21; Leiden: Brill, 2005) 173-84. Wassen favors the view that the offense was intercourse during pregnancy.

priest, purity issues related to skin disease, flux, and childbirth, agricultural issues, the suspected adulteress and the betrothed slave woman, the
Jubilee Year, oaths and vows, reproof, witnesses, and so on.[11] Issues of ritual purity and other priestly concerns are especially prominent in the fragments found at Qumran, and strengthen the impression that these fragments derive from a different recension of the rule from what we find in
the Genizah manuscripts. Hempel infers that "these traditions originated
with priestly groups" before the formation of any sectarian movement.[12]
Since the priestly concerns are especially prominent in the fragments
found at Qumran, however, we should also reckon with the possibility that
they were a secondary development in this halakic tradition.

Much of this tradition is reminiscent of the rabbinic principle of
"building a fence around the law." Louis Ginzberg inferred that these were
the teachings of "an unknown Jewish sect" that emerged from among the
Pharisees.[13] Many scholars have suggested that this sect was engaged in polemics against the Pharisees.[14] Charlotte Hempel has argued that the Laws
of the *Damascus Rule,* unlike the Admonition, are "on the whole, free of
overt polemics."[15] But she is also aware that "it lies in the nature of
halakhic exposition, of course, that the interpretations arrived at often differ from the halakhic decisions taken in other groups."[16] Indeed, it is likely
that differences in the interpretation of religious law were a major factor in
the emergence of the movement for a new covenant. The need for a new
covenant arose precisely out of disagreement about the interpretation of
the Laws. We should expect then that interpretation along the lines of
these laws that were applicable to all Israel must have been going on for
some time before the need for a new covenant became apparent. It does
not follow, however, that any law that is applicable to all Israel must pre-
date the new association. The sectarian movement was still concerned with
the correct interpretation of the law that applied to all Israel, not just with
its own regulations, and presumably it continued to refine its rulings on
these issues.

11. See Hempel, *Damascus Texts,* 34-39.
12. Hempel, *Laws,* 70.
13. Ginzberg, *Unknown Jewish Sect,* xvi-xxi.
14. See Albert I. Baumgarten, "Pharisees," *EDSS* 2.657-63, especially 661-62.
15. Hempel, *Laws,* 72.
16. Ibid.

Laws in the Admonition

As Fraade has noted, the Laws are given a narrative context by the Admonition.[17] Some of these rulings may have originated before any separatist movement came into being, but they are now part of the understanding of the Torah that gives this group its *raison d'être*. The Admonition contains a section on "the three nets of Belial" (CD 4:12–5:15): fornication, wealth, and defilement of the temple. These "nets" are expounded on the basis of a particular interpretation of scriptural passages. "Taking two wives in their lifetime," whether by polygamy or remarriage, counts as "fornication," because "the principle of creation is 'male and female he created them.'"[18] This interpretation involves an extrapolation from the biblical text. Polygamy was never condemned in biblical law. Again, Lev 18:13, "Do not approach your mother's sister," is taken to entail a prohibition of relations between niece and uncle.[19] The temple is defiled by laxity regarding sexual relations with menstruant women. Again CD 6:14b–7:4a lists a series of issues pertaining to "the exact interpretation of the Torah." These include abstaining from "wicked wealth," from the wealth of the temple, and from stealing from the poor, but also observance of the Sabbath day and the day of fasting. Many of these issues are addressed in more detail in the Laws. Also those who live in camps according to the rule of the land, and marry

---

17. Fraade, "Law, History, and Narrative," *38.

18. See Lawrence H. Schiffman, *Reclaiming the Dead Sea Scrolls* (Philadelphia: Jewish Publication Society, 1994) 130. The passage has been debated endlessly. The suffix on *bḥyyhm*, "in their lifetime," is masculine. If this is correct, the passage would seem to preclude both polygamy and remarriage. Many scholars, including Schiffman, think that this is a scribal error, and that the passage prohibits taking a second wife while the first one is alive. J. A. Fitzmyer, "Divorce among First-Century Palestinian Jews," *ErIsr* 14 (H. L. Ginsberg Volume) (1978): 106*-10*, takes the suffix as inclusive. Some scholars disregard the word "in their lifetime" and contend that the passage refers only to polygamy, and not to remarriage after divorce. So Wassen, *Women in the Damascus Document*, 118, admits that "if taken literally, the accusation against 'taking two wives in their lives' proscribes any second marriage within a man's lifetime." Nonetheless, she argues that the passage prohibits only polygamy since "divorce has always meant freedom to remarry in Jewish legislation" (ibid., 117). But the legislation in CD is clearly at variance with the prevalent norms in Jewish society! Adiel Schremer, "Qumran Polemic on Marital Law: CD 4:20-5:11 and Its Social Background," in Baumgarten et al., eds., *Damascus Document*, 147-60, also opts for the view that only polygamy is in view, but fails to provide an explanation of the word "in their lifetime."

19. See Wassen, *Women in the Damascus Document*, 120-22.

and beget children, are enjoined to do so in accordance with the Torah (CD 7:7-8).

That the correct interpretation of the law was indeed the *raison d'être* of the new community is shown in CD 3:12-16. While the members of the original covenant of God with Israel had become guilty and were destroyed,

> for those who held fast to God's ordinances, who remained of them, God established his covenant with Israel forever, revealing to them hidden things in which all Israel had strayed: his holy Sabbaths, the glorious appointed times, his righteous testimonies, his true ways, and the desires of his will, which a person shall do and live by them. He opened before them and they dug a well of abundant water.

Later we are told:

> The well is the Torah, and those who dig it are the returnees of Israel who depart from the land of Judah and dwell in the land of Damascus . . . and the "staff" is the interpreter of the Torah . . . and the "nobles of the people" are those who come to dig the well with the staves that the staff decreed, to walk in them in the entire time of evil. (CD 6:4-10, trans. J. Baumgarten)

Notable in CD 3 is the prominence of the cultic calendar: "his holy Sabbaths, the glorious appointed times." The subject of calendars is an important one in the Dead Sea Scrolls. Some nineteen texts are devoted to calendrical issues, and many more touch on the subject at some point.[20] These texts attest both a 364-day solar calendar and a 354-day lunar one, but the religious festivals are dated in accordance with the solar one.[21] This was at variance with the practice of the Jerusalem temple. The *Pesher,* or biblical commentary, on Habakkuk, which was one of the first scrolls found at Qumran, famously describes a confrontation between the Righteous Teacher and the Wicked Priest, when the latter disrupted the Teacher's observance of the Day of Atonement. The Wicked Priest, who is usually assumed to be a high priest, obviously did not observe the holy day on the

---

20. 4Q317-330, 4Q561. 4Q321 is divided into two texts, and 4Q324 into four. See James C. VanderKam, *Calendars in the Dead Sea Scrolls: Measuring Time* (London: Routledge, 1998) 110.

21. Ibid., 112.

same date.[22] Calendrical differences were a major impetus to sectarian formation. If a group did not observe the festivals at the same time as everyone else, then it effectively separated itself from the rest of the people.[23]

4QMMT and Sectarian Separation

Right interpretation of the Torah is also the issue that leads to sectarian separation in the text called *Some of the Works of the Torah,* 4QMMT, a fragmentary text found in six manuscripts in Qumran Cave 4 (4Q394-399). The first public presentation of this text, at a conference in Jerusalem in 1984, led to a revolution in the study of the Scrolls, as it states explicitly that the group represented by the author "have separated ourselves from the majority of the people" because of halakic disagreements.[24] The issues in question are primarily ones of holiness and purity (the holiness of Jerusalem and the "camp," the purity of liquid streams, sacrifice and tithing, forbidden sexual unions, etc.).[25] Some twenty issues are cited. A whole section of the text is devoted to laying out the solar calendar, although this may be a separate document annexed to 4QMMT secondarily.[26] While the

22. This was noted already in 1951 by Shemaryahu Talmon, "Yom hakippurim in the Habakkuk Scroll," *Biblica* 32 (1951): 549-63. See also Talmon, "The Calendar of the Covenanters of the Judean Desert," in idem, *The World of Qumran from Within: Collected Studies* (Jerusalem: Magnes, 1989) 147-85; and idem, "Calendars and Mishmarot," *EDSS* 1.108-17.

23. Philip R. Davies, "Sects from Texts: On the Problems of Doing a Sociology of the Qumran Literature," in Jonathan G. Campbell, William John Lyons, and Lloyd K. Pietersen, eds., *New Directions in Qumran Studies: Proceedings of the Bristol Colloquium on the Dead Sea Scrolls* (Library of Second Temple Studies 52; London: T&T Clark, 2005) 78, notes that the solar calendar is already found in the Astronomical Book of Enoch and in *Jubilees,* neither of which indicates separation from the temple. As he comments, "presumably in some way their authors lived with a calendar they disapproved of." Nonetheless the calendrical difference seems to have been a major factor in the secession of the sect of the new covenant. While CD 11:17-21 contains prescriptions relating to sacrifice, it does not imply acceptance of the current cultic calendar.

24. Elisha Qimron and John Strugnell, eds., *Qumran Cave 4,* vol. V: *Miqṣat Ma'aśe ha-Torah* (DJD 10; Oxford: Clarendon, 1994) 59 (Composite text, C 7). On the impact of the presentation of this text see Schiffman, *Reclaiming the Dead Sea Scrolls,* xvii.

25. See the essay on "The Halakha" by Elisha Qimron, in DJD 10, 123-77.

26. See John Strugnell, "MMT: Second Thoughts on a Forthcoming Edition," in Eugene Ulrich and James VanderKam, eds., *The Community of the Renewed Covenant* (CJA 10;

scriptural basis of the disputed issues is not made explicit, it is evidently assumed throughout. The issues raised are "precepts of the Torah." They are presented by juxtaposing opposing arguments, "we say" as opposed to "they do." In all cases the views of the "we" group are stricter than those of their opponents. The views of the opponents generally correspond to those attributed to the rabbis in the Mishnah, and are consequently thought to be those of the Pharisees.[27] The text concludes: "We have written to you some of the precepts of the Torah according to our decision, for your welfare and the welfare of your people. For we have seen (that) you have wisdom and knowledge of the Torah . . . so that you may rejoice at the end of time, finding that some of our practices are correct."[28]

Most scholars have accepted the editors' suggestion that this text, which may be viewed as a halakic treatise, was addressed to an individual leader of Israel, most probably a Hasmonean high priest.[29] The conclusion reads:

> and also we have written to you some of the works of the Torah which we think are good for you and for your people, for we have seen that that you have wisdom and knowledge of the Torah. Reflect on all these matters and seek from him that he may support your counsel and keep far from you the evil scheming and the counsel of Belial, so that at the end of time, you may rejoice in finding that some of our words are true. And it shall be reckoned to you as justice when you do what is upright and good before him, for your good and that of Israel. (4QMMT C 26-32, my trans.)

Most scholars believe that the addressee in this passage must have been a ruler of Israel.[30] Fraade argues that since the text was preserved in multiple copies it must have been used as a document for intramural instruction, to address and reinforce communal self-understanding, and questions

---

Notre Dame, IN: University of Notre Dame Press, 1994) 61-62; Hanne von Weissenberg, "4QMMT: The Problem of the Epilogue" (diss., Helsinki, 2006) 141.

27. Eyal Regev, *Sectarianism in Qumran: A Cross-Cultural Perspective* (RelSoc 45; Berlin: de Gruyter, 2007) 98.

28. Composite text C 26-30; DJD 10, 63.

29. Qimron and Strugnell, DJD 10, 121. Compare Schiffman, *Reclaiming the Dead Sea Scrolls*, 83-95. The initial suggestion of the editors that this text was a letter is widely rejected. See already DJD 10, 113-14; and now von Weissenberg, "4QMMT," 146-70.

30. See, e.g., Regev, *Sectarianism*, 104.

whether it was necessarily addressed to an outsider.[31] It is, of course, possible that a document composed for the benefit of a high priest was subsequently used for instruction within the sect. In any case, it provides the author's understanding of the reasons for separation from the rest of Israel.

Eyal Regev, who accepts the view that the treatise is addressed to a high priest, regards it as a "pre-sectarian" text, on the grounds that there would have been no such attempt to communicate with the authorities after the sect had seceded.[32] This is not necessarily so. The text states explicitly that the "we" party had already separated itself from the majority of the people. Neither is it necessary to assume that 4QMMT was written at or close to the point of separation, although this is possible. All the text requires is that the author thought that the high priest of the day might be sympathetic to the positions of the sect. We shall return to the possible historical implications of this text below in chapter 3.

The exact relationship of this text to the movement described in the *Damascus Rule* is not immediately clear.[33] The two documents share many concerns, such as the exclusion of the blind and deaf from the community, the prohibition of some marital combinations as "fornication," and of accepting sacrifices from non-Jews.[34] At the same time, each document raises many issues that are not paralleled in the other, and there is no evidence of literary interdependence. Lawrence Schiffman attributes the correspondences to a common halakic tradition, which he identifies as Sadducean.[35] In view of the multiple copies of both documents found at Qumran, some relationship is highly probable. For the present, however, it will suffice to note that *the kinds of issues* that lead to sectarian separation in 4QMMT are quite similar to those cited in the *Damascus Rule*. They are

31. Steven Fraade, "To Whom It May Concern: 4QMMT and Its Addressee(s)," *RevQ* 19 (2000): 507-26.

32. Regev, *Sectarianism*, 107, 158-60.

33. Strugnell warns that "we will find no small differences if we try to identify the beliefs and practices of the protagonists here and those in the Qumrân corpus," "MMT: Second Thoughts," 71.

34. I find it difficult to see why Regev, *Sectarianism*, 109, says that "MMT has weak ideological connections with the Damascus Document and Community Rule," and simultaneously finds it "hard to deny its connection to the pre-Qumranic corpus" (ibid., 107).

35. L. H. Schiffman, "The Place of 4QMMT in the Corpus of Qumran Manuscripts," in John Kampen and Moshe J. Bernstein, eds., *Reading 4QMMT: New Perspectives on Qumran Law and History* (SBLSymS 2; Atlanta: Scholars Press, 1996) 90-94.

primarily disputes about the correct interpretation of the Torah, especially in matters pertaining to purity, and about the cultic calendar.

The Laws and the Life of the Sect

Fraade has cautioned that the Laws are not necessarily a reliable guide to the actual setting and practice of the movement that produced them. The point may be illustrated from a few controversial examples. The laws of the Sabbath include a provision that "No one should offer anything upon the altar on the Sabbath, except the sacrifice of the Sabbath, for thus is it written 'except your offerings of the Sabbath.' No one should send to the altar a sacrifice, or an offering, or incense, or wood, by the hand of a man impure from any impurities, so allowing him to defile the altar . . ." (CD 11:17-21). Philip Davies argued that one of the things that distinguished CD from "the Qumran community" represented by 1QS is that it "legislates for participation in the Temple cult."[36] Fraade argues that this is not necessarily so: "Even if the 'authors' of these rules considered the Temple to be defiled, by the impurities of those who entered or served there, and even if they did not perform sacrificial worship, they might still have found it meaningful, or even obligatory to expound the rules relevant to the offering of sacrifices on the Sabbath and the proper procedures for approaching and entering the holy place of worship."[37] Rabbinic Judaism continued to legislate for the sacrificial cult long after it had ceased to exist.

The explicitly sectarian injunction about the temple in CD 6:11b-14a is notoriously ambiguous:

> But all those who have been brought into the covenant shall not enter the temple to kindle his altar in vain. They will be the ones who close the door, as God said, "Whoever amongst you will close my door so that you do not kindle my altar in vain!" unless they take care to act in accordance with the exact interpretation of the law for the age of wickedness.[38]

36. Davies, *Damascus Covenant*, 19, 134-35. Cf. also CD 9:14.

37. Fraade, "Law, History, and Narrative," *51.

38. See the review of previous discussions by Davies, *Damascus Covenant*, 136-37. The interpretation of the passage hangs on the translation of the phrase *ky 'm,* which normally

This passage certainly expresses a critical attitude toward current temple practice, but does not condemn temple worship as such. Whether it implies a boycott of the temple until such time as the laws are properly observed, however, remains uncertain,[39] and that issue cannot be decided by appeal to the temple legislation in the Laws. While a boycott may be implied, the passage can also be construed so as to permit some continued use of the temple in accordance with the "proper" sectarian halakah.

Several laws deal with relations with Gentiles, for example, CD 12:6b-11a.[40] Jerome Murphy-O'Connor, following Samuel Iwry, took this as evidence that the legislation "was designed for a community living in a gentile environment."[41] Again, the conclusion is not a safe one. Interaction with Gentiles, with its attendant problems, was at least a theoretical possibility for any Jew in the Hellenistic Roman period, whether living in Judea or elsewhere.

Finally, laws dealing with women have attracted attention, because of the common assumption that this is an Essene document, and the emphasis on the celibacy of the Essenes in the Greek and Latin sources. There is plenty of evidence that the "new covenant" did not require celibacy, and in any case Josephus acknowledges that not all Essenes were celibate. Nonetheless, a number of the references to women arise in the context of expounding scripture. For example, the discussion of women's oaths in CD 16:10-12 is based on Num 30:7-9. Hempel is correct that "great caution is required when inferring present-day realities from the references to women in halakhic exposition."[42]

---

means "unless," but is often ignored by translators, who begin a new sentence in line 14: "they should take care to act."

39. *Pace* Hultgren, *From the Damascus Covenant,* 537, 541, who assumes that a boycott is implied, and takes this to mark an important development in the history of the sect.

40. See L. H. Schiffman, "Legislation Concerning Relations with Non-Jews in the Zadokite Fragments and in Tannaitic Literature," *RevQ* 11 (1989): 379-89.

41. J. Murphy-O'Connor, "The Essenes and Their History," *RB* 81 (1974): 223; S. Iwry, "Was There a Migration to Damascus? The Problem of ישראל שבי," *ErIsr* 9 (Albright Festschrift) (1969): 85.

42. Hempel, *Laws,* 37.

The New Covenant

The *Damascus Rule* is concerned with the law of Moses, as it should apply to all Israel,[43] but it is also concerned with an elite group within Israel, who recognize that the law is not being properly observed. The goal of this group is the correct interpretation and fulfillment of the laws, in accordance with their own teachings. They formalize their commitment to the exact interpretation of the Torah by entering into a new covenant, an idea that had a scriptural basis in Jer 31:31: "The days are surely coming, says the Lord, when I will make a new covenant with the house of Israel and the house of Judah."[44] This covenant is still based on the law of Moses, but those who are Israelites by birth do not automatically qualify. It is potentially a covenant for all Israel (15:5), even proselytes.[45] The individual "must impose upon himself to return to the law of Moses with all his heart and soul" (15:12). He must also impose the oath of the covenant on his son, when he reaches the age of enrollment (15:5-6). The swearing in is supervised by an official who is called *mebaqqer,* or inspector: "On the day when he talks to the Inspector of the many, they shall enroll him with the oath of the covenant which Moses established with Israel, the covenant to revert to the law of Moses with the whole heart and with the whole soul, to do what is found during the whole period of his approach" (15:7b-10a).

There are some restrictions on membership: "no one who is stupid or deranged (should enter); and no one feeble[-minded and insane,] those with eyes too weak t[o see,] the lame [or] one who stumbles, o[r a deaf

---

43. Hultgren, *From the Damascus Covenant,* 196-205, makes much of the fact that the covenant is for all Israel, and argues that it was meant to include the (proto-) Samaritans. It is not apparent to me that there is any specific concern for (proto-) Samaritans in CD, although they are not specifically excluded either.

44. On the scriptural basis of the new covenant see further Hultgren, *From the Damascus Covenant,* 77-140.

45. CD 14:4, 6. P. R. Davies, "The 'Damascus Sect' and Judaism," in John C. Reeves and John Kampen, eds., *Pursuing the Text: Studies in Honor of Ben Zion Wacholder on the Occasion of His Seventieth Birthday* (JSOTSup 184; Sheffield: Sheffield Academic Press, 1994) 75, claims that the reference is to "a proselyte to the sect, and thus one in the process of initiation into it," but there is no parallel for such usage. See Hempel, "Community Structures in the Dead Sea Scrolls: Admission, Organization, Disciplinary Procedures," in Peter W. Flint and James C. VanderKam, eds., *The Dead Sea Scrolls after Fifty Years: A Comprehensive Assessment* (2 vols.; Leiden: Brill, 1998–99) 2.77.

person,] or an un[der a]ge boy, none of these should one allow to enter the congregation, for the ho[ly] angels. . . ."[46]

Members, or at least some of them, "live in camps according to the order of the land and marry and have children" (CD 7:6-7). It is, then, a family-based movement, not the kind of quasi-monastic community usually inferred from the *Community Rule*. But members are subject to community discipline.

The "camps" in which the members live seem to be conceived on the model of the organization of Israel in the wilderness, as described in the book of Numbers. "The rule for the assembly of the camps" (CD 12:22-23) specifies that the members "shall be ten in number as a minimum to (form) thousands, hundreds, fifties, and tens." Wherever there is a quorum of ten, there should be a priest "learned in the book of Hagy . . . and by his authority all shall be governed." The following verses qualify the authority of the priest. He may be replaced by a Levite who is an expert, except in cases involving leprosy. More importantly, he seems to be subordinated to the Inspector or *mebaqqer*. Hempel is probably right that there is some redactional development here, reflecting development in the structure of communal organization.[47] While priests play an important role in some parts of the Laws, the Inspector is normally the focus of authority in the camps.[48] There is mention of a *Maskil,* or Instructor, in 12:20b-22a and again in 13:22, but the *Maskil* does not seem to have any distinct role here. Either he is the same person as the Inspector, or the title is introduced here from the *Community Rule,* where the *Maskil* has a more central role.

The role of the Inspector is spelled out in CD 13:7b-20a: "He shall instruct the many in the works of God. . . . He shall be as kind to them as a father to his children and guard all those who have gone astray like a shepherd his flock, and he shall undo all the fetters that bind them so that there shall not be anyone oppressed and broken in his congregation." It is not clear what is entailed by undoing the fetters that bind them. Exorcism comes to mind as a possibility.

This rather pastoral view of the Inspector's role gives way to the more practical aspects of supervision in 13:11-12: "He shall examine every-

---

46. CD 15:15-17; 4Q266 8 i 6-9. There is a similar restriction on membership in the council of the community (*'ṣt hyḥd*) in the eschatological *Rule of the Congregation* (1QSa), also because of the presence of angels.

47. Hempel, *Laws,* 113.

48. Regev, *Sectarianism,* 166-69.

one who joins his congregation as to their deeds, their insight, their strength, their might and their property, and he shall write them down according to their inheritance in the lot of light (my trans.)."[49]

In fact, he exercises tight control over his congregation. No one may bring anyone into the congregation without his permission. Members cannot engage in trade without his approval, and they need his permission to marry or divorce. He is empowered to discipline their children. He enforces a strict separation from outsiders.

In light of this tight control, it is surprising that the "many" do not have to share all their possessions. They are required to contribute at least two days' salary per month (CD 14:12-13). From this common fund they care for the needy and the elderly, for "everything is the task of the association *(ḥbr)*." In a provision reminiscent of the early Christians in Acts we are told that the man who lies knowingly with respect to riches is liable to punishment.[50] This is only one of many offenses for which specific punishment is prescribed.[51] A fuller penal code is found in the fragments of the *Damascus Rule* from Cave 4, and it is similar to what is found in the *Community Rule* (1QS 6:24–7:25). Issues addressed in both rules include lying about wealth, insulting a fellow member, bearing a grudge, speaking folly, interrupting the speech of a fellow member, falling asleep during a session of the "many," leaving a session as many as three times, walking naked in the presence of another or exposing oneself, guffawing foolishly, gesticulating with the left hand, slandering fellow members or the community as a whole, and "deviation of one's spirit."[52] The punishment is specified in number of days, and presumably consisted of suspension from the assembly. Some offenses were grounds for dismissal: despising the judgment of the "many," "fornicating" with one's wife in a way that is not

---

49. Here again there may be some assimilation to the *Serek*, as the dualism of Light and Darkness does not figure prominently in CD.

50. The length of punishment is given variously as 60 days in CD and 100 days in 4Q266.

51. CD 14:18b-22; 4Q266 10 i-ii; Q467 9 6; 4Q468 11 I-ii; 4Q460 7 i. See J. M. Baumgarten, "The Cave 4 Versions of the Qumran Penal Code," *JJS* 43 (1992): 268-76; Hempel, *Laws*, 141-48; eadem, "The Penal Code Reconsidered," in M. J. Bernstein, F. García Martínez, and J. Kampen, eds., *Legal Texts and Legal Issues: Second Meeting of the IOQS, Cambridge, 1995* (Leiden: Brill, 1997) 337-48.

52. The passages are found in 1QS 6:24-7:25; CD 14:20; 4QD[a] 18:3-4; 4QD[b] 12; and 4QD[e] 11 i. See Hempel, "Penal Code Reconsidered," 338-41. See also the amalgam of rules from both rules preserved in 4Q265.

in accordance with the law, or murmuring against the "fathers" of the congregation. One who murmurs against the "mothers," however, is only suspended for ten days.

In the context of the *Damascus Rule,* these regulations would presumably apply to the assembly of the camps, as this rule does not require that members live permanently in community. It is possible that the *Damascus Rule* (D) was influenced by the *Serek ha-Yahad* (S) at some points. (For example, references to "the many" are more typical of S than of D.) But it is also noteworthy that D prescribes penalties for some offenses that are not found in S. These include "fornication with one's wife" and murmuring against "fathers" and "mothers." The D code, then, is explicitly formulated for an association that allows marriage and has female members, whereas S makes no reference to either. Hempel infers that "the penal code originated with the parent movement of the 1QS community."[53] At least the provisions were tailored for two different kinds of community. We shall return to the question of priority below.

In addition to the local "camps," there is provision for an assembly of all the camps (CD 14:3-18a). There is a priest at the head of the "many" and an Inspector, who must be knowledgeable in all the regulations of the law. Each of these officials must be between 30 and 60 years of age. The assembly of all the camps, then, reflects the same kind of authority structure as we find in the individual camps.[54]

Those who reject the rulings of the movement, or do not abide by them, are subject to expulsion, as is made clear in the conclusion of the text in 4Q266 11 5-8: "And anyone who rejects these regulations, (which are) in accordance with all the statutes found in the law of Moses, shall not be reckoned among all the sons of his truth; for his soul has despised righteous instruction. Being in rebellion, let him be expelled from the presence of the many." The new covenant, in effect, creates a new community, with its own rites of admission and expulsion.

To enter into this covenant is to return to the Torah of Moses. In CD 6:4-11 we are told that the Torah is the well mentioned in Num 21:18: "a well which the princes dug, which the nobles of the people delved with the staff. The well is the law. And those who dug it are the returnees of Israel *(šby yśr'l).*" It is apparent that the congregation embodied, and to some degree

---

53. Hempel, "Penal Code Reconsidered," 348.
54. Hempel, *Laws,* 136.

arose because of, a distinctive tradition of interpretation of the Torah. But it is apparent that some additional instruction was required. In CD 15:10-11 we are told that no one should make a candidate for admission know the precepts until he stands before the Inspector. The candidate could hardly be completely ignorant of the Torah. The precepts in question must be the distinctive rulings of the congregation. The officials of the congregation are supposed to be proficient in "the Book of Hagu/Hagi" (or "Medita-tion"). It is not clear exactly what this book contains, but it would seem to contain some revelation over and above the Torah. Moreover, the distinc-tive teachings of the movement are attributed to revelation in CD 3:12-16: "God established his covenant with Israel forever, revealing to them hid-den matters in which all Israel had gone astray." The claim that these things were revealed is not incompatible with the idea that they were derived from scripture by interpretation (although the understanding of interpre-tation in the Scrolls is quite different from that of the later rabbis). We shall meet claims of divinely inspired exegesis again in the sectarian scrolls. The Torah itself was revealed to all Israel, and insofar as its interpretation was transparent and not in dispute it constituted a category of revealed law *(nigleh)*. But in many cases its true interpretation was hidden from Israel *(nistar)* and could only be revealed through inspired exegesis. In the words of Schiffman, "The sect divided the law into two categories — the *nigleh*, 'revealed,' and the *nistar*, 'hidden.' The revealed laws were known to all Is-rael, for they were manifest in Scripture, but the hidden laws were known only to the sect and were revealed solely through sectarian exegesis."[55]

Precedents for the New Covenant

The group described in the *Damascus Document* was not the first move-ment in Second Temple Judaism to call for a "return" to a strict interpreta-tion of the law of Moses. Something analogous is found in the books of Ezra and Nehemiah.[56] In Neh 10:29 certain people "enter into a curse and

55. Schiffman, *Reclaiming the Dead Sea Scrolls,* 247.
56. Blanton, *Constructing a New Covenant,* 33-36. He notes that neither D nor S ac-knowledges the covenant renewal of Ezra-Nehemiah, as they did not wish to countenance a successful attempt at covenant renewal during the Persian period. Hultgren, *From the Da-mascus Covenant,* 196, claims that "the structure of the Damascus covenant is almost identi-cal to Asa's covenant in 2 Chr 15:9-15," but the similarity lies only in the swearing of an oath

an oath to walk in God's law, which was given by Moses the servant of God, and to observe and do all the commandments of the Lord our God and his ordinances and his statutes."[57] As in CD, these people agree to abide by a particular interpretation of the law, one that prohibits them from intermarriage with foreign peoples. They also undertake to support the temple with various contributions and offerings. In Ezra 10:8 we find that people who did not comply with Ezra's directives could be banned from "the congregation of the exiles." The situation of Ezra and Nehemiah differs from that of the *Damascus Document*, insofar as both have the backing of the Persian government and have control of the temple. The movement described in the *Damascus Document* has power to enforce internal discipline and to expel members who fail to conform, but it does not have power over the society at large, and so it relies on the threat of divine punishment. It also offers the prospect of reward in the afterlife, an idea that is not attested in Ezra and Nehemiah.

The "congregation of the exiles" in Ezra and Nehemiah was made up of families, who separated themselves from the people of the land, in the sense that they did not mingle with them. Did the *Damascus Document* require any greater degree of separation? CD 4:2 says that "the priests are the converts of Israel who left the land of Judah," but the passage is notoriously ambiguous and the language may be entirely symbolic. Again, we do not know whether the references to the new covenant in the land of Damascus have any geographical value. References to Damascus are found only in the *Damascus Rule*, in the Admonition section of CD, and in 4Q266 3 iii 20, where it parallels CD 7:19.[58] CD 7:19 follows a citation of Amos 5:26-27: "I will deport the Sikkut of your King and the Kiyyun of your images away from my tent to Damascus *(m'hly dmśq)*." (This reading differs from the

---

to seek the Lord, and the appeal to all Israel. Asa does not constitute an association with a distinct membership over against the rest of the people of the land. According to the Chronicler, his covenant was embraced enthusiastically by "all Judah."

57. Michael Duggan, *Covenant Renewal in Ezra-Nehemiah (Neh 7:72b–10:40): An Exegetical, Literary, and Theological Study* (SBL Dissertation Series 164; Atlanta: SBL, 2001). The analogy with the Dead Sea Scrolls was already noted by Morton Smith, "The Dead Sea Sect in Relation to Judaism," *New Testament Studies* 7 (1961): 347-60. See also Alexei Sivertsev, "Sects and Households: Social Structure of the Proto-Sectarian Movement of Nehemiah 10 and the Dead Sea Sect," *CBQ* 67 (2005): 59-78; idem, *Households, Sects, and the Origins of Rabbinic Judaism* (JSJSup 102; Leiden: Brill, 2005) 94-118; Hultgren, *From the Damascus Covenant*, 141-63.

58. There are seven references in CD: 6:5, 19; 7:15, 19; 8:21 par. 19:34; 20:12.

Masoretic text, which has "beyond Damascus," *mhl'h ldmśq.*) The passage goes on to identify the Sikkut of the King as the books of the law, and the Kiyyun of the images as the books of the prophets, but it offers no interpretation of Damascus. Instead, we are told that the Star of Balaam's oracle "is the Interpreter of the Law who will come to Damascus." "Damascus" has been interpreted in various ways.[59] Most often, it has been taken as a cipher for Qumran.[60] Jerome Murphy-O'Connor popularized the view that it was a cipher for Babylon.[61] Michael Wise has revived the view that it refers to a literal exile of the Teacher to Damascus.[62] Geza Vermes underlined the exegetical derivation of the term and concluded: "If in fact they went somewhere else, they still called this place 'the land of Damascus,' because their exegesis of Holy Scripture obliged them to do so."[63] In fact, all we can conclude is that "Damascus" is an exegetical term derived from Amos 5:26-27 to describe the community's place of exile where the faithful devote themselves to the study of the law. We cannot even conclude safely that a specific place is involved. "Damascus" may simply indicate the state of withdrawal from the rest of Jewish society ("the land of Judah").[64] Nothing in the Laws of the *Damascus Rule* suggests that the members had physically withdrawn from society, to the wilderness or elsewhere.

We are told that some members of the new covenant "reside in camps

59. For an overview, see Hempel, *Damascus Texts,* 58-60; Blanton, *Constructing a New Covenant,* 79-86.

60. So Frank Moore Cross, *The Ancient Library of Qumran* (3rd ed.; BibSem 30; Sheffield: Sheffield Academic Press, 1995) 72.

61. Jerome Murphy-O'Connor, "The Essenes and Their History," *RB* 81 (1974): 221; so also Davies, *Damascus Covenant,* 122-23; idem, "The Birthplace of the Essenes: 'Where Is Damascus'?" in *Sects and Scrolls: Essays on Qumran and Related Topics* (SFSHJ 134; Atlanta: Scholars Press, 1996) 95-111. Davies admits that the origin of the Essenes as a sect cannot be traced to Babylon, only the roots of their ideology ("Birthplace," 105). See the critique by Michael A. Knibb, "The Exile in the Literature of the Intertestamental Period," *HeyJ* 17 (1976): 249-72.

62. Michael O. Wise, *The First Messiah* (San Francisco: HarperSanFrancisco, 1999) 136-38. So also Blanton, *Constructing a New Covenant,* 90.

63. Geza Vermes, *Scripture and Tradition in Judaism: Haggadic Studies* (SPB 4; Leiden: Brill, 1973) 44.

64. Liv Ingeborg Lied, "Another Look at the Land of Damascus: The Spaces of the *Damascus Document* in the Light of Edward W. Soja's Thirdspace Approach," in Campbell et al., eds., *New Directions in Qumran Studies,* 101-25, concludes that Damascus is "a place of rescue for the remnant during the time of evil," and must be understood as both an exile and a blessing.

in accordance with the rule of the land and marry and have children" (7:6-7). These people are evidently not members of a quasi-monastic community, such as has been imagined in the case of Qumran. The regulations at the end of the document include provision for marriage and divorce (CD 13:16-17), and for the instruction of children (4Q266 frag. 9 iii 6) and even regulate sexual relations between married people (4Q267 frag. 9 vi 4-5; 4Q270 frag. 7 i 12-13). Nehemiah's covenant also restricted the freedom to marry, by banning intermarriage. The Damascus covenant, however, is much more intrusive. A man could be expelled from the community for "fornicating with his wife," engaging in sexual intercourse in a manner or at a time that was not approved, and would presumably have to divorce his wife in the process. (Enforcement of this law would seem to depend on the testimony of the wife.)[65] Members were not even free to marry or divorce without informing the *mebaqqer* (13:16-17). Consequently, even though the movement was family-based in the sense that members joined as families and did not have a communal life, Cecilia Wassen concludes that it was anti-family to a degree: "Some aspects of the traditional authority of the husband as a *pater familias* were diminished in favour of the communal authority, leaving husband and wife relatively powerless."[66] Again, while the requirement that members contribute two days' salary stops well short of sharing all possessions, it requires a tighter degree of communal control than is suggested in the covenant of Nehemiah.

Were Some Members Celibate?

It is quite clear that celibacy was not the norm in the movement described in the *Damascus Rule*. Accordingly, scholars who identify this movement as Essene argue that it represents the "marrying Essenes," of whom Josephus also spoke.[67] Nonetheless, many scholars have detected a reference to another, celibate, order in CD 7. The argument has been outlined as follows by Joseph Baumgarten:

65. See Wassen, *Women in the Damascus Document*, 181-82. On the testimony of women see 1QSa 1:11, and Philip Davies and Joan Taylor, "On the Testimony of Women in 1QSa," *DSD* 3 (1996): 223-35.
66. Wassen, *Women in the Damascus Document*, 205.
67. See, e.g., Geza Vermes, *The Complete Dead Sea Scrolls in English* (rev. ed.; London: Penguin, 2004) 26-48.

CD 6.11–7.6 contains an extended list of duties incumbent upon adherents of the sect identified as "they that walk in these in the perfection of holiness." They are given the promise that "the covenant of God shall stand faithfully with them to keep them alive for thousands of generations" (7.6; 19.20). This is immediately followed by the provision "And if they dwell in camps according to the order of the land and take wives and beget children, they shall walk according to the Law" (7.6-7). . . . The only valid conclusion to be drawn from all this is that the editor of CD placed this provision after the promise to those who walk in perfect holiness quite deliberately. Its adversative formulation beginning with the conditional "And if" indicates that the previously mentioned aspirants to perfect holiness did not dwell in scattered dwelling places in the conventional manner of the land, did not take wives, and did not beget children.[68]

This argument has been subjected to a thorough critique by Wassen.[69] She argues that the comparison in CD 7 is between two groups, those who "walk in perfect holiness" and "all those who despise" in 7:9, who will be subject to judgment and will not live for a thousand generations. The reference to those who live in camps in CD

does not form a part of this overall comparison between the just and the wicked, and does not serve as an antithesis to the first group. . . . the reference to those who live in camps (CD VII 6b-9a) looks out of place . . . since the reference to the camp group breaks up the nice parallelism between the promise of the reward for the obedient and the warning about evils which will afflict the transgressors. The most reasonable conclusion is that the segment is an interpolation, as some scholars claim.[70]

---

68. J. M. Baumgarten, "Qumran-Essene Restraints on Marriage," in Lawrence H. Schiffman, ed., *Archaeology and History in the Dead Sea Scrolls: The New York University Conference in Memory of Yigael Yadin* (JSPSup 8; Sheffield: JSOT Press, 1990) 18. Compare Elisha Qimron, "Celibacy in the Dead Sea Scrolls and the Two Kinds of Sectarians," in Julio Trebolle Barrera and Luis Vegas Montaner, eds., *The Madrid Qumran Congress: Proceedings of the International Congress on the Dead Sea Scrolls, Madrid, 18-21 March 1991* (STDJ 11; Leiden: Brill, 1992) 287-94 (290-91).

69. Wassen, *Women in the Damascus Document,* 125-28.

70. Ibid., 126; cf. J. Murphy-O'Connor, "A Literary Analysis of the Damascus Document VI, 2-VIII, 3," *RB* 78 (1971): 222.

Moreover, she points out that the expression "men of perfect holiness" occurs three times in CD 20 (2, 5, 7), in the context of a discussion of those who undertake to walk in perfect holiness and then transgress. Also in CD 2:15-16 all the addressees are offered the possibility of walking perfectly on all his paths.[71] She concludes that elsewhere in CD expressions similar to "all those who walk in these in holy perfection" do not allude to a separate group within the community, but to the entire congregation.

Wassen may well be right that the reference to the camps is added secondarily, and she is also probably right that the people in the camps are viewed as a subgroup of those who live in perfect holiness, in the sense that they too are contrasted with the sinners. But she does not explain the "adversative formulation beginning with the conditional 'And if,'" on which Baumgarten based his argument. In her view "those who marry and live in camps are singled out, *from among the first group,* in order for the redactor to emphasize that the whole family, including women and children," should observe both the laws of the Torah and the community regulations. But the conditional "if" nonetheless implies that not all members lived in camps and married and had children. Rather than contrast the two groups, the intention of the passage seems to be to reassure those who marry and have children that they too can walk in perfection. There is no other hint of an unmarried group in the *Damascus Rule.* If this passage is indeed a secondary addition it may reflect a later stage in the development of the movement, when the perfection of holiness came to be associated with a celibate lifestyle, and it was necessary to add that faithful married members would also be delivered from the judgment.

An Eschatological Dimension

Eschatological expectation played a significant motivating role in the new covenant.[72] This is perhaps most evident in the prediction that those who "turned back" and abandoned the movement would be destroyed within forty years of the death of the Teacher (CD 20:14). The *Damascus Rule* as-

71. Wassen, *Women in the Damascus Document,* 124-25. She also points to CD 14:2, which promises deliverance to all the righteous, without distinction, but that passage does not use language of perfection or holiness.

72. I have discussed this aspect of the Scrolls at length elsewhere: *Apocalypticism in the Dead Sea Scrolls* (London: Routledge, 1997) 52-70.

sumes that "the end of days" is imminent, when there shall arise "a messiah of Aaron and Israel" (CD 20:1). We need not dwell here on the debate as to whether this expectation involved one individual or two.[73] The novelty, in either case, was the expectation of a messianic *priest*, which shows the importance this group attached to the temple and its cult. The messianic references are made in passing, and assume rather than argue for messianic expectation. It should be clear, however, that the movement described in the *Damascus Rule* is not messianic in the sense that early Christianity was: the movement does not arise because an actual messiah was believed to have come. Rather, eschatology in the *Damascus Rule* adds a sense of urgency to the laws, and reassures the members that while their interpretation was rejected by the authorities of the day, it would soon be vindicated.

The Origin of the New Covenant

The *Damascus Rule* provides only oblique evidence of the history of the movement it describes.[74] The closest we come to a narrative about the origin of this group is in CD 1. God, we are told, hid his face from Israel and from his sanctuary because the people were unfaithful, "and he delivered them up to the sword. But when he remembered the covenant with the forefathers, he saved a remnant for Israel and did not deliver them up to destruction." (This pattern of destruction followed by the deliverance of a remnant is reiterated in CD 2–3.) Then

> in the age of wrath, three hundred and ninety years after having delivered them up into the hand of Nebuchadnezzar, king of Babylon, he visited them and caused to sprout from Israel and from Aaron a shoot of the planting, in order to possess his land.[75]

73. See J. J. Collins, *The Scepter and the Star: The Messiahs of the Dead Sea Scrolls and Other Ancient Literature* (Anchor Bible Reference Library; New York: Doubleday, 1995) 74-82. I regard it as probable that two messiahs were intended.

74. On the difficulties of reconstructing history from the *Damascus Rule* see Maxine L. Grossman, *Reading for History in the Damascus Document: A Methodological Study* (STDJ 45; Leiden: Brill, 2002).

75. On the problems posed by this passage, see Davies, *Damascus Covenant*, 63; J. J. Collins, "The Origin of the Qumran Community: A Review of the Evidence," in idem, *Seers, Sibyls, and Sages in Hellenistic-Roman Judaism* (JSJSup 54; Leiden: Brill, 1997) 250-51. Davies

This passage has been widely interpreted to mean that this movement arose from Israel and from Aaron in the early second century BCE.[76] It is doubtful, however, that the number of 390 years can be pressed in this way. It is a symbolic number, derived from Ezek 4:5, and in any case we do not know how the author of this text understood the chronology of the postexilic period.[77] It does seem clear, however, that a considerable period of time had elapsed between the exile and the rise of this group. If the period of punishment was 390 years, even as a round, symbolic number, the group can hardly have arisen in the Babylonian exile or in the Persian period, as some scholars have argued.[78] Even if this number is a secondary gloss, it still reflects the movement's own understanding of its history. The argument that its roots should in some sense be sought in the exile derives in part from its self-designation as *šby yśr'l*, "the returnees [or perhaps the captivity] of Israel." But as Michael Knibb especially has shown, several apocalyptic texts of the second century BCE conceive of the exile as an unredeemed state lasting down to their own time. Accordingly, an "exilic consciousness" has no chronological value.[79] Neither can any chronological conclusions be drawn from the very general analogies between CD and Ezra-Nehemiah, which point at most to some common concerns that persisted throughout the Second Temple period.[80] The Damascus covenant

---

sees the reference to 390 years as a gloss. In this he is followed by Hultgren, *From the Damascus Covenant*, 533.

76. See, e.g., James C. VanderKam, *The Dead Sea Scrolls Today* (Grand Rapids: Eerdmans, 1994) 100. Wacholder, *New Damascus Document*, 147: "in this chronological scheme, the point in time is 597 B.C.E. plus three hundred and ninety years, which equals 207 B.C.E., with an additional twenty years of blindness to arrive at 187 B.C.E. as the anticipated year of Israel's full repentance." Wacholder argues that the 390 years were not yet complete.

77. This point is generally granted even by scholars who still think the number is approximately correct, e.g., Cross, *Ancient Library*, 104-5; Vermes, *Complete Dead Sea Scrolls*, 58-59.

78. J. Murphy-O'Connor, "The Damascus Document Revisited," *RB* 92 (1985): 224-30; Davies, *Damascus Covenant*, 203.

79. Knibb, "Exile in Literature"; idem, "Exile in the Damascus Document," *JSOT* 25 (1983): 99-117. Compare Daniel 9 or the Apocalypse of Weeks in *1 Enoch* 93.

80. *Pace* Hultgren, *From the Damascus Covenant*, 141-232. I find his suggestion that "the Damascus covenant was the group that continued to uphold the ideal vision of the Chronicler and his party when the Jerusalem priesthood followed a different path" (p. 234) rather bizarre. Chronicles shows none of the halakic interests that Hultgren himself shows were fundamental to D, and its vision was centered on the temple cult, which is pushed into the background in quite different circumstances in D.

was ultimately quite different, in its organization but also in its motivation, from the covenant of Nehemiah.

Apart from the 390 years, however, CD gives no indication of the date at which this development took place. It also fails to provide reference to any rulers whose identity might be discovered from other sources, even through coded names such as "Wicked Priest." It does mention a figure called "the Teacher of Righteousness," and he will reappear, in conjunction with various other figures, in the *pesharim,* or biblical commentaries, which permit some speculation about his date.[81] The earliest manuscript of the *Damascus Rule* found at Qumran (4Q266) dates to "the first half or middle of the first century BCE."[82] Presumably the movement had its origin some considerable time before that. The *Damascus Rule,* however, is not concerned to locate the movement historically, but only to give an account of its internal development.

God, we are told, caused to sprout from Aaron and Israel a root of planting (1:7). "They realized their iniquity and knew that they were guilty [men]; but they were like blind persons and like those who grope for a path over twenty years." Accordingly, this group is often described by modern scholars as "a penitential movement."[83] David Lambert has objected to this designation, noting that the initiative is said to come from God, whose salvific intervention is prior to any action on their part.[84] The priority of the divine initiative is reiterated in CD 2:11, 3:13, and 6:2. Those who were chosen then responded by realizing their guilt. This response leads to another divine intervention — the sending of the Teacher of Righteousness. Throughout this text there is a dialectic of divine and human initiative. The movement is not penitential in the sense in which that word is used in medieval Christianity, and is not focused on feeling sorry for sin. But it does involve a conversion in practice, a turning away from a way of life that is perceived as sinful and a "return" to the strict observance of the law of Moses.

81. See below, chapter 3.

82. Baumgarten "Damascus Document," in Charlesworth and Reitz, eds., *Damascus Document II,* 1.

83. VanderKam's statement is typical: "it is evident that before the Qumran settlement was built a new penitential movement came into being in Palestine" (*Dead Sea Scrolls Today,* 100). Compare also the standard translation of the expression *šby yśr'l* as "the penitents of Israel."

84. D. Lambert, "Did Israel Believe That Redemption Awaited Its Repentance? The Case of *Jubilees* 1," *CBQ* 68 (2006): 631-50, especially 646-50.

The period of blindness and groping is said to last "twenty years," or half a generation.[85] Then God raised up for them a "Teacher of Righteousness." The name is an allusion to Hos 10:12 ("for it is time to seek the Lord, that he may come and rain righteousness on you"),[86] but the meaning might better be indicated by a phrase such as "the right teacher," the one who could interpret the will of God correctly for his followers. We will hear more of this individual in the *pesharim*. In view of his authority in the congregation, he must be identified with the "Interpreter of the Law" who is mentioned in CD 6:7, in a passage to which we have already referred: the Interpreter is the "staff" for digging the well of the law. The "returnees of Israel" dig the well of the law with the staves that the staff decreed, which is to say that they interpret the law in light of his teachings.

The passage in CD 6 has generated some confusion, as it goes on to speak of another figure who will "teach righteousness in the end of days" (6:11). In the early days of research on the Scrolls, this passage gave rise to some rather wild speculation that the historical Teacher was expected to return at the end of days.[87] A consensus developed, however, that the figure expected at the end of days cannot be identified with the Teacher who played a role in the beginning of the community. Rather, that Teacher is referred to in this passage as the Interpreter of the Law, and the eschatological figure remains in the future.

This consensus was challenged by Philip Davies, who argued that this passage comes from an early stratum of the document, before the advent of the historical Teacher.[88] The historical Teacher, then, claimed to be the fulfillment of the expectation expressed in CD 6:11, and so might be re-

---

85. Again, Davies, *Damascus Covenant*, 63, regards the number as a secondary gloss, but it still reflects an understanding current within the community.

86. The Hebrew verb *yrh* has the sense of "rain" in Hosea, but can also mean "teach," hence *mwrh*, "Teacher."

87. So especially A. Dupont-Sommer, *The Essene Writings from Qumran* (trans. G. Vermes; Gloucester, MA: Peter Smith, 1973) 131 n. 6: "The Teacher of Righteousness is dead but will reappear 'at the end of days' . . . The expectation of the Teacher's return, formulated so clearly here, was one of the fundamental articles of belief in the credo of the New Covenant." See further G. Jeremias, *Der Lehrer der Gerechtigkeit* (SUNT 2; Göttingen: Vandenhoeck & Ruprecht, 1963) 275-81; J. Carmignac, "Le retour du Docteur de Justice à la fin des jours?" *RevQ* 1 (1958–59): 235-48.

88. Davies, *Damascus Covenant*, 124; idem, "The Teacher of Righteousness at the End of Days," *RevQ* 13 (1988) 313-17. Davies's position is assumed without argument by Hultgren, *From the Damascus Covenant*, 537.

garded, loosely, as a messianic figure. But elsewhere "Interpreter of the Law" appears as the title for an eschatological figure. In the *Florilegium* (4Q174) he will appear with the Branch of David at the end of days. In CD 7:18 the "star" of Balaam's oracle is identified as the "Interpreter of the Law." This suggests that such titles as "Teacher of Righteousness" and "Interpreter of the Law" could be used variously to refer to figures past or future, and that they are interchangeable.

The *Community Rule* requires that an "Interpreter of the Law" be present in every group of ten" (1QS 6:6). The *Damascus Rule*, as preserved, retains the expectation of "one who will teach righteousness at the end of days," even though the career of the historical Teacher is clearly past. It envisages two Teachers, one of whom was dead at the time of the final redaction and one who was still to come. It is gratuitous to multiply Teachers without cause, by identifying the Interpreter of the Law as yet a third figure who preceded the historical Teacher.[89] The *Damascus Rule* as we have it looks back to the Teacher.[90] At least the form of the document found in CD manuscript B was edited after his death, as it predicts that from "the day of the gathering in of the unique teacher" until the end of all his opponents would be about forty years (CD 20:15; cf. 19:33–20:1).[91] It is possible that this passage was added to update the document, but there can be no doubt that the *Damascus Rule* was compiled within the Teacher's community (that is, the community of the Teacher mentioned in CD 1).[92]

89. See the criticism of Davies's proposal by Michael Knibb, "The Teacher of Righteousness — A Messianic Title?" in P. R. Davies and R. T. White, eds., *A Tribute to Geza Vermes: Essays on Jewish and Christian Literature and History* (JSOTSup 100; Sheffield: JSOT Press, 1990) 51-65; and J. J. Collins, "Teacher and Messiah? The One Who Will Teach Righteousness at the End of Days," in Ulrich and VanderKam, eds., *Community of the Renewed Covenant*, 194.

90. Charlotte Hempel, "Community Origins in the Damascus Document in the Light of Recent Scholarship," in D. W. Parry and E. Ulrich, eds., *The Provo International Conference on the Dead Sea Scrolls: Technological Innovations, New Texts and Reformulated Issues* (STDJ 30; Leiden: Brill, 1999) 328, tries to find a pre-Teacher stratum in passages such as CD 2:8-13 that mention only one stage in the rise of the community. But as she herself recognizes, one could argue that the author or compiler did not have to give the full story every time he mentioned it.

91. See Joseph A. Fitzmyer, "The Gathering In of the Community's Teacher," *Maarav* 8 (1992): 223-28; contra B. Z. Wacholder, "Does Qumran Record the Death of the *Moreh*? The Meaning of *he'aseph* in *Damascus Covenant* XIX,35, XX,14," *RevQ* 13 (Mémorial Jean Carmignac; 1988): 323-30. See also Hanan Eshel, "The Meaning and Significance of CD 20:13-15," in Parry and Ulrich, eds., *Provo International Conference*, 330-36.

92. Davies, *Damascus Covenant*, 200, also assigns the reference to the Teacher in CD 1:11 to a "Qumranic recension," although he has no adequate literary argument for doing so.

We are not told exactly what the Teacher did in terms of organizing the community. Some scholars have inferred from the period of blindness that the movement was not organized into a structured community until the Teacher arrived. So Shemaryahu Talmon credits the Teacher with "transforming the loose group-cohesion of the founding members into a structured socioreligious system."[93] On this hypothesis, the community structures described in the Laws (the "new covenant") would have been introduced by the Teacher. Charlotte Hempel, in contrast, attributes these structures to the "parent group" that existed prior to the Teacher's arrival.[94] We shall find a different form of community structure known as the *yaḥad,* with a more elaborate process of admission, in the *Community Rule.* The Teacher is not mentioned in the *Community Rule,* but he is associated with the *yaḥad* in the *pesharim,* and a reference to "the unique Teacher" *(mwrh hyḥyd)* in CD 20:1 is usually thought to be either a mistake or a play on "Teacher of the *Yaḥad."* Hempel's argument is based on the assumption that the *yaḥad* was "the Teacher's community." The organization described in the *Damascus Rule,* then, was "the communal organization of the pre-Teacher group."[95] In this case the Damascus covenant would have been formed some twenty years before the coming of the Teacher, according to the schema in CD 1. But the Teacher is venerated in the *Damascus Rule,* while he is not mentioned at all in the *Community Rule.* Moreover, both rules continued to be copied through the first century BCE, and so the *Damascus Rule* community does not seem to have been displaced by the *yaḥad.* Hempel may be right, but it is also possible that the movement was not organized into a structured association until the Teacher arrived, that it was he who inaugurated the "new covenant," and that the *yaḥad* was a later outgrowth of his movement.[96]

93. S. Talmon, *The World of Qumran from Within* (Jerusalem: Magnes, 1989) 284.

94. Hempel, *Laws,* 150.

95. Ibid.

96. Hultgren, *From the Damascus Covenant,* 53-62, 533, distinguishes between the Damascus covenant (= "the new covenant") and "the pre-Qumran community that arose from within the Damascus covenant" (= "the covenant," which boycotted the temple). He assumes that the insertion of the 390 years in CD 1 entails a revised understanding of the "root of planting," which originally referred to "the Damascus covenant" but now refers to "the pre-Qumran community." I find this reconstruction gratuitously complicated. The text speaks of only one "parent community," which arose some twenty years before the coming of the Teacher.

Other Witnesses to the New Covenant?

The *Damascus Rule* is not the only document of Second Temple Judaism that speaks of the emergence of an elect group within Judaism. The Apocalypse of Weeks in *1 Enoch* speaks of "the chosen righteous from the eternal plant of righteousness," which is given "sevenfold teaching concerning his whole creation" (*1 En.* 93:10). In another Enochic apocalypse, the Animal Apocalypse, "small lambs" are born and begin to "open their eyes" (*1 En.* 90:6). Later, horns grow upon these lambs, and a big horn grows on one of the sheep, who is usually taken to symbolize Judas Maccabee.[97] The book of Daniel speaks of "wise teachers" (*maśkilim*) who resist the persecution of Antiochus Epiphanes (Dan 11:33; 12:3, 10). *Jubilees* speaks of a turning point in history when "the children will begin to study the laws, and to seek the commandments, and return to the path of righteousness" (*Jub.* 23:26). A further example is found in the fragmentary *Pseudo-Daniel* text (4Q243-244) from Qumran.[98] At one time scholars tended to assume that all these texts, and also CD 1, were referring to a single group, the Hasidim, who are known from the books of Maccabees.[99] But the main thing known about the Hasidim is that they were militant supporters of Judas Maccabee.[100] Of the texts in question, only the Animal Apocalypse in *1 Enoch* exhibits a compatible ideology, and there is no evidence in the books of Maccabees that the Hasidim were interested in Enoch.

While the Hasidim have receded in recent scholarship, however, many scholars still posit a link between the development described in the

97. G. W. E. Nickelsburg, *1 Enoch 1* (Hermeneia; Minneapolis: Fortress, 2001) 400.

98. See further J. J. Collins, "Pseudepigraphy and Group Formation in Second Temple Judaism," in Esther G. Chazon and Michael E. Stone, eds., *Pseudepigraphic Perspectives: The Apocrypha and Pseudepigrapha in Light of the Dead Sea Scrolls* (STDJ 31; Leiden: Brill, 1999) 43-58.

99. For example, Martin Hengel, *Judaism and Hellenism* (trans. John Bowden; 2 vols.; Philadelphia: Fortress, 1974) 1.175-80; A. Lacocque, "The Socio-Spiritual Formative Milieu of the Daniel Apocalypse," in A. S. van der Woude, ed., *The Book of Daniel in the Light of New Findings* (BETL 106; Leuven: Peeters, 1993) 315-43.

100. 1 Macc 2:42; 2 Macc 14:6. They also seem to be identified with a group of scribes who sought peace in 1 Macc 7:12-14. See John Kampen, *The Hasideans and the Origin of Pharisaism* (SBLSCS 24; Atlanta: Scholars Press, 1988). According to Étienne Nodet, "*Asidaioi* and Essenes," in A. Hilhorst, É. Puech, and E. Tigchelaar, eds., *Flores Florentino: Dead Sea Scrolls and Other Early Jewish Studies in Honour of Florentino García Martínez* (JSJSup 122; Leiden: Brill, 2007) 81, they seek peace, but not at any cost.

Damascus Rule and the groups mentioned in the pseudepigraphic writings, especially *1 Enoch*. In 1984 Devorah Dimant suggested that the Animal Apocalypse was an early sectarian work that refers to the emergence of the Teacher of Righteousness.[101] In 1987 Philip Davies, who a decade earlier had debunked the all-embracing portrayal of the Hasidim, threw caution to the winds and declared that it seemed "unnecessarily pedantic" not to call the authors of the Enochic texts and *Jubilees* "Essenes."[102] The "Groningen Hypothesis" advanced by Florentino García Martínez in 1990 also tried "clearly to distinguish between the origins of the Qumran group and the origins of the parent group, the Essene movement, and to trace back to the apocalyptic tradition of the third century BCE the ideological roots of the Essenes."[103] In 1998 Gabriele Boccaccini went further and claimed that "Enochic Judaism is the modern name for the mainstream body of the Essene party, from which the Qumran community parted as a radical dissident, and marginal offspring."[104]

The books of Enoch (that is, the books that make up the collection known as *1 Enoch*) and *Jubilees* are found in multiple copies at Qumran, except for *1 Enoch* 37–71 (= the *Similitudes of Enoch*). It is reasonable to assume that there is some continuity between the authors of these texts and the "new covenant." The latter movement inherited from *Enoch* and Daniel an apocalyptic view of history, and the belief in reward and punishment after death.[105] More significantly, calendrical disputes, and advocacy of the 364-day solar calendar, figure prominently in *Enoch* and *Jubilees*. The festal calendar was one of the matters revealed to the members of the new covenant in CD 3. The Enoch tradition was also very critical of the Jerusalem temple. According to *1 En.* 89:73, the offerings in the restored temple after

---

101. D. Dimant, "Qumran Sectarian Literature," in M. E. Stone, ed., *Jewish Writings of the Second Temple Period* (CRINT 2/2; Philadelphia: Fortress, 1984) 544-45.

102. P. R. Davies, *Behind the Essenes: History and Ideology in the Dead Sea Scrolls* (BJS 84; Atlanta: Scholars Press, 1987) 109. For his earlier debunking of the Hasidim: "Hasidim in the Maccabean Period," *JJS* 28 (1977): 127-40.

103. F. García Martínez and A. S. van der Woude, "A Groningen Hypothesis of Qumran Origins and Early History," *RevQ* 14 (1990) 537. García Martínez had already proposed the Groningen hypothesis in "Qumran Origins and Early History: A Groningen Hypothesis," *Folia orientalia* 25 (1988): 113-26. Both articles are now reprinted in his *Qumranica Minora* (STDJ 63; Leiden: Brill, 2007) 3-52.

104. Gabrile Boccaccini, *Beyond the Essene Hypothesis* (Grand Rapids: Eerdmans, 1998) 16.

105. See further Collins, *Apocalypticism in Dead Sea Scrolls*, 12-29.

the exile were impure. There can be no doubt that the members of the new covenant were familiar with that literature and influenced by it in significant ways. The *Damascus Rule* refers to the story of the Watchers in CD 2:18.

Nonetheless, it is difficult to identify the "plant root" of the *Damascus Rule* with *Enoch*'s "chosen righteous from the eternal plant of righteousness," even despite the similar terminology.[106] For the Enoch literature (Boccaccini's "Enochic Judaism"), Enoch, not Moses, was the revealer *par excellence.* Moreover, the interpretation of the law of Moses, the very *raison d'être* of the Damascus covenant, is conspicuously absent from the Enoch literature.[107] It is arguable that the movement that produced the Enoch literature eventually acquired an interest in the law of Moses, but there is little indication of such interest in the books attributed to Enoch.[108] Equally, there is no indication of an interest in speculation about heavenly bodies or otherworldly geography in the *Damascus Rule.* The Judaism of the *Damascus Rule* cannot be described as "Enochic Judaism."[109]

A stronger case can be made for continuity between *Jubilees* and the *Damascus Rule. Jubilees* is essentially a retelling of the book of Genesis and Exodus 1–15. While it picks up the Enochic elaboration of the myth of the Watchers and reworks it, it has a pervasive interest in halakic issues, and the "children" mentioned in chapter 23 are devoted to the study of the law.

106. See further my essays, "Enoch, the Dead Sea Scrolls, and the Essenes: Groups and Movements in Judaism in the Early Second Century B.C.E.," in Gabriele Boccaccini, ed., *Enoch and Qumran Origins* (Grand Rapids: Eerdmans, 2005) 345-50; and "Enochic Judaism and the Sect of the Dead Sea Scrolls," in John J. Collins and Gabriele Boccaccini, eds., *The Early Enoch Literature* (JSJSup 121; Leiden: Brill, 2007) 283-99.

107. Nickelsburg, *1 Enoch 1,* 50: "To judge from what the authors of 1 Enoch have written, the Sinaitic covenant and Torah were not of central importance for them." Cf. G. W. E. Nickelsburg, "Enochic Wisdom: An Alternative to Mosaic Torah?" in J. Magness and S. Gitin, eds., *Hesed ve-Emet: Studies in Honor of Ernest S. Frerichs* (BJS 320; Atlanta: Scholars Press, 1998) 123-32.

108. For a gradual increase in interest in the Mosaic Torah in the Enoch tradition, see Andreas Bedenbender, *Der Gott der Welt tritt auf den Sinai* (Arbeiten zur neutestamentlichen Theologie und Zeitgeschichte 8; Berlin: Institut Kirche und Judentum, 2000) 215-58. Gabriele Boccaccini, "Enochians, Urban Essenes, Qumranites: Three Social Groups, One Intellectual Movement," in Collins and Boccaccini, eds., *Early Enoch Literature,* 301-27, speaks rather of an Enochic movement, in which the book of *Jubilees* plays a mediating role.

109. Boccaccini now agrees that "it is unlikely that the authors of the Enoch apocalypses and the sectarian rule books once belonged to the same group or organization" ("Enochians, Urban Essenes, Qumranites," 315).

Jubilees argues explicitly for a 364-day calendar, and calendrical issues are also important in the *Damascus Rule*. CD 16:3-4 states explicitly that "the explication of the times" is specified in "the Book of the Divisions of the Times in their Jubilees and in their weeks." This is generally recognized as an allusion to *Jubilees*. Boccaccini sees *Jubilees* as a transitional text between the early Enoch literature and the Scrolls.[110] *Jubilees* certainly reworks the myth of the Watchers, and most scholars agree that it is ideologically close to the sectarian scrolls.[111] The Enoch literature, however, is only one of the sources on which *Jubilees*, and *a fortiori* the *Damascus Rule*, drew.

Jubilees does not refer to any community structure or to any new covenant within Israel. Martha Himmelfarb has argued that it should not be regarded as sectarian at all, since it seems to envision the salvation of all Israel, not just of the elect.[112] But it certainly has sectarian tendencies. As Michael Segal has shown, it engages in harsh polemic against Jews who interpret the Torah differently. For example, *Jub.* 15:26 declares that "anyone who is born, the flesh of whose private parts has not been circumcised by the eighth day does not belong to the people of the pact which the Lord made with Abraham but to the people (meant for) destruction (trans. J. VanderKam)." The passage goes on in verses 33-34 to rail against Israelites who do not circumcise their sons properly. This kind of polemic is in keeping with what we find in the Admonition of the *Damascus Rule*, and more emphatic than what we find in the Laws. It may not be possible to prove that *Jubilees* was written or redacted within the new covenant, but Segal seems justified in concluding that "*Jubilees* was redacted within the same stream of Judaism within which one can locate the Qumran sect, and in a similar ideological climate."[113]

Another text that may reflect the concerns of the movement described in the *Damascus Rule* in its early stages is the *Temple Scroll*

110. Ibid., 317.

111. For example, M. Testuz, *Les idées religieuses du livre des Jubilés* (Geneva: Minard, 1960), especially 179-83 on correspondences with the *Damascus Document*. See most recently Michael Segal, *The Book of Jubilees: Rewritten Bible, Redaction, Ideology and Theology* (JSJSup 117; Leiden: Brill, 2007) 97-143, on the reworking of the Watchers story, and 322 on the relationship to Qumran.

112. M. Himmelfarb, *A Kingdom of Priests: Ancestry and Merit in Ancient Judaism* (Philadelphia: University of Pennsylvania Press, 2006) 80-83.

113. Segal, *Book of Jubilees*, 322.

(11QT).[114] This long text is presented as a revelation of God to Moses. It takes its name from its lengthy prescriptions relating to the temple and the sacrificial cult, but it goes on to reformulate biblical laws on a wide range of topics, many dealing with issues of purity, others with issues of polity, including the Law of the King, in columns 57–59.[115] In several cases, laws in the *Temple Scroll* parallel laws in the *Damascus Rule*.[116]

The *Temple Scroll* forbids the king to remarry during his first wife's lifetime (11QT 57:17-19). CD 4:19–5:2 makes this restriction universal.[117]

CD 12:1-2 prohibits sexual relations in the city of the sanctuary. According to 11QT 45:7-12, before entering the temple, anyone who has had a seminal emission must undergo a three-day purification period. Both texts require a seven-day purification period for a woman who has had sexual relations during menstruation. Both texts prohibit uncle-niece marriages.

There are further correspondences on several other issues, including the impurity of the dead, priestly gifts, and the slaughter of pregnant animals.[118] Moreover, the *Temple Scroll*, like *Jubilees*, follows a 364-day solar calendar.[119] There are also significant points of contact between the *Temple Scroll* and 4QMMT.[120] At the same time, many issues discussed in the *Temple Scroll* are not raised in the other texts, and vice versa.

The *Temple Scroll* gives no hint of any sectarian organization. It is not overtly polemical in the manner of the *Damascus Rule* or 4QMMT. It presents its laws as divine revelation, rather than as exegesis. For all these

114. Y. Yadin, *The Temple Scroll* (3 vols. in 4; Jerusalem: Israel Exploration Society, 1977–83), supplemented by E. Qimron, *The Temple Scroll: A Critical Edition with Extensive Restorations* (Jerusalem: Israel Exploration Society, 1996).

115. For a literary analysis of the scroll see M. O. Wise, *A Critical Study of the Temple Scroll from Qumran Cave 11* (SAOC 49; Chicago: Oriental Institute of the University of Chicago, 1990).

116. L. H. Schiffman, "The Zadokite Fragments and the Temple Scroll," in Baumgarten et al., eds., *Damascus Document*, 133-45.

117. See above, n. 18.

118. There are also some cases of incongruity, where the treatments of a common issue do not correspond. See L. H. Schiffman, "The Law of Vows and Oaths (Num. 30. 3-15) in the Zadokite Fragments and the Temple Scroll," *RevQ* 15 (1991): 199-214.

119. On the close relation between the *Temple Scroll* and *Jubilees*, see James C. VanderKam, "The Temple Scroll and the Book of Jubilees," in George J. Brooke, ed., *Temple Scroll Studies* (JSPSup 7; Sheffield: Sheffield Academic Press, 1989) 211-36.

120. L. H. Schiffman, "The Temple Scroll and the Systems of Jewish Law of the Second Temple Period," in Brooke, ed., *Temple Scroll Studies*, 245-50.

reasons, it is now usually regarded as a presectarian text. Nonetheless, it would seem to be representative of the kinds of concerns that led to the formation of the new covenant.

Schiffman has argued that the halakic tradition reflected in the *Damascus Rule, Temple Scroll,* and 4QMMT is Sadducean in origin.[121] In a number of cases, the rulings in these texts correspond to those of the Sadducees against those of the Pharisees. For example, the Pharisees allowed one who has already immersed and performed all necessary purification rituals to come in contact with pure food outside the sanctuary, before the end of his purification period. (This principle is called *tevul yom.*) This position is rejected in the *Temple Scroll* and 4QMMT, and also in the *Damascus Rule.*[122] The Pharisees held that impurity does not travel back from a receptacle along a liquid stream. The Sadducees disagreed.[123] 4QMMT agrees with the Sadducean position. The prohibition of marriage between uncle and niece (CD 5:7-9; 11QT 66:15-17) is a polemic against the position of the Pharisees as found in the Talmud.[124] The number of examples is not great, but the halakah of this tradition seems to disagree consistently with the positions later attributed to the Pharisees, and, at least in a number of striking cases, to agree with that of the Sadducees.[125] This does not necessarily mean that the authors were Sadducees, only that they shared a tradition of legal interpretation with the Sadducees. This observation does not preclude the possibility that the authors might be Essenes, or belong to some other sect, as other factors would have to be taken into consideration to establish sectarian identity.[126] Nonetheless, the fact that they shared common traditions

---

121. For example, L. H. Schiffman, "The Sadducean Origins of the Dead Sea Scrolls," in H. Shanks, ed., *Understanding the Dead Sea Scrolls* (New York: Random House, 1992) 35-49.

122. 4Q266 6 ii 1-4. Schiffman, "Systems of Jewish Law," 247; idem, "Zadokite Fragments," 139. See also J. M. Baumgarten, "The Pharisaic-Sadducean Controversies about Purity and the Qumran Texts," *JJS* 31 (1980): 157-70; Y. Sussmann, "Appendix 1: The History of the Halakha and the Dead Sea Scrolls," in DJD 10, 187-88.

123. *m. Yadayim* 4:7. See Schiffman, "Systems of Jewish Law," 250-51; Sussmann, "Appendix 1," 188.

124. Schiffman, "Zadokite Fragments," 140.

125. James C. VanderKam, "The People of the Dead Sea Scrolls: Essenes or Sadducees?" in Shanks, ed., *Understanding the Dead Sea Scrolls,* 50-62, questions some of the examples adduced by Schiffman (two of four examples from *m. Yadayim* 4:6-7), but he does not discuss some of Schiffman's main examples, such as *tevul yom.*

126. This is clearly recognized by Sussmann, "Appendix 1," 195-96.

with the Sadducees is significant. It suggests that the development of the new covenant took place in the same general milieu as the early controversies between Pharisees and Sadducees about halakic issues.

Sons of Zadok?

The *Damascus Document* was originally labeled a "Zadokite" work by Schechter.[127] Many scholars have shared the view that the movement had its origin in a dispute over the high priesthood. The traditional line of high priests was disrupted during the so-called Hellenistic Reform and the persecution by Antiochus Epiphanes, and the office was subsequently usurped by the Hasmoneans, when Jonathan Maccabee became high priest in 152 BCE. Frank Cross was one of many scholars who saw these events as the background for the rise of the sectarian movement:

> The key to any sound reconstruction of the historical circumstances which gave rise to the Essene movement lies in an adequate explanation of the peculiarly priestly character of the early schismatic community. . . . The founder of the sect, the Righteous Teacher, was himself a priest. The "opposite number" of the Righteous Priest was the Wicked Priest, the archpersecutor of the sect. The priests of Qumrân regarded the Jerusalem sanctuary as defiled, its priests false, its calendar unorthodox. In the end of days the Essene (Zadokite) priesthood would be re-established in the New Jerusalem, the false priesthood overthrown for ever.[128]

Consequently, the separation of this sect from the rest of Judaism is often assumed to date from the time when the Hasmoneans assumed the high priesthood, in the mid-second century BCE.

This reconstruction of events is based in part on the opposition between the Teacher and the Wicked Priest in the *pesharim*, but its primary support is found in a passage in CD 3:21–4:4:

> As God swore to them by means of Ezekiel the prophet, saying, "the priests and the Levites and the sons of Zadok who maintained the ser-

---

127. Schechter, *Fragments of a Zadokite Work.*

128. Cross, *Ancient Library*, 100-101. Cross dated the schism to the time of Simon Maccabee rather than Jonathan.

vice of my temple when the children of Israel strayed far away from me; they shall offer me the fat and the blood." The priests are the returnees of Israel who left the land of Judah, and the Levites are those who joined them, and the sons of Zadok are the chosen of Israel, the men of renown, who stand at the end of days.[129]

There is also mention of an individual named Zadok in CD 5:5: David had not read the book of the law, because it was sealed until Zadok took office. A teacher named Zadok is known to have lived about 200 BCE, and Ben Zion Wacholder has argued that this figure was the founder of the sect.[130] Hence his followers were the "sons of Zadok." Most scholars, however, have assumed that the Zadok mentioned in CD 5 was the priest appointed by David (2 Sam 15:24-29). In any case, it is unsafe to infer from CD that the members of this movement were Zadokite priests. The reference is scriptural (cf. Ezek 44:15-31), and need not be taken literally, any more than the reference to Damascus, which we have already discussed.[131] The "sons of Zadok" are the chosen of Israel, who stand at the end of days, and so would seem to be an honorific title for the whole community.[132] Moreover, "sons of Zadok" was not a common way of referring to the actual high priests of the Second Temple era. Apart from the utopian vision of Ezekiel 40–48, the only references prior to the Dead Sea Scrolls are the mention of a chief priest Azariah of the house of Zadok in 2 Chron 31:10 and a reference in Sir 51:13 whose authenticity is disputed.[133]

No doubt, priests played a part in the movement of the new covenant: it was said to spring from Aaron and Israel, and it expected a messiah or messiahs "of Aaron and Israel." Its great concern with issues of purity is typically priestly. Moreover, we shall meet the expression "sons of Zadok"

---

129. Cross offers his translation of this passage in ibid., 101.

130. Wacholder, *New Damascus Document*, 5, 196-97. Zadok is mentioned in *Abot de Rabbi Nathan* 5.

131. See P. R. Davies, "Sons of Zadok," in *Behind the Essenes*, 51-72, especially 53-54.

132. So already Georg Klinzing, *Die Umdeutung des Kultus in der Qumrangemeinde und im Neuen Testament* (SUNT 7; Göttingen: Vandenhoeck & Ruprecht, 1971) 132-42.

133. See Alice Hunt, *Missing Priests: The Zadokites in Tradition and History* (LHB/OTS [= JSOTSup] 452; London: T&T Clark, 2006) 11. Saul Olyan, "Ben Sira's Relationship to the Priesthood," *HTR* 80 (1987): 275, notes that Zadok is "conspicuously absent" from Ben Sira. See also the discussion by Maria Brutti, *The Development of the High Priesthood during the Pre-Hasmonean Period: History, Ideology, Theology* (JSJSup 108; Leiden: Brill, 2006) 110-15, who notes the uncertainty surrounding the supposed Zadokite line.

again in the *Community Rule*, where it is used rather differently. The reference in the *Damascus Rule*, however, does not necessarily require that Zadokite lineage was an issue for the author. Neither is there any hint in the *Damascus Rule* that a dispute over the high priestly office played any part in the origin of the movement.

A Split in the Community?

Recent treatments of the early history of the movement described in the *Damascus Rule* have made much of a supposed "split" in the movement, which led to the separation of the Teacher and his followers ("the Qumran community") from the rest of the "Essenes." This reconstruction has figured prominently in the Groningen hypothesis advanced by Florentino García Martínez and in the more recent work of Gabriele Boccaccini, who sees the split as between "Enochic Judaism" and "Qumran." There is very little evidence for such a split in the texts. The scholarly theory has evolved from analyses of references to a figure called "the man of the lie."

It is apparent from the *Damascus Document* that the Teacher clashed with another prominent teacher called "the man of the lie," "spouter of lies," or "the liar": "This is the time about which it has been written, 'like a stray heifer, so has Israel strayed, when the scoffer arose, who poured over Israel waters of lies and made them stray into a wilderness without a path'" (CD 1:14-15). CD 20:14-15 refers to those who turned back with the man of the lie. Hartmut Stegemann argued that the latter figure was a leader within the movement who refused to accept the authority of the Teacher, and led a breakaway group that became the Pharisees.[134] Murphy-O'Connor saw him as a leader of "non-Qumran Essenism," which refused to follow the Teacher to the desert, and even suggested that he be identified with Judah the Essene.[135] Hence the idea has arisen that there was a split in the "Essene" movement, and that the Teacher's group broke away from the main body of the Essenes.

We shall return later to the question whether it is appropriate to

---

134. H. Stegemann, *Die Entstehung der Qumran Gemeinde* (Bonn: published privately, 1971) 227-28. Hultgren, *From the Damascus Covenant,* 307, regards him as an influential proto-Pharisaic teacher but not the founder of Pharisaism.

135. J. Murphy-O'Connor, "The Essenes and Their History," *RB* 81 (1974): 235; idem, "Judah the Essene and the Teacher of Righteousness," *RevQ* 10 (1981): 579-86.

speak here of Essenes at all. But even the idea that the man of the lie and the Teacher were rival teachers in the same movement is dubious. It is based on a passage in *Pesher Habakkuk* (1QpHab 5:8-12):

> The interpretation of it concerns the House of Absalom and their partisans, who were silent at the rebuke of the Teacher of Righteousness and did not support him against the man of the lie — who rejected the Law in the midst of all their council. (Trans. M. P. Horgan)

The passage is ambiguous as to which party was administering the rebuke. It has been argued that such a rebuke would be administered only within a community of which both men were members.[136] But this is not necessarily so. Another *pesher* refers to a "law" that the Teacher sent to the Wicked Priest, who is usually assumed to have been a high priest, and not a member of the Teacher's community.[137] The "house of Absalom" appears to be neutral and noncommittal. The references in the *Damascus Rule* do not suggest that the feud was an internal one. In CD 1:14 the man of mockery is said to spout waters of falsehood "to Israel" and lead them astray. He did not merely resist the claims of the Teacher but preached a different message. His audience was not just a congregation or community but Israel. In CD 4:19-20 the "builders of the wall" who have followed the spouter are said to be trapped in two of the nets of Belial. The disagreement, then, is not only over the authority of the Teacher but involves some of the halakic issues that separated this movement from the rest of Israel. It is probable that those whom the man of the lie led astray included some who had belonged to the movement described in CD 1. CD 20:14-15 speaks of "the men of the war who turned back with the man of the lie." The same column says that those who rejected "the new covenant in the land of Damascus" would receive the same judgment as their companions who turned back with the men of scoffing. These traitors to the new covenant, however, should not be simply identified with the followers of the man of the lie. The latter are only one of three groups of traitors distinguished in *Pesher Habakkuk* (1QpHab 2:1-10).

The *pesharim* emphasize the success of the man of the lie.[138] He led many astray (4QpPs[a] 1:26; 1QpHab 10:9) and built a city of vanity and es-

---

136. Jeremias, *Lehrer der Gerechtigkeit*, 85-86.
137. 4QpPs[a] 4:8-9. See further Collins, "Origin of Qumran Community," 255.
138. Stegemann, *Entstehung*, 44-45.

tablished a congregation of deceit (1QpHab 10:10). From this it would seem that he was credited with building up a movement, not merely retaining the loyalty of an old movement against the challenge of the Teacher, or causing a split in the movement. Stegemann's thesis that the followers of the man of the lie became the Pharisees has some evidence to support it.[139] They are said to be "seekers after smooth things" (CD 1:18). The Hebrew expression *dršy ḥlqwt* has often been taken as a play on the Pharisaic interest in halakot, or legal teachings, although this is also disputed.[140] In the *pesharim,* the "seekers" are opponents of the Hasmonean king Alexander Jannaeus, as the Pharisees are known to have been. Be that as it may, it is far from clear that the man of the lie was a member of the same community as the Teacher. All we can say is that he was a rival teacher, who rejected the Teacher's claims and won over some of his followers.

It is doubtful, then, whether the *Damascus Document* can be adduced as evidence for a split in the movement that it describes. In any case, the document is clearly compiled by the followers of the Teacher: it is not the rule of a community that rejected him. The differences between the communities described by the *Damascus Rule* and the *Community Rule* cannot be explained by the hypothesis that the Teacher broke away from the community described in the *Damascus Rule.*[141]

We shall return later to the question whether the Teacher's movement should be identified as Essene. The main arguments in favor of such an identification are based on the *Community Rule* rather than on the *Damascus Rule,* and concern the elaborate procedures for admission attributed to the Essenes, among other things. For the present, it may suffice to say that there is little or no basis for referring to the movement described in the *Damascus Rule* as Essene, and even less for applying that name to earlier texts such as *Jubilees* or the *Temple Scroll,* which do not speak of an organized community at all.

---

139. Ibid., 250. See A. I. Baumgarten, "Pharisees," *EDSS* 1.661-62.

140. See John P. Meier, "Is there *Halaka* (the Noun) at Qumran?" *JBL* 122 (2003): 150-55.

141. Boccaccini, "Enochians, Urban Essenes, Qumranites," 319, argues that the absence of the Similitudes of Enoch from the Qumran library shows that a split had taken place between Qumran and Enochic Judaism. But it is not certain that the Similitudes derive from an Enochic movement that is continuous with the other books found in *1 Enoch,* all of which are earlier by two centuries or more. Moreover, the Similitudes were composed later than most of the literature found at Qumran. Its absence is not necessarily due to deliberate rejection.

Conclusion

In summary, what we find in the *Damascus Rule* is a movement dedicated to the strict observance of the Torah of Moses, which lends urgency to its observance by the expectation of an eschatological judgment. It is a family-based movement, but it is also an organized community that makes extensive demands on its members, and to a great degree undercuts the authority of the paterfamilias. It restricts relations with the outside world, but has not withdrawn to anything resembling a monastic way of life. Marriage is the norm, although it is regulated and restricted.

The *Damascus Rule* is tantalizingly vague about historical information. It is apparent that the movement existed for some time before the Teacher of Righteousness came along. It is not clear, however, whether any of the communal organization found in CD derives from the time before his coming. The earlier stage of the movement may be reflected in such texts as *Jubilees* and the *Temple Scroll.* There also appears to be an affinity with the Sadducean tradition of halakic interpretation, but this does not require that the authors were Sadducees. Whether there was any historical or sociological continuity with the authors of the early Enoch literature is more questionable. The *Damascus Rule* is certainly not "Enochic Judaism," but has its focus on the Torah of Moses.

Many ideas about this movement that have gained wide currency in recent years appear to be ill-founded. It is not apparent that "sons of Zadok" was a genealogical designation for the members, or any segment of them, only an honorific title with reference to Ezekiel. Neither is there any reference to a dispute about the high priesthood. The theory that the arrival of the Teacher led to a split between the Teacher's community and the rest of the parent movement has very little evidence to support it. The *Damascus Rule,* taken on its own, provides little basis for identifying this movement as "Essene."

But the *Damascus Rule* does not stand alone. It is evidently related to the *Community Rule (Serek ha-Yahad)* and other related texts such as the so-called *Messianic Rule* (1QSa). The relationship between these texts points to some measure of diachronic development, even though the older texts continued to be copied throughout the first century BCE. We will turn to the *Serek* and its related texts in the following chapter.

CHAPTER TWO

The Yaḥad

Popular perceptions of "the Qumran community" are based above all on the document known as the *Community Rule* (*Serek ha-Yaḥad*, also known as 1QS or the *Manual of Discipline*), which was one of the scrolls in the initial discovery in Qumran Cave 1. Ten further copies were found in Cave 4.[1] The most elaborate form of the document is found in 1QS. It includes

a statement of the aims of the community, 1:1-15;
a description of an entrance ritual, or covenant renewal ceremony, in 1:16–3:12;
an instruction on the two spirits of light and darkness, in 3:13–4:26;
rules for community life, 5:1–7:25;
a program for a new community, 8:1–9:26;
an instruction on times of prayer, followed by a concluding hymn, 9:26b–11:22.

This full form of the text is paralleled in 4QS^b (4Q256), which preserves fragments of all these sections except for the *Instruction on the Two Spirits,* but has a shorter form of the text. For example, where 1QS 5:2 says that the men of the community are "subject to the authority of the sons of Zadok, the priests who safeguard the covenant, and to the authority of the

---

1. James H. Charlesworth, ed., *The Dead Sea Scrolls: Hebrew, Aramaic, and Greek Texts with English Translations,* vol. 1: *Rule of the Community and Related Documents* (PTSDSSP; Louisville: Westminster John Knox, 1994); Philip S. Alexander and Geza Vermes, *Qumran Cave 4,* vol. XIX: *Serekh ha-Yaḥad and Two Related Texts* (DJD 26; Oxford: Clarendon, 1998).

multitude of the men of the community who hold fast to the covenant," 4QS^b says only that they are subject to the authority of the "many" *(rabbim).* Other copies differ in various ways. 4QS^d (4Q258) evidently lacked the opening covenantal ceremony and the *Instruction on the Two Spirits.* 4QS^e concluded with the calendrical text 4QOtot (4Q319) instead of the hymnic material found in 1QS 10–11. Each of these manuscripts, however, has some form of the rules in 1QS 5–9, which form the core of the *Serek.*

There has been some debate as to how these different forms of the *Serek* developed. Sarianna Metso argues that "two different lines of tradition, both of which are older than that of 1QS, are represented by the manuscripts 4QS^{b,d} (4Q256, 258) and 4QS^e (4Q259)."[2] These manuscripts, however, are dated later than 1QS on the basis of paleography (handwriting).[3] Philip Alexander has argued that the paleographic dating reflects the more probable order of composition.[4] We shall return to this issue below. If Metso is right, as I believe she is, then it would seem that older forms of the text were not simply replaced by newer ones, but continued to be copied. This phenomenon is of some significance for our understanding of the nature and coherence of the community involved, and also for our understanding of the nature and purpose of the *Serek.*

At least in the form found in 1QS, the *Serek* is not simply a rule book. While a greater proportion of the text consists of community rules than is the case in CD, it also includes extensive instructional and motivational material. Alexander suggests that "it is best taken as a manual of instruction to guide the Maskil in his duties towards the community."[5] Nonetheless, it is also a rule book, at least in part, and it contains detailed information about the nature and purpose of the association that it describes.

2. Sarianna Metso, *The Textual Development of the Qumran Community Rule* (STDJ 21; Leiden: Brill, 1997) 152. See also her essay, "In Search of the Sitz im Leben of the Qumran Community Rule," in D. W. Parry and E. C. Ulrich, eds., *The Provo International Conference on the Dead Sea Scrolls* (STDJ 30; Leiden: Brill, 1999) 306-15; and her overview, *The Serekh Texts* (CQS 9; London: T&T Clark, 2007).

3. On the paleographic dates of the manuscripts see F. M. Cross, "Appendix: Paleographical Dates of the Manuscripts," in Charlesworth, ed., *Rule of the Community,* 57.

4. Philip Alexander, "The Redaction-History of *Serek ha-Yaḥad:* A Proposal," *RevQ* 17 (Milik Festschrift) (1996): 437-53.

5. Ibid., 439. So also Geza Vermes, *The Complete Dead Sea Scrolls in English* (rev. ed.; London: Penguin, 2004) 97; Carol Newsom, *The Self as Symbolic Space: Constructing Identity and Community at Qumran* (STDJ 54; Leiden: Brill, 2004) 102.

The Relationship to the *Damascus Rule*

The rules in the *Serek* have some features in common with the *Damascus Rule*. Here, as in CD, the person joining the community must "swear a binding oath to return to the law of Moses, according to all that he commanded, with his whole heart and whole soul" (1QS 5:8-9).[6] Both rules portray the association on the model of Israel in the wilderness, organized in "thousands, hundreds, fifties, and tens."[7] As in CD 13, the association is organized in communities with a minimum number of ten members (1QS 6:3-4). Both have strict disciplinary codes. Nonetheless, it becomes apparent that a different kind of community is envisioned in the *Serek*. There is no mention of women or children, and there is a greater degree of communal activity.[8] The members are said to eat, bless, and take counsel together. They also relieve one another interpreting the Torah, night and day, and keep watch together for one-third of each night. Members apparently are required to turn over all their possessions to the inspector, although they are still credited to their accounts (6:19-20). This greater cohesiveness and tighter community structure is reflected in the designation for the community, *yahad*, which means "union" or "togetherness."

The word *yahad* occurs more than fifty times in 1QS, the most complete manuscript of the *Serek*. It also occurs 7 times in 1QSa, the *Rule of the Congregation*, and 3 times in 1QSb, the *Scroll of Blessings*. It occurs several times in *pesharim* and related texts, such as 4Q174 *(Florilegium)*, 4Q177 *(Catena)*, and 4Q252 *(Pesher Genesis)*, but only once in CD (assuming that "the men of the *yahid*," literally "the unique one," in CD 20:32 is a mistake for "the men of the *yahad*").[9] There are also 4 occurrences in 4Q265, a text that combines elements of the *Serek* and the *Damascus Rule*. Most of the

---

6. Compare 4Q256 frag. 5:6-7; 4Q258 frag. 1, col. 1, line 6. The differences between the manuscripts with regard to the "sons of Zadok" do not affect this point.

7. 1QS 2:21-22; cf. Exod 18:21; Deut 1:15. See S. Metso, "Qumran Community Structure and Terminology as Theological Statement," *RevQ* 20 (2002): 437.

8. See Alexei Sivertsev, *Households, Sects, and the Origins of Rabbinic Judaism* (JSJSup 102; Leiden: Brill, 2005) 130-40; Russell C. D. Arnold, *The Social Role of Liturgy in the Religion of the Qumran Community* (STDJ 60; Leiden: Brill, 2006) 29-36.

9. There is also a reference to "the unique Teacher" *(moreh hayyahid)* in CD 20:1, 14, which may conceivably be a mistake for *moreh hayyahad*, but is more likely to be a play on it. These references are redactional in any case. Martin Abegg, *The Dead Sea Scrolls Concordance* (2 vols.; Leiden: Brill, 2003) 1.308, also reconstructs an occurrence of *yahad* in 4Q270 (4QD^e).

occurrences in the *Serek* are in such phrases as "the men of the *yaḥad*" or "the council of the *yaḥad*," and occasional references to "the *yaḥad* of God." Shemaryahu Talmon suggested another precedent in Ezra 4:3, where Zerubbabel and the leaders of the Jewish community rebuff the offer of the Samaritans to help rebuild the temple by saying "we *yaḥad* will build."[10] (In this case the word is usually translated as "alone," admittedly an unusual usage.) While the suggestion that *yaḥad* might have served as the name of the exclusive community of returned exiles is attractive, the word is not otherwise attested in the books of Ezra and Nehemiah, and so the suggestion has not won acceptance.[11] The choice of this specific Hebrew word is better explained by analogy with Deut 33:5, although the Scrolls never refer to "the *yaḥad* of the tribes."[12]

This name for the association is attested only indirectly in the *Damascus Rule,* in passages that may be redactional. In the latter rule, the preferred name for the organization was '*edah,* "congregation." Similarly, the term *maśkil,* which figures prominently in the *Serek,* appears only twice, "in the headings of heavily redacted passages," in the *Damascus Rule.*[13] The *mebaqqer,* who has a central role in CD, is mentioned only briefly in 1QS 6:12, 20.

The relationship between the two rules has been explained in various ways. Milik and Cross affirmed the priority of the *Serek,* and this view has recently been revived by Eyal Regev.[14] The priority of the *Damascus Rule*

10. Shemaryahu Talmon, "The Qumran יחד — A Biblical Noun," in idem, *The World of Qumran from Within* (Jerusalem: Magnes, 1989) 53-60.

11. There is one other nominal occurrence, in 1 Chron 12:18 (Eng. 17), where David tells the Judahites and Benjaminites that if they have come to him in friendship he will have "a heart for union" with them.

12. The suggestion of Hartmut Stegemann ("The Qumran Essenes — Local Members of the Main Jewish Union in Late Second Temple Times," in J. Trebolle Barrera and L. Vegas Montaner, eds., *The Madrid Qumran Congress* [2 vols.; STDJ 11; Leiden: Brill, 1992] 1.83-166) that "*Ha-yaḥad* meant a confederation of all existing Jewish groups, their union in a new religious body, which had never existed before" (p. 155), has found no followers.

13. Metso, "Qumran Community Structure," 439.

14. J. T. Milik, *Ten Years of Discovery in the Wilderness of Judaea* (trans. J. Strugnell; SBT 1/26; London: SCM, 1959) 83-93; F. M. Cross, *The Ancient Library of Qumran* (3rd ed.; BibSem 30; Sheffield: Sheffield Academic Press, 1995) 71 n. 2; so also Hartmut Stegemann, *The Library of Qumran: On the Essenes, Qumran, John the Baptist, and Jesus* (Grand Rapids: Eerdmans, 1998) 107-8, 150-52. Cf. Eyal Regev, "The *Yaḥad* and the Damascus Covenant: Structure, Organization and Relationship," *RevQ* 21 (2003): 233-62; idem, *Sectarianism in Qumran: A Cross-Cultural Perspective* (RelSoc 45; Berlin: de Gruyter, 2007) 163-96.

has been maintained especially by Philip Davies, Michael Knibb, and Charlotte Hempel.[15] Hempel has provided the most thorough comparison of the community structures.

Admission Procedures

The central feature of the admission process in the *Damascus Rule* is the swearing of an oath to return to the law of Moses (CD 15:5b-6a). Hempel has noted that a similar simple process of admission by swearing an oath is found 1QS 5:7c-9a:

> every one who enters into the Council of the Community, shall enter into the covenant of God in the sight of all those who devote themselves. He shall take upon his soul by a binding oath to return to the Torah of Moses, according to all which he has commanded with all heart and with all soul, according to everything which has been revealed from it to the Sons of Zadok, the priests who keep the covenant and seek his will, and according to the multitude of the men of their covenant. (Trans. J. H. Charlesworth)

This simple process contrasts with the elaborate, multistage process of admission described in 1QS 6:13b-23.[16] In the latter passage the postulant is initially examined by "the man appointed *(paqid)* at the head of the many."[17] Later he is subjected to another examination by the members of the association (the "many" or *rabbim*). He may not approach the "purity"

---

15. Davies, *Damascus Covenant,* 173-201; Knibb, "The Place of the Damascus Document," in M. O. Wise et al., eds., *Methods of Investigation of the Dead Sea Scrolls and the Khirbet Qumran Site* (ANYAS 722; New York: New York Academy of Sciences, 1994) 153-60; Hempel, *The Laws of the Damascus Document: Sources, Traditions, and Redaction* (STDJ 29; Leiden: Brill, 1998) 101, 150; idem, "Community Structures in the Dead Sea Scrolls: Admission, Organization, Disciplinary Procedures," in Peter W. Flint and James C. VanderKam, eds., *The Dead Sea Scrolls after Fifty Years* (2 vols.; Leiden: Brill, 1998–99) 2.67-92. So also Stephen Hultgren, *From the Damascus Covenant to the Covenant of the Community* (STDJ 66; Leiden: Brill, 2007) 233-318.

16. Some scholars, admittedly, have seen the two passages as continuous. See Hempel, "Community Structures," 72.

17. This individual, the *paqid,* probably corresponds to the *mebaqqer.* See Metso, "Qumran Community Structure," 439-40.

of the "many" until he has completed a probationary year.[18] At that point his property is handed over to the *mebaqqer,* who must register it to his account and keep it separate. He is still not allowed to partake of the drink of the *rabbim* until he has completed a second year. Then he is examined again, and if accepted he is registered in the order of his rank, and his property is merged with that of the community. This procedure is considerably more developed than what is described in CD 15, which provides for instruction by the *mebaqqer* for only one year. Hempel argues persuasively that the "short form" of the admission procedure in 1QS 5 is "a case of an earlier piece of communal legislation having been preserved in 1QS alongside the later and more elaborate procedure," and that the legislation in question derives from the "parent" community described in CD 15.[19] The older requirement for admission, swearing an oath, is not contravened by the more elaborate procedure, but is rather supplemented. The *Damascus Rule* already required that the *mebaqqer* examine admittees, with regard to character, intelligence, and wealth (CD 13:11). We may suppose that the *yaḥad* initially had a similar, simple procedure, and later devised a more elaborate one. The more exacting process of admission reflects a higher standard for the community, although it has the same basis in the law of Moses as the *Damascus Rule.*

Property

The demands of the *yaḥad* are also stricter in the matter of property. The *Damascus Rule* required only the surrender of two days' wages. The *Serek* apparently envisions full community of property. It is true that a few passages have been taken to imply some continued private property. 1QS 7:6-7 says that a member who is wasteful of community property must restore it, but he could possibly do this by work rather than by drawing on private property of his own. 1QS 7:24-25 threatens any member who associates with someone who has been expelled, "in his purity or in his wealth," but

---

18. On "the purity of the many" see Friedrich Avemarie, " *'Tohorat ha-Rabbim' and 'Mashqeh ha-Rabbim'*: Jacob Licht Reconsidered," in M. Bernstein, F. García Martínez, and J. Kampen, eds., *Legal Texts and Legal Issues* (STDJ 23; Leiden: Brill, 1997) 215-29. The reference is often taken to mean the pure food, but it cannot be limited to this.

19. Hempel, "Community Structures," 72.

the reference is obscure. In any case it is clear that the *Serek* makes greater demands on the property of the members than does the *Damascus Rule*.

Marriage and Family

There is also a clear difference between the two rules in the matter of family life. The movement described in the *Damascus Rule* was clearly family-based. The *Serek*, in contrast, makes no mention of women and children. The only reference to procreation, "fruitfulness of seed" *(prwt zr')*, occurs in the *Instruction on the Two Spirits* (1QS 4:7). Fruitfulness is a common blessing in the Hebrew Bible (Gen 49:25; Deut 7:13; 28:4; 30:9; Isa 49:20; 53:10), as we might expect in a culture where immortality was achieved through progeny. Similarly, in *1 En.* 10:17 we are told that "all the righteous will escape, and they will live until they beget thousands." Preben Wernberg-Møeller regards the expression here as figurative, and comments that "the idea of plenty of progeny is so common in Jewish eschatological speculations . . . that it is reasonable to believe that our community took over this idea, quite irrespective of whether they practiced marriage or not."[20] It is true, however, that the *Serek* never forbids marriage or requires celibacy. Regev has argued that later sectarian groups which required celibacy, such as the Shakers, made the requirement quite explicit.[21] Such a major departure from Jewish tradition would not have been left unmentioned. But the absence of any reference to women is also astonishing, especially in a document as concerned with purity issues as the *Serek*. In the end the silence of the text is not conclusive evidence either way. It is clear, however, that family life is not important in the *Serek* in the way that it is in the *Damascus Rule*. The *yaḥad* cannot be described as a family-based organization. Here again the difference between the two rules is more readily understandable if the older form of organization is reflected in the *Damascus Rule*.

---

20. Preben Wernberg-Møeller, *The Manual of Discipline: Translated and Annotated with an Introduction* (STDJ 1; Leiden: Brill, 1957) 79.

21. Regev, *Sectarianism*, 254.

Attitude to the Cult

The *Serek* also reflects a more advanced state of alienation from the temple cult than was attested in the *Damascus Rule*.[22] In the *Damascus Rule* the temple cult was criticized, even rejected, but the theme of the community as a replacement for the cult was not developed.[23] In 1QS 8:4b, however, we read: "when these are in Israel, the council of the community shall be established on truth, as an everlasting plantation, a holy house for Israel and a council of supreme holiness for Aaron, true witnesses for the judgment and elect of good will to atone for the land and to render the wicked their retribution (my trans.)." The function of atoning, which was traditionally exercised by the temple cult, is here claimed for the *yaḥad*.[24] Here again the direction of the development seems clear, from the critical demands for reform in the *Damascus Rule* toward a greater degree of separation and replacement.

All the features considered so far suggest that there is indeed continuity between the new covenant described in the *Damascus Rule* and the *yaḥad* described in the *Serek,* and that the new covenant represents the earlier stage, when the movement was less sharply separated from the rest of Judah. Regev, however, has recently argued for the reverse development. His argument, in brief, is that "the *yaḥad* was semi-egalitarian whereas the Damascus Covenant was highly hierarchical," and that sectarian movements tend to evolve in the direction of greater hierarchy, not greater egalitarian-

---

22. On the importance of the cult in sectarian disputes see now Paul Heger, *Cult as the Catalyst for Division: Cult Disputes as the Motive for Schism in the Pre-70 Pluralistic Environment* (STDJ 65; Leiden: Brill, 2007).

23. See CD 4:17-18; 5:6-7; 6:13-14 (4Q266 3 ii 17-19). 4Q266 11 1-5, par. 4Q270 7 i 15-19, seems to prescribe repentance, instead of temple offerings, for inadvertent sin, but does not speak of the life of the community as a means of atonement. See Hillary Evans Kapfer, "The Relationship between the Damascus Document and the Community Rule: Attitudes toward the Temple as a Test Case," *DSD* 14 (2007): 152-77.

24. See Newsom, *Self as Symbolic Space,* 157-60; and the older treatments of Bertil Gärtner, *The Temple and the Community in Qumran and the New Testament* (Cambridge: Cambridge University Press, 1965); and Georg Klinzing, *Die Umdeutung des Kultus in der Qumrangemeinde und im Neuen Testament* (SUNT 7; Göttingen: Vandenhoeck & Ruprecht, 1971). See also L. H. Schiffman, "Community Without Temple: The Qumran Community's Withdrawal from the Jerusalem Temple," in B. Ego, A. Lange, and P. Pilhofer, eds., *Gemeinde ohne Tempel/Community without Temple: Zur Substituierung und Transformation des Jerusalemer Tempels und seines Kults im Alten Testament, antiken Judentum und frühen Christentum* (Tübingen: Mohr Siebeck, 1999) 267-84.

ism.[25] His argument is based on the role assigned to the *rabbim*, or "many," in the *Serek*. In 1QS 6:7 we encounter "the rule for the session of the 'many.'" They shall sit "each in his order. The priests shall sit first, the elders second, and the rest of all the people shall sit each in his order. And thus they shall be asked concerning judgment, concerning any counsel, and anything which is for the 'many,' each man presenting his knowledge to the council of the community (trans. J. H. Charlesworth)."[26] We are further told that "at a session of the 'many' no man may say anything which is not according to the interest of the 'many'" (6:11). Moreover, as we have already seen, the "many" have a decisive role in the admission of new members in 1QS 6:18, 21. There is, then, a communal dimension to the decision-making process in the *Serek*. Nonetheless, it is clear that the "many" are by no means egalitarian. They sit each according to his rank, and carefully maintain distinctions between the priests, the elders, and the rest of the people. We also hear of "the man who is the *mebaqqer* over the 'many'" (6:12), who also has the role of bursar (6:18). This individual is probably identical with the person appointed *(paqid)* at the head of the "many" in 6:14, who examines the postulants, but is usually distinguished from the Maskil (1QS 3:13; 9:12), who seems to take over the teaching role that was filled by the *mebaqqer* in the *Damascus Rule*. Moreover, one of the functions of the Maskil is to "separate and weigh the sons of righteousness according to their spirits" (9:14).[27] So while the *Damascus Rule* does not speak of the "many" or assign them a role in decision making, it is not clear that it is more hierarchical. The *Serek* is thoroughly hierarchical, and has a more developed set of community officials.

The Sons of Zadok

An important issue in the question of hierarchy in the *Serek* is the role assigned to the sons of Zadok. According to 1QS 5:2, the "men of the *yaḥad*" are answerable to "the sons of Zadok, the priests who keep covenant, according to the multitude of the men of the *yaḥad*, who hold fast to the cov-

---

25. Regev, "*Yaḥad* and Damascus Covenant," 233.

26. Regev tries to distinguish between the *rabbim* and the council of the community, but the two are clearly synonymous.

27. See Carol A. Newsom, "The Sage in the Literature of Qumran: The Functions of the *Maśkîl*," in John G. Gammie and Leo G. Perdue, eds., *The Sage in Israel and the Ancient Near East* (Winona Lake, IN: Eisenbrauns, 1990) 373-82.

enant (trans. J. H. Charlesworth)." In 1QS 5:9 those who enter the covenant swear to return to the Torah of Moses "according to everything which has been revealed from it to the sons of Zadok, the priests who keep the covenant and seek his will, and according to the multitude of the men of their covenant (trans. J. H. Charlesworth)." These references to the sons of Zadok, however, are absent from two of the manuscripts of the *Serek* from Cave 4, 4QS[b] (4Q256) and 4QS[d] (4Q258). In 4QS[d] those who form a *yaḥad* are "answerable to the authority of the 'many' about everything concerning Torah," and they swear to return to the Torah according to everything revealed to the council of the men of the *yaḥad*. In these passages either the references to the sons of Zadok were inserted secondarily, or they were excised in a secondary recension.[28] The question arises whether this change reflects an actual change in the leadership of the community, and its hierarchical or egalitarian character.

Philip Alexander has argued that the references to the sons of Zadok belong to the original form of the *Serek*.[29] 1QS, which preserves the fullest form of the text, is dated paleographically to the first quarter of the first century BCE.[30] 4QS[b] and 4QS[d] are dated to the last quarter of that century.[31] One of the most popular theories of the origin of the sect holds that it originated in reaction to the disruption of the Zadokite high priesthood at the time of the Maccabean revolt, and the subsequent usurpation of the office by the Hasmoneans. On this theory it would make sense that Zadokite priests would have figured very prominently in the movement initially, but that they would have faded from prominence after the first generation. But this reconstruction of the origin of the sect is based primarily on inferences from the *pesharim*, or biblical commentaries. Other texts that discuss the causes of separation, such as the *Damascus Rule* and

---

28. For the former see G. Vermes, "Preliminary Remarks on Unpublished Fragments of the Community Rule from Qumran Cave 4," *JJS* 42 (1991): 250-55; idem, "The Leadership of the Qumran Community: Sons of Zadok — Priests — Congregation," in H. Cancik, H. Lichtenberger, and P. Schaefer, eds., *Geschichte-Tradition-Reflexion: Festschrift für Martin Hengel zum 70. Geburtstag* (3 vols.; Tübingen: Mohr Siebeck, 1996) 1.375-84; S. Metso, *The Textual Development of the Qumran Community Rule* (STDJ 21; Leiden: Brill, 1997) 78, 80. For the latter see Alexander, "Redaction-History," 437-53.

29. Alexander, "Redaction-History."

30. F. M. Cross, "The Development of the Jewish Scripts," in G. E. Wright, ed., *The Bible and the Ancient Near East: Essays in Honor of William Foxwell Albright* (Garden City, NY: Doubleday, 1965) 169-71.

31. Cross, "Appendix," in Charlesworth, ed., *Rule of the Community*, 57.

4QMMT, do not refer to a dispute about the high priesthood at all. We have seen in the previous chapter that the reference to the "sons of Zadok" in CD 3:21–4:4 is a biblical allusion, applied to "the chosen of Israel" as an honorific title, and not necessarily an indication of priestly genealogy. Consequently, the idea that the initial leaders of the movement were disaffected Zadokite priests rests on doubtful foundations.[32]

Moreover, the textual variation with regard to the sons of Zadok must be seen in the context of numerous other variations between the longer form of the text in 1QS and the shorter form in $4QS^b$ and $4QS^d$.[33] For example, in 1QS 5:11-13 the necessity of separating from the men of deceit is supported by a pastiche of biblical phrases that have no counterpart in $4QS^b$ or $4QS^d$:

> for they cannot be accounted in his covenant, since they have neither sought nor inquired after him through his statutes, in order to know the hidden things in which they erred, incurring guilt, nor the revealed things which they treated arrogantly, arousing anger for judgment and incurring vengeance by the curses of the covenant, to bring upon themselves mighty acts of judgment leading to eternal destruction without a remnant. (Trans. J. H. Charlesworth)

In the words of Metso: "A comparison between the manuscripts 1QS and $4QS^{b,d}$ reveals a process of redaction in 1QS, the purpose of which was to provide a Scriptural legitimation for the regulations of the community and to reinforce the community's self-understanding."[34] When all the variations are taken into account, it seems easier to explain the longer forms as expansions, despite the anomaly of the paleographic dating. Consequently, it is possible to argue that the shorter text reflects a more egalitarian form of community organization, which was later disrupted by the ascendancy of the sons of Zadok.[35]

32. Compare Hultgren, *From the Damascus Covenant*, 317: "There is no evidence that the Zadokites had any special authority in the *yaḥad* at the very beginning." Also Robert Kugler, "Priesthood at Qumran," in Flint and VanderKam, eds., *Dead Sea Scrolls after Fifty Years*, 2.113-14; Charlotte Hempel, "The Sons of Aaron in the Dead Sea Scrolls," in Anthony Hilhorst, Émile Puech, and Eibert Tigchelaar, eds., *Flores Florentino: Dead Sea Scrolls and Other Early Jewish Studies in Honour of Florentino García Martínez* (JSJSup 122; Leiden: Brill, 2007) 223-24.

33. Metso, *Textual Development*, 76-90.

34. Ibid., 105.

35. So Regev, "*Yaḥad* and Damascus Covenant," 242; Hultgren, *From the Damascus*

The significance of the textual variation can be questioned, however. Metso, who has produced the most thorough study of the textual variation in the *Serek*, concludes that "there cannot be any decisive difference" in the implied community structures, since "the *rabbim* includes both priests and (lay) men."[36] Moreover, the short form of the *Serek* assigns special authority to the "sons of Aaron."[37] For example, 1QS 5:21-22 reads:

> And they shall examine their spirits within the community, between each man and his neighbor according to his insight and his works in the Torah, under the authority of the sons of Aaron, who dedicate themselves within the community to establish his covenant and to observe all his statutes which he commanded to do, and upon the authority of the multitude of Israel who dedicate themselves to return to his covenant through the community. (Trans. J. H. Charlesworth)

Although the duplication of authority in this passage seems superfluous, the same reading is reflected in 4QS[d] (beginning with "and their works in the Torah, under the authority of the sons of Aaron"). In the words of Nathan Jastram, "the hierarchical nature of the community is unmistakable."[38] We must assume that the priests, the sons of Aaron, carried special authority within the "many" *(rabbim)*. The longer form of the text, in 1QS, places greater emphasis on priestly authority by the added references to the sons of Zadok; but as Metso argues, "the motive for replacing הרבים with a longer wording was undoubtedly theological: the redactor(s) wished to stress the purpose of הרבים as the true keepers of the covenant."[39] This would accord with the symbolic use of the expression "sons of Zadok" in CD.

Covenant, 317. Further evidence of a "Zadokite redaction" has been proposed by R. Kugler, "A Note on 1QS 9:14: The Sons of Righteousness or the Sons of Zadok," *DSD* 3 (1996): 315-20; and C. Hempel, "The Earthly Essene Nucleus of 1QSa," *DSD* 3 (1996): 263-67.

36. Metso, *Textual Development,* 122.

37. See especially Hempel, "Sons of Aaron." On the distribution of "sons of Aaron" and "sons of Zadok" see also H.-J. Fabry, "Zadokiden und Aaroniden in Qumran," in F. L. Hossfeld and L. Schwienhorst-Schönberger, eds., *Das Manna fällt auch heute noch: Beiträge zur Geschichte und Theologie des Alten, Ersten Testaments: Festschrift für Erich Zenger* (Herders biblische Studien 44; Freiburg: Herder, 2004) 201-17; Kugler, "Priesthood at Qumran," 97-103.

38. N. Jastram, "Hierarchy at Qumran," in Bernstein et al., eds., *Legal Texts and Legal Issues,* 355.

39. Metso, *Textual Development,* 78.

Whether the expression "sons of Zadok" necessarily implies any genealogical relationship to the pre-Maccabean high priestly line must be considered doubtful. That line is not commonly called "Zadokite" in literature of the Second Temple period after Ezekiel (e.g., Chronicles, Ezra-Nehemiah, Ben Sira, the books of Maccabees).[40] A hymn inserted in some manuscripts of Ben Sira between 51:12 and 51:13 gives thanks to God who chose the sons of Zadok to be priests, but this hymn is generally recognized as a secondary addition, of uncertain provenance. As Saul Olyan has shown, "Zadok is conspicuously absent" from the rest of the book of Ben Sira, although Aaron is extolled.[41] It is quite possible that the Hasmonean usurpers of the high priesthood could also claim Zadokite lineage.[42] Phinehas, who is invoked as a model in 1 Macc 2:26, 54, was son of Eleazar, son of Aaron, the same line from which Zadok was descended (1 Chron 24:3). There is little evidence that the sect, in any of its phases, arose from a dispute over the high priestly succession. It is quite possible that the insertion of "the sons of Zadok" into the *Serek* does not reflect the rise to power of a particular priestly group, but is an honorific title, similar to the usage in the *Damascus Rule*.

There can be no doubt, however, that priests figure prominently both in the *Damascus Rule* and in the *Serek*. While the degree of priestly leadership may have fluctuated over time, even the short form of the *Serek* assigns

---

40. Alice Hunt, *Missing Priests: The Zadokites in Tradition and History* (New York: T&T Clark, 2006) 11. Cf. J. Baumgarten, "The Heavenly Tribunal and the Personification of Sedeq in Jewish Apocalyptic," *ANRW* 2.19.1.233-36, who argues that "sons of Zadok" in the Scrolls does not refer to priestly lineage but is a claim of theological status. D. R. Schwartz, "On Two Aspects of a Priestly View of Descent at Qumran," in Lawrence H. Schiffman, ed., *Archaeology and History in the Dead Sea Scrolls: The New York University Conference in Memory of Yigael Yadin* (JSPSup 8; Sheffield: JSOT Press, 1990) 157-79, insists that lineage is the issue. J. Liver, "The 'Sons of Zadok the Priests' in the Dead Sea Sect," *RevQ* 6 (1967): 3-32, allows that there may have been Zadokites in the community, but denies that their lineage was the reason for the separation of the sect. See Kugler, "Priesthood at Qumran," 97.

41. Saul Olyan, "Ben Sira's Relationship to the Priesthood," *HTR* 80 (1987): 275.

42. Deborah W. Rooke, *Zadok's Heirs: The Role and Development of the High Priesthood in Ancient Israel* (Oxford: Oxford University Press, 2000) 281-82; James C. VanderKam, *From Joshua to Caiaphas: High Priests after the Exile* (Minneapolis: Fortress, 2004) 270 n. 90; Alison Schofield and James C. VanderKam, "Were the Hasmoneans Zadokites?" *JBL* 124 (2005): 73-87. The Zadokite line was descended from Aaron's son Eleazar. According to 1 Chronicles 23, sixteen of the twenty-four priestly courses were descended from Eleazar, so there are two chances out of three that Joiarib, the ancestor of the Hasmoneans, belonged to the same priestly house as Zadok, that of Eleazar.

special authority to the priests.[43] Despite the role of the "many" *(rabbim)* in decision making, the community structure described in the *Serek* (the *yaḥad*) is never egalitarian, and there is no reason to regard it as more primitive than what we find in the *Damascus Rule*. On the contrary, the *yaḥad* is more complex in its process of admission, places greater demand on its members with regard to property and community life, and reflects a greater degree of withdrawal from the temple cult. All of this suggests that the *yaḥad* is a more developed form of the association described in the *Damascus Rule*.

The relationship between the two rules, and the communities they describe, cannot, however, be explained simply in terms of diachronic development. Both rules were copied throughout the first century BCE. Presumably, the *Damascus Rule* was not rendered entirely obsolete by the *Serek*. The relationship of the *yaḥad* to the older association of the new covenant is complex, and much remains unclear. The *Damascus Rule* was edited by followers of the Teacher of Righteousness. The Teacher is not mentioned in the *Serek,* but he is linked firmly to the *yaḥad* in the *pesharim.* That the community regulations in the two rules overlap also argues strongly in favor of continuity. I see no evidence whatever that the differences between the two rules should be attributed to a schism within the movement. Rather, it would seem that the movement evolved in ways that led to some diversity within its community structures.

The *Yaḥad* and "the Qumran Community"

It has been commonplace in scholarship on the Dead Sea Scrolls to identify the *yaḥad* with the (celibate) community that lived at Qumran, and the "camps" of the *Damascus Rule* with the "marrying Essenes," dispersed throughout the land. So, for example, the article on "community organization" in the *Encyclopedia of the Dead Sea Scrolls* begins: "The Qumran community *(ha-yaḥad)* was organized. . . ."[44] In the words of Geza Vermes:

43. For an attempt to distinguish different stages in the authority of the priests see Kugler, "Priesthood at Qumran," 93-116, especially 101-2. Hempel, "Sons of Aaron," 224, argues that "a number of passages dealing with the earliest forms of communal life lack interest in the genealogical background of the priestly leadership altogether." Much of the argument depends on a rather fine analysis of redactional layers.

44. J. H. Charlesworth, "Community Organization in the Rule of the Community," *EDSS* 1.133.

"The Community Rule legislates for a group of ascetics living in a kind of 'monastic' society, the statutes of the Damascus Document for an ordinary lay existence."[45] This explanation is certainly too simple. The *Serek* is quite explicit that members of the *yaḥad* are dispersed in multiple dwellings:

> In this way shall they behave in all their places of residence. Whenever one fellow meets another, the junior shall obey the senior in work and in money. They shall eat together, together they shall bless and together they shall take counsel. In every place where there are ten men of the council of the community, there should not be missing among them a priest. . . . And in the place in which the ten assemble there should not be missing a man to interpret the law day and night, always, one relieving another. (1QS 6:1c-8a)

The quorum of ten corresponds to the prescription for the "camps" in CD 12:22–13:7. The passage is attested in 4QS[d], although the text is fragmentary.[46]

Scholars have dealt with this passage in various ways. Hempel argues that it "is of a heterogeneous character and contains some rather early and organizationally primitive material alongside some apparently later additions."[47] Metso has argued similarly that the reference to communities with a quorum of ten is likewise a relic of older legislation.[48] If we accept

---

45. Vermes, *Complete Dead Sea Scrolls,* 26. The suggestion that the *Manual of Discipline* was designed for a "monastic" order was made already by Millar Burrows in the press release announcing its discovery in April, 1948.

46. For the following see my articles, "Forms of Community in the Dead Sea Scrolls," in Shalom M. Paul et al., eds., *Emanuel: Studies in Hebrew Bible, Septuagint, and Dead Sea Scrolls in Honor of Emanuel Tov* (VTSup 94; Leiden: Brill, 2003) 97-111; "The *Yaḥad* and 'the Qumran Community,'" in Charlotte Hempel and Judith M. Lieu, eds., *Biblical Traditions in Transmission: Essays in Honour of Michael A. Knibb* (JSJSup 111; Leiden: Brill, 2006) 81-96. Torleif Elgvin has also argued that "The *Yaḥad* Is More than Qumran," in G. Boccaccini, ed., *Enoch and Qumran Origins: New Light on a Forgotten Connection* (Grand Rapids: Eerdmans, 2005) 273-79, on the grounds that some of the sectarian scrolls were copied before the establishment of the settlement at Qumran.

47. Hempel, "Interpretative Authority in the Community Rule Tradition," *DSD* 10 (2003): 63. Cf. already M. A. Knibb, *The Qumran Community* (Cambridge Commentaries on Jewish Writings of the Jewish and Christian World 200 BC to AD 200, 2; Cambridge: Cambridge University Press, 1988) 115.

48. S. Metso, "Whom Does the Term Yaḥad Identify?" in Hempel and Lieu, eds., *Biblical Traditions in Transmission,* 213-35.

the thesis that the *Damascus Rule* reflects an older form of sectarian organization than the *yaḥad,* then it is reasonable to infer that the reference to groups of at least ten in the *Serek* was derived from the older rule. The question that concerns us here, however, is not so much the source of this passage as its function within the *Serek.* On one view, which I hold, *yaḥad* was an umbrella term for several communities of variable size.[49] On the alternative view, the term rather referred to a single large community (usually called "the Qumran community"), and the passage in 1QS 6 is included as "an earlier, time-honored set of directives" that is anachronistic in the context of the *Serek.*[50] The "rule for the assembly of the many" that begins in 1QS 6:8b seems to envision a large community, with multiple priests. But this is not incompatible with the continued existence of multiple smaller communities. The assembly may be conceived in the same way as "the assembly of all the camps" in CD, or, alternatively, it may be the rule for any assembly of *yaḥad* members, on the assumption that large communities were the norm. The provision that members could meet in small groups with a quorum of ten is never contravened in the *Serek,* and I see no reason to regard it as anachronistic.

A different line of argument questions the relationship between these smaller groups and the supposed larger community at Qumran. It is often noted that the word for "their places of residence" *(mgwryhm)* "suggests a more or less temporary lodging."[51] Jerome Murphy-O'Connor actually suggested that the reference was to huts or tents in which community members lived at Qumran, at least ten to a tent.[52] 1QS 6:3 refers to "every place where there shall be ten men *from* the council of the community" *(mʿṣt hyḥd).* Metso takes the preposition "from" in a locative sense, and spins out a scenario of "traveling Essenes": "members of the יחד (i.e. members *from* the council of the community, מעצת היחד) while they were visiting areas outside large Essene settlements such as the one at Qumran, . . . would have

49. Collins, "Forms of Community," 104; idem, "*Yaḥad* and 'Qumran Community,'" 85-86.

50. So Metso, "Whom Does the Term Yaḥad Identify?" 227. The passage is found in 4QS[d], which Metso takes to reflect the oldest form of the *Serek.*

51. A. R. C. Leaney, *The Rule of Qumran and Its Meaning* (London: SCM, 1966) 180. Leaney assumed that the following passage, which is introduced as "the rule for the session of the Many," relates to "the larger community at Qumran."

52. J. Murphy-O'Connor, "La genèse littéraire de la *Règle de la Communauté,*" *RB* 76 (1969): 528-49, especially 536.

been in contact with Essenes living in towns and villages and lodging in settlements small enough that gathering the quorum of ten would have been an issue."[53] She refers here to Josephus, *J.W.* 2.124: "They have no one city, but many settle in each city; and when any of the sectarians come from elsewhere, all things they have lie available to them." But Josephus clearly assumes that Essenes, apparently of the same order, live in many cities, so the parallel lends no support to the view that only the visitors were members of the *yaḥad.* Neither does the *Serek* say anything to indicate that the passage refers to situations where members are traveling, and I do not think that the word *mgwryhm,* literally "their places of sojourning," can be taken to imply travel out of the community.[54] It is surely easier to accept that the preposition "from" is partitive, and that members living in villages and towns, in smaller communities, were just as much members of the *yaḥad* as those in a larger community such as the one commonly supposed to have lived at Qumran.[55] This assumption also frees us from the need to suppose that the passage in 1QS 6:1c-8a is only a fossil of an earlier time, and not reflective of the community described in the rest of the *Serek.*

The view that that the *yaḥad* was an association dispersed in multiple settlements may also explain why different editions of the *Serek* continued to be copied, and why the more primitive form found in 4QS[d] was not simply superseded by the more developed edition found in 1QS. Not all the scrolls found at Qumran were copied on site. Some may have been brought there from different settlements of the *yaḥad,* which may have been operating with different editions of the *Community Rule.*[56] In short, the different forms of the *Serek* were not being copied side by side in the same com-

---

53. Metso, "Whom Does the Term Yaḥad Identify?" 225.

54. *Pace* Metso. The statement "in this way shall they behave in all their places of sojourning" relates immediately to the practice of reproof in the preceding verses, and it would make little sense to suppose that this law applied only to travelers.

55. Regev, "*Yaḥad* and Damascus Covenant," 236, recognizes that the *Serek* provides for a number of smaller communities, but his argument that the phrase "council of the community" refers to a local community, rather than to the association as a whole, is untenable, as he himself also now recognizes (*Sectarianism,* 184).

56. As suggested by Alison Schofield, "Rereading S: A New Model of Textual Development in Light of the Cave 4 Serekh Copies," *DSD* 15 (2008): 96-120; idem, *From Qumran to the Yaḥad: A New Paradigm of Textual Development for the Community Rule* (STDJ 77; Leiden: Brill, 2009). Schofield suggests that the fluctuating prominence of the "sons of Zadok" may reflect the fact that priests were more prominent in some settlements than in others. On the view argued above, this suggestion is unnecessary.

munity, but may have been in effect in different communities at the same time.[57] Scrolls from various communities would then have been brought to Qumran for hiding in time of crisis.

An Elite Group?

The *Serek,* then, assumes that the *yaḥad* has multiple places of residence. Does it provide any evidence for a specific community, such as has usually been supposed to have existed at Qumran?

Although the text never indicates a specific location, it does speak of a group that is to go to the wilderness to prepare there the way of the Lord. From the early days of scholarship on the Scrolls, scholars have seen here a specific reference to the settlement by the Dead Sea.[58]

The passage is found in 1QS 8.[59] The opening section (8:1-4a) announces that there shall be "in the council of the community twelve men and three priests, perfect in everything that has been revealed from all the law" (8:1). This section is followed by three paragraphs, each of which begins with the phrase, "when these are in Israel."

The first of these, beginning in 8:4b, claims for the sectarian group the function of atonement, which was traditionally proper to the temple cult, as we have already noted above. It will be "a holy house for Israel, and the foundation of a holy of holies for Aaron." It will offer a pleasant aroma, and will be accepted to atone for the land. There is a further temporal clause in 8:10b-11: "when these have been established in the foundation of the community for two full years in perfection of way they will be separated as holy in the midst of the council of the men of the community, and every matter hidden from Israel but which has been found out by the Interpreter, he should not keep hidden from them for fear of a spirit of defection."

---

57. This observation undercuts the question raised by Philip Davies, "Redaction and Sectarianism in the Qumran Scrolls," in idem, *Sects and Scrolls: Essays on Qumran and Related Topics* (SFSHJ 134; Atlanta: Scholars Press, 1996) 157: "if the 'rule' is a rule, there can be only one version in effect at any one time. The paradox obliges us to reconsider our premises: is 1QS a 'community rule' at all?"

58. The reference to the founding of the settlement at Qumran is still assumed by Hultgren, *From the Damascus Covenant,* 315.

59. For the following see Collins, "*Yaḥad* and 'Qumran Community,'" 88-91. Translations of 1QS 8 in this section are my own.

The second paragraph begins in 8:12b: "when these are a community in Israel[60] . . . they shall be separated from the midst of the dwelling of the men of iniquity, to go to the wilderness to prepare there the way of Him, as it is written, 'in the wilderness prepare the way of. . . .' This is the study of the law, which he commanded by the hand of Moses. . . ."

The third paragraph, beginning in 9:3, reads: "when these are in Israel in accordance with these rules in order to establish the spirit of holiness in truth eternal. . . ." This passage is not found in 4QSᵉ, which lacks 8:15–9:11. The paragraph beginning in 9:3 seems to duplicate 8:4b-10, and may be a secondary insertion.[61]

In the early days of Scrolls scholarship, the twelve men and three priests were understood as an inner council.[62] It is not apparent, however, that they have any administrative role. In an influential article published in 1959, E. F. Sutcliffe, S.J., dubbed them "The First Fifteen Members of the Qumran Community."[63] In this he was followed by Murphy-O'Connor, who labeled the passage "an Essene manifesto."[64] This view has been widely, though not universally, accepted. Michael Knibb spoke for many when he wrote:

> This material thus appears to be the oldest in the Rule and to go back to the period shortly before the Qumran community came into existence; it may be regarded as reflecting the aims and ideals of conservative Jews who were disturbed by the way in which the Maccabean leaders were conducting affairs, and whose decision to withdraw into the wilderness was motivated by the desire to be able to observe strictly God's laws in the way that they believed to be right. It probably dates from the middle of the second century BC.[65]

Nonetheless, this view does not withstand a close analysis of the text.

1QS 8:1, "In the council of the community (there shall be) twelve men and three priests," can be read in either of two ways. The twelve men

---

60. The word *lyḥd,* "a community," is inserted above the line and appears to be missing from 4QSᵈ. See Alexander and Vermes, DJD 26, 107.

61. So Metso, *Textual Development,* 72.

62. So Milik, *Ten Years,* 100.

63. E. F. Sutcliffe, S.J., "The First Fifteen Members of the Qumran Community," *JSS* 4 (1959): 134-38.

64. Murphy-O'Connor, "Genèse Littéraire." Cf. also Knibb, *Qumran Community,* 129.

65. Knibb, *Qumran Community,* 129.

and three priests can be taken to constitute the council of the community, as Sutcliffe and Murphy-O'Connor read it. But it is also possible to take the verse to mean that the twelve men and three priests are a special subgroup within the council of the *yaḥad*. (The council of the *yaḥad* is simply the *yaḥad* itself.) This is indeed how they are understood in 1QS 8:10-11: "When these have been established in the fundamental principles of the community for two years in perfection of way, they shall be set apart as holy within the council of the men of the community." They are not, then, a council in the sense of an administrative or executive body. Rather, they are an elite group set aside for special training. The establishment of such a group is necessary for the completion of the *yaḥad*: "when these exist in Israel the council of the community is established in truth" (8:5). The group in question cannot be taken to constitute the whole *yaḥad*, at any stage of its existence.[66] Rather, as A. R. C. Leaney already saw, "the community or movement out of which it arose must have been represented by groups dispersed throughout the land."[67] The elite group does not break away from the *yaḥad*, nor does it found a separate organization. It may be said to found a new community, but it is a community that is an integral part of the broader *yaḥad*.

The ideal of the *yaḥad* is summed up again in 1QS 9:5-6: "At that time the men of the community shall separate themselves as a holy house of Aaron, that they may be united as a holy of holies, and as a house of community *(byt yḥd)* for Israel, as those who walk in perfection." "The men of the community" are the entire *yaḥad*, and walking in perfection is required of the entire *yaḥad* elsewhere in the *Serek*.[68] It is the whole *yaḥad*, not just the elite group that constitutes its pinnacle, that makes up the holy house. But 1QS 8:10-11 says quite clearly that certain people who have been established in the community for two years will be set apart as holy in its midst. In the extant text, the antecedent is the group of twelve men and

---

66. See further Collins, "Forms of Community," 105-7; idem, "*Yaḥad* and 'Qumran Community,'" 88-90; also Shane A. Berg, "An Elite Group within the *Yaḥad*: Revisiting 1QS 8–9," in Michael Thomas Davis and Brent A. Strawn, eds., *Qumran Studies: New Approaches, New Questions* (Grand Rapids: Eerdmans, 2007) 161-77.

67. Leaney, *Rule of Qumran*, 210-11.

68. Metso, "Whom Does the Term Yaḥad Signify?" 230. Cf. 1QS 1:8; 2:2; 3:9; etc. Note, however, the observation of Berg, "Elite Group," 171: "it is significant that the collocation of 'holiness' and 'perfection' occurs only four times in 1QS — all of which are in columns 8–9 and all of which refer to the elite group."

three priests. Metso claims that this passage is "more naturally understood as a reference to the period of two years of probation that is required of all new community members."[69] But this would require that the statement in question is out of context, and that this section of the *Serek* is a collection of statements that are only loosely related. Such a view of the *Serek* may be possible. 4Q265, which contains a parallel to 1QS 8:1,[70] does seem to be a random collection of laws and statements. But a reading that posits coherence in the passage should be preferred. It seems to me, then, that 1QS 8 does indeed posit the existence of an elite group within the *yaḥad*, which is said to consist of twelve men and three priests.

Unfortunately, we do not know what part this group played in the history of the movement. The numbers have symbolic significance, referring to the twelve tribes and three priestly families,[71] and we cannot be sure that this group ever came to be. Moreover, the command to prepare in the wilderness the way of the Lord is taken from scripture, and is interpreted allegorically in the text:

> As it is written: In the desert prepare the way of . . ., in the wilderness make level a highway for our God. This is the study of the law which he commanded through the hand of Moses, in order to act in compliance with all that has been revealed from age to age, and according to what the prophets have revealed through his holy spirit.[72]

Symbolism does not preclude literal enactment, and the fact that this text was found beside an inhabited site in the wilderness is hard to dismiss as mere coincidence. Accordingly, the suspicion persists that the retreat of this pioneering group to the wilderness marked the beginning of "the Qumran community." If so, it should be noted that it did not arise from a schism in a parent group, and did not by itself constitute the *yaḥad* but was part of a larger whole. It would also, of course, have to have grown in size. But while the identification of this group with the founding of the Qumran community is attractive, it is by no means certain. As we shall see

---

69. Cf. Knibb, *Qumran Community*, 133.

70. "When there are in the community council fifte[en men] . . . the community coun[cil] will be firmly established."

71. Milik, *Ten Years*, 100.

72. See George J. Brooke, "Isaiah 40:3 and the Wilderness Community," in Brooke and F. García Martínez, eds., *New Qumran Texts and Studies* (STDJ 15; Leiden: Brill, 1994) 117-32.

in chapter 5, the identification of Qumran as a sectarian settlement is the subject of raging controversy, and the problems are especially acute in the Hasmonean period, when the *Serek* was composed.

It is true, as Metso has argued, that the aims of this group can hardly be distinguished from those of the broader *yaḥad*. All were supposed to walk in perfection of the way; all were supposed to pursue a life of holiness. But to say that the entire *yaḥad* was consecrated to a life of holiness is not to deny that different degrees of holiness were possible. The great concern for holiness in the *Serek* evidently related to the fact that it envisions the *yaḥad* as a substitute for the temple cult. Traditionally, the whole temple was holy, but there was still an area marked off as "the holy of holies." Even if all Jerusalem was regarded as holy, the temple was still especially holy. According to the editors' reconstruction of 4QMMT, Israel is holy, but the priests are most holy and should not intermarry with those who are merely holy.[73] The holiness of the whole body is enhanced by the existence of a part that is especially holy. As Carol Newsom has observed, with reference to this passage, "As a description of the most dedicated and highest form of community life, it serves not merely as yet one more account of community procedure but rather as an expression of its highest potential and its telos."[74]

In the case of this elite group, the intensification of holiness is reflected in the retreat to the desert. In part, it is a return to the situation of Israel in the wilderness at the time of the original Sinai revelation. It dramatizes the separation of the *yaḥad* from the people of iniquity. Hindy Najman has suggested an analogy with the thought of Philo, who explained the remote location of the Sinai revelation by arguing that "he who is about to receive the holy laws must first cleanse his soul and purge away the deep-set stains which it has contracted through contact with the motley promiscuous horde of men in cities. And to this he cannot attain except by dwelling apart, nor that at once, but only long afterwards" (*Decalogue* 10-11).[75] Philo's philosophical presuppositions were, of course, quite different from anything found in the Dead Sea Scrolls. For him, the goal was the separation of the soul from the corporeal world, for a life of contemplation. The *Serek* shows no familiarity with the Platonic idea of the soul.

---

73. 4QMMT composite text, B 17-82. See Elisha Qimron and John Strugnell, eds., *Qumran Cave 4*, vol. V: *Miqṣat Maʿaśe Ha-Torah* (DJD 10; Oxford: Clarendon, 1994) 172-73.

74. Newsom, *Self as Symbolic Space,* 153.

75. Hindy Najman, "Philosophical Contemplation and Revelatory Inspiration in Ancient Judean Traditions," *SPA* 19 (2007): 103.

Nonetheless, contemplation also had its place in the life of the *yaḥad*. The analogy with Philo is useful as it reminds us that the goal of the *yaḥad* was not only the reformation of Israel by proper observance of the Torah, but also the spiritual transformation of its members. In this respect the *yaḥad* anticipates by several hundred years the rise of Christian monasticism, which would flourish literally in the desert, although it is not possible to show any historical continuity between the two phenomena. The context of monasticism would be quite different from that of the *yaḥad*, and even that of Philo, insofar as it was not concerned with the Torah or the restoration of Israel. But there is nonetheless an analogy in some respects.

The aspect of personal transformation is also highlighted in the hymn at the end of the *Serek*:

> As for me, to God belongs my judgment; in his hand is the perfection of my behavior with the uprightness of my heart; and with his just acts he cancels my iniquities. For from the source of his knowledge he has disclosed his light, and my eyes have observed his wonders, and the light of my heart the mystery that is to be *(rz nhyh)*. . . . From the spring of his justice is my judgment and from the wonderful mystery is the light of my heart. My eyes have gazed on that which is eternal, wisdom hidden from humankind, knowledge and prudent understanding (hidden) from the sons of man, fount of justice and well of strength and spring of glory (hidden) from the assembly of flesh. (1QS 11:2-7)

As Newsom has argued, the placement of this hymn at the end of the *Community Rule* suggests that it represents the culmination of formation within the community. "The character constructed for the Maskil in the instructions and hymn is one that embodies the values of the sect in a particularly pronounced fashion."[76] The experience articulated in this hymn is paradigmatic for the community.

The ideal of the *yaḥad*, then, has a mystical aspect that is not in evidence in the new covenant of the *Damascus Rule*. It entails fellowship with the angels, not only in worship but in the entire life of the community.[77]

---

76. Newsom, *Self as Symbolic Space*, 173.

77. See my essay, "The Angelic Life," in Turid Karlsen Seim and Jorunn Økland, eds., *Metamorphoses: Resurrection, Body and Transformative Practices in Early Christianity* (Berlin: de Gruyter, 2009) 291-310. Cf. already Collins, *Apocalypticism in the Dead Sea Scrolls*, 130-49; Regev, *Sectarianism*, 351-76.

The ideal of the angelic life has important implications for the question of celibacy, to which we will return in chapter 4, when we consider whether the *yaḥad* should be identified with the Essenes.

The *Rule of the Congregation* (1QSa)

In addition to the *Serek* and the *Damascus Rule,* we must consider another text in connection with the development of the sectarian movement in the Dead Sea Scrolls. This is the *Rule of the Congregation,* 1QSa. This short rule book is introduced as "the rule for all the congregation of Israel at the end of days." Accordingly, it is usually taken as a rule for a future, messianic age. Hartmut Stegemann, however, has argued that the authors of the sectarian scrolls believed they were living in "the end of days" and that this was not a rule for a future time but rather "an early rule-book of the Essenes."[78] The more recent publication of other manuscripts of the *Rule of the Congregation,* in cryptic script, by Stephen Pfann, supports an early date for this document.[79] Its place in the development of the Qumran rule books, however, remains controversial.

Stegemann's suggestion that it was a rule for the present rather than for the future appeals to the thorough study of the phrase *aḥarit hayamim* by Annette Steudel.[80] Steudel shows that the phrase can refer to events that are already past and to time continuing in the present, but she adds: "In addition to all previous implications, there are also events which are expected *within the* אחרית הימים *as lying in the future.* First of all, this concerns the coming of the messiahs, who are still awaited."[81] Stegemann's contention that the rule refers to the present time of the author is

---

78. Hartmut Stegemann, "Some Remarks to 1QSa, 1QSb, and Qumran Messianism," *RevQ* 17 (1996): 488. In *Library of Qumran,* 113, he calls it "The Essenes' Oldest Congregational Rule." His main argument for the antiquity of this rule is that, on his interpretation, it does not envision a priestly messiah.

79. Stephen J. Pfann, "Cryptic Texts," in *Qumran Cave 4,* vol. XXVI: *Cryptic Texts and Miscellanea, Part 1* (DJD 36; Oxford: Clarendon, 2000) 515-74 (= 4Q249a-i). Pfann dates these manuscripts to the second century BCE (ibid., 522-23) and claims that the lack of any copies of the *Community Rule* and the *Damascus Covenant* in cryptic script argues for the priority of the *Rule of the Congregation.*

80. A. Steudel, "אחרית הימים in the Texts from Qumran," *RevQ* 16 (1993): 225-46.

81. Ibid., 230 (emphasis added).

disproven by the explicit references to the messiah in 1QSa 2:11-22. In no other text from Qumran is the messiah said to be actually present. This is a rule for a future age, one that has not yet come to pass. In part Stegemann is misled by his presuppositions of what a messianic age must entail. 1QSa addresses problems presented by the presence of people with various blemishes and impurities. But the messianic age is not the new creation. It is an intermediate era, which is utopian in some respects, but in which the conditions of the old order still obtain.[82]

There are also problems with Stegemann's claim that 1QSa is "the Essenes' oldest congregational rule." According to this rule, the congregation is to be governed by the regulation of the sons of Zadok, whose authority is also asserted in 1QS 5. As we have seen, however, the references to the sons of Zadok are missing from some of the manuscripts of the *Community Rule* from Cave 4. These references must be seen in the context of other scriptural allusions in 1QS that are lacking in the shorter form of the text. It is easier to understand why these allusions would have been added than to suppose that they were systematically eliminated in some manuscripts. But the references to the sons of Zadok in 1QSa are plausibly assigned to the same redactional stage as those in 1QS.[83] If this is correct, the shorter form of the *Community Rule* found in 4QS[b,d] is likely to be older than 1QSa. Moreover, the statement that the sons of Zadok atone for the land in 1QSa 1:3 echoes 1QS 8:10. The allusions to the *yaḥad* in 1QSa are scarcely intelligible without prior acquaintance with some form of the *Community Rule*.

Hempel has offered a more sophisticated variant of Stegemann's proposal. The *Rule of the Congregation* is messianic in its present form, but it includes an early nucleus that was intended as the rule for a community in the present, which should be associated with the community behind the Laws of the Damascus Document, which she takes to go back to "the Essene parent movement of the Qumran community."[84] The most obvious point of affinity is that both 1QSa and the *Damascus Rule* presuppose family life and provide for women and children. Other points of affinity ad-

---

82. See my essay, "'He Shall Not Judge by What His Eyes See': Messianic Authority in the Dead Sea Scrolls," *DSD* 2 (1995): 145-64. The priestly messiah is simply the high priest of the messianic age. Stegemann's claim that 1QSa does not envision a priestly messiah would require the odd situation of a messianic age without a high priest.

83. Charlotte Hempel, "The Earthly Essene Nucleus of 1QSa," *DSD* 3 (1996): 257-59.

84. Ibid., 253-69.

duced by Hempel include the use of "all Israel" terminology; the term "congregation" *('dh)*, which occurs seven times in CD; reference to the book of Hagu (1QSa 1:7; CD 10:6; 13:2); and the exclusion of physically disabled people from the congregation.

That there is some relationship between 1QSa and the Damascus texts cannot be doubted, but there is also an important link between 1QSa and the *Community Rule,* which Hempel acknowledges only in a footnote.[85] This is the mention of "the council of the community" *('ṣt hyḥd)* three times in 1QSa 1:6–2:11, as well as a variant, "the council of holiness," which is found once. This terminology is familiar from the *Community Rule,* and is not found at all in the fragments of the *Damascus Rule* at Qumran, and is only reflected in manuscript B of CD. The "council of the community" is not coterminous with the congregation. Those summoned to it are "the wi[se men] of the congregation, the learned and the intelligent, men whose way is perfect and men of ability," together with the chiefs and officials (1QSa 1:28-29).[86] These, we are told, are "the men of renown, the members of the assembly summoned to the Council of the Community in Israel before the sons of Zadok the Priests" (1QSa 2:2). It is from their assembly (1QSa 2:4: *qhl 'lh:* "the assembly of these")[87] that those smitten with any human uncleanness are excluded: "none of these shall come to hold office among the congregation of the men of renown, for the Angels of Holiness are [with] their [congregation]" (1QSa 2:8-9). It is with this group that the messiah shall sit and eat (2:11). The rule for the assembly in the presence of the messiah in the latter part of column 2 applies whenever there is a quorum of ten, and the messiah is present. The reference is not to a single "messianic banquet," but neither is it to any gathering of ten Israelites.

In short, 1QSa, like the *Damascus Rule* and the *Community Rule,* sets some people aside as more holy than others. This elite group is called "the council of the community," which is the name of the sect in the *Community Rule,* and is also identified with "the sons of Zadok and the men of their covenant." The usual assumption that this rule is intended for all Is-

---

85. Ibid., 267 n. 31.

86. The translations of 1QSa in this paragraph and the next are my own.

87. So correctly Florentino García Martínez, *The Dead Sea Scrolls Translated* (trans. Wilfred G. E. Watson; Grand Rapids: Eerdmans, 1994) 127; Vermes, *Complete Dead Sea Scrolls,* 159, translates "the assembly of God."

rael at a future time[88] is quite correct, but fully half of the document relates to the special role that "the council of the community" retains in "the end of days." The concern of the text for "all Israel" must be seen in context. The author hoped for a time when all Israel would live "according to the law of the sons of Zadok the Priests and of the men of their Covenant who have turned aside [from the] way of the people, the men of His Council who keep His Covenant in the midst of iniquity, offering expiation [for the Land]" (1QSa 1:2-3). We should expect, then, that the rules for all Israel in the future would to a great degree correspond with the rules of the new covenant in the present, at least for those members who married and had children, as envisioned in the *Damascus Rule.*[89] The affinities between the *Rule of the Congregation* and the *Damascus Rule,* however, must be balanced by an appreciation of the role in 1QSa of "the council of the community," which continues to enjoy a special place in "the end of days." That women and children are present in the eschatological "congregation" does not carry any implication about their presence in the *yaḥad* in the time before the coming of the messiah, nor indeed in the "council of the community" in the eschatological time.

The relation of this text to both the *Damascus Rule* and the *Community Rule* shows again the difficulty, if not the impossibility, of assigning these rules to different movements, or regarding them as different sects.

Conclusion

Although much is unclear about the relation between the *Damascus Rule* and the *Community Rule* or *Serek ha-Yaḥad,* there is obviously a relationship between them. Arguments that they reflect two different sects are unpersuasive both because of parallels in terminology and organization and because fragments of both are found in Qumran Cave 4. I agree with those who find the more primitive form of community organization reflected in the *Damascus Rule,* although the issue is clouded by the fact that that Rule

88. As expounded by, e.g., Lawrence H. Schiffman, *The Eschatological Community of the Dead Sea Scrolls* (SBLMS 38; Atlanta: Scholars Press, 1989).

89. See further my essay, "The Construction of Israel in the Sectarian Rule Books," in Alan J. Avery-Peck, Jacob Neusner, and Bruce Chilton, eds., *Judaism in Late Antiquity,* part 5: *The Judaism of Qumran: A Systemic Reading of the Dead Sea Scrolls,* vol. 1: *Theory of Israel* (Handbuch der Orientalistik 1/56; Leiden: Brill, 2001) 25-42.

seems to have undergone some revision in light of the *Serek*. The popular theory that the *Damascus Rule* represents an order that practiced marriage, while the *Serek* was the rule for celibates, requires some qualification, but is substantially correct. The *Damascus Rule* is primarily concerned with households. It allows for some other members who walk in perfect holiness, but says little about their way of life, and it is possible that the one passage that distinguishes this group was a secondary addition. The *Serek*, in contrast, is primarily concerned with those who walk in perfect holiness. While it allows for multiple communities with a quorum of ten members, in the manner of the "camps" of the *Damascus Rule*, it makes no mention of women or children. It reflects a more intense preoccupation with holiness, and provides for an elite group that pursues it to a higher degree in the wilderness. The heightened quest for holiness arises in large part from the view that the community life is a substitute for the temple cult, in atoning for the land. This view is not yet found in the *Damascus Rule*, and reflects a more complete break with the temple cult.

I see no reason to attribute the differences between the two rules to a schism. Since both rules continued to be copied, it would seem that the kind of family-based movement envisioned in the *Damascus Rule* was not simply superseded, but continued to exist in tandem with the more intensive communities of the *yaḥad*.

Appendix: Analogous Movements and Associations

Both the new covenant of the *Damascus Rule* and the more developed *yaḥad* were voluntary associations: one was not simply born into them. Voluntary associations proliferated in the Hellenistic world and were of various kinds, ranging from guilds of craftsmen to devotees of a particular deity. In the case of many of these associations, statutes have been preserved, which provide analogies for the rule books found at Qumran. These analogies have been explored by Moshe Weinfeld in a slim monograph.[90]

90. Moshe Weinfeld, *The Organizational Pattern and the Penal Code of the Qumran Sect: A Comparison with the Guilds and Religious Associations of the Hellenistic Period* (NTOA 2; Fribourg: Éditions Universitaires, 1986). Weinfeld provided examples from seventeen associational statutes. Note also the earlier studies of Hans Bardtke, "Die Rechtsstellung der Qumran-Gemeinde," *TLZ* 86 (1961): 93-104; and Carl Schneider, "Zur Problematik des Hellenistischen in den Qumrāntexten," in Hans Bardtke, ed., *Qumran-Probleme* (Berlin:

Further analogies have been suggested in the case of philosophical schools.[91]

Associations involved regular common meals and administrative meetings. Members did not usually live together, except in exceptional cases.[92] Prospective members went through a phase of testing, and admission was typically determined by a vote of the assembly of the members. Members typically swore an oath to abide by the statutes of the association. Priests often pronounced blessings over the food. Members were required to pay an entrance fee and to contribute to the common fund. Failure to pay would result in exclusion. Many of the analogies to the *yaḥad* concern the maintenance of order at meetings. As a representative example, Weinfeld cited in full the statutes of the Iobacchi (a drinking club, dedicated to Bacchus or Dionysus), from 178 CE.[93] According to the statutes of the Iobacchi:

> No one may be an Iobacchus unless he is first registered in the usual manner with the priest and is approved by a vote of the Iobacchi as being clearly worthy and fit to be a member of the Bacchic Society.
>
> The entrance-fee shall be fifty denarii and a libation for one who is not the son of a member. . . .
>
> The Iobacchi shall meet on the ninth of each month and on the anniversary of its foundation and on the festivals of Bacchus and on any extraordinary feast of the god, and each member shall take part in word or act or honorable deed, paying the fixed monthly contribution for the wine. . . .
>
> No one may either sing or create a disturbance or applaud at the gathering, but each shall say and act his allotted part with all good order and quietness under the direction of the priest or the archbacchus.[94]

Akademie, 1963) 299-314. See now the critical discussion by Yonder M. Gillihan, "Civic Ideology among the Covenanters of the Dead Sea Scrolls and Other Greco-Roman Voluntary Associations" (Ph.D. diss., University of Chicago, 2007) 48-64.

91. Albert Baumgarten, "Graeco-Roman Voluntary Associations and Ancient Jewish Sects," in Martin Goodman, ed., *Jews in a Greco-Roman World* (Oxford: Clarendon, 1998) 93-111.

92. Bardtke, "Rechtsstellung," 98, mentions an exception in the case of the Poseidoniasts at Delos.

93. Weinfeld, *Organizational Pattern,* 51-54; Wilhelm Dittenberger, *Sylloge Inscriptionum Graecarum* (3rd ed.; 4 vols.; Leipzig: Hirzelium, 1916–24) no. 1109.

94. Weinfeld, *Organizational Pattern,* 51-52.

No one is allowed to deliver a speech without the permission of the priest. The penalty for breach of these regulations is typically a fine.

There are obvious analogies between these regulations and those of the *yaḥad,* as found in 1QS 5–7 and parallels. The *Community Rule* is also concerned with good order at meetings. There are also differences. Weinfeld noted that Greco-Roman voluntary associations often specify sacrifices and oblations to be offered on holidays. They typically provide for funerals and burials. They are much concerned with the payment of dues. They typically lack the religio-moralistic rhetoric of the Jewish sect.[95] There is a closer analogy between the associations and the family-based movement of the *Damascus Rule* than between the associations and the *yaḥad,* which is a "greedier" organization, making more totalitarian demands on its members.[96] Nonetheless, Sandra Walker-Ramisch has argued that the sectarian ideology of the *Damascus Rule* is in sharp contrast to the typical stance of the Greco-Roman associations: "This sectarian ideology places CDC [Cairo Damascus Composition] in an oppositional, indeed antagonistic, relation to the larger system of which it is a part, and thus the structured social group . . . represented by CDC has a social function and exhibits social behavior fundamentally different from those of the collegia."[97] The most significant difference between the *Damascus Rule* and the pagan associations is the emphasis on separation from the rest of the society in the Jewish texts.

Another major difference concerns the degree of communal property. Matthias Klinghardt has argued that the *yaḥad* was a "synagogue community" that came together at regular intervals to bless, eat, and take counsel together, as indicated in 1QS 6.[98] In order to maintain this position he has to argue that "since the submission of private property to the *yachad* is mentioned only in connection with the initiation, this is most likely what is called in Greek associations the *'eisélysion,'* the entrance fee."[99] But this does

95. Ibid., 46-47.

96. Baumgarten, "Graeco-Roman Associations," 98, says, with reference to the Greek accounts of the Essenes rather than to the Scrolls, that "an Essene had no identity but as a member of his movement. He had sacrificed his personality to a greedy institution."

97. Sandra Walker-Ramisch, "Graeco-Roman Voluntary Associations and the Damascus Document," in John S. Kloppenborg and Stephen G. Wilson, eds., *Voluntary Associations in the Graeco-Roman World* (London: Routledge, 1996) 142.

98. Matthias Klinghardt, "The Manual of Discipline in the Light of Statutes of Hellenistic Associations," in Wise et al., eds., *Methods of Investigation,* 251-70.

99. Ibid., 255.

not seem to be a possible interpretation of 1QS 6:19, which says that the property and possessions of the person entering the community shall be given into the hand of the *mebaqqer* (inspector), who has charge of the property of the *rabbim* (many), and 6:22, which prescribes that at a later stage of the process his property must be merged. It seems quite clear that what is envisioned here is not an entrance fee but communal property. Klinghardt's idea of a "synagogue community" may be tenable in the case of the community of the new covenant as described in the *Damascus Rule*, although even there the community is "greedier," and makes more extensive demands on its members, than the typical synagogue. In the case of the *yaḥad*, as described in 1QS and the related rules, this explanation is not tenable at all.[100]

Community of property is often encountered as a literary trope or philosophical ideal in classical antiquity. Plato upholds the ideal for the Guardians of his Republic.[101] They were supposed to live and eat together (*Republic* 416E, 449C). He reaffirmed the ideal of the common life in the *Laws* (739C). The practice of the common life was associated especially with the Pythagoreans. According to Iamblichus, "they placed their possessions in common."[102] Pythagoras is said to have taught that friends should hold things in common, but several ancient writers claim that this led to the practice of common property among his followers.[103] The Pythagoreans were also said to be an exclusive society, greatly concerned with purity. There was a lengthy process of initiation in several stages.[104] After an initial examination, there was a period of probation for three years. Then there was a second period of probation in silence for five years. The

---

100. Klinghardt, ibid., 259, suggests that the various manuscripts that have been classified as copies of the *Community Rule* are actually "similar statutes of different groups." This suggestion does not take account of the degree of similarity among the different exemplars.

101. Plato, *Republic* 416D. See Hans-Josef Klauck, "Gütergemeinschaft in der Klassischen Antike, in Qumran und im Neuen Testament," *RevQ* 11 (1982): 48-49.

102. Iamblichus, *De Vita Pythagorica* 30. See Justin Taylor, S.M., *Pythagoreans and Essenes: Structural Parallels* (Collection de la Revue des Études Juives 32; Louvain: Peeters, 2004) 15.

103. Diogenes Laertius 8.10b; Porphyry, *Life of Pythagoras* 20. For recent studies of Pythagoras and Pythagoreanism see J. A. Philip, *Pythagoras and Early Pythagoreanism* (Toronto: University of Toronto Press, 1966); Charles Kahn, *Pythagoras and the Pythagoreans: A Brief History* (Indianapolis: Hackett, 2001).

104. Iamblichus, *Vita Pythagorica* 71-74. Taylor, *Pythagoreans and Essenes*, 20-21.

candidate's possessions were then handed over to officials appointed for this purpose. Candidates who were rejected received double their property, and a tomb was prepared for them as if they were dead. There was provision for expulsion from the community. In all of this (except for the tomb!), the Pythagorean way of life resembled both that of the Essenes, as described by Philo and Josephus, and that of the *yaḥad* as described in the *Community Rule*.

The main sources for the Pythagorean way of life, Diogenes Laertius, Porphyry, and Iamblichus, date from the third century CE. How far they reflect the practice of actual Pythagorean communities is disputed. Such communities were alleged to have existed from the fifth century BCE, but the evidence is uncertain. Pythagoras established a society in Croton, in the toe of Italy in the late sixth century BCE, but his followers eventually encountered violent opposition, and were scattered about 450 BCE.[105] It is widely accepted that Pythagoreanism as a social phenomenon died out no later than the fourth century BCE.[106] Pythagorean philosophy influenced Plato; and Nigidius Figulus, a friend of Cicero and founder of Neoplatonism, is said to have revived Pythagoreanism in Rome in the first century BCE.[107] Evidence of actual Pythagorean communities, however, is scant to nonexistent.[108] Peter Kingsley, in a controversial study, has argued that Pythagorean communities never ceased to exist, but continued as underground units, sometimes no larger than a household.[109] But even Justin

---

105. Fritz Graf, "Pythagoras, Pythagoreanism," in Simon Hornblower and Anthony Spawforth, eds., *Oxford Classical Dictionary* (3rd ed.; Oxford: Oxford University Press, 1999) 1283-85; cf. Iamblichus, *Vita Pythagorica* 248-66.

106. Walter Burkert, "Hellenistische Pseudopythagorica," *Philologus* 105 (1961): 16-43, 226-46.

107. Cicero, *Timaeus* 1. John Dillon and Jackson Hershbell, *Iamblichus on the Pythagorean Way of Life* (SBL Texts and Translations 29, Graeco-Roman Religion Series 11; Atlanta: Scholars Press, 1991) 15. Moses Hadas, *Hellenistic Culture: Fusion and Diffusion* (New York: Columbia University Press, 1959) 193-96, argued that there was a vigorous Pythagorean revival at this time. For a counterargument see D. Musial, " '*Sodalicium Nigidiani*': Les pythagoriciens à Rome à la fin de la République," *Revue de l'histoire des religions* 218 (2001): 339-67.

108. Moderatus of Gades in the first century CE is said to have promoted Pythagorean teaching and attracted students. See Dillon and Hershbell, *Iamblichus*, 15; Taylor, *Pythagoreans and Essenes*, 102.

109. Peter Kingsley, *Ancient Philosophy, Mystery, and Magic: Empedocles and Pythagorean Tradition* (Oxford: Oxford University Press, 1995) 322.

Taylor, who finds Kingsley's proposal "plausible," admits that "in the absence of positive evidence, it must remain speculative."[110]

There was, however, a literary tradition, transmitted in philosophical circles.[111] The existence of some tradition about the Pythagorean way of life is clear from Josephus, who says that the Essenes followed a way of life taught by Pythagoras (*Ant.* 15.371). Some scholars in the late nineteenth and early twentieth century took this claim quite seriously, and argued for extensive Pythagorean influence on Judaism, especially in Alexandria.[112] It is quite likely that both Josephus's account of the Essenes and Philo's account of the Therapeutae were colored to some degree by Pythagorean traditions. It is much less likely that the actual development of a Judean sect was influenced by either the social reality or the literary ideal of Pythagoreanism. While the parallels between the *yaḥad* and the Pythagoreans, especially in the matter of shared possessions, are intriguing, they should probably be understood as strictly parallel developments, each of which developed similar institutions for different reasons, in different cultural contexts.[113]

The analogies between the rules and the voluntary associations concern primarily matters of organization and procedure, and do not speak to the *raison d'être* of any particular association. If we are concerned with the latter, the closest analogies are likely to be found within the context of Judaism. Two such analogies have been proposed. One concerns the Therapeutae described by Philo in *On the Contemplative Life*. Since the closest analogies to the Therapeutae are found in the ancient accounts of the Essenes, we will defer that discussion to chapter 4. The other analogy concerns the *ḥavurah*,

110. Taylor, *Pythagoreans and Essenes*, 104.

111. See ibid., 9-11, on the sources of the later Lives of Pythagoras.

112. Eduard Zeller, *Philosophie der Griechen in ihrer geschichtlichen Entwicklung*, vol. 2 (Leipzig: Riesland, 1923) 89-93; Isidore Lévy, *La légende de Pythagore de Grèce en Palestine* (Paris: Champion, 1927). See also André Dupont-Sommer, "Le problème des influences étrangères sur la secte juive de qoumrân," *Revue d'histoire et de philosophie religieuses* 35 (1955): 75-92. Dupont-Sommer cited the Essene practice of praying toward the sun as an example of Pythagorean influence. See now the critical discussion by Gillihan, "Civic Ideology," 44-48.

113. Cf. Gillihan, "Civic Ideology," 47-48, who concludes that if there was any influence it was more likely to be literary than social. Contra Taylor, *Pythagoreans and Essenes*, 106, who finds it "reasonable to suppose that the close structural parallels between the Pythagorean and the Essene ways of life are to be explained finally by contacts between the two, specifically by the influence of the former on the latter." He suggests that Alexandria was the main channel of communication.

or table fellowship, attested in rabbinic sources and thought to derive from the practice of the Pharisees in the Second Temple period.

The Ḥavurah

Of the various voluntary associations that have been adduced, the one that is closest to the kinds of concerns that gave rise to the *yaḥad* is undoubtedly the Pharisaic/rabbinic *ḥavurah*.[114] This kind of fellowship was distinguished by its strictness in setting aside priestly portions and tithes, and in observing ritual purity. The *ḥavurah* is known only from a few passages in rabbinic literature. The primary sources are as follows:

Mishnah Demai 2:2:
He that imposes on himself to be reliable must give tithe from what he eats and from what he sells and buys, and he may not be the guest of an outsider. R. Judah says, Even he that is the guest of an outsider may still be reckoned trustworthy. They replied, He would not be reliable in what concerns himself, how then could he be trustworthy in what concerns others?

Mishnah Demai 2:3:
He that imposes upon himself to be a *ḥaver* may not sell to an outsider either wet or dry (produce), nor buy from him (produce that is) wet; and he may not be the guest of an outsider (*'am ha'areṣ*, literally, "people of the land") nor may he receive him as a guest in his own garment.

Tosefta Demai 2:2:
He that imposes upon himself four things is accepted to be a *ḥaver*: not to give a heave-offering or tithes to an outsider, not to prepare his pure food in the house of an outsider, and to eat even ordinary food in purity.

---

114. Saul Lieberman, "The Discipline in the So-Called Dead Sea Manual of Discipline," *JBL* 71 (1952): 199-206; Chaim Rabin, *Qumran Studies* (Oxford: Oxford University Press, 1957) 12-21; Jacob Neusner, "The Fellowship (חבורה) in the Second Jewish Commonwealth," *HTR* 53 (1960): 125-42; idem, *Fellowship in Judaism: The First Century and Today* (London: Vallentine, Mitchell, 1963); Aharon Oppenheimer, "Haverim," *EDSS* 1.333-36; Steven D. Fraade, "Qumran *Yaḥad* and Rabbinic *Havurah*: A Comparison Reconsidered," paper presented at the SBL annual meeting in San Diego, November, 2007.

Tosefta Demai 2:10-12:

And he is accepted first with regard to "wings" and is afterward accepted for purities.[115] If he only imposes upon himself the obligations concerning the "wings" he is accepted; if he imposes upon himself the obligations concerning pure food, but not yet concerning "wings, " he is not considered reliable, even for pure food.

Until when is a man accepted? The school of Shammai says: for liquids, thirty days, for clothing, twelve months. The school of Hillel says: for either, thirty days. (Trans. J. Neusner)

These meager testimonies come from a time much later than the Dead Sea Scrolls. The Mishnah was compiled toward the end of the second century CE, the Tosefta sometime after that. It is commonly supposed that the *havurah* existed already in the first century CE, and perhaps earlier. The only textual support for this view lies in the references to Hillel and Shammai. It is not implausible that the Pharisees had some such fellowship, but the actual texts come from a later time.

The texts suggest some analogies between the *yahad* and the *havurah*. The *haver* was required to "take upon himself." It is possible that this implied an oath, such as we find in the *yahad* or in the *Damascus Rule*, but this is not certain.[116] The obligations had to be undertaken in the presence of the *havurah*. There is some period of testing, and admission was gradual. There was a distinction between the level of purity required for sharing liquids and for sharing solid food and other things. It is apparent that some degree of separation from outsiders is required.

It is also apparent, however, that the *havurah* did not require the same degree of separation from outsiders that is required in the *yahad*, or even in the *Damascus Rule*. The process of admission is perhaps more developed than what we find in the *Damascus Rule*, but much less developed than what we find in 1QS. Nothing is said in the rabbinic sources about the kind of community discipline that is required in either the *Damascus Rule* or the *Serek* rules from Qumran.

The *havurah* is relevant to the study of the sectarian communities described in the Scrolls, insofar as it also was a "purity community," which

---

115. The meaning of "wings" has not been established. The traditional explanation is that it means "hands" — the ritual washing of hands. It has also been suggested that it means "clothing." See Rabin, *Qumran Studies*, 19.

116. Lieberman, "Discipline," 200.

separated to some degree from the rest of Judaism for this reason. There were also some correspondences in terminology. For example, the *haverim* also referred to their members as the *rabbim*, or "many," and used the verb "to draw near" *(qrb)* for admission to membership. They also differentiated degrees of purity, and provided for gradual admission. The degree of separation, however, was considerably less in the case of the *havurah*, and the kind of association involved was much less "greedy" than what we find in the Scrolls. It is not apparent that the *haverim* had any quarrel with the temple cult, unlike their counterparts in the Scrolls. The *havurah* was not a sect, in the sense of being at odds with the rest of Judaism. It sought to practice Jewish law more strictly than did the common people, but it did not regard "the people of the land" *('m h'rṣ)* as "sons of the pit."

None of these analogies, then, can be held to explain the rise of the movement of the new covenant or the *yahad*. The sectarian movement shared some of the Pharisaic concerns about purity. The procedures they adopted for their meetings are similar to those of other voluntary associations in the Hellenistic world. Whether this similarity is due to influence, or is a strictly parallel development, is not clear. Most intriguing are the parallels with the Pythagoreans, as these are portrayed in the literary tradition, but the possibility of Pythagorean influence on the Judean sect seems remote.

CHAPTER THREE

The Historical Context

Our study of the "new covenant" described in the *Damascus Rule* and of the *yaḥad* described in the *Serek ha-Yaḥad* or *Community Rule* suggests a fairly complex process of development that must have taken some time to unfold. The fullest manuscript of the *Community Rule*, 1QS, is dated on paleographic grounds to the first quarter of the first century BCE. While this dating is not precise, we may take it at least as approximately correct. If we allow both for a process of development from shorter forms of the *Serek*, and for the existence of an earlier "parent movement" attested in the *Damascus Rule*, then the origins of the movement can hardly be later than the late second century BCE. Beyond that rather general conclusion, however, little can be said with confidence about the early history of the movement.

To be sure, there has long existed a consensus on the origin and early history, and this is still maintained with great confidence in some quarters.[1] According to that consensus, the earliest beginnings of the movement should be dated around the time of the Maccabean crisis. CD 1 says that God delivered Israel into the hand of Nebuchadnezzar for 390 years. While it is recognized that this figure is symbolic (it derives from Ezek 4:5), it is often accepted as approximately correct, and taken to point to a date in the early second century BCE. CD also says that the members of the move-

---

1. For an overview see James C. VanderKam, "Identity and History of the Community," in Peter W. Flint and VanderKam, eds., *The Dead Sea Scrolls after Fifty Years: A Comprehensive Assessment* (2 vols.; Leiden: Brill, 1998-99) 2.507-23; Philip R. Callaway, *The History of the Qumran Community: An Investigation* (JSPSup 3; Sheffield: Sheffield Academic Press, 1988) 11-27. The consensus view has been defended recently by Hanan Eshel, *The Dead Sea Scrolls and the Hasmonean State* (Grand Rapids: Eerdmans, 2008) 1-27.

ment initially were like blind men groping their way for twenty years. The decisive event that galvanized the movement was the coming of the Teacher of Righteousness. This in turn is supposed to have been a reaction to the usurpation of the high priesthood by Jonathan Maccabee in 152 BCE. Jonathan is then identified as the "Wicked Priest" mentioned in the *pesharim*, or commentaries, on the prophets. The archeology of the site of Qumran, as explained by Roland de Vaux, was thought to lend support to this reconstruction of the history. This consensus was formulated with minor variations by J. T. Milik, Frank Cross, and Geza Vermes.[2]

There have, of course, been other proposals.[3] In the 1950s and 1960s Cecil Roth and G. R. Driver tried to explain the Scrolls against the background of the First Jewish Revolt against Rome.[4] More recently, Robert Eisenman and Barbara Thiering have sought to explain them against the background of early Christianity.[5] If one at all accepts paleography as a tool of dating, however, these settings are too late. As we shall see below, the historical figures who are mentioned by name in the Scrolls all date to the pre-Christian period, mainly to the first century BCE. The only credible alternative to the second-century dating of the Teacher is one that places him in the first half of the first century BCE. Such a dating was advocated early on by André Dupont-Sommer, and has recently been revived by Michael Wise.[6]

2. J. T. Milik, *Ten Years of Discovery in the Wilderness of Judaea* (trans. J. Strugnell; SBT 1/26; London: SCM, 1959) 44-98; F. M. Cross, *The Ancient Library of Qumran* (3rd ed.; BibSem 30; Sheffield: Sheffield Academic Press, 1995; 1st ed. 1958) 88-120; G. Vermes, *Les manuscrits du désert de Juda* (2nd ed.; Paris: Desclée, 1954; 1st ed. 1953) 70-104. Compare Vermes, *The Complete Dead Sea Scrolls in English* (rev. ed.; London: Penguin, 2004) 49-66. Cross identified Simon Maccabee, rather than Jonathan, as the Wicked Priest.

3. An excellent review of scholarship on the subject can be found in VanderKam, "Identity and History," 501-31. A summary of the debates in the early years of scrolls scholarship can be found in M. Burrows, *The Dead Sea Scrolls* (New York: Viking, 1955) 123-223.

4. Cecil Roth, *The Historical Background of the Dead Sea Scrolls* (Oxford: Blackwell, 1958); G. R. Driver, *The Judaean Scrolls: The Problem and a Solution* (Oxford: Blackwell, 1965).

5. Barbara E. Thiering, *Redating the Teacher of Righteousness* (Sydney: Theological Explorations, 1979); idem, *The Qumran Origins of the Christian Church* (Sydney: Theological Explorations, 1983); Robert E. Eisenman, *Maccabees, Zadokites, Christians and Qumran: A New Hypothesis of Qumran Origins* (Leiden: Brill, 1983).

6. A. Dupont-Sommer, *The Dead Sea Scrolls: A Preliminary Survey* (trans. E. Margaret Rowley; Oxford: Blackwell, 1952) 91-93; Michael O. Wise, "Dating the Teacher of Righteousness and the *Floruit* of His Movement," *JBL* 122 (2003): 53-87. See also idem, *The First Messiah* (San Francisco: HarperSanFrancisco, 1999) 37-60; Wise, Martin Abegg, and Ed

The flood of publications following the release of all unpublished scrolls in 1991 has shed little direct light on this issue. No new texts have been found that mention the Teacher, or that provide chronological information about the origin of the community. The most authoritative surveys of Scrolls studies in recent years have reaffirmed the consensus that the activity of the Teacher should be placed in the mid-second century.[7] Nonetheless, much has changed in the study of the Scrolls since Cross and Milik wrote. Several of the pillars on which the consensus was based have eroded, and there is good reason to ask whether it still deserves the status it has enjoyed.[8]

Eroded Pillars

Several of the considerations used to support a mid-second-century date have been called in question in recent years. To begin with, many scholars assumed that the archeology of the site of Qumran could provide a key to the history of the community.[9] That assumption is now widely chal-lenged,[10] but in any case the archeology can no longer be taken to require a mid-second-century origin for the community. De Vaux had proposed that the settlement at Qumran had been established in the mid-second century BCE, but he admitted that the earliest phase was poorly attested. The small amount of pottery from Period Ia is indistinguishable from that of Ib and there are no coins associated with it.[11] Jodi Magness points out

---

Cook, *The Dead Sea Scrolls: A New Translation* (San Francisco: HarperSanFrancisco, 1996) 26-35.

7. So, e.g., Lawrence H. Schiffman, *Reclaiming the Dead Sea Scrolls* (Philadelphia: Jew-ish Publication Society, 1994) 83-95; James C. VanderKam, *The Dead Sea Scrolls Today* (Grand Rapids: Eerdmans, 1994) 99-108; and, tentatively, James VanderKam and Peter Flint, *The Meaning of the Dead Sea Scrolls* (San Francisco: HarperSanFrancisco, 2002) 275-92. A vigorous defense of the consensus, insofar as it depends on the *pesharim,* can be found in James H. Charlesworth, *The Pesharim and Qumran History: Chaos or Consensus?* (Grand Rapids: Eerdmans, 2002).

8. See my essay, "The Time of the Teacher: An Old Debate Renewed," in Peter W. Flint, Emanuel Tov, and James C. VanderKam, eds., *Studies in the Hebrew Bible, Qumran, and the Septuagint Presented to Eugene Ulrich* (VTSup 101; Leiden: Brill, 2006) 212-29.

9. Callaway, *History of the Qumran Community,* 29-51.

10. See chapter 5 below.

11. R. de Vaux, *Archaeology and the Dead Sea Scrolls* (Oxford: Oxford University Press, 1973) 4-5. See the summary by VanderKam, "Identity and History," 501-4.

that neither the pottery nor the coins provide evidence for any settlement before 100 BCE, and concludes that "it is reasonable to date the initial establishment of the sectarian settlement to the first half of the first century B.C.E. (that is, sometime between 100–50 B.C.E.)."[12] It should be noted that the *yaḥad* was not a single settlement, at Qumran or elsewhere, and there is no hard evidence linking the Teacher to the site of Qumran. The beginnings of the *yaḥad*, and the activity of the Teacher at least in part, should be dated to a time before the settlement of the site (assuming that Qumran was a settlement of the sect).[13] Nonetheless, the archeological evidence does not provide any solid support for the second-century dating of the Teacher or the community.

Neither is a mid-second-century dating required by the paleography of the Scrolls. Paleographic dating is at best relative. Even its proponents typically allow a margin of plus or minus 25 years. Wise has argued that scripts might evolve differently at different locations, and that many of the scrolls may have been copied at sites other than Qumran.[14] Be that as it may, the most widely accepted dating, that of Cross, places the great majority of the sectarian texts in the first century BCE.[15] The suggested date for 1QS, 100–75 BCE, may require an earlier date for some parts of the composition, since it is a composite document and has clearly undergone a process of development, as can be seen by comparison with the fragments from Cave 4. But there is still a margin of error in this dating, and if the lower end of the spectrum should be correct the beginning of the process need be no earlier than approximately 100 BCE, or the last decades of the second century BCE.[16] Attempts to establish the date of manuscripts by radiocarbon analysis generally support the paleographic dating, but claim

12. J. Magness, *The Archaeology of Qumran and the Dead Sea Scrolls* (Grand Rapids: Eerdmans, 2002) 65.

13. Torleif Elgvin, "The *Yaḥad* Is More than Qumran," in G. Boccaccini, ed., *Enoch and Qumran Origins: New Light on a Forgotten Connection* (Grand Rapids: Eerdmans, 2005) 273-79.

14. Wise, "Dating the Teacher," 55-60.

15. See the summary by Wise, ibid., 61.

16. Stephen Pfann has argued for a very early date for 4Q249, which he identifies as a manuscript of 1QSa, the *Rule of the Congregation*. See Stephen J. Pfann et al., *Qumran Cave 4*, vol. XXVI: *Cryptic Texts and Miscellanea, Part 1* (DJD 36; Oxford: Clarendon, 2000) 515-74. The manuscript, however, is in cryptic script, and comparative material is provided only by the heading, and so the basis for the paleographic dating is exceedingly small.

even less precision, and there have been enough anomalies and problematic results to show that this kind of analysis is not definitive either.[17]

The 390 Years of CD 1

The only passage in the entire corpus of the Scrolls that appears to give chronological information about the rise of the sect is the opening column of the *Damascus Document,* which mentions a period of 390 years after the conquest of Jerusalem by Nebuchadnezzar.[18] But all scholars acknowledge that the number is symbolic, derived from Ezek 4:5. Moreover, it is widely thought to be related to the schema of seventy weeks of years (= 490 years) of Daniel 9. In CD 1 it is followed by a period of wandering for twenty years, then by the career of the Teacher, and finally we are told that "from the day of the gathering in of the unique teacher until the destruction of all the men of war who turned back with the man of the lie there shall be about forty years" (CD 20:14). If we allow the stereotypical figure of forty years for the career of the Teacher, this brings us to 490 years as the length of the period from the exile to the beginning of the eschatological age.[19] This schema was based on scriptural exegesis, not on chronological re-

17. See G. Doudna, "Dating the Scrolls on the Basis of Radiocarbon Analysis," in Flint and VanderKam, eds., *Dead Sea Scrolls after Fifty Years,* 1.430-71; VanderKam and Flint, *Meaning of Dead Sea Scrolls,* 27-33; Joseph Atwill and Steve Braunheim, "Redating the Radiocarbon Dating of the Dead Sea Scrolls," *DSD* 11 (2004): 143-57. The issues raised by Atwill and Braunheim are not entirely offset by the response of Johannes van der Plicht, "Radiocarbon Dating and the Dead Sea Scrolls: A Comment on 'Redating,'" *DSD* 14 (2007): 77-89.

18. On the difficulties of using the *Damascus Document* as a historical source, see M. L. Grossman, *Reading for History in the Damascus Document: A Methodological Study* (Leiden: Brill, 2002).

19. See, among many, F. F. Bruce, *Biblical Exegesis in the Qumran Texts* (Grand Rapids: Eerdmans, 1959) 59-62; Antti Laato, "The Chronology in the *Damascus Document* of Qumran," *RevQ* 15 (1992): 605-7; idem, *A Star Is Rising: The Historical Development of the Old Testament Royal Ideology and the Rise of the Jewish Messianic Expectations* (University of South Florida International Studies in Formative Christianity and Judaism 5; Atlanta: Scholars Press, 1997) 306-7; Geza Vermes, "Eschatological World View in the Dead Sea Scrolls and in the New Testament," in Shalom M. Paul et al., eds., *Emanuel: Studies in the Hebrew Bible, Septuagint, and Dead Sea Scrolls in Honor of Emanuel Tov* (VTSup 94; Leiden: Brill, 2003) 481-82. This interpretation of the chronology of the *Damascus Document* is disputed by Ben Zion Wacholder, *The Dawn of Qumran* (Monographs of Hebrew Union College 8; Cincinnati: Hebrew Union College Press, 1983) 108-9, 179.

search. The book of Daniel itself calculates the period from the Babylonian exile (beginning either from the first deportation in 597 BCE or the destruction of Jerusalem in 586) to the persecution of Antiochus Epiphanes (168–164 BCE) as 490 years. (This figure is arrived at by interpreting Jeremiah's prophecy that Jerusalem would be desolate for 70 years as 70 *weeks* of years.)[20] In fact, the author is mainly concerned with the last "week" of seven years. His reasoning is that if the final divine intervention is at hand, then Jeremiah's prophecy must be about to be fulfilled, and the numbers are adjusted accordingly. There is no reason to believe that the 390 years of CD is any more reliable as a chronological indicator than Daniel's 490 years.[21]

Besides, we do not know how the author understood the chronology of the Second Temple period. As Vermes has pointed out, "all the extant evidence proves that Jews of the early post-biblical age possessed no correct knowledge of the length of the duration of Persian rule."[22] Even Demetrius the Chronographer, a Hellenistic Jewish writer of the third century BCE, whose use of numbers was not at all symbolic, said that the time from the fall of Samaria (dated to 722 BCE by modern historians) to the reign of Ptolemy IV (221–204 BCE) was 573 years and nine months, and the time from the fall of Jerusalem (dated to 586 BCE by modern historians) to Ptolemy IV was 338 years and three months.[23] In the latter case, his calculation was about 27 years too short. It has been suggested that CD follows the same chronological calculation as Demetrius.[24] In that case, 390 years after

20. Jer 25:11, 12; 29:10. See John J. Collins, *Daniel* (Hermeneia; Minneapolis: Fortress, 1993) 349.

21. See already John J. Collins, "The Origin of the Qumran Community: A Review of the Evidence," in idem, *Seers, Sibyls, and Sages in Hellenistic-Roman Judaism* (JSJSup 54; Leiden: Brill, 1997) 250; idem, "Time of the Teacher," 215. The statement of Eshel, *Dead Sea Scrolls and Hasmonean State*, 43 n. 35, that "Wise and Collins do not discuss one of the three major arguments for the identification of the Wicked Priest with Jonathan the Hasmonean, namely, the 390 years of col. 1 of the *Damascus Document*," is not correct.

22. Vermes, "Eschatological World View," 482 n. 4. Compare Eshel, *Dead Sea Scrolls and Hasmonean State*, 31.

23. Clement of Alexandria 1.141.1-2. He gives the interval between the fall of Samaria and that of Jerusalem, inconsistently, as 128 years 6 months. On the chronological problems raised by the text see Elias Bickerman, "The Jewish Historian Demetrios," in Jacob Neusner, ed., *Christianity, Judaism, and Other Greco-Roman Cults* (5 vols.; SJLA 12; Leiden: Brill, 1975) 3.72-84, especially 80-84.

24. So Laato, "Chronology," 607-9; Hartmut Stegemann, "The Qumran Essenes —

the fall of Jerusalem would yield a date of approximately 170/169 BCE, which would fit quite well with the usual reconstruction of sectarian origins. (The Teacher would have come approximately twenty years later.) But Demetrius lived in a very different cultural, and linguistic, environment in Alexandria, where he was influenced by the scholarly methods of Alexandrian grammarians.[25] His use of numbers is entirely different from what we find in CD. His calculations had little impact on later tradition.[26] Josephus, who, unlike the author of CD, wrote in Greek and was familiar with a range of Greek literature, variously gives the time between the return from the Babylonian exile (539 or 538 BCE) and the death of the Hasmonean king Aristobulus I in 103 BCE as 481 (*Ant.* 13.301) or 471 years (*J.W.* 1.70), an error of either 46 or 36 years by modern calculation. The rabbinic *Seder Olam Rabbah* 30 assigns only 34 years to the period of Persian rule. It would be remarkable indeed if the Hebrew *Damascus Document*, alone among Jewish writings of the Hellenistic period, followed the calculations of the Alexandrian Jewish chonographer Demetrius. Scholars have had recourse to Demetrius only as a way of bolstering a date for sectarian origins that had been postulated on other grounds. But these other grounds, which postulate a quarrel over the high priesthood as a factor in the origin of the sect, do not withstand scrutiny either.

The 390 years of CD 1, then, is a symbolic number for the period of time between the destruction of Jerusalem and the beginning of the last times. It is probably safe to say that a considerable time had elapsed since the destruction, but the number cannot be pressed to yield even an approximate date.[27]

Local Members of the Main Jewish Union in Late Second Temple Times," in Julio Trebolle Barrera and Luis Vegas Montaner, eds., *The Madrid Qumran Congress: Proceedings of the International Congress on the Dead Sea Scrolls, Madrid, 18-21 March 1991* (2 vols.; STDJ 11; Leiden: Brill, 1992) 1.141-42; idem, *The Library of Qumran: On the Essenes, Qumran, John the Baptist, and Jesus* (Grand Rapids: Eerdmans, 1998) 123; Annette Steudel, *Der Midrasch zur Eschatologie aus der Qumrangemeinde (4QMidrEschat*[a,b]*)* (STDJ 13; Leiden: Brill, 1994) 206; Armin Lange, *Weisheit und Prädestination in den Textfunden von Qumran* (STDJ 18; Leiden: Brill, 1995) 22.

25. For a discussion of Demetrius see J. J. Collins, *Between Athens and Jerusalem: Jewish Identity in the Hellenistic Diaspora* (rev. ed.; Grand Rapids: Eerdmans, 2000) 33-35.

26. Vermes, "Eschatological World View," 482-83 n. 4.

27. It is remarkable that a scholar such as Hanan Eshel, who is fully aware of the symbolism and of the lack of an accurate chronology in this period, can still take this passage as a major argument for dating the origin of the movement to the mid-second century BCE,

A Dispute over the High Priesthood?

Perhaps the most significant revision in the discussion of the origin of the movement in recent years has concerned the Zadokite priesthood.[28] It has been widely assumed that the usurpation of the high priesthood by the Maccabees was a decisive factor in the formation of the sect.[29] The high priestly succession had been disrupted during the so-called Hellenistic Reform by Jason (who was from the high priestly family) and Menelaus (who was not), as reported in 2 Maccabees 4. After the death of Menelaus, Alcimus held the office for some three years (162–160 or 159 BCE).[30] After this, there was a period known as the *intersacerdotium,* when the office of high priest was vacant, until Jonathan Maccabee was appointed high priest by the Syrian king Alexander Balas.[31] Hartmut Stegemann argued that there must have been at least a *de facto* high priest, to perform the ceremonies of the High Holy Days, especially Yom Kippur.[32] Moreover, both the Teacher (in 1QpHab 2:8; 4QpPs[a] 2:19; 3:15) and his opponent, dubbed "the Wicked Priest" (in 1QpHab 8:16; 9:16; 11:12), are referred to as "the priest" in the biblical commentaries, or *pesharim.* Stegemann argued that this was a technical term, and that it proves that both of these figures were high priests.[33] In this he was supported by Jerome Murphy-O'Connor, who likewise argued that the absolute use of "the priest" always designated the high priest.[34] Hence these scholars concluded that "the Wicked Priest" meant "the illegitimate high priest," and that the Teacher must have been an otherwise unknown high priest during the *intersacerdotium.*

---

and blithely conclude that "in any case, the group probably came into being before the Hasmonean revolt, most likely about the year 170 BCE" (Eshel, *Dead Sea Scrolls and Hasmonean State,* 31). Such is the power of the received scholarly consensus.

28. See Alice Hunt, *Missing Priests: The Zadokites in Tradition and History* (Library of Hebrew Bible/Old Testament Studies 452; New York: T&T Clark, 2006) 166-75.

29. This hypothesis was first proposed by Vermes, *Manuscrits du désert de Juda,* 79. See VanderKam, "Identity and History," 509-10.

30. See James C. VanderKam, *From Joshua to Caiaphas: High Priests after the Exile* (Minneapolis: Fortress, 2004) 226-44.

31. Josephus, *Ant.* 13.146. See VanderKam, *From Joshua to Caiaphas,* 244-50.

32. Stegemann, *Library of Qumran,* 147.

33. Hartmut Stegemann, *Die Entstehung der Qumrangemeinde* (Bonn: published privately, 1971) 102 nn. 328 and 329.

34. Jerome Murphy-O'Connor, "The Damascus Document Revisited," *RB* 92 (1985): 239.

This argument does not hold. In Ezra 7:11; 10:10, 16, Ezra is called "the priest," but on his arrival in Jerusalem he is said to have delivered gold, silver, and vessels to Meremoth son of Uriah, who is also called "the priest." Both cannot have been high priest simultaneously. Michael Wise has surveyed the evidence adduced by Stegemann, and also the evidence of coins and inscriptions, and concluded:

> the great mass of evidence — from the usage for known early postexilic high priests to the Hasmonean coins and the ossuary inscriptions — points to the conclusion that the way to say "high priest" was HKHN HGDL. The conclusion has to be that the references to the T[eacher] of R[ighteousness] as HKHN do not intend to suggest that he was ever a functioning — or nonfunctioning — high priest.[35]

There are a couple of exceptions to this. In the Hebrew text of Sir 50:1, Simon, son of Onias, is called simply "the priest" *(hkhn).* (However, the Greek translation, *hiereus ho megas,* "the great priest," may presuppose a Hebrew text that read *hkhn hgdwl).* A silver coin from the fourth century BCE reading *ywḥn[n] hkhn* has been taken to refer to a high priest.[36] But these exceptional occurrences do not show that "the priest" always meant "the high priest." In the words of James VanderKam, "the definite form of the noun alone does not serve as a consistent, foolproof means for identifying someone as a high priest."[37] VanderKam concludes his discussion of the *intersacerdotium* by stating that "we have no textual evidence that anyone, much less the Teacher, was Jonathan's immediate predecessor."[38]

In fact, there is no explicit support in the texts for the view that the high priestly succession was a reason for the development of the sect.[39]

---

35. Michael O. Wise, "The Teacher of Righteousness and the High Priest of the Intersacerdotium: Two Approaches," *RevQ* 14 (1990): 602.

36. Dan Barag, "A Silver Coin of Yohanan the High Priest and the Coinage of Judea in the Fourth Century B.C.," *Israel Numismatic Journal* 9 (1986–87): 4-21; Lange, *Weisheit und Prädestination,* 23 n. 99; Eshel, *Dead Sea Scrolls and Hasmonean State,* 56-57 n. 74.

37. VanderKam, *From Joshua to Caiaphas,* 247. So also Eshel, *Dead Sea Scrolls and Hasmonean State,* 57 n. 74.

38. VanderKam, *From Joshua to Caiaphas,* 250. His point is not that the Teacher could not possibly have served as high priest, but that we have no evidence that he did. *Pace* Lange, *Weisheit und Prädestination,* 23, such titles as "Righteous Teacher," "Unique Teacher," or "Interpreter of the Torah" are not attested as traditional titles of the high priest.

39. See already Collins, "Origin of Qumran Community," 247.

The reasons for separation given in the *Damascus Document* and 4QMMT concern the cultic calendar and matters of legal observance. At no point is any mention made of the legitimacy of the high priest. Neither can the use of the sobriquet "the Wicked Priest" in the *pesharim* be taken to imply that the high priest was illegitimate.[40] As we shall see, the *pesharim* often qualify the wickedness of the Priest in question, and at no point do they accuse him of usurping the high priesthood.[41] It seems highly unlikely that this issue would go unmentioned, if it were a major reason for the formation of the sect.

Moreover, while the "sons of Zadok" appear as authoritative figures in 1QS 5, they are not mentioned in some of the parallel fragments from Cave 4. Sarianna Metso has argued persuasively that the shorter form of the text is the more original.[42] We must reckon, then, with the possibility that the Zadokites were not the original leaders of the sect. Moreover, as we have seen, "sons of Zadok" appears to be an honorific title for the community, rather than an indication of lineage. Much remains unclear about the history of the leadership of the community, but the evidence of the Cave 4 fragments further weakens the case that the sect originated in a dispute over the high priesthood. In any case, VanderKam has argued that the Hasmoneans may have been Zadokites, since they belonged to the line of Joiarib, the first of the twenty-four priestly groups in 1 Chron 24:7-19, and Phinehas, who was from the same line as Zadok, is glorified in 1 Macc 2:26, 54.[43] The Hasmoneans

---

40. Contra Stegemann, *Entstehung*, 109.

41. Compare Alison Schofield and James VanderKam, "Were the Hasmoneans Zadokites?" *JBL* 124 (2005): 73-87: "while the community opposed Hasmonean ruler-priests, there is no surviving indication that they considered them *genealogically* unfit for the high priesthood" (83).

42. S. Metso, *The Textual Development of the Qumran Community Rule* (STDJ 21; Leiden: Brill, 1997) 105; eadem, "In Search of the Sitz im Leben of the Community Rule from Qumran Cave 4," in D. W. Parry and E. C. Ulrich, eds., *The Provo International Conference on the Dead Sea Scrolls* (STDJ 30; Leiden: Brill, 1999) 306-15. See above, chapter 2.

43. VanderKam, *From Joshua to Caiaphas,* 270 n. 90. Of the 24 priestly houses, 16 were from the line of Eleazar, as were Phinehas and Zadok. See Schofield and VanderKam, "Were the Hasmoneans Zadokites?" 73-87; and Deborah Rooke, *Zadok's Heirs: The Role and Development of the High Priesthood in Ancient Israel* (Oxford: Oxford University Press, 2000) 281-82. Eshel, *Dead Sea Scrolls and Hasmonean State,* 55, does not represent the argument of Schofield and VanderKam accurately. He holds that "since we do not find explicit statement saying that the Hasmoneans were Zadokites, we should assume that they were not from this family."

were not Oniads; they did not belong to the family that had occupied the office in the third century BCE. But they may still have been Zadokite by genealogy. Conversely, it has been noted that "Zadokite" was by no means a standard or common way of referring to the high priestly line in the Second Temple period.[44] The appeal to "sons of Zadok" in the Scrolls is primarily a claim of spiritual superiority rather than genealogical legitimacy.

The recognition that the usurpation of the high priesthood was not a causative factor in the origin of the sect is extremely important for the present discussion. Not only does it remove a major reason for dating the Teacher to the mid-second century BCE. It also allows for the possibility that the conflict between the Teacher and the Wicked Priest was not the original rift that caused the separation of the sect but may have occurred sometime later.

Historical Allusions

Michael Wise is surely right that the most reliable evidence for dating is provided by historical allusions in the texts. This is only true, however, if the allusions are found in texts that bear on the subject under discussion, and if the references are explicit enough to warrant confident identification. Such allusions, unfortunately, are very few. The main issue in question is the date of the activity of the Teacher, since this is the only episode in the formation of the sect that involves other characters who might possibly admit of historical identification.

Wise has provided the most extensive catalogue to date of the historical allusions in the Scrolls, listing thirty-two allusions in all.[45] Half of these, however, are from nonsectarian texts, and only a few of the sectarian references bear on the date of the Teacher. The great majority of explicit references point to the first century BCE. There are clear references to Alexander Jannaeus ("the lion of wrath, who hangs men alive") in *Pesher Nahum*, which also mentions Demetrius, king of Greece. Other texts refer

---

44. So especially Hunt, *Missing Priests*. She suggests that "there never was a priestly dynasty until the Oniads and these Oniads were ousted by a new dynasty . . . the Hasmoneans" (190). Also Maria Brutti, *The Development of the High Priesthood during the Pre-Hasmonean Period: History, Ideology, Theology* (JSJSup 108; Leiden: Brill, 2006) 110-15.

45. Wise, "Dating the Teacher," 67-81. See also Gregory L. Doudna, *4Q Pesher Nahum: A Critical Edition* (JSPSup 35; London: Sheffield Academic Press, 2001) 701-5.

to Salome Alexandra (Shelamzion; 4Q332), who reigned from 76 to 67 BCE; the Roman general Aemilius Scaurus, who served under Pompey (4Q333); and Peitholaus, a Jewish general active in the mid-first century BCE (4Q468e). There are several references to the coming of the Romans, which culminated in Pompey's capture of Jerusalem. Surprisingly, there is no clear allusion to Herod, or to any event or person later than 37 BCE.[46] Wise concludes that the preponderance of references to the first century BCE "certainly speaks to the question of the Teacher's movement's *floruit*, and unless there is good historical reason to interpose a long period between that *floruit* and the time of the founder, it speaks also to the dating of the Teacher."[47] But while one may readily grant the first part of that claim, the second does not follow. Proponents of the second-century dating have never denied that the sect flourished in the first century BCE. De Vaux posited a significant expansion of the Qumran settlement at that time. It is gratuitous to assume that the Teacher must have been active at the peak of the literary productivity of the sect. (New Testament scholars do not assume that Jesus must have lived at the time the Gospels were written.) Historical allusions can determine the time of the Teacher only if they refer to him or to someone known to be contemporary with him.

The *Pesharim* as Historical Sources

The Teacher is mentioned only in the *Damascus Document* and the *pesharim* (on Habakkuk, Psalms, and Micah). Hopes of establishing the time of his activity rest primarily on references to conflict between the Teacher and two other figures, the "liar" and the "Wicked Priest." Discussion has focused mainly on the latter. Since the early days of Scrolls research, the title *hkhn hrš*, "the wicked priest," is understood to be a pun on *hkhn hr'š*, "the chief priest."[48] If this figure was a high priest, then he might be identified more easily than a more obscure figure (such as the liar). It

---

46. Doudna, *4Q Pesher Nahum*, 701, concludes that the Scrolls were deposited in the caves around 40 BCE, which, on his theory, would mean that they were deposited in the lifetime of the Teacher, although the *Damascus Rule* seems to refer to him as a figure of the past. Nonetheless, the lack of later references is intriguing.

47. Wise, "Dating the Teacher," 82.

48. Karl Elliger, *Studien zum Habakuk-Kommentar vom Toten Meer* (Beiträge zur historischen Theologie 15; Tübingen: Mohr Siebeck, 1953) 266.

should be noted, however, that the title might, in principle, refer to different individuals in different passages.[49] Most scholars have tried to identify a single Wicked Priest.

As many scholars have noted, the *pesharim* are highly problematic as historical sources.[50] Except for the mention of Demetrius in *Pesher Nahum*, they do not name names. Rather, they use cryptic titles such as "the Teacher" and "the Wicked Priest."[51] More fundamentally, they are commentaries, and so they are constrained to a degree by the text that is being explained. From the early days of Scrolls scholarship, there has been a debate as to how far the interpretations provided in the *pesharim* are derived exegetically, and how far they are imported on the basis of supposed revelation.[52] In recent years, scholars have tended to emphasize the exegetical character of the commentaries.[53] George Brooke has noted the use of secondary biblical quotations, and cautioned: "Before jumping to

49. The view that there were multiple Wicked Priests has been advanced especially by A. S. van der Woude, "Wicked Priest or Wicked Priests? Reflections on the Identification of the Wicked Priest in the Habakkuk Commentary," *JJS* 33 (1982): 349-59. See the criticism of this position by T. H. Lim, "The Wicked Priests of the Groningen Hypothesis," *JBL* 112 (1993): 415-25; idem, *Pesharim* (CQS 3; New York: Continuum, 2002) 70-72. Lim agrees with van der Woude, however, that more than one high priest was envisioned. Van der Woude responded in "Once Again: The Wicked Priests in the *Habakkuk Pesher* from Cave 1 of Qumran," *RevQ* 17 (1996): 375-84.

50. See, e.g., Callaway, *History of the Qumran Community*, 135-71; George J. Brooke, "The Pesharim and the Origins of the Dead Sea Scrolls," in M. O. Wise et al., eds., *Methods of Investigation of the Dead Sea Scrolls and the Khirbet Qumran Site: Present Realities and Future Prospects* (ANYAS 722; New York: New York Academy of Sciences, 1994) 339-53.

51. H. Bengtsson, *What's in a Name? A Study of the Sobriquets in the Pesharim* (Uppsala: Uppsala University Press, 2000).

52. The exegetical character of the *pesharim* was emphasized especially by W. H. Brownlee, *The Midrash Pesher of Habakkuk* (SBLMS 24; Missoula, MT: Scholars Press for SBL, 1979). The claim of revelation is emphasized by Elliger, *Studien*, 150-56; and Otto Betz, *Offenbarung und Schriftforschung in der Qumransekte* (Tübingen: Mohr, 1960) 36-59.

53. George J. Brooke, "The Kittim in the Qumran Pesharim," in Loveday Alexander, ed., *Images of Empire* (JSOTSup 122; Sheffield: Sheffield Academic Press, 1991) 135-59; idem, "Pesharim and Origins"; B. Nitzan, *Pesher Habakkuk: A Scroll from the Wilderness of Judaea (1QpHab): Text, Introduction and Commentary* (Hebrew) (Jerusalem: Bialik Institute, 1986); Shani Berrin, *The Pesher Nahum Scroll from Qumran: An Exegetical Study of 4Q169* (STDJ 53; Leiden: Brill, 2004) 9-19; Jutta Jokiranta, "Pesharim: A Mirror of Self-Understanding," in K. De Troyer and A. Lange, eds., *Reading the Present in the Qumran Library: The Perception of the Contemporary by Means of Scriptural Interpretations* (SBLSymS 30; Atlanta: SBL, 2005) 23-34.

conclusions, therefore, about the history that may or may not be reflected in reading between the lines of the pesharim, it is important first of all to identify which literary sources are being used by the interpreter."[54] Philip Davies raised a more fundamental question.[55] On the one hand, he raised the possibility that the interpreters might "infer 'events' from the biblical text." On the other hand, he noted correspondences between passages in the *Hodayot* and 1QpHabakkuk, especially in passages relating to the Teacher, and suggested that "historical events" in the life of the Teacher may have been inferred from the *Hodayot,* on the assumption that the so-called Teacher Hymns were read as reflecting the Teacher's experience. In his most recent discussion of the subject, he suggests that the Wicked Priest was an entirely fictitious character.[56]

All parties agree that "the pesharim are not history in the normal sense of the word."[57] The issue is not only that they provide "interpreted history"; all history involves interpretation. Rather the issue is that the historical information they provide is oblique and indirect — and usually in code. They provide no coherent narrative to put the allusions in historical context. It is not the purpose of the *pesharim* to provide historical information as such. Rather, it is their purpose to reassure the members of the *yahad* that history was unfolding as had been foretold by the prophets, and that they would be vindicated in the not too distant future.[58] In the process, the commentaries reaffirm the identity and rightness of the sectarian movement.[59]

Nonetheless, historical information plays an essential role in the

54. Brooke, "Pesharim and Origins," 343.

55. Davies, "History and Hagiography," in idem, *Behind the Essenes: History and Ideology in the Dead Sea Scrolls* (BJS 94; Atlanta: Scholars Press for Brown University, 1987) 87-105.

56. Davies, "What History Can We Get from the Scrolls, and How?" in Charlotte Hempel, ed., *Proceedings of the Birmingham Dead Sea Scrolls Conference, October 2007,* forthcoming.

57. Jokiranta, "Pesharim," 27.

58. Bilhah Nitzan, "The Pesher and Other Methods of Instruction," in Z. J. Kapera, ed., *Mogilany 1989: Papers on the Dead Sea Scrolls Offered in Memory of Jean Carmignac,* part II: *The Teacher of Righteousness* (Kraków: Enigma, 1991) 213, writes that the *pesher* "was intended to show that . . . all that occurs in the reality of history . . . does not deviate or contradict the words of the ancient prophets and visionaries." But the demonstration of the reliability of prophecy is a means to the end of providing reassurance to the community.

59. This point is emphasized especially by Jokiranta, "Pesharim."

rhetoric and logic of the *pesharim*. In order to show that prophecy was being fulfilled, they needed to show correspondences between the prophetic
text and history as known from other sources. In this respect, they resemble the use of *ex eventu* prophecy in apocalyptic literature (e.g., Daniel 11).
The effectiveness of the argument depends on the reader's ability to recognize the allusions. *Pesher Nahum* uses some actual names (Antiochus,
Demetrius) and has some transparent allusions (e.g., the Lion of Wrath
who hangs men alive is easily identified as Alexander Jannaeus, who crucified eight hundred of his opponents). In the words of Timothy Lim, it
gives the reader "the clearest indication that the pesherist was indeed interested in history. His commentary was not just an exegetical and literary
play on the words and oracles of the prophet Nahum, but in it was also a
concern for contemporary life and events."[60] In this case we are fortunate
to have a narrative of the relevant events in Josephus's *Antiquities*.[61] In the
case of the Teacher and the Wicked Priest, we have no independent narrative. But in this case too the allusions must have been intelligible in light of
a narrative that was known in the community.

The idea that commentators might infer historical events from
hymnic material is not unreasonable in itself. The prose account of the
crossing of the sea in Exodus 14 is most probably inferred from the poem
in Exodus 15.[62] Baruch Halpern has argued persuasively that the prose account of the death of Sisera in Judges 4 is inferred from the Song of
Deborah in Judges 5.[63] Halpern argued that the authors of the prose texts
should properly be regarded as historians: they were attempting to reconstruct history from the material available to them. The hymns were allusive, and did not give clear accounts of the incidents to which they refer.
The prose accounts clarify the specific details, even if they do so by constructing imaginative accounts that are ultimately fictitious. The *pesher*,
however, is almost as allusive as the hymn on which it supposedly relies.
The logic of the *pesher* requires that the reader recognize the allusions and
find correspondences between the prophetic text and the historical narrative known to the reader. But the *pesharim* are not constructing that narra-

60. Lim, *Pesharim*, 64.

61. *Ant.* 13.372-83. See Berrin, *Pesher Nahum Scroll*, 104-9.

62. F. M. Cross, *Canaanite Myth and Hebrew Epic* (Cambridge: Harvard University
Press, 1973) 123-44.

63. Baruch Halpern, *The First Historians: The Hebrew Bible and History* (San Francisco: Harper & Row, 1988) 76-104.

tive, only alluding to it in an elliptic way. They are scarcely intelligible to the modern reader who does not know that narrative, and they would have been unintelligible in antiquity if the referents of the stereotypical language were not known in the community.

Scholars such as Brooke have quite rightly emphasized the difficulty of extracting historical information from the *pesharim*. Nonetheless, the commentaries allude consistently to a historical narrative that they presuppose (or at least to a narrative that they supposed to be historical, whether it was objectively accurate or not). It should be possible, then, to catch glimpses of that narrative between the lines. Even Davies allows that "wherever there is presented as an interpretation of a biblical text information which is not derivable from the text but seems gratuitous, then that information may be regarded as potentially of historical value."[64] In view of the logic of the *pesharim*, and the importance of the fulfillment of prophecy, it is unlikely that major characters such as the Wicked Priest or the liar were invented out of whole cloth. It is certainly legitimate to try to decipher these references, even if the task is difficult and the results uncertain.

The Wicked Priest Reconsidered

Debates about the identity of the Wicked Priest have focused primarily on four Hasmonean rulers.[65] The earliest of these is *Jonathan Maccabee*.[66] He became leader of the Maccabean movement after the death of his brother Judas in 161 BCE. In 152 BCE he was appointed high priest by the Syrian king Alexander Balas, who sent him a purple garment and a diadem as tokens of princely rank. He was captured treacherously by Tryphon, a former general of Alexander Balas and the guardian of his son Antiochus. He was held as a hostage for a time, to extract payments from the Judeans, but he was murdered in 143/142 BCE.

---

64. Davies, *Behind the Essenes*, 92. See the comments of Lim, *Pesharim*, 68, who cautions that material that can be derived from the text may also have historical value.

65. Van der Woude, "Wicked Priest or Wicked Priests?" identified six different figures, Judas Maccabee, Alcimus, Jonathan Maccabee, Simon Maccabee, John Hyrcanus, and Alexander Jannaeus, as Wicked Priests.

66. 1 Macc 9:23–13:30; Josephus, *J.W.* 1.48-49; *Ant.* 13.1-212. See Emil Schürer, *The History of the Jewish People in the Age of Jesus Christ (175 B.C.–A.D. 135)* (rev. and ed. Geza Vermes, Fergus Millar, and Martin Goodman; 3 vols. in 4; Edinburgh: T&T Clark, 1973–87) 1.174-78.

Simon Maccabee succeeded his brother. In exchange for allegiance to the Syrian king Demetrius, he won exemption from taxes and the political liberation of Judea. Beginning in 143/142, documents and treaties were dated according to the years of Simon, high priest and prince of the Jews.[67] He and two of his sons, Mattathias and Judas, were murdered by his son-in-law, Ptolemy son of Abubus, governor of Jericho, during a banquet in his honor in the fortress Dok, near Jericho, when they were all drunk.

Alexander Jannaeus, grandson of Simon and son of John Hyrcanus, ruled from 103 to 76 BCE.[68] He attacked the cities on the coast of Syria. They appealed to Ptolemy Lathyrus, who had been driven from Egypt by his mother Cleopatra and was at that time ruling Cyprus. Ptolemy defeated Jannaeus in battle, but was forced to withdraw by his mother. Jannaeus waged new campaigns and made conquests east of the Jordan and in Philistia, including Gaza. The Pharisees, however, led a revolt against him, on the grounds that he was not fit to be high priest, and he responded by having some six thousand people killed. The conflict continued, however. Accord-ing to Josephus, he killed fifty thousand people over a period of six years. Finally, his Jewish opponents sent for help to Demetrius Akairos. Demetrius invaded, and defeated Jannaeus in battle near Shechem. The Jews then rallied to Jannaeus, and Demetrius withdrew. But his conflict with his Jewish opponents continued. According to Josephus, he had some eight hundred of them crucified, and killed their wives and children before their eyes, while he feasted with his concubines. Eventually he fell ill from heavy drinking and was afflicted with quatrain fever for three years. On his deathbed, he advised his queen, Salome Alexandra, to make peace with the Pharisees.

Hyrcanus II served as high priest during the reign of his mother, Salome Alexandra (76–67 BCE), the widow of Alexander Jannaeus.[69] After his mother's death he assumed the duties of ruler, but was attacked by his younger brother Aristobulus and was forced to abandon his claim both to the kingship and to the high priesthood. He was restored to the high priesthood by Pompey, after the capture of Jerusalem in 63 BCE, and continued in the office until 40 BCE, as a Roman vassal.[70] Then he was taken

---

67. 1 Macc 13:31–16:22; Josephus, *J.W.* 1.50-53; *Ant.* 13.213-29; Schürer, *History,* 1.189-99.

68. Josephus, *J.W.* 1.85-106; *Ant.* 13.320-406; Schürer, *History,* 1.219-28.

69. Josephus, *J.W.* 1.107-19; *Ant.* 13.405-32; Schürer, *History,* 1.229-32.

70. Josephus, *J.W.* 1.159-273; *Ant.* 14.80-369; Schürer, *History,* 1.267-80.

prisoner by the Parthians, who had allied themselves with Antigonus, son of Aristobulus II and nephew of Hyrcanus II. Antigonus cut off the ears of Hyrcanus to render him unfit for the high priesthood. The Parthians then installed Antigonus as king (40–37 BCE). When Herod came to power, and Antigonus was executed by the Romans, Hyrcanus II was allowed to return to Judea, although he could no longer act as high priest (Josephus, *Ant.* 15.21). After the battle of Actium, Herod had him put to death.

Many allusions in the *pesharim* are either too specific or not specific enough to be helpful to the historian. 1QpHab 11 describes a highly specific encounter between the Wicked Priest and the Teacher on the Day of Atonement (according to the latter's calendar).[71] Unfortunately, we have no other information about this incident that would enable us to identify when it took place.[72] In contrast, the statement that God will condemn the Wicked Priest to complete destruction, because he dealt wickedly with the council of the community (1QpHab 12:2-3), is far too general. There are, however, several passages that seem, prima facie, to be more promising.

1QpHab 8

1QpHab 8 offers the following interpretation of Hab 2:5-6:

> And moreover, wealth betrays a haughty man, and he is unseemly, who opens his soul wide like Sheol; and like death he cannot be sated. And all the nations are gathered about him, and all the peoples are assembled to him. Do not all of them raise a taunt against him and interpreters of riddles about him, who say: "Woe to the one who multiplies what is not his own! How long will he weigh himself down with debt?" (VACAT) Its interpretation concerns the Wicked Priest, who was called by the true name at the beginning of his standing, but when he ruled in Israel his heart became large, and he abandoned God, and betrayed the statutes for the sake of wealth. And he stole and amassed the wealth

---

71. Callaway, *History of Qumran Community*, 160-61, denies that the Teacher was necessarily following a sectarian calendar, but his denial requires the implausible assumption that a high priest would have traveled to the Teacher's place of exile on the official Day of Atonement.

72. Davies, "History and Hagiography," 94, argued that this passage was influenced by 1QH^a 12. See the comments of Brooke, "Pesharim and Origins," 344; and Lim, *Pesharim*, 68.

of the men of violence who had rebelled against God, and he took the wealth of peoples to add to himself guilty iniquity. And the abominable ways he pursued with every sort of unclean impurity.[73]

The accusation of taking what was not his own and the allusion to the nations are explicit in the biblical text. The commentary, however, adds several items that have no apparent biblical basis, beginning with the identification of the figure in question as a priest. The *pesher* distinguishes two stages in the career of the Wicked Priest: he was called by the name of truth when he first arose, but when he ruled in Israel he became arrogant. This is hardly a necessary inference from the prophet's statement that "wealth betrays a haughty man."[74] The prophet implies that the man was haughty even before he took the property of others. The statement that he was called "by the true name" when he first arose may mean only that he had a good reputation. The "beginning of his standing" (*'mdw*) refers to his assumption of office (presumably the priestly office).[75] We may reasonably infer that he was not regarded as illegitimate because of genealogy. His "wickedness" is rather a matter of rapacious conduct, which became manifest when he ruled (*mšl*) in Israel. This formulation may imply that he only began to rule in Israel sometime after he assumed the priestly office, but this is not necessarily so. It may be that his character changed in the course of his rule. There has been much debate over the precise meaning of the verb *mšl* here.[76] It may be significant that the priest is never said to be king (*mlk*). But again, *mšl* can refer to kingly rule, as it does in 4QpIsa[a] frags. 8-10 3 25, in the context of Isaiah 11. Finally, he is said to seize the wealth of "the men of violence" as well as that of the nations. Even though the reference to the wealth of the nations can be inferred easily from the biblical text, it is still significant, since it is on the basis of this reference that the passage is taken to refer to the Wicked Priest.

73. Translation of M. P. Horgan, "Habakkuk Pesher (1QpHab)," in James H. Charlesworth, ed., *The Dead Sea Scrolls: Hebrew, Aramaic, and Greek Texts with English Translations*, vol. 6B: *Pesharim, Other Commentaries, and Related Documents* (PTSDSSP; Louisville: Westminster John Knox, 2002) 175.

74. Eshel, *Dead Sea Scrolls and Hasmonean State*, 41: "It is striking that the verse from Habakkuk does not describe an originally good person who then sinned; it would seem therefore, that the author of the *Pesher on Habakkuk* had his own reason for stressing that the Wicked Priest was not originally wicked."

75. See Collins, "Origin of Qumran Community," in *Seers, Sibyls, and Sages*, 244.

76. See especially Milik, *Ten Years*, 65-66; Stegemann, *Entstehung*, 100-104.

In light of these observations, is it possible to identify the priest in question? Jonathan Maccabee presumably came to office with a good reputation, in view of his role in the struggle for liberation from Syria. He may plausibly be assumed to have seized property of the hellenizers (the men of violence) and of Gentiles. Since he never became king, the choice of verb is not problematic. The passage could also be applied plausibly to his brother Simon. Alexander Jannaeus was constantly engaged in warfare both with Gentiles and with Jewish enemies (the Pharisees), and presumably seized their wealth as opportunity offered. The followers of the Teacher may have hoped for better things from him initially, in view of his opposition to the Pharisees. Josephus says that Jannaeus was appointed king after the death of Aristobulus, because he seemed best fitted for that office by reason of age and evenness of temper (*Ant.* 13.320), although the latter quality was not much in evidence in his subsequent career. In his case, we might have expected the title "king," but it should be noted that while he used that title on his bilingual coins, he also minted coins that bore only a Hebrew legend and claimed only the priesthood: *yhwntn hkhn hgdl wḥbr yhwdym*: "Jonathan the high priest and the association of the Judeans."[77]

Finally, Hyrcanus II was appointed high priest, without kingly power, by his mother, Alexandra Salome (76–67 BCE). It is questionable whether he could be said to rule in Israel while his mother, Salome Alexandra, was queen, but Josephus says that "even in her lifetime his mother had entrusted the kingdom" to him (*J.W.* 1.120). The *yaḥad* may have expected him to continue the policies of his father, which were notoriously hostile to the Pharisees, and felt betrayed when he implemented his mother's policy and gave power to the rival sect. He was a weak ruler, however, and is not known to have been especially rapacious.

Any of the Hasmonean high priests under consideration could conceivably have been called by the name of truth when they first arose, but the charge of rapaciousness is perhaps most appropriate for Alexander Jannaeus.

This passage is followed by the quotation of Hab 2:7-8a: "Will it not be . . . that your cre[di]tors will arise? And will those who make you tremble awake, and will you become their booty? For you have plundered many nations, but all the rest of the peoples will plunder you." The lemma sug-

---

77. Y. Meshorer, *Ancient Jewish Coinage*, vol. 2: *Herod the Great through Bar Cochba* (Dix Hills, NY: Amphora, 1982) 123-34.

gests that the figure in question will suffer retribution at the hands of the nations. The interpretation poses several problems. First, the addressee is identified as "the priest who rebelled," and this figure is usually and plausibly identified with the Wicked Priest. The passage continues: *ngwʿw bmšpṭy ršʿh wšʿrwrywt mḥlym rʿym ʿśw bw nqmwt bgwyt bśrw*. Maurya Horgan translates: "his injury on account of wicked judgments. And horrors of evil diseases were at work in him, and acts of vengeance on his carcass of flesh."[78] The verb *ʿśw* can be taken impersonally, as in Horgan's translation. If a subject is implied, it is not clear whether the perpetrators are human or angelic. The reference to diseases brings to mind the fate of Alexander Jannaeus, who died after a prolonged bout of quatrain fever brought on by excessive drinking (*Ant.* 13.398). The passage could also be applied credibly to Hyrcanus II, the last Hasmonean high priest, whose ears were mutilated so that he would be unfit for the priesthood (*Ant.* 14.366). Milik argued that it was historically plausible that the circumstances of Jonathan Maccabee's death also fit this description: "That he was tortured, it is true, is not mentioned by Josephus, but it is a most probable deduction."[79] Be that as it may, we have no evidence that would warrant the application of this passage to Jonathan.

The last part of the lemma, "for you have plundered many nations, but all the rest of the peoples will plunder you," is repeated, and applied more broadly to "the last priests of Jerusalem," that is, the priests who were contemporary with the author of the *pesher*. We are told that "in latter days their wealth together with their plunder will be given into the hand of the army of the Kittim." The future tense of the prophetic text is retained, although in the preceding passage the tense was changed to the past.[80] This prediction was fulfilled in the Roman conquest of Jerusalem, and it is difficult to avoid the assumption that it was written after the fact.[81] If that is correct, the "last priests" would presumably include Aristobulus II and Hyrcanus II.

---

78. Horgan, "Habakkuk Pesher," 177.

79. Milik, *Ten Years*, 69.

80. On the use of tenses in the *Habakkuk Pesher* see Loren T. Stuckenbruck, "Temporal Shifts from Text to Interpretation: Concerning the Use of the Perfect and Imperfect in the *Habakkuk Pesher* (1QpHab)," in Michael Thomas Davis and Brent A. Strawn, eds., *Qumran Studies: New Approaches, New Questions* (Grand Rapids: Eerdmans, 2007) 124-49.

81. Wise takes this passage as a reference not to the conquest by Pompey but to the plunder of Jerusalem by Herod's Roman allies in 37 BCE. Wise, "Dating the Teacher of Righteousness," 81.

1QpHab 9

The afflictions suffered by the Wicked Priest are taken up again in 1QpHab 9 in an exposition of Hab 2:8b: "On account of human bloodshed and violence (done to) the land, the town, and all its inhabitants." The interpretation, we are told, "concerns the Wicked Priest, whom — because of the wrong done to the Teacher and the men of his counsel — God gave into the hand of his enemies to humble him with affliction *(ngʿ)* for annihilation in bitterness of soul, because he had acted wickedly against his chosen ones."

It is largely on the basis of this passage that the Wicked Priest has been identified with Jonathan Maccabee, who was captured by the Syrian general Trypho, held for a time, and then killed.[82] It seems less apt for Simon, who also died at the hands of his enemies, but in a drunken stupor.[83] It could also be applied appropriately to Hyrcanus II, whose mutilation could reasonably be called a *ngʿ*, or "affliction." The mutilation was inflicted by the nephew of Hyrcanus, Antigonus, but the uncle was in the custody of Parthians at the time.[84] Hyrcanus survived for several years after this incident. The Parthians took him prisoner (Josephus, *J.W.* 1.273). They treated him leniently, and allowed him to live in the large Jewish community in Babylon, where he was honored as high priest and king (*Ant.* 15.15). He was nonetheless a prisoner, and the conditions of his confinement were not necessarily known to the author of the *pesher*. When Herod became king of Judea in 31 BCE, Hyrcanus was allowed to return. At first, he was treated with honor, and used to lend legitimacy to Herod's regime. After the battle of Actium in 30 BCE, when Herod's patron Antony was defeated and Herod again felt vulnerable, Hyrcanus was viewed as a potential rival and was put to death.[85] Josephus comments that "in his old age, he came to an unworthy end" (*Ant.* 15.181). The *pesher* on Habakkuk is plausibly dated somewhere in the later phase of Hyrcanus's life. If he is the Wicked Priest referred to in this passage, then we should probably assume that the *pesher* was composed before his return to Judea, and that his Parthian captivity was assumed to be final.

---

82. 1 Macc 12:46-48; 13:23; Josephus, *Ant.* 13.191-93, 209.

83. 1 Macc 16:16; Josephus, *Ant.* 13.228.

84. Josephus, *J.W.* 1.269-70; *Ant.* 14.366. See VanderKam, *From Joshua to Caiaphas*, 369-70.

85. *Ant.* 15.165-78. See VanderKam, *From Joshua to Caiaphas*, 371-72.

The view that the Wicked Priest was given into the hands of foreigners derives support from the *pesher* on Psalm 37. The lemma in question is Ps 37:32-33: "The wicked one lies in ambush for the righteous one and seeks to murder him. Yahweh will not abandon him into his hand, nor will he let him be condemned as guilty when he comes to trial." The lemma says nothing about the fate of the wicked one. The pesherist identifies the righteous one with the Teacher, but adds, obviously with reference to the Wicked Priest, that "[God will] pay [him] his due, giving him into the hand of the ruthless ones of the Gentiles. . . ." As often in the *pesharim*, the import of the tenses is uncertain. The prediction may be after the fact, or may express a hope for the future. If the reference is taken quite literally, the only candidates would seem to be Jonathan Maccabee, Hyrcanus II, or the latter's brother Aristobulus, who was taken prisoner to Rome. If the passage is taken as a genuine prediction, it could refer to any of the Hasmoneans. Nonetheless, when this passage is read in conjunction with 1QpHab 9, the most reasonable interpretation is that the Wicked Priest suffered some bodily affliction at the hands of Gentiles.

1QpHab 11

One other passage about the Wicked Priest, in 1QpHab 11, requires comment. The lemma is taken from Hab 2:16: "You will be sated with shame rather than glory. Drink then, you yourself, and totter. The cup of Yahweh's right hand will come around to you and disgrace (will come) upon your glory." The interpretation is translated as follows by Horgan: "Its interpretation concerns the priest whose shame prevailed over his glory, for he did not circumcise the foreskin of his heart, but he walked in the ways of inebriety in order that the thirst might be consumed, but the cup of the wrath of [Go]d will swallow him up, ad[d]ing [t]o [all] his [s]ha[me]. . . ."[86]

The reference to drunkenness is suggested by the text. Milik pointed out that the interpretation draws on Deut 29:18: *lm'n spwt hrwh w't hṣm'h,* "to devastate the dry and the irrigated land together." He noted that the phrase is repeated in the curse on apostates in 1QS 2:14 in a metaphorical sense, and concluded that here too it is a metaphor for unfaithfulness.[87]

86. Horgan, "Habakkuk Pesher," 181.
87. Milik, *Ten Years,* 69-70.

The *pesher* does not cite Deuteronomy directly, but alters it to say that the priest "walked in the ways of inebriety." This may be metaphorical, but it would be all the more apt if the priest in question had a reputation for drinking. Jannaeus, as we have seen, became ill from heavy drinking in his latter years. The passage might conceivably be applied to Simon Maccabee, who was drunk at a banquet when he was killed, but we do not know that he was a habitual drunkard. Here again, the imperfect (future) is used for the destruction, but the tense may be carried over from the biblical lemma.

The Identification of the Wicked Priest

While none of these allusions is unequivocal, some fit one Hasmonean ruler better than another. The problem is that they do not all bring to mind the same figure. If the drunkenness is taken literally, it would suggest Alexander Jannaeus, as would the charge that he took the wealth of the Gentiles. But Jannaeus did not literally suffer at the hand of Gentiles. It may be that more than one Wicked Priest is in view. For our purposes, the crucial question is the identity of the figure with whom the Teacher had his dispute. The wrong done to the Teacher is explicitly mentioned in 1QpHab 9:8-12, in connection with the figure who was given into the hand of his enemies. Again in the *pesher* on Psalm 37, the conflict with the Teacher is mentioned in connection with the priest who would be given into the hand of the ruthless ones of the Gentiles. If these references can be taken literally, and the latter one is not a prediction, then the Wicked Priest in these passages can only be identified with either Jonathan Maccabee or Hyrcanus II. Both of these figures functioned as high priest without royal status, except for a very brief interlude in the case of Hyrcanus II.

Jonathan Maccabee was certainly given into the hand of his enemies, who might reasonably be called "the ruthless ones of the Gentiles." The surviving accounts of Jonathan provide no basis for the references to drunkenness or to bodily affliction. More significantly, we should have to posit a long gap between the activity of the Wicked Priest and the events of the first century, which figure prominently in the *pesharim*. It is true that Josephus first mentions the Jewish sects in the context of Jonathan's reign in the *Antiquities* (13.171), but he introduces them much later in his account of the Jewish War, in the context of the early first century CE (*J.W.* 2.119-66). Joseph Sievers has argued persuasively that the notice in *Antiq-*

uities 13 is a secondary addition and out of context.[88] Josephus gives no indication that Jonathan (or his brother Simon) was engaged in controversy with any of these sects.[89] Rather, Jonathan was preoccupied with the Syrians, and his only Jewish opponents were the hellenizers, early in his career. The case for Jonathan as Wicked Priest has always rested heavily on the assumption that the basic dispute that led to the secession of the sect was over the high priesthood, and we have seen that this thesis is unfounded.

At the other end of the spectrum, several of the references apply rather well to Hyrcanus II. He was given into the hands of his enemies and suffered grievous bodily harm. He is not known to have walked in the ways of drunkenness, but this language may be metaphorical or may refer to a different priest, Alexander Jannaeus. The conquest of Judea by the Romans, which figures so prominently in the *pesharim*, happened in his time. He may well have still been alive when the *pesharim* were written.

Many scholars have ruled Hyrcanus II out of account on the grounds that he is simply too late. The archeological evidence suggests that Qumran was settled in the time of Alexander Jannaeus, and some sectarian scrolls are dated paleographically to the early first century BCE. Even allowing for imprecision in the methods of dating, it is difficult to suppose that the sect originated as late as the reign of Hyrcanus II. This objection, however, must be qualified by two considerations. First, the conflict with the Wicked Priest did not necessarily take place at the beginning of the history of the sect. It may have occurred late in the Teacher's life, and he may have been active for thirty or forty years before that. Since the movement existed for some twenty years before the arrival of the Teacher (CD 1:9-10), some sectarian texts might conceivably precede the conflict with the

---

88. Joseph Sievers, "Josephus, First Maccabees, Sparta, the Three *Haireseis* — and Cicero," *JSJ* 32 (2001): 24-51. The passage in question is paraphrasing 1 Maccabees 12, but omits the letter to Arius of Sparta. Sievers argues that this created a gap in a manuscript that had already been formatted, i.e., in a second edition. Cf. Eshel, *Dead Sea Scrolls and Hasmonean State*, 40.

89. The earliest instance of sectarian conflict in Josephus concerns the Pharisees and John Hyrcanus (*Ant.* 13.288-98). Sievers also regards this story as a secondary insertion that does not fit the context. So also Étienne Nodet, "*Asidaioi* and Essenes," in A. Hilhorst, É. Puech, and E. Tigchelaar, eds., *Flores Florentino: Dead Sea Scrolls and Other Early Jewish Studies in Honour of Florentino García Martínez* (JSJSup 122; Leiden: Brill, 2007) 71-73. Eshel, *Dead Sea Scrolls and Hasmonean State*, 51, claims that Jonathan Maccabee "subscribed to a Pharisaic outlook," but he gives no reference to support this claim, and I am not aware of any.

Wicked Priest by half a century. There is no mention of the Wicked Priest in either CD or the *Serek,* nor indeed in any text other than the *Pesharim.* Second, Hyrcanus II was high priest under Salome Alexandra (76–67 BCE). If the conflict occurred at the beginning of this period, the chronological difficulty would be lessened significantly.

The hypothesis that the Wicked Priest with whom the Teacher quarreled was Hyrcanus II was originally proposed by André Dupont-Sommer.[90] His interpretation of the *Habakkuk Pesher* was notoriously problematic (he argued that the Teacher was expected to return from the dead), and this helped to discredit his identification of the Wicked Priest.[91] The hypothesis was revived, without reference to Dupont-Sommer, by Michael Wise.[92] But Wise's book, *The First Messiah,* was written in a popular, semifictional style and was not taken seriously by many scholars. The possibility that Hyrcanus II was the Wicked Priest who came in conflict with the Teacher, however, deserves serious consideration. It is not without difficulties, but it fits the admittedly sketchy evidence better than any of the other proposals.

A Dispute with the Pharisees?

A few other factors may have some bearing on the question of chronology. The *pesharim* mention another contemporary of the Teacher, known as "the man of the lie." He is presumably the same person who is mentioned in CD 1:14-21 as "the scoffer" who "poured out over Israel waters of lies," and whose followers are said to "seek smooth things." In *Pesher Nahum,* the "seekers after smooth things" are the opponents of Alexander Jannaeus, who invited Demetrius Akairos to intervene in Judea. They are further referred to as "Ephraim." There is a long-standing consensus that they should be identified with the Pharisees. The expression "seekers after smooth things," *dršy ḥlqwt,* is plausibly taken as a derogatory play on the Pharisaic halakah, a form of legal interpretation that the followers of the Teacher regarded as too lenient.[93] Consequently, "the man of the lie" has

---

90. A. Dupont-Sommer, *The Essene Writings from Qumran* (trans. G. Vermes; Gloucester, MA: Peter Smith, 1973) 351-57.

91. See the comments of VanderKam, "Identity and History," 514.

92. Wise, *First Messiah,* 67-73.

93. Berrin, *Pesher Nahum Scroll,* 91-99. A. I. Baumgarten, "Seekers after Smooth

often been taken as the founder of the Pharisaic movement.[94] Since Josephus reports that the Pharisees were active in the reign of John Hyrcanus (*Ant.* 13.288-98), this identification would seem to push the activity of the Teacher back into the second century. But all we can reasonably infer about "the man of the lie" is that he was a Pharisaic teacher who engaged in dispute with the Teacher, and seduced some of the latter's followers. The belief that he founded a new movement rests on a slim foundation. He is accused of "building a city of emptiness" and establishing a congregation with falsehood" in 1QpHab 10:10, but this does not necessarily require that he was the initial "builder" of the movement. The Pharisees may have been in existence for several decades before the "liar" confronted the Teacher. Wise identifies him as Shimeon ben Shetach, who was active in the time of Alexander Jannaeus.[95] The specific identification cannot, of course, be proven, but the suggestion is not implausible. All we can safely assume is that the "liar" was an influential Pharisaic leader.

It has been widely assumed in the scholarship of the late twentieth century that the liar and the Teacher were once members of the same community. Here again, the evidence is less than conclusive. In 1QpHab 5:8, Hab 1:13b ("why do you heed traitors, but are silent when a wicked one swallows up one more righteous than he?") is applied to "the house of Absalom and the men of their council, who were silent at the rebuke of the Righteous Teacher and did not support him against the man of the lie, who rejected the Torah in the midst of all their counsel." Gert Jeremias argued that the word "rebuke" *(twkḥt)* implies that this was an inner-community dispute.[96] 1QS 9:16 decrees that "one must not engage in rebuking or disputation with the men of the pit" *(lw' lhwkyḥ wlhtrbb 'm 'nšy hšḥt)*. But the "liar" was not necessarily constrained by the rule of the *yaḥad*, if indeed it

---

Things," *EDSS* 2.857-58; J. C. VanderKam, "Those Who Look for Smooth Things, Pharisees, and Oral Law," in Paul et al., eds., *Emanuel*, 465-77; Lawrence H. Schiffman, "Pharisees and Sadducees in *Pesher Naḥum*," in Marc Brettler and Michael Fishbane, eds., *Minḥah le-Naḥum: Biblical and Other Studies Presented to Nahum M. Sarna in Honour of His 70th Birthday* (JSOTSup 154; Sheffield: Sheffield Academic Press, 1993) 272-90; Charlesworth, *Pesharim*, 97-98; Bengtsson, *What's in a Name?* 110-35. Doudna, *4Q Pesher Nahum*, 577-99, identifies the Seekers as the rulers of Jerusalem.

94. So especially Stegemann, *Entstehung*, 253. These identifications are disputed by Doudna, *4Q Pesher Nahum*, 639-74.

95. Wise, *First Messiah*, 68-73.

96. Gert Jeremias, *Der Lehrer der Gerechtigkeit* (SUNT 2; Göttingen: Vandenhoeck & Ruprecht, 1963) 85-86; followed by Stegemann, *Entstehung*, 48-49.

was in force at the time of this encounter. In CD 1:14 he is said to spout waters of falsehood "to Israel" and lead them astray. He did not merely resist the claims of the Teacher to leadership within his own community, but actively preached a different message to all Israel. In CD 4:19-20 his followers are said to be trapped in two of the nets of Belial. The disagreement is not only over the authority of the teacher, but involves some of the halakic issues that separated the sect from the rest of Israel.

Moreover, there is evidence that the Teacher at least once reached out to his opponents in an attempt to persuade them. According to 4QpPs[a] frags. 1-10 4:8-9, the Wicked Priest sought to murder the Teacher "and the Torah which he sent to him." Most probably this was the same "Torah" that was rejected by the man of the lie. Elisha Qimron and John Strugnell made the attractive proposal that the document in question is none other than the text we know as 4QMMT, and the proposal has been taken up by such diverse scholars as Michael Wise and Hanan Eshel.[97] This text, variously dubbed "the Halakhic Letter" or "the Letter of the Teacher of Righteousness to the Wicked Priest," appears to be addressed to a leader in Israel: "We have (indeed) sent you some of the precepts of the Torah according to our decision, for your welfare and the welfare of your people."[98] The man of the lie, it would seem, argued against this interpretation of the Torah, and may have contributed to the violent reaction of the Wicked Priest.

Scholars generally agree that the interpretation of the Torah found in 4QMMT is opposed to that of the Pharisees.[99] In the words of Lawrence Schiffman, "When mishnaic texts preserve Pharisee-Sadducee conflicts over the same matters discussed in the *Halakhic Letter,* the views of the letter's authors match those of the Sadducees."[100] We need not conclude that

---

97. Elisha Qimron and John Strugnell, *Qumran Cave 4*, vol. V: *Miqṣat Maʿaśe Ha-Torah* (DJD 10; Oxford: Clarendon, 1994) 175; Wise, *First Messiah*, 65-68; Hanan Eshel, "4QMMT and the History of the Hasmonean Period," in J. Kampen and M. J. Bernstein, eds., *Reading 4QMMT: New Perspectives on Qumran Law and History* (SBLSymS 2; Atlanta: SBL, 1996) 53-65; Eshel, *Dead Sea Scrolls and Hasmonean State*, 46-47.

98. 4QMMT C 26-28, trans. Qimron and Strugnell, DJD 10, 63. This view of the purpose of MMT is challenged by Stephen Fraade, "To Whom It May Concern: 4QMMT and Its Addressee(s)," *RevQ* 19 (2000): 507-26, who argues that the text could have been used for instruction of the members of the community. This hypothesis does not, however, undermine the view that the text was originally addressed to outsiders.

99. See Qimron and Strugnell, DJD 10, 123-77; Y. Sussmann, "Appendix 1: The History of the Halakha and the Dead Sea Scrolls," in DJD 10, 179-200.

100. Schiffman, *Reclaiming the Dead Sea Scrolls*, 87.

the authors were Sadducees,[101] but at least they were anti-Pharisaic. Eshel notes astutely that "if we assume that the addressee of the letter was a Pharisee and that MMT is 'the Law and the Torah' sent from the Teacher of Righteousness to the Wicked Priest mentioned in 4QpPsᵃ, then we cannot identify the Wicked Priest with Alexander Jannaeus[,] who was a Sadducee."[102] When Jannaeus was dying in 76 BCE, however, he urged his widow Salome Alexandra to make peace with the Pharisees. She did so, and entrusted them with the government. According to Josephus "she permitted the Pharisees to do as they liked in all matters, and also commanded the people to obey them; and whatever regulations, introduced by the Pharisees in accordance with the tradition of their fathers, had been abolished by her father-in-law Hyrcanus, these she again restored. And so, while she had the title of sovereign, the Pharisees had the power" (*Ant.* 13.408-9). She appointed Hyrcanus II high priest and he served in that capacity until 67 BCE. He later had a second term from 63 to 40. We should not be surprised if the reversal of royal attitude toward the Pharisees and their rulings provoked a protest from the other sects. This is perhaps the time in Hasmonean history when a high priest was most likely to take action against people who were contesting the Pharisaic halakah. Josephus says that the Pharisees tried to persuade the queen to kill those who had urged Alexander to put the eight hundred to death, and that they themselves assassinated some of them. This struggle for sectarian hegemony provides a plausible context for the conflict between the Teacher and both the Wicked Priest and the man of the lie. In contrast, we have no evidence for sectarian conflict in the time of Jonathan Maccabee. Even though Josephus introduces the three schools of thought in the time of Jonathan in *Ant.* 13.171, it is only at the end of the long reign of John Hyrcanus (135/134–104 BCE) that sectarian affiliation becomes an important issue for the high priest, when he encounters criticism from the Pharisees (*Ant.* 13.288-98). Even that reference is problematic, because of its similarity to a story told about Alexander Jannaeus and the Pharisees in *b. Qiddushin* 66a. Hyrcanus and Jannaeus are each accused of being unfit for the high priesthood because his mother was a captive. Some have argued that the story about Hyrcanus and the Pharisees is secondary, and derived from the story of the conflict

---

101. Other factors besides halakah would have to be taken into account. See the comments of VanderKam and Flint, *Meaning of Dead Sea Scrolls*, 250-52.

102. Eshel, "4QMMT and History," 62.

between Jannaeus and the Pharisees. (Josephus would have derived the story from oral tradition, where the two kings had been confused.) In that case, the first authentic reference to sectarian conflict should be dated to the time of Jannaeus.[103] But even if the story of the conflict between Hyrcanus and the Pharisees is essentially historical, as many scholars believe,[104] there is no evidence of sectarian conflict in the time of Jonathan Maccabee.

Another factor in calculating the approximate date of the conflict between the Teacher and the Wicked Priest concerns the time of the death of the Teacher. According to the *Damascus Document,* "from the day of the gathering in of the Teacher of the Community until the end of all the men of war who deserted to the liar, there shall pass about forty years." The *pesher* on Psalm 37 (frags. 1-10 2) tells us that at the end of forty years all the wicked will be consumed. It seems reasonable to infer that the "end" or time of divine intervention was expected forty years after the death of the Teacher. 1QpHab 7:7 interprets Hab 2:3a to mean that "the last period will be prolonged." Admittedly, the biblical text provides a basis for this interpretation ("if it tarries, wait for it"), but the interpretation expresses more concern about the delay than does the text. If we may assume that CD, *Pesher Psalms,* and *Pesher Habakkuk* share a common understanding on this matter, we may perhaps infer that the Teacher died about forty years before the composition of *Pesher Habakkuk.* Unfortunately, we do not know just when the *pesher* was composed. It clearly presupposes the conquest of Jerusalem by the Romans in 63 BCE. If Hyrcanus II is the Wicked Priest, then the *pesher* was written after he was mutilated while in Parthian custody in 40 BCE. Wise argues that 1QpHab 9:4-7 alludes to the plundering of Jerusalem by the Roman army under Sosius in 37 BCE.[105] This is possible, but hardly certain.[106] There is no reference in the *pesharim* to the reign of Herod (37–4 BCE), and so they were probably composed in the 30s,

---

103. Nodet, "*Asidaioi* and Essenes," 70-74. Sievers, "Josephus, First Maccabees, Sparta," 241-51, also regards the story about the Pharisees as a secondary addition to *Antiquities* 13.

104. Anthony J. Saldarini, *Pharisees, Scribes and Sadducees in Palestinian Society: A Sociological Approach* (Wilmington, DE: Glazier, 1988) 86 n. 17, concludes "that it is likely that the conflict with John Hyrcanus is historical." So also Schürer, *History,* 1.214, who acknowledges that the story bears the stamp of a legend.

105. Wise, "Dating the Teacher," 81.

106. Jerusalem was also plundered by Crassus in 54–53 BCE (Josephus, *J.W.* 1.179).

at the latest. If the Teacher died in 76 BCE or later (after the death of Alexander Jannaeus), the forty years would not be fulfilled until after 36. The identification of Hyrcanus II as the Wicked Priest, then, is not impossible on chronological grounds. If the reference is indeed to Hyrcanus II, then the pesherist was not writing about events that happened a century before his time, but about a figure who was still alive.

The Prayer for King Jonathan

Some passages in the *pesharim* fit Hyrcanus II remarkably well, and these are the passages that speak of conflict with the Teacher and say that the Wicked Priest was given into the hand of his enemies. As we have seen, however, it is difficult to find any one figure for whom all the passages about the Wicked Priest are appropriate. The passage in 1QpHab 8, and also the passage about drunkenness in col. 11, apply quite well to Alexander Jannaeus. It should be noted that neither of these passages mentions conflict with the Teacher.[107]

In Wise's reconstruction, the Teacher's followers would not have regarded Jannaeus as a Wicked Priest, but were rather his enthusiastic supporters.[108] He bases this opinion on 4Q448, the so-called *Prayer for King Jonathan*, which reads: 'wr qdš 'l ywntn hmlk, translated by the editors as: "Guard (or: Rise up), O Holy One, over King Jonathan."[109] The passage continues: "and all the congregation of your people Israel who are in the four winds of heaven, let them all be at peace and upon your kingdom may your name be blessed." The "King Jonathan" in question can only be Alexander Jannaeus; Jonathan Maccabee was never king.[110] It is somewhat sur-

---

107. I. R. Tantlevskij, *The Two Wicked Priests in the Qumran Commentary on Habakkuk* (QC Appendix C; Kraków: Enigma, 1995), identifies two wicked priests, Jonathan and Jannaeus, but does not address the anomaly of the chronological gap between the time of Jonathan and the other historical references in the *pesharim*.

108. Wise, Abegg, and Cook, *Dead Sea Scrolls*, 26-32.

109. E. Eshel, H. Eshel, and A. Yardeni, "A Qumran Scroll Containing Part of Psalm 154 and a Prayer for the Welfare of King Jonathan and His Kingdom," *IEJ* 42 (1992): 199-229; E. Eshel, H. Eshel, and A. Yardeni, "448: 4QApocryphal Psalm and Prayer," in Esther Eshel et al., *Qumran Cave 4, vol. 6: Poetic and Liturgical Texts, Part 1* (DJD 11; Oxford: Clarendon, 1998) 421; Eshel, *Dead Sea Scrolls and Hasmonean State*, 101-15.

110. Eshel, Eshel, and Yardeni, "448," 412-15; Eshel, *Dead Sea Scrolls and Hasmonean State*, 105.

prising to find a prayer for Alexander Jannaeus in the Dead Sea Scrolls, in light of the sect's negative relationship with the Hasmoneans.[111] It is quite conceivable, however, that the Teacher and his followers would pray for Jannaeus when he was engaged in conflict with their archrivals, the Pharisees, and especially when he was confronted with the invasion of a foreign king.[112] It is also conceivable that their attitude toward him changed over time, and that they came to regard him in retrospect as a Wicked Priest.

But it is also possible to read the passage in question as a prayer *against* King Jonathan:

> Wake up, Holy One, against Jonathan the king,
> and as for the whole congregation of Thy people
> — Israel who is in the four winds of heaven —
> let them all have peace
> and upon Thy kingdom shall be blessed Thy Name.[113]

The crucial argument here concerns the preposition *'l*, which usually has an adversative sense (against) when it is used in conjunction with the verb *'wr* (rise up).[114] This reading makes for an awkward disjunction between "Jonathan the king" and "the whole assembly of your people Israel," but this awkwardness must be weighed against the usual usage of the preposition and verb.[115] On this rendering, the psalm may indeed be sectarian, but it is not favorable to Jannaeus. Rather, it invokes the aid of God against a wicked ruler, although it refers to him as king rather than as priest.[116]

---

111. Eshel, *Dead Sea Scrolls and Hasmonean State*, 113, argues that the composition was not sectarian, and that it was brought to Qumran by someone who later joined the sect. This proposal does not explain why it was preserved by the sect.

112. Eshel, ibid., argues that the occasion was the invasion by Ptolemy Lathyrus. Column A of the same composition refers to the campaign of Sennacherib. Eshel argues that the scribe saw a link between the campaign of Sennacherib and that of Lathyrus.

113. Translation of Emmanuelle Main, "For King Jonathan or Against? The Use of the Bible in 4Q448," in Michael E. Stone and Esther G. Chazon, eds., *Biblical Perspectives: Early Use and Interpretation of the Bible in Light of the Dead Sea Scrolls* (STDJ 28; Leiden: Brill, 1998) 130. See also J. Strugnell and D. J. Harrington, "Qumran Cave 4 Texts: A New Publication," *JBL* 112 (1993): 498. Compare A. Lemaire, "Le roi Jonathan à Qoumrân (4Q448 B-C)," in E. M. Laperrousaz, ed., *Qoumrân et les manuscrits de la mer morte: Un cinquantenaire* (Paris: Cerf, 1997) 57-70.

114. Main, "For King Jonathan or Against?" 121-22. Compare Lemaire, "Roi Jonathan."

115. VanderKam, *From Joshua to Caiaphas*, 336, accepts Main's reading.

116. Doudna, *4Q Pesher Nahum*, 735-36, misses the force of the argument about the

The interpretation of this prayer must remain uncertain. Even if it is correctly read as a prayer *for* Alexander Jannaeus, however, it does not preclude the possibility that the sect later came to regard him as a wicked priest.

Conclusion

In light of the foregoing discussion, the references to the Wicked Priest in the *pesharim* can be explained if they refer to Alexander Jannaeus in some cases and to Hyrcanus II in others. The passages that mention a conflict with the Teacher are most plausibly taken to refer to Hyrcanus II. The conflict most probably occurred toward the end of the Teacher's career and the beginning of Hyrcanus's first term as high priest. While scholars generally prefer a simpler hypothesis that requires only one Wicked Priest, there is no reason why the label should not be attached to more than one individual. To be sure, the evidence is less than clear-cut. In view of the stereotypical and allusive language of the *pesharim*, all conclusions about the Teacher and the Wicked Priest must remain tentative, and the issues are likely to remain controversial.[117]

The negative conclusions can be stated with more confidence than the positive. Many of the arguments for dating the Teacher and the Wicked Priest to the mid-second century BCE can no longer be accepted. Most significantly, the theory that the Teacher's movement originated in a conflict over succession to the high priesthood is without basis in the texts. Once this is recognized, there is no reason to suppose that the conflict between the Teacher and the Wicked Priest (or the dispute with the man of the lie) took place at the beginning of the history of the sect. The long-accepted identification of the Wicked Priest with Jonathan Maccabee suffers from the anomalous gap of more than fifty years that separates him from any other identifiable person or event reflected in the *pesharim*, which were probably composed in the lifetime of Hyrcanus II. Moreover, the shifting

---

use of the words *'wr 'l.* Both words individually can be used with positive connotations, but the combination is invariably negative. The preposition *'l* occurs later in the psalm with reference to the kingdom (of God), but the word *'wr* is not used in that context, and so the two passages are not parallel.

117. Doudna, *4Q Pesher Nahum*, 683-54, argues that Hyrcanus II was the Teacher of Righteousness!

political fortunes of the Pharisees in the reigns of Alexander Jannaeus and Salome Alexandra provide a far more plausible setting for sectarian disputes than the time of Jonathan Maccabee.

It should be emphasized that the origin of the Teacher's movement, *a fortiori* the parent community, must certainly have been earlier than the time of Hyrcanus II, and should probably be placed toward the end of the second century BCE. But that movement did not arise because of a dispute over the high priesthood. Rather, it arose over a distinctive interpretation of the Mosaic law, which was in conflict with that of the Pharisees and also with the majority of the people. The Wicked Priest was not the catalyst for the emergence of the sect. To judge by his absence from the Scrolls apart from the *pesharim,* he did not play a great role in the life of the sect, except for one confrontational episode. But for the authors of the *pesharim,* the death of Jannaeus and the capture and disfigurement of Hyrcanus II provided fine examples of divine retribution, and served to show that prophecy was being fulfilled and that the Teacher and his followers would be vindicated in the end.

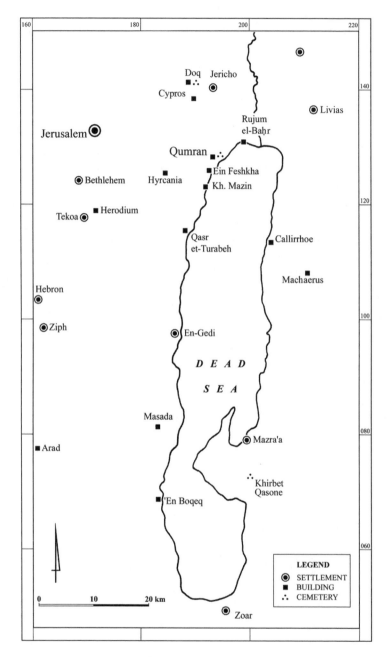

Fig. 1: Dead Sea region

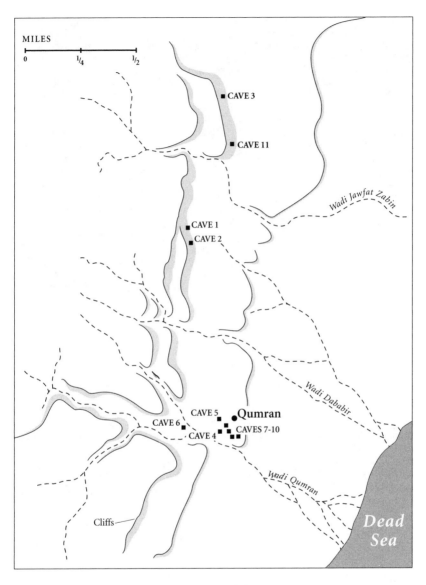

Fig. 2: Palestine, location of the Qumran caves

Fig. 3: View of Cave 4 at Qumran
Courtesy of Jodi Magness

Fig. 4: Northern and western sides of the tower at Qumran
Courtesy of Jodi Magness

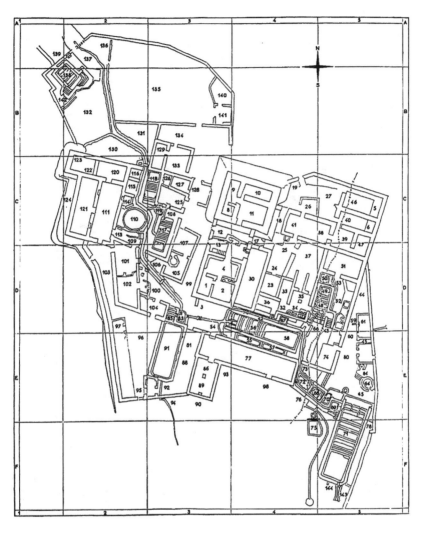

Fig. 5: Schematic plan of Qumran according to de Vaux, showing loci

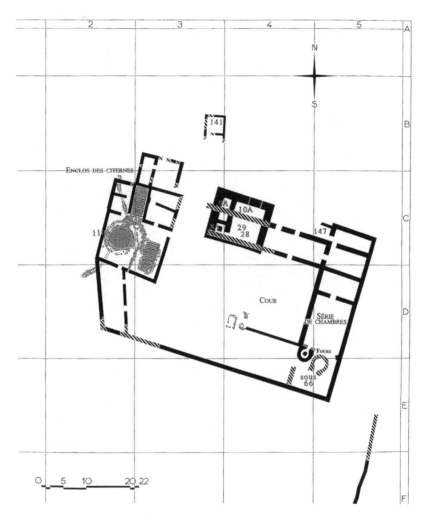

Fig. 6: Plan of Khirbet Qumran in Period Ia,
according to Humbert and Chambon

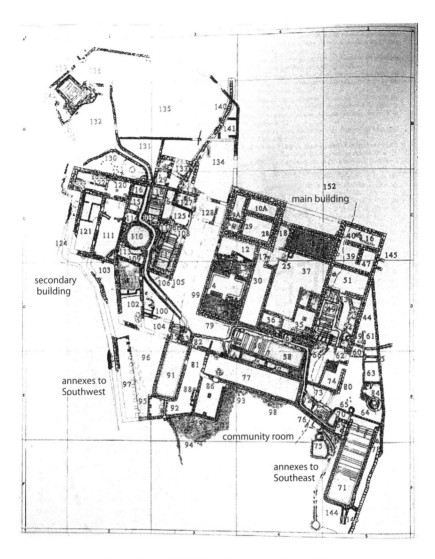

Fig. 7: Plan of Khirbet Qumran in Period Ib,
according to Humbert and Chambon

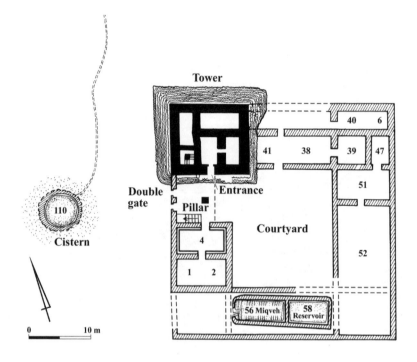

Tower

40 **6**

41 **38** **39** **47**

51

Double gate

Entrance

Pillar

110

Cistern

4

Courtyard

52

1 **2**

56 Miqveh **58 Reservoir**

0   10 m

Fig. 8: Plan of Qumran in the Hasmonean period,
according to Hirschfeld

Fig. 9: View of the miqveh or stepped pools in L48-L49

Courtesy of Jodi Magness

Fig. 10: The toilet in L51 at the time of de Vaux's excavations

Fig. 11: View of the cemetery at Qumran
Courtesy of Catherine Murphy

CHAPTER FOUR

The Essenes

Few matters relating to the Dead Sea Scrolls have aroused such heated and sustained debate as the proposed identification of the new covenant with the Essenes. The identification was proposed almost immediately after the Scrolls were discovered, by such diverse scholars as Millar Burrows, Eleazar Sukenik, and André Dupont-Sommer, and has continued to command a scholarly consensus.[1] It has been challenged not only by maverick scholars such as Norman Golb, but also by "mainstream" figures such as Shemaryahu Talmon, Larry Schiffman, and Albert Baumgarten.[2] It has been passionately defended by Israeli archeologists, such as Magen Broshi and Hanan Eshel.[3] Several scholars have argued that "the Qumran com-

---

1. See Stephen Goranson, "Others and Intra-Jewish Polemic as Reflected in Qumran Texts," in Peter W. Flint and James C. VanderKam, eds., *The Dead Sea Scrolls after Fifty Years: A Comprehensive Assessment* (2 vols.; Leiden: Brill, 1998–99) 2.534; Millar Burrows, *The Times* of London, April 12, 1948; Eleazar Sukenik, *Megillot Genuzot mi-Tokh Genizah Qedumah she-Nimṣe'ah be-Midbar Yehudah: Seqirah Rishonah* (Jerusalem: Bialik Institute, 1948) 16; A. Dupont-Sommer, *The Dead Sea Scrolls: A Preliminary Survey* (trans. E. Margaret Rowley; Oxford: Blackwell, 1952).

2. Norman Golb, *Who Wrote the Dead Sea Scrolls?* (New York: Scribner, 1995); Shemaryahu Talmon, "The Community of the Renewed Covenant," in Eugene Ulrich and James VanderKam, eds., *The Community of the Renewed Covenant: The Notre Dame Symposium on the Dead Sea Scrolls* (CJA 10; Notre Dame, IN: University of Notre Dame Press, 1994) 8; Lawrence H. Schiffman, *Reclaiming the Dead Sea Scrolls* (Philadelphia: Jewish Publication Society, 1994) 78-81; Albert Baumgarten, "Who Cares and Why Does It Matter? Qumran and the Essenes, Once Again," *DSD* 11 (2004): 174-90.

3. Magen Broshi, "Essenes at Qumran? A Rejoinder to Albert Baumgarten," *DSD* 14 (2007): 24-33; Magen Broshi and Hanan Eshel, "Qumran and the Dead Sea Scrolls: The Con-

munity" was an offshoot of the Essenes.[4] Most recently Eyal Regev has suggested that "the Essenes were a later development of the Qumran movement."[5]

Scholars frequently discuss the parallels between the ancient accounts and the Dead Sea Scrolls, with scant attention to the literary contexts in which the accounts of the Essenes are found.[6] Steve Mason has objected strongly to this procedure on methodological grounds.[7] He argues, quite correctly, that Josephus's account must be understood in its own context before it can be mined for information about other matters. In this regard, his argument is in line with recent trends in the study of history writing, which tend to emphasize the literary character of historiographical works.[8] He also objected to the very widespread tendency to "correct" Josephus in light of the Scrolls, on the assumption that the latter are primary Essene documents.[9]

---

tention of Twelve Theories," in D. R. Edwards, ed., *Religion and Society in Roman Palestine: Old Questions and New Approaches* (London: Routledge, 2004) 162-69.

4. See above, chapter 1.

5. Eyal Regev, *Sectarianism in Qumran: A Cross-Cultural Perspective* (RelSoc 45; Berlin: de Gruyter, 2007) 264.

6. See, e.g., Todd S. Beall, *Josephus' Description of the Essenes Illustrated by the Dead Sea Scrolls* (SNTSMS 58; Cambridge: Cambridge University Press, 1988). This is also true of my own discussion, "Essenes," *ABD* 2.619-26. The following discussion incorporates material from my essay, "Josephus on the Essenes: The Sources of His Evidence," in Zuleika Rodgers with Margaret Daly-Denton and Anne Fitzpatrick McKinley, eds., *A Wandering Galilean: Essays in Honour of Sean Freyne* (JSJSup 132; Leiden: Brill, 2009).

7. Steve Mason, "Essenes and Lurking Spartans in Josephus' *Judean War:* From Story to History," in Zuleika Rodgers, ed., *Making History: Josephus and Historical Method* (JSJSup 110; Leiden: Brill, 2007) 219-61. See also Steve Mason, "What Josephus Says about the Essenes in His *Judean War,*" http://orion.mscc.huji.ac.il/orion/programs/Masonoo-1.shtml. Part of this essay (roughly, the latter half) appeared under the same title in Stephen G. Wilson and Michel Desjardins, eds., *Text and Artifact in the Religions of Mediterranean Antiquity: Essays in Honour of Peter Richardson* (Studies in Christianity and Judaism 9; Waterloo: Wilfrid Laurier University Press, 2000) 434-67. Page references in this essay are to the printed version unless otherwise indicated. Compare also Joan E. Taylor, "Philo of Alexandria on the Essenes: A Case Study of the Use of Classical Sources in Discussions of the Qumran-Essene Hypothesis," *SPA* 19 (2007): 1-28.

8. For example, Hayden White, *Metahistory: The Historical Imagination in Nineteenth-Century Europe* (Baltimore: Johns Hopkins University Press, 1973); idem, *Tropics of Discourse: Essays in Cultural Criticism* (Baltimore: Johns Hopkins University Press, 1978).

9. For example, E. P. Sanders, *Judaism: Practice and Belief 63 BCE–66 CE* (Philadelphia: Trinity Press International, 1992) 341-79. Examples could be multiplied. Mason's objection

The thrust of Mason's argument is that the account of the Essenes is thoroughly Josephan, part of the historian's rhetorical and apologetic presentation of Judaism. He does not suggest that Josephus invented all this material out of whole cloth (although he does suggest this in the case of the passage on "marrying Essenes" in *J.W.* 2.160-61). Rather, he assumes that Josephus wrote on the basis of his personal knowledge of a contemporary group of Jews.[10] In this he goes against a long tradition in Josephan scholarship, which holds that Josephus, and also Philo, depended on literary, ethnographic accounts of the Essenes, written for a Gentile readership, possibly by Gentile authors.[11] Mason is not alone in his dissent from this tradition,[12] but he has given the strongest arguments against it to date. At stake is the degree to which Josephus can be assumed to know what he was talking about, whether he wrote from his own observation or relied on secondhand accounts by others who may have had little if any firsthand knowledge of the sect.

Philo and Pliny

Josephus was not the first writer in antiquity to formulate an account of the Essenes, nor even the first Jewish author to do so. Philo Judaeus, who flourished about half a century earlier, has left us two passages describing a group that he calls "Essaeans," *Quod Omnis (That Every Good Person Is Free)* 75-91, and *Hypothetica* 11.1-8 (= *Apology for the Jews*).[13] Josephus also

---

was anticipated by Georges Ory, *À la recherche des Esséniens: Essai critique* (Paris: Cercle Ernest-Renan, 1975) 75.

10. In personal correspondence, Mason insists that he is not denying the possibility that Josephus used sources to supplement his knowledge of the Essenes, but only the possibility of delineating them.

11. For example, Gustav Hölscher, "Josephus," PW 9/2.1949; Walter Bauer, "Essener," PWSup 4.386-430, repr. in idem, *Aufsätze und kleine Schriften* (ed. G. Strecker; Tübingen: Mohr Siebeck, 1967) 1-59. For the history of scholarship on this issue in the nineteenth century, see Siegfried Wagner, *Die Essener in der wissenschaftlichen Diskussion vom Ausgang des 18. bis zum Beginn des 20. Jahrhunderts* (BZAW 79; Berlin: de Gruyter, 1960) 202-9.

12. See also Tessa Rajak, "Ciò che Flavio Giuseppe Vide: Josephus and the Essenes," in Fausto Parente and Joseph Sievers, eds., *Josephus and the History of the Greco-Roman Period: Essays in Memory of Morton Smith* (SPB 41; Leiden: Brill, 1994) 141-60 (repr. in Rajak, *The Jewish Dialogue with Greece and Rome: Studies in Cultural and Social Interaction* [AGJU 48; Leiden: Brill, 2002] 219-40. References are to the original publication).

13. For the passages see Geza Vermes and Martin Goodman, *The Essenes According to*

uses the name "Essaean" with reference to individuals,[14] and in *Ant.* 15.371-79 he begins by referring to "those we call Essaeans" but goes on to speak of "Essenes" (in the passage about a seer named Menahem). There is no doubt that Philo uses the name "Essaean" to designate a sect or religious community, and Josephus appears to use the term in this way at least in *Antiquities* 15. The two forms of the name, *Essaioi* and *Essēnoi*, are simply variants, representing two common Greek adjectival endings, and no great significance can be attached to the variation.[15]

The two passages in Philo are the oldest extant accounts of the Essenes.[16] Philo's interest in the Essaeans was primarily moral and philosophical.[17] The extant passages contain nothing comparable to the description of procedures for admission and expulsion in Josephus's longest account in *Jewish War* 2.

The two surviving Philonic accounts cover most of the same themes. The Essaeans live in villages (but the passage in *Hypothetica* also allows that they live in many towns). They support themselves by agricultural work and crafts. They live a common life and have no private property: "almost alone among all mankind, they live without goods and without property; and this by preference, and not as a result of a reverse of fortune" (*Quod Omnis* 77). They put their salaries in a common fund and care for the sick and the aged. Each account supplies some details lacking in the other. We read in *Hypothetica* that no Essaean takes a woman, because marriage is detrimental to the common life: "shrewdly providing against the sole or principal obstacle threatening to dissolve the bonds of communal life, they banned marriage at the same time as they ordered the practice

---

the *Classical Sources* (Sheffield: Sheffield Academic Press, 1989) 19-31. Translations in this section are from this source. A good recent discussion can be found in Taylor, "Philo of Alexandria on Essenes."

14. Josephus, *J.W.* 1.78; 2.113; cf. *Ant.* 13.311; 17.346 with reference to the Essene prophets, Judas and Simon; *J.W.* 2.567; 3.11, John the Essene.

15. See Mason, "What Josephus Says about Essenes," 426-27.

16. It appears that Philo also wrote a longer account that has not survived. At the beginning of his treatise on the Therapeutae in *Contemplative Life* he says that he has discussed the Essenes, who pursue the active life, and now turns to the life of contemplation. It is unlikely that either of the surviving passages on the Essaeans was the counterpart of the lengthy treatise on the Therapeutae. Unfortunately nothing can be said about the missing treatise.

17. Madeleine Petit, "Les Esséens de Philon d'Alexandrie," in Devorah Dimant and Uriel Rappaport, eds., *The Dead Sea Scrolls: Forty Years of Research* (STDJ 10; Leiden: Brill, 1992) 139; Taylor, "Philo of Alexandria on Essenes," 8.

of perfect continence." Consequently there are no young children among the Essaeans. They constitute a voluntary association of mature men.[18] The account in *Quod Omnis* specifies the number of Essaeans as over four thousand, and claims that they "do not offer animal sacrifice, judging it more fitting to render their minds holy."[19] It also mentions their rejection of slavery and of oaths, and their strict observance of the Sabbath. Despite these variations in emphasis, the two Philonic accounts seem quite compatible with one another.

It is unlikely that Philo had any personal acquaintance with the Essenes in Palestine,[20] although he, like Josephus, put his own stamp on the material he used. The identity and nature of his source is unknown.[21] Philo's account shares some key points with the oldest extant account by a Gentile, the Roman polymath Pliny the Elder. Pliny famously wrote that the Essenes "are a people *(gens)* unique of its kind and admirable beyond all others in the world, without women and renouncing love entirely, without money, and having for company only the palm trees."[22] He conspicuously fails to say that they were Jewish, and may not have recognized them as such.[23] It is now considered unlikely that Pliny was ever in Palestine.[24]

18. Taylor, "Philo of Alexandria on Essenes," 21-23, argues that Philo does not say that Essenes cannot have married in earlier life, but that when they join the Essene community they do not bring wives with them.

19. *Quod Omnis* 75. Taylor, "Philo of Alexandria on Essenes," 12-13, argues that this does not mean that they repudiated sacrifices as such, but only contrasts the kind of offerings they make with those of the priests in the temple.

20. Despite the very tentative suggestion of Petit, "Esséens de Philon d'Alexandrie," 139-55. Petit devotes much of her article to the attempt to identify Jewish oral traditions that might have been known to Philo, with little result.

21. Stephen Goranson, "Posidonius, Strabo and Marcus Vipsanius Agrippa as Sources on Essenes," *JJS* 45 (1994): 295-98, suggests that Philo derived his account of the Essenes from Strabo, who in turn drew on Posidonius, and also used Agrippa's work, and that Josephus derived some of his information from Strabo. Strabo, who lived in the second half of the last century BCE and the early decades of the first century CE, wrote an account of the Jews and Judea in his *Geography*, of which fragments are cited by Josephus, but Strabo does not seem to have visited the country.

22. Pliny, *Nat. Hist.* 5.73; Vermes and Goodman, *Essenes*, 32-33.

23. Menahem Stern, *Greek and Latin Authors on Jews and Judaism* (3 vols.; Jerusalem: Israel Academy of Sciences and Humanities, 1974–84) 1.480; Robert A. Kraft, "Pliny on Essenes, Pliny on Jews," *DSD* 8 (2001): 258.

24. Older scholarship thought that he was in Palestine with Vespasian, on the basis of an inscription from Arados in Syria, which now appears to have been misread. See Stern,

In any case, he relied on sources in compiling his *Natural History*.[25] His account presupposes the destruction of the Jewish War, but his source may have been much older. His description of the Essenes comes in the context of a geographical description of Judea. Stephen Goranson has suggested that it was derived from the world map and commentary of Marcus Vipsanius Agrippa, son-in-law of Augustus and friend of Herod the Great.[26] Josephus reports that Agrippa visited Judea in 14 BCE, and that Herod showed him the fortresses Alexandreion, Herodion, and Hyrcania, so he must have been close to the Dead Sea. Agrippa died in 12 BCE. Pliny cites Agrippa several times in books 3–6 of his *Natural History*. It is quite plausible, then, even if not provable, that Agrippa was the source of Pliny's geographical account of the Dead Sea region. If so, the account of the Essenes would date from before the turn of the era. I should emphasize that Pliny was writing a geographical account. That he only mentions Essenes in the vicinity of the Dead Sea is due to the fact that he was describing that region, and does not preclude the existence of other Essene communities.

The Passages in Josephus

Josephus refers to Essenes in six passages in his account of the *Jewish War*, which is dated to 75–81 CE; five times in his *Jewish Antiquities*, which was published some 15 years later (93 CE); and once in his *Life*, which was added to the *Antiquities*.[27] These references are of different kinds.

Greek and Latin Authors, 1.466; Stephen Goranson, "Rereading Pliny on the Essenes: Some Bibliographic Notes," http://orion.mscc.huji.ac.il/symposiums/programs/Goranson98 .shtml, note 4.

25. R. König and G. Winkler, *Plinius der ältere: Leben und Werk eines antiken Naturforschers* (Munich: Heimeran, 1979) 53: "We must not forget that Pliny gives us primarily book knowledge, even when he could easily have acquired better insight as an observer"; my trans. Cf. Roland Bergmeier, *Die Essener-Berichte des Flavius Josephus* (Kampen: Kok Pharos, 1993) 21.

26. Goranson, "Posidonius, Strabo and Marcus Vipsanius Agrippa," 297. On Agrippa's map see J. J. Tierney, "The Map of Agrippa," *Proceedings of the Royal Irish Academy*, vol. 63-C no. 4 (1963): 151-66.

27. The passages are conveniently collected by Vermes and Goodman, *Essenes*, 34-57; and also by Beall, *Josephus' Description*, 12-33. See also the synopsis provided by Mason, "What Josephus Says about Essenes," 424-25.

In *Life* 10–11 Josephus claims that he knew the Essenes from personal experience: "at about the age of sixteen I wished to get experience of the schools of thought to be found among us. There are three of these — Pharisees, the first, Sadducees the second, Essenes the third — as we have often remarked. I thought that in this way, by learning about all of them, I would choose the best. I therefore made myself hardy and, with much trouble, went through the three courses." After this, we are told, he lived for three years with a hermit named Bannus in the wilderness, and then returned to the city in his nineteenth year and embraced the rules of the Pharisees.[28] If he really had tried out the lifestyle of each of the "schools" we might suppose that his account of the Essenes was informed by his own experience.[29] But the passage in *Life* is problematic. Many scholars have noted that this account is full of rhetorical commonplaces. (Josephus presents himself as a *Wunderkind*, whom the chief priests consulted on matters of law.)[30] If he spent three years with Bannus, he cannot have spent much time getting acquainted with the three philosophies, and in any case he cannot have gone through the process of Essene initiation that he describes in *Jewish War* 2, which required a full three years, culminating with solemn oaths.[31] Of course Josephus may have known Jews who were Essenes, just as he surely knew Pharisees and Sadducees, and he could, in principle, have had reliable informants (although he claims that members of the sect swore "to reveal nothing to outsiders"). He was not, however, writing from experience as an insider.

28. Steve Mason, "Was Josephus a Pharisee? A Reexamination of Life 10–12," *JJS* 40 (1989): 31-46, argues that Josephus merely followed the Pharisaic school as a function of his entry into public life. Nonetheless, this is the only time he affiliates himself in any way with one particular school. See also Mason, *Flavius Josephus on the Pharisees: A Composition-Critical Study* (SPB 39; Leiden: Brill, 1991) 325-56; idem, *Life of Josephus: Translation and Commentary* (Flavius Josephus Translation and Commentary 9; Leiden: Brill, 2001) 21.

29. This position was defended by Kenneth Atkinson, "Josephus the Essene on the Qumran Essenes and Related Jewish Sectarians along the Dead Sea," paper read at the SBL annual meeting in San Diego, November 18, 2007.

30. See, e.g., Steve Mason, *Josephus and the New Testament* (2nd ed.; Peabody, MA: Hendrickson, 2003) 39-41; idem, *Life of Josephus*, 17-18; Morton Smith, "The Description of the Essenes in Josephus and the Philosophumena," *HUCA* 29 (1958): 277-78.

31. Bergmeier, *Essener-Berichte*, 20; Shaye J. D. Cohen, *Josephus in Galilee and Rome: His Vita and Development as a Historian* (Leiden: Brill, 1979) 107. Tessa Rajak, *Josephus the Historian and His Society* (London: Duckworth, 1983) 34-39; idem, "Ciò che Flavio Giuseppe Vide," 144, is exceptional in overruling this objection, on the grounds that he may have learned the rudiments of each philosophy in a few months.

Five of the passages in *Jewish War* are brief, incidental references. Four of them relate incidents involving individual Essenes: Judas (1.78-80), Simon (2.113), both seers, and John the Essene, a general in the war against Rome, who is mentioned twice (2.567; 3.11). The fifth incidental reference is to the Essene Gate in Jerusalem (5.145). While Josephus presumably drew on his own knowledge of the events of the Jewish War, the accounts of the three seers must of necessity have come from some source, whether written or oral.[32] It has been argued that the revolutionary, John the Essaean, was not a member of the sect but rather a native of Essa or Gerasa in Transjordan. He is mentioned in association with other generals who are identified by their origin, Niger the Perean and Silas the Babylonian (*J.W.* 3.11).[33] The seers Judas and Simon are said to be "Essaean by race" (*genos*).[34] Pliny refers to the Essenes as *gens,* but in his long account in *Jewish War* 2 Josephus is careful to state that "they are Jews by race" (2.119; he does, however, refer to them as "this *genos*" in *Ant.* 15.371).

If we leave aside the references to John the Essene, and to the Essene Gate (which do not say anything about the nature of the sect), the only references to Essenes in *Jewish War,* outside of the long passage in book 2, are the brief references to the seers Judas and Simon, who are "Essaeans by race." If John was not a member of the sect, then there is no reference to the sect in *Jewish War* after book 2.

The remaining passage in Josephus (*J.W.* 2.119-61) is his fullest account of the Essenes. It covers their attitude to sex and marriage, common life, cultic observances, procedures for admission and expulsion, and beliefs about the afterlife. It begins with the statement: "Indeed, there exist among

---

32. They are often attributed to Nicolaus of Damascus, a major source for his account of Herod. See Bergmeier, *Essener-Berichte,* 18. On Nicolaus see Stern, *Greek and Latin Authors,* 1.227-60; Ben Zion Wacholder, *Nicolaus of Damascus* (University of California Publications in History 75; Berkeley: University of California Press, 1962). On Josephus's use of Nicolaus see D. R. Schwartz, "Josephus and Nicolaus on the Pharisees," *JSJ* 13 (1983): 157-71. Stern, *Greek and Latin Authors,* 1.229, claims that "it is the consensus of scholars, e.g. Schürer, Hölscher and Thackeray, that Nicolaus' writings constitute the main source of the *Bellum Judaicum* for the whole period between Antiochus Epiphanes and the accession of Archelaus." Vermes and Goodman, *Essenes,* 37, doubt that Nicolaus's *History* extended to the downfall of Archelaus, which is the setting of the anecdote about Simon.

33. Abraham Schalit, *Namenwörterbuch zu Flavius Josephus* (Leiden: Brill, 1968) 46; Mason, "What Josephus Says about Essenes," 428.

34. In contrast, Menahem, in *Ant.* 15.373-79, is clearly identified as "one of the Essenes," and is responsible for the respect in which they were held by King Herod.

the Jews three schools of philosophy: the Pharisees belong to the first, the Sadducees to the second, and to the third belong men who have a reputation for cultivating a particularly saintly life, called Essenes." The immediate occasion for the discussion of the three "schools" is a reference to Judas of Galilee (2.117-18), who is described as "a sophist who founded a sect of his own, having nothing in common with the others." The other schools, then, are introduced as a foil for the revolutionaries.[35] But they are not treated in equal detail. The last one mentioned, the Essenes, is described first, and occupies more than forty paragraphs (2.120-61). The account of the Pharisees and Sadducees together receives a mere five (162-66). The Essenes are said to be "Jews by race" *(genos)*, which seems superfluous, since in the preceding sentence they were identified as one of the three schools of philosophy among the Jews.[36] The account is given in the present tense, except for an aside by Josephus on their endurance during the war against Rome.[37] The most striking thing about this passage, however, is its length, relative to the brief treatments of the Pharisees and Sadducees.

When we turn to the *Antiquities,* we find that the passages about Judas and Simon are paralleled in *Ant.* 13.311 and 17.346. An incident involving another Essene seer, Menahem, is reported in *Ant.* 15.371-79. Menahem is said to have foretold that Herod would be king of the Jews. For this reason, Herod treated all Essenes with respect. As in *Jewish War,* the individual Essenes singled out for mention are all seers.

The remaining passages in *Antiquities,* 13.171-72 and 18.11, like the passage in *Jewish War* 2, speak of three "sects" (*haireseis, Ant.* 13.171-72) or "philosophies" (*Ant.* 18.11, which lists them in reverse order as the Essenes, the Sadducees, and the Pharisees). In *Antiquities* 13 each "sect" receives one sentence, regarding its views on fate and free will. In *Antiquities* 18 the Essenes get the longest account (five paragraphs, 18-22), but not by much. The Pharisees receive four paragraphs (12-15), and the Sadducees two (16-17). Each account highlights the beliefs of the group regarding fate/free will and life after death, although some other details are also included. These themes are also highlighted in the account of the Pharisees and Sadducees in *Jewish War* 2.

---

35. Compare Mason, *Flavius Josephus on Pharisees,* 122: "he wants to dissociate mainstream Judaism from the rebel psychology."

36. Note, however, that he uses the word *genos* to refer to the individual Essaeans Judas and Simon, and also uses it with reference to the sect in *Ant.* 15.371. Pliny refers to the Essenes as a *gens.* Josephus may be correcting a misapprehension here.

37. Smith, "Description of the Essenes," 279.

The main description of the sect in *Antiquities* is found in 18.18-22, again in the context of a description of the three "philosophies." This account is much shorter than the one in *Jewish War* 2, and does not address such matters as admission and expulsion. It has its closest parallels in the accounts given by Philo, especially the one in *Quod Omnis* 75-91. It is not clear why Josephus substituted this account for the more detailed one in *Jewish War*. Morton Smith regarded the variation between *Jewish War* and *Antiquities* as significant: "had Josephus himself written the account in the War he would probably not, when he came to write the Antiquities, have replaced his own work by a copy or condensation of somebody else's."[38] It may be, however, that he saw no need to repeat the lengthy passage in *Jewish War*, and simply wished to vary his account.[39]

Philo and Josephus

More important for our immediate purpose is the relation between Philo's account and that of Josephus in *Antiquities* 18. The correspondences are extensive: praise of their moral character, the estimate of membership at four thousand, distinctive doctrine (that God is the cause of all, or of all good things), distinctive sacrifices, agricultural practice, uniqueness, common fund and avoidance of money, celibacy, rejection of slavery, communal life, common meals, mutual service.[40] Scholars have explained these correspondences in either of two ways: either Josephus used Philo directly (Walter Bauer, Tessa Rajak) or both drew on a common source (Morton Smith, Roland Bergmeier, Randal Argall). The difference in names *(Essaioi, Essēnoi)* is not decisive, since Josephus could easily have switched to the preferred form of the name. Neither is the fact that the two authors do not maintain the same sequence.[41] If one or both of them could change

38. Ibid.

39. See the reflections on this issue by Rajak, "Ciò che Flavio Giuseppe Vide," 148.

40. See Randal A. Argall, "A Hellenistic Jewish Source on the Essenes," in Argall, Beverly A. Bow, and Rodney A. Werline, eds., *For a Later Generation: The Transformation of Tradition in Israel, Early Judaism, and Early Christianity* (Harrisburg: Trinity Press International, 2000) 22-23. Argall excludes the account in *Jewish War* 2 from consideration here, and also Philo's account in *Hypothetica,* except for the topic of celibacy (*Hypothetica* 11.14).

41. Argall, ibid., maintains that the two accounts maintain the same approximate order, but the correspondence is certainly not complete.

the sequence of topics in their source, Josephus could presumably change the order he found in Philo. Josephus, however, includes some details that are found neither in Philo nor in *Jewish War* 2. These include the notice that the Essenes choose priests "to prepare the bread and food" and the comparison to the Dacians (*Ant.* 18.22). Priests may well have supervised the preparation of food, to ensure its purity, but it is unlikely that Josephus would have cast them in a culinary role if he were not following a source. He does not otherwise compare the Essenes to the Dacians; elsewhere he prefers the Pythagoreans.

The one topic on which Philo and Josephus may be thought to disagree, the attitude to temple sacrifice, may also be explained by the hypothesis of different explanations of a common source.[42] Philo says that "they have shown themselves especially devout in the service of God, not by offering sacrifices of animals, but by resolving to sanctify their minds."[43] Josephus says that "they send offerings to the temple, but perform their sacrifices using different customary purifications. For this reason, they are barred from entering into the common enclosure, but offer sacrifice among themselves." (Note that Josephus uses the present tense here, twenty years after the destruction of the temple.) Neither passage is free of ambiguity. Philo's statement can be read as a categorical rejection of animal sacrifice, but it has also been taken to mean only that sacrifice was not the focal point of their worship.[44] The passage in Josephus is uncertain because of a textual problem. The *Epitome* (an abbreviation of the *Antiquities* thought to date from the 10th century) and the Latin translation of Josephus read "they do not perform their sacri-

---

42. The problems involved in the accounts of the Essene view of sacrifice are discussed by Jamal-Dominique Hopkins, "Josephus, the Dead Sea Scrolls, and the Qumran Essenes: Examining a Jewish Sectarian Movement," paper read at the SBL annual meeting in San Diego, November 14, 2007; and also in his dissertation, "Sacrifice in the Dead Sea Scrolls: Khirbet Qumran, the Essenes and Cultic Spiritualization" (diss., Manchester, 2005) (which I have not seen).

43. *Quod Omnis* 75 (trans. F. H. Colson, in *Philo,* vol. IX [LCL; Cambridge: Harvard University Press, 1960]). The translation of Vermes and Goodman, *Essenes,* 21, "they do not offer animal sacrifice," is a misleading rendering of the Greek participle.

44. For the former see Vermes and Goodman, *Essenes,* 21; for the latter, Beall, *Josephus' Description,* 118. Argall, "Hellenistic Jewish Source," 20, argues that it is unlikely that Philo would have commended the sect for purely spiritual worship, given his well-known views on the need for literal observance (*Migration of Abraham* 89-93). So also Taylor, "Philo of Alexandria on Essenes," 13.

fices."[45] Even if we reject this variant, which may have been an attempt to harmonize Josephus with Philo, it is less than clear whether the Essenes offered animal sacrifices by themselves or rather made some other kind of offerings. The discrepancy between Philo and Josephus may be resolved if we suppose that their common source noted that the Essenes were barred from participation in the temple sacrifices, and our two authors each interpreted this in his own way.[46]

Whether Josephus depended directly on Philo in *Antiquities* 18, or, as I think more likely, both drew on a common source, there can be no doubt that Josephus used a source here. This does not, of course, require that he cited the source verbatim.

Sources in Dispute

The main dispute about Josephus's sources for the Essenes, however, has centered not on *Antiquities* but on *Jewish War*. The long account of the Essenes in *Jewish War* 2 has its closest parallel in Hippolytus, *Refutation of All Heresies* 9.18-28.[47] Morton Smith and Matthew Black argued independently of each other that the two accounts drew on a common source.[48] More recently, however, Christoph Burchard and Roland Bergmeier have argued strongly and persuasively that Hippolytus was dependent on Josephus.[49] Moreover, Smith subsequently changed his mind and concluded that he was "probably mistaken in supposing Hippolytus inde-

45. See Matthew Black, *The Scrolls and Christian Origins* (1961; repr. BJS 48; Atlanta: Scholars Press, 1983) 39-40.

46. So Argall, "Hellenistic Jewish Source," 20.

47. Vermes and Goodman, *Essenes,* 62-73.

48. Smith, "Description of the Essenes," 273-313; Matthew Black, "The Account of the Essenes in Hippolytus and Josephus," in W. D. Davies and D. Daube, eds., *The Background of the New Testament and Its Eschatology* (Cambridge: Cambridge University Press, 1956) 172-82; idem, *Scrolls and Christian Origins,* 187-91.

49. Christoph Burchard, "Zur Nebenüberlieferung von Josephus' Bericht über die Essener Bell 2,119-61 bei Hippolyt, Porphyrius, Josippus, Niketas Choniates und anderen," in Otto Betz et al., eds., *Josephus-Studien: Untersuchungen zu Josephus, dem antiken Judentum und dem Neuen Testament* (Göttingen: Vandenhoeck & Ruprecht, 1974) 77-96; idem, "Die Essener bei Hippolyt: Hippolyt, Ref. IX 18, 2-28, 2 und Josephus, Bell. 2, 119-161," *JSJ* 8 (1977): 1-41; R. Bergmeier, "Die drei jüdischen Schulrichtungen nach Josephus und Hippolyt von Rom," *JSJ* 34 (2003): 443-70.

pendent of Josephus."[50] It does not appear, then, that the parallels with Hippolytus throw any light on the source of Josephus's information.

The most extensive recent attempt to identify the sources of Josephus's account is that of Bergmeier. He posits four sources:

The anecdotes about Essene prophets, which he attributes to Nicolaus of Damascus.

The "Three School Source," which gave brief accounts of the beliefs of Pharisees, Sadducees, and Essenes.

A Hellenistic Jewish "Essaean" source used by Philo, and by Josephus in *Antiquities* 18 and to a limited degree in *Jewish War* 2.

A "pythagorizing" source, from which Josephus drew most of his account in *Jewish War* 2 and which can also be detected in Philo's account of the Therapeutae in *On the Contemplative Life* and in Pliny, *Nat. Hist.* 5.15.73.[51]

Bergmeier supports his source-critical analysis by listing some 51 *hapax legomena* in *J.W.* 2.119-66.[52]

Bergmeier's analysis has been criticized on several counts. Randal Argall focused on the Hellenistic Jewish "Essaean" source.[53] He agreed

---

50. Morton Smith, "Helios in Palestine," *ErIsr* 16 (1982): 199*-214* (the citation is from n. 24). Smith was persuaded by the account of Cohen, *Josephus in Galilee and Rome*, 24-47, of the paraphrastic way Josephus used his sources that there would not be so much verbal agreement if Hippolytus were using a common source rather than drawing directly on Josephus. See further my essay, "The Essenes and the Afterlife," in Florentino García Martínez, Annette Steudel, and Eibert Tigchelaar, eds., *From 4QMMT to Resurrection: Mélanges qumraniens en hommage à Émile Puech* (STDJ 61; Leiden: Brill, 2006) 35-53. C. D. Elledge, *Life after Death in Early Judaism: The Evidence of Josephus* (WUNT 2/208; Tübingen: Mohr Siebeck, 2006) 91-93, still accepts Smith's original hypothesis of a common source, apparently unaware of Smith's retraction.

51. Bergmeier, *Essener-Berichte*, 114-15. Cf. idem, "Zum historischen Wert der Essenerberichte von Philo und Josephus," in Jörg Frey and Hartmut Stegemann, eds., *Qumran Kontrovers: Beiträge zu den Textfunden vom Toten Meer* (Paderborn: Bonifatius, 2003) 11-22. Other scholars who have recently affirmed Josephus's reliance on sources include Per Bilde, "The Essenes in Philo and Josephus," in Frederick H. Cryer and Thomas L. Thompson, eds., *Qumran between the Old and New Testaments* (JSOTSup 290; Sheffield: Sheffield Academic Press, 1998) 64-65; and Catherine M. Murphy, *Wealth in the Dead Sea Scrolls and in the Qumran Community* (STDJ 40; Leiden: Brill, 2002) 408-9.

52. Bergmeier, *Essener-Berichte*, 108-13.

53. Argall, "Hellenistic Jewish Source," 19.

with Bergmeier that specific pieces of information in *Ant.* 18.18-22 and in Philo's *Quod Omnis* 75-91 occur in similar clusters and in much the same relative order, but he offered a more modest reconstruction of the source, drawing only on *Quod Omnis* 75-91 and *Ant.* 18.18-22.

Jörg Frey acknowledges that Josephus used sources, but he objects to the confidence with which Bergmeier delineates them.[54] Bergmeier admits that he cannot support his thesis with a full linguistic analysis of Josephus, and Frey questions whether one can delineate sources with confidence in light of this. Most problematic, in Frey's view, is Bergmeier's "pythagorizing" source. Bergmeier's proposal requires that Philo used this source in his account of the Therapeutae, but not in his description of the Essenes, while Josephus used it in *Jewish War* but not in *Antiquities*. Pliny would also have drawn on this source for his account of the settlement by the Dead Sea. Frey concludes that this theory goes beyond the bounds of possible source-critical reconstruction.[55] Nonetheless, Frey grants that it is plausible that the disproportionately long account of the Essenes in *Jewish War* 2 drew on a source. He denies that either the extent of the source or its provenance can be determined with confidence. Yet he grants that the hellenizing and pythagorizing features of the ancient accounts are literary embellishments, whether they are attributed to the authors or to their sources. They represent the perspective of an outsider, not a historically reliable account of the Essenes. Frey, like many scholars before him, argues that this "outsider perspective" can and should be corrected by comparison with the texts of the *yaḥad* in the Dead Sea Scrolls, which he takes to be authentic Essene documents.[56]

The most far-reaching critique of Bergmeier, and of any attempt to identify sources in Josephus's account of the Essenes, is that of Steve Mason.[57] Despite conceding that "no one doubts that Josephus used sources for most of his work,"[58] Mason dismisses Bergmeier's approach as a relic of nineteenth-century German historiography, which routinely looked for underlying sources. Contemporary Josephan scholarship, in contrast,

---

54. Jörg Frey, "Zur historischen Auswertung der antiken Essenerberichte: Ein Beitrag zum Gespräch mit Roland Bergmeier," in Frey and Stegemann, eds., *Qumran Kontrovers*, 23-57, especially 34-46.

55. Ibid., 44.

56. Ibid., 46-55.

57. Above, n. 10.

58. "What Josephus Says about Essenes" (Internet version), 7.

views Josephus as an author, and asks first for the meaning of a passage in context. Mason complains at length of the detrimental influence of the Dead Sea Scrolls on Josephan scholarship in this respect, as it has encouraged scholars to disregard the context in Josephus and mine the passage for parallels to the Qumran rule books. The main focus of his critique, however, concerns the criteria used by Bergmeier and others for identifying sources.

The different forms of the name, *Essaios* and *Essēnos,* are simply variants. Both forms are used in the passage in *Antiquities* 15, in such a way as to suggest that the current Judean usage was *Essaios.* (It begins by referring to *hoi par' hēmin Essaioi.*) Josephus prefers *Essēnos* when referring to the group, because this form was more familiar to his Roman readers. Pliny uses the Latin equivalent, *Esseni.* The variant forms of the names cannot be correlated with sources. Philo uses *Essaios* for the group; Josephus uses it primarily for individuals (except in *Antiquities* 15).

The virtues highlighted in the first two Essene oaths, piety toward the Deity and justice toward humanity, are Hellenistic commonplaces. That they are also commonplace in Philo is of no significance for identifying a Jewish-Hellenistic source.[59]

The list of 51 *hapax legomena* in the account in *Jewish War* 2 has no probative value, since the subject matter of this passage is exceptional in Josephus. A stylometric analysis of this passage by David S. Williams (focusing on the frequency of particles, conjunctions, and the like) finds it "demonstrably Josephan."[60] It should be noted, however, that Williams still regarded it likely that Josephus used source material in this passage, although he did not simply copy it but rewrote it significantly.[61]

The heart of Mason's argument is an extended attempt to show that the account of the Essenes in *Jewish War* 2 is thoroughly Josephan in character.[62] Josephus wrote with apologetic intent in the wake of the war

---

59. *Pace* Bergmeier, *Essener-Berichte,* 36-37.

60. David S. Williams, "Josephus and the Authorship of *War* 2.119-61 (on the Essenes)," *JSJ* 25 (1994): 221. See also idem, *Stylometric Studies in Flavius Josephus and Related Literature* (Jewish Studies 12; Lewiston, NY: Edwin Mellen, 1992).

61. Williams, "Josephus and Authorship," 221: "Two possibilities remain: (a) Josephus wrote *War* 2.119-161 as a free composition; or (b) Josephus used source material to write *War* 2.119-161. The latter possibility seems more likely."

62. Mason, "What Josephus Says about the Essenes," 433-48. See also André Paul, "Flavius Josèphe et les Esséniens," in Dimant and Rappaport, eds., *Dead Sea Scrolls,* 126-38.

against Rome, with a view to showing that Judeans at their best were exemplary world citizens. So the Essenes behave with *semnotēs*, which is one of Josephus's favorite terms for appealing to his Roman audience. They show self-control (*enkrateia*, among other terms) in their attitudes toward the passions, sex, and women. The Essene community of goods illustrates the Jewish pursuit of *koinōnia* (*Ag. Ap.* 2.151, 208), which is the opposite of *misanthrōpia*, the vice with which Jews were often charged. The statement that the Essenes revere the sun as a deity is in accordance with Josephus's tendency elsewhere to personify the sun and treat it as a representation of God. The Essenes bathe in frigid water, as Josephus did when he was with Bannus in the wilderness. The sobriety and restraint of the common meals is in accordance with Josephus's general emphasis on the restraint of Jewish sacrificial meals. The prominence of priests accords with his own claim of priesthood. The description of the Essenes as "fair administrators of anger, able to restrain temper, masters of fidelity, servants of peace" (*J.W.* 1.135) serves Josephus's narrative aims perfectly. The emphasis on piety and justice is typical of Josephus's presentation of Judaism after the war against Rome. Other oaths, for example, "to refrain from banditry," also fit his purpose of showing that Jewish ideals were antithetical to those of the revolutionaries. Also typical of Josephus is the emphasis on precision *(akribeia)* in the interpretation of the Law. Compare the veneration of Moses elsewhere in his writings. The language used for the Essenes' belief in the afterlife accords with Josephus's own views in *J.W.* 3.372-74, where he says that "all of us have mortal bodies composed of perishable matter," "a soul is a portion of God housed in a body," and that "those who die naturally are allotted the holiest heavenly place."[63] It should be noted, however, that Josephus affirms resurrection in bodily form, a belief that he attributes to the Pharisees but not to the Essenes.[64] The statement about the Essenes' ability to predict the future fits his reports of individual Essene prophets. He himself also claimed to be able to predict the future, like the Essenes, on the basis of the prophetic statements in the Scriptures. The dis-

63. *J.W.* 3.374. See Joseph Sievers, "Josephus and the Afterlife," in Steve Mason, ed., *Understanding Josephus: Seven Perspectives* (JSPSup 32; Sheffield: Sheffield Academic Press, 1998) 20-34; Elledge, *Life after Death*, 53-80.

64. *J.W.* 2.163. See G. W. E. Nickelsburg, *Resurrection, Immortality, and Eternal Life in Intertestamental Judaism* (Harvard Theological Studies 26; Cambridge: Harvard University Press, 1972) 168; and my essay, "Essenes and Afterlife," 44.

cussion of the occult powers of the Essenes with respect to roots is paralleled in the account of Solomon in *Ant.* 8.44-49.

Mason concludes his discussion of the passage in *Jewish War* 2 by suggesting that the report on "the marrying Essenes" was invented by Josephus out of whole cloth, since the celibate ideal would have been impractical, and Josephus obviously did not adhere to it himself.[65]

Mason has shown conclusively that Josephus put his own stamp on this material, and that it serves a clear purpose in the argument of *Jewish War* as a whole. He has effectively refuted some criteria for distinguishing sources — the varying usage of *Essaioi* and *Essēnoi,* and the occurrence of *hapax legomena.* Mason is also right on the methodological issue: the passage must be understood in its Josephan context before it can be used as historical evidence or compared with the Dead Sea Scrolls. Questions remain, however, about the source of Josephus's detailed information, and the disproportionate length of the account of the Essenes relative to those of the Sadducees and Pharisees.

Josephus's Knowledge of the Essenes

We have seen above that Josephus's claim, in *Life,* to have gained personal experience of all three sects is problematic. "But," writes Mason, "we do not need *Life* 10-12 to see that Josephus claims to know the Essenes very well. This Jerusalemite aristocrat, who claims to be a leader of his people, says that *many* Essenes settle in *each* city."[66] But the fact that there were Essenes in Jerusalem and other towns does not mean that their beliefs or communal practices were well known to all. According to the account in *Jewish War* 2, members of the sect swore to reveal nothing to outsiders. Some aspects of their lifestyle could be observed easily enough, such as whether they married, or participated in the temple cult. But outsiders could not normally be expected to know the details of their communal organization or beliefs. Presumably some Essenes must have divulged something to outsiders, unless the accounts that we have are pure fiction. But Josephus would at least have needed an oral informant, if not a written source, to produce the detailed account that we find in *Jewish War* 2.

---

65. "What Josephus Says about Essenes," 447-48.
66. Ibid., 436.

The Disproportionate Length of the Account

The most obvious reason for suspecting that Josephus was following a source on the Essenes in *Jewish War* 2 is the disproportionate length of the account. The disproportion is striking, because of the juxtaposition with the much shorter accounts of the other two sects, and is therefore not analogous to other cases where the historian describes some events in more detail than others. Mason argues that "by proportioning his narrative as he does, Josephus makes it plain that he is much more interested in describing the Essenes than the other two groups."[67] The life of holiness *(semnotēs)* that they exhibit may be said to provide the most striking contrast to the revolutionary philosophy of Judas. Yet, apart from this passage, the Essenes play a minimal role in *Jewish War*. If John the Essene was not a member of the sect, the only subsequent reference is a passing mention of the Essene Gate. If Josephus's goal in introducing the three schools was "to dissociate mainstream Judaism from the rebel psychology,"[68] his purpose would have been better served by a balanced exposition of the virtues of all three. It is true that he is never critical of the Essenes, but this may be explained by the fact that their role in Judean politics seems to be restricted to an occasional prediction. The length of the description in *Jewish War* 2 is not only disproportionate relative to that of the other sects, but also relative to the role the Essenes play in the history as a whole. One obvious way of explaining this discrepancy is to suppose that he had at his disposal a longer account of the Essenes than of the Pharisees or Sadducees. This explanation does not require that we accuse Josephus of incoherence, or of including material just because it was available. He clearly shaped it for his purposes and integrated it into his history. But it is difficult to see why he should have included such disproportionate detail if he were composing the passage entirely *de novo*.

The impression that Josephus was following a source here is strengthened by the extraneous character of the passage about marrying Essenes. As Mason recognizes, nothing in the preceding account even hints at the existence of such people. Surely if Josephus wanted to introduce them, he could have mentioned them in the context of the first discussion of the Essene attitude to women.[69] Rather, this passage gives the

---

67. Mason, *Flavius Josephus on Pharisees*, 123.
68. Ibid., 122.
69. Compare Taylor, "Philo of Alexandria on Essenes," 22 n. 76: "it would have been

impression that it is tacked on as an epilogue to a prefabricated account. The body of Josephus's account agrees with Philo and Pliny in declaring that the Essenes rejected marriage. This is also the case in his later account in *Antiquities* 18. The description, or descriptions, of the Essenes that circulated in the Hellenistic-Roman world evidently did not mention marrying Essenes. It seems to me, then, that the paragraph in *J.W.* 1.160 is most easily explained as a correction of the received account. If Essenes had lived in every Judean city before the war, most Judeans must have known whether they married. (This would not be true of Pliny or Philo, who had much less opportunity to observe.) It is easier to suppose that Josephus supplied such a correction than to accept Mason's rather desperate argument that Josephus invented marrying Essenes out of whole cloth.

Not much can be said about the nature or provenance of Josephus's source. He could conceivably have gotten his hands on an Essene rule book, and supplied the hellenizing presentation himself. Or he may have known a Greek account that already developed analogies with Pythagoreans and Greek ideals. Many of the ideals Mason identified as Josephan were in fact more widely shared in the Hellenistic-Roman world, as he readily notes.[70] For example, many features of the account are paralleled in passages about the Spartans in Xenophon and Plutarch.[71] These ideals could have shaped a description of the Essenes by some Greek ethnographer, or they could have been introduced into the account by Josephus himself.[72] We do not know just what he had before him. What we can say

---

surprising for Josephus to invent something that complicates his description without adding anything to his rhetoric on the Essenes. Additionally, according to Mason's reading, Josephus would contradict something he has stated earlier."

70. See Martin Hengel, *Judaism and Hellenism: Studies in Their Encounter in Palestine during the Early Hellenistic Period* (trans. John Bowden; 2 vols.; Philadelphia: Fortress, 1974) 1.247. Doron Mendels, "Hellenistic Utopia and the Essenes," *HTR* 72 (1979) 207-22, documents several parallels between the Essenes and the utopia of Iambulus, but argues that the similarity is due to the utopian ideals of the historical Essenes, whom he identifies with the sect known from the Dead Sea Scrolls.

71. Cf. Xenophon, *Lacedaemonians*, passim; Plutarch, *Instituta Laconica* (*Moralia*, 236-40). The parallels are documented by Mason, "Essenes and Lurking Spartans."

72. On Greek ethnography see Gregory E. Sterling, *Historiography and Self-Definition: Josephos, Luke-Acts and Apologetic Historiography* (Novum Testamentum Supplement 64; Leiden: Brill, 1992) 20-54 and the literature there cited; idem, "'Athletes of Virtue': An analysis of the Summaries in Acts (2:41-47; 4:32-35; 5:12-16)," *JBL* 113 (1994): 688.

with some confidence is that he did not write this detailed account on the basis of his personal observation of the Essenes.

A "Three School" Source?

In this conclusion I generally agree with Jörg Frey that Josephus relied on sources, but that we cannot now delineate them as specifically as Bergmeier has tried to do. He evidently drew on different sources for the accounts in *Jewish War* 2 and *Antiquities* 18. Bergmeier also posits a source that consists of brief descriptions of the three Jewish philosophies.[73] The topos of three schools is known to us only from Josephus, and it could have originated with him. Bergmeier's argument rests on the relationship between the accounts in *Jewish War* and *Antiquities*. This putative source focused on the philosophical positions of the three schools with regard to fate and the soul. In *Jewish War* 2 Josephus informs us that the Pharisees affirm both fate and human responsibility, while the Sadducees dispense with fate. There is no corresponding statement about the position of the Essenes. In *Antiquities* 18, however, the account of the Essenes begins with the statement that "the doctrine of the Essenes is wont to leave everything in the hands of God." A similar brief statement, contrasting the positions of the three schools on the question of fate, occurs in *Ant.* 13.171-72. Each of these passages in *Antiquities* is introduced by a statement about the three schools. It seems likely, then, that already when he wrote *Jewish War* Josephus had an account that contrasted the views of the three schools on the question of fate, but omitted the summary of Essene views in favor of the longer account of their way of life. It is *possible* that Josephus himself had authored the account that addressed the question of fate, but he cannot have done so specifically for *Jewish War,* and we do not know of an earlier occasion on which he might have composed it.

Neither Josephus nor Philo, nor Pliny, had much if any firsthand acquaintance with the Essenes. This conclusion is not negated by Mason's quite convincing demonstration that Josephus integrated his material on the Essenes into his own work, so that it contributed to his apologetic agenda. It does not require that we accept every detail of Bergmeier's analysis, or that we share his confidence in delineating the sources. It does

73. Bergmeier, *Essener-Berichte,* 60-64.

seem likely, however, that for his descriptions of the Essenes Josephus drew on at least two distinct sources, one in *Jewish War* 2 and one in *Antiquities* 18, and probably also on a third, a brief characterization of the philosophical tenets of the "three schools."

The Essenes and the Scrolls

Location

The identification of the Essenes with the sectarian movement described in the Scrolls was suggested first of all by the geographical notice of Pliny, who describes an Essene settlement on the western shore of the Dead Sea. Pliny continues: "Below them was the town of Engada [Engedi]. . . . From there, one comes to the fortress of Masada, situated on a rock, and itself near the lake of Asphalt." Pliny's account progresses from north to south, beginning with the Jordan River and proceeding southward to Masada.[74] This would suggest that "below them" means "south of them," and that the Essenes were located north of Engedi, in the vicinity of Qumran. Some scholars have argued that the preposition *infra* (below) does not mean to the south, but on a lower level. Yizhar Hirschfeld identified a site in the hills overlooking Engedi as the Essene settlement, but while this site has some agricultural installations it does not seem to have housed a community such as Pliny describes.[75] Pliny's account presents some difficulties: he knows that Jerusalem and Engedi have been destroyed but writes as if the Essene community were still flourishing, although Qumran was also destroyed when he wrote. Nonetheless, Qumran remains the most plausible site for the community of Essenes that Pliny describes. If Pliny relied on the world map and commentary of Marcus Vipsanius Agrippa (see the discussion above), this would suggest that there was an Essene community in this region before the turn of the era.

---

74. Stern, *Greek and Latin Authors*, 1.480-81.

75. Yizhar Hirschfeld, "A Settlement of Hermits above Engedi," *TA* 27 (2000): 103-55; and the rejoinder by David Amit and Jodi Magness, "Not a Settlement of Hermits or Essenes: A Response to Y. Hirschfeld, 'A Settlement of Hermits above En Gedi,'" *TA* 27 (2000): 273-85. See further Jodi Magness, *The Archaeology of Qumran and the Dead Sea Scrolls* (SDSSRL; Grand Rapids: Eerdmans, 2002) 41.

Communal Life

Quite apart from the issue of location, the Scrolls provide several striking parallels to the accounts of the Essenes. These parallels concern both the structure of community life and ideas and beliefs. Some parallels concern commonplaces that one would expect to find in any association, such as deference to elders, the prohibition of spitting in an assembly, or provision for expulsion.[76] Even the common meal, presided over by a priest, is not necessarily distinctive. Such common meals were a standard feature of voluntary associations in the Hellenistic world, and are also attested in Judaism in the case of the *haverim* known from rabbinic literature who practiced table fellowship for the sake of purity.[77] But other affinities are more significant.

Both Philo and Josephus emphasize that the Essenes held their property in common, while Pliny says that they lived "without money." Josephus writes: "For it is a law that those entering the sect transfer their property to the order; consequently, among them all there appears neither abject poverty nor superabundance of wealth, but the possessions of each are mingled, and there is, as among brothers, one property common to all."[78] The motif of common property is found in Greek descriptions of Spartans, Pythagoreans, and other utopian groups,[79] and Josephus elsewhere praises *koinōnia* or fellowship as the opposite of *misanthrōpia*, and says that Jewish laws encourage the sharing of possessions in common *(tōn ontōn koinōnian).*[80] But the only parallel to the Essene practice in a contemporary Jewish source is found in the *Community Rule.*[81] 1QS 1:11-12 states that all who join the community "will convey all their knowledge, their energies, and their riches" to the *yahad.* 1QS 5:2 specifies that the members constitute a *yahad* in law and possessions. Most specifically, 1QS

---

76. On spitting see Mason, "Essenes and Lurking Spartans," 249-50.

77. See chapter 2 above.

78. *J.W.* 2.122; cf. *Ant.* 18.20; Philo, *Hypothetica* 10.4; *Good Person* 77.

79. See above, chapter 2; Hans-Josef Klauck, "Gütergemeinschaft in der klassischen Antike, in Qumran und im Neuen Testament," *RevQ* 11 (1982–85): 47-79; Justin Taylor, *Pythagoreans and Essenes: Structural Parallels* (Leuven: Peeters, 2004) 41-43.

80. *Ag. Ap.* 2.291. Cf. Mason, "What Josephus Says about Essenes" (Internet version), 4.

81. Beall, *Josephus' Description,* 44. The sharing of possessions in early Christianity (Acts 2:44-45) is not part of a community structure in the same way, and arises from imminent eschatological expectation.

6:17-22 specifies that a postulant should not share in the possessions of the many in his first, probationary year. After his first full year, his possessions and his earnings will be brought to the common fund by the *mebaqqer*, but will be credited to his account and not used for the many. Finally, after he has completed a second year successfully, he is registered in the community, "to mingle his wealth" *(l'rb 't hwnw)*. Even the Hebrew terminology of "mingling" brings to mind the Greek account of the Essenes *(anamemigmenōn)*, granted the difference in language. It should be noted that the parallel here is with the *yaḥad*, as described in the *Community Rule* or *Serek ha-Yaḥad*, rather than with the *Damascus Rule*, which required only the contribution of two days' salary a month.

Process of Admission

Another striking parallel with the *Community Rule* lies in the description of a multi-year process of admission.[82] According to Josephus, this process takes three years:

> Now for those who are eager to join their sect, entrance is not immediate; but while he remains outside for a year, they place him under their way of life. . . .
> After he has given proof of his self-control in this time, they bring him closer to their way of life: he participates in the purer waters for purification, but he is not yet received into the common ways of living. For after this demonstration of perseverance, his character is tested for two more years, and if he is deserving, then he is admitted into the community. But before he may touch the common meal, he must take awesome oaths. *(J.W. 2.137-38)*

We may compare with this the admission process described in 1QS 6:13b-23:

> And anyone from Israel who freely volunteers to enroll in the council of the community, the man appointed at the head of the many shall

---

82. Candidates for admission to the rabbinic *ḥavurah* also had to undergo a probationary period, but "the sources do not give an exact description of the entry stages and how long they lasted" (Aharon Oppenheimer, "Haverim," *EDSS* 1.333).

test him with regard to his insight and his deeds. If he suits the discipline he shall let him enter into the covenant so that he can revert to the truth and shun all injustice, and he shall teach him all the precepts of the community. And then when he comes in to stand in front of the many, they shall be questioned, all of them, concerning his affairs. And depending on the outcome of the lot in the council of the many he shall be included or excluded. When he is included in the community council, he must not touch the purity of the many until they test him about his spirit and about his deeds, until he has completed a full year; neither should he share in the possession of the many. When he has completed a year within the community, the many will be questioned about his affairs, concerning his insight and his deeds in connection with the law. And if the lot results in him entering the council of the community, according to the priests and the majority of the men of the covenant, they shall also bring near his possessions and his earnings to the hand of the Inspector *(mebaqqer)* of the earnings of the many. And they shall credit it to his account, but they shall not use it for the many. He must not touch the drink of the many until he completes a second year among the men of the community. And when this second year is complete, he will be examined by command of the many. And if the lot results in him joining the community, they shall enter him in the order of his rank among his brothers for the law, for the judgment, for purity and for the placing of his possessions. And his advice will be for the community, as will his judgment.

There are minor differences between these two processes of admission. Josephus specifies that the initial probationary period before admission to the community is to last one year. In the *Community Rule* the length of this period is not specified. After this, both regulations require two more years. Josephus mentions purificatory baths at the end of the probationary period. These are not mentioned in the rule, although they were surely required at some stage. The rule indicates examinations at the end of each subsequent year, with gradual admission, first to "the purity of the many" (usually taken to mean the pure food),[83] and then to "the drink

---

83. Friedrich Avemarie, " '*Tohorat ha-Rabbim*' and '*Mashqeh ha-Rabbim*': Jacob Licht Reconsidered," in Moshe Bernstein, Florentino García Martínez, and John Kampen, eds., *Legal Texts and Legal Issues: Proceedings of the Second Meeting of the International Organization for Qumran Studies, Cambridge 1995, Published in Honour of Joseph M. Baumgarten* (STDJ

of the many." Josephus mentions admission to the common food only at the end of the process. Eyal Regev infers that "the Essene probation period was longer, and furthermore their inclusion in communal practices progressed in an inverse order: new Essene converts were first permitted to participate in ritual baths, and only at a later stage in communal meals, in contrast to the order of inclusion in the *yaḥad*."[84] But this is a matter of inference from the gaps in the two accounts. The rule is not explicit as to when the postulant was admitted to the purificatory baths, and Josephus may have conflated the final two years.[85] Neither can much significance be attached to the fact that Josephus mentions some things that are not mentioned in the rule — the fact that postulants are given a shovel for burying their excrement, and a white garment.[86] Neither account of the admission procedures is necessarily exhaustive, and it is also possible that there was some variation in time and place. Josephus wrote more than a century after the composition of the Hebrew rule book, and even his sources may have been composed considerably later than the Qumran rule.[87] The similarity of the two accounts remains impressive and distinctive. There is even some similarity in terminology: Josephus says that after the initial probationary year the novice "draws closer" *(proseisin)* to the way of life. 1QS 6:16 says that he will either "draw near" *(qrb)* or depart. Here again the analogy is with the *yaḥad*, as described in the *Community Rule*, rather than with the *Damascus Covenant*.

23; Leiden: Brill, 1997) 215-29. Avemarie allows that we cannot exclude the possibility that it has a broader meaning.

84. Regev, *Sectarianism*, 251.

85. So Beall, *Josephus' Description*, 75.

86. Albert Baumgarten, "The Temple Scroll, Toilet Practices, and the Essenes," *Jewish History* 10 (1996): 9-20, makes much of the fact that the *Temple Scroll* and the *War Scroll* require permanent latrines, but as Regev notes it is not clear that either of these texts represents the practice of the *yaḥad*. See Regev, *Sectarianism*, 251 n. 37. On the white garments of the Essenes, see Eibert Tigchelaar, "The White Dress of the Essenes and Pythagoreans," in F. García Martínez and G. P. Luttikhuizen, eds., *Jerusalem, Alexandria, Rome: Studies in Honour of A. Hilhorst* (JSJSup 82; Leiden: Brill, 2003) 301-21. Tigchelaar concludes that "there is no direct evidence that the Qumranites dressed in white. Nonetheless, indications in the texts preserved at Qumran do suggest that they too would have shared the same criticisms toward and avoidance of coloured clothes" (as the Essenes and Pythagoreans).

87. This point is emphasized especially by Atkinson, "Josephus the Essene."

Multiple Settlements

Josephus states clearly that the Essenes "have no one city, but many settle in each city" (*J.W.* 2.124). Similarly, Philo says that "they live in a number of towns in Judaea, and also in many villages and large groups."[88] Mason comments: "One of the biggest casualties of the Qumran-Essene hypothesis is Josephus' plain statement here."[89] But, as we have seen, both the *Damascus Rule,* which speaks of "camps," and the *Community Rule* (1QS 6) provide for small communities with a quorum of ten. The multiplicity of settlements is another point of affinity between the *yaḥad* and the Essenes.

Social Structure and Leadership

Regev has argued that "Josephus' Essenes differ from both the *yaḥad* and the Damascus Covenant in their social structure and types of leadership."[90] While the role of the Essene elders resembles the total authority of overseers and priests in the *Damascus Rule,* elders are seldom mentioned in the Hebrew rule books, and they are not assigned much authority. He argues that the *yaḥad* "had a democratic and semi-egalitarian social structure with no governing individual leader."[91] But as we have seen, Regev exaggerates the egalitarian character of the *yaḥad,* where the *maskil* and *paqid,* and to a lesser extent the *mebaqqer* (if he is not identical to the *paqid*), had important leadership roles. If we bear in mind that the Greek accounts of the Essenes were written by outsiders, the substitution of "elders" for other figures of authority is not a decisive difference. Neither can great weight be placed on Mason's observation that priests are mentioned only in connection with blessings over food and more generally with food preparation.[92] We might have expected Josephus to give priests a more prominent role, but if, as I have argued, he was following a source here the point has less significance. The source was obviously impressed with the

---

88. *Hypothetica* 11.1. Elsewhere Philo says that they "live in villages and avoid the cities" (*Quod Omnis* 76), but in that case he may be projecting onto them his own prejudices on city life. Compare *Decalogue* 10-11; *Contemplative Life* 2.18-20.

89. Mason, "Essenes and Lurking Spartans," 244.

90. Regev, *Sectarianism,* 249.

91. Ibid., 250.

92. Mason, "Essenes and Lurking Spartans," 243.

emphasis on hierarchy among the Essenes, and was aware of the presence of priests, but it may not have reflected the nuances of the hierarchy in full detail.

Oaths

Josephus claims that the Essenes refrain from swearing (*J.W.* 2.135), and yet says they do swear oaths on admission to the sect (2.139). The two positions are not necessarily contradictory: the prohibition may apply only to an individual swearing in everyday life.[93] The Hebrew rule books do not note the prohibition, but both prescribe an oath on joining the sect.[94] Some of the oaths mentioned by Josephus are unremarkable: to practice piety toward the Deity, to observe justice. But some items have noteworthy parallels in the *Community Rule*: "to hate the wicked always, to conceal nothing from the members of the sect, and to reveal nothing to outsiders . . . to transmit none of the doctrines except as he himself received them . . . and to preserve in like manner both the books of their sect and the names of the angels" (*J.W.* 2.139-42).

In the *Community Rule* those who enter the covenant are to love all the sons of light and hate all the sons of darkness (1QS 1:9-10). The characteristics of the spirit of light include "careful behavior in wisdom concerning everything, concealment concerning the truth of the mysteries of knowledge" (1QS 4:6). In 1QS 9:16-17 we are told of the Maskil: "and thus shall be his love and thus shall be his hatred. He should not reproach or argue with the men of the pit, but instead hide the counsel of the law in the midst of the men of injustice." The Scrolls do not mention a requirement of secrecy with regard to the names of the angels, but as Beale remarks, they are "replete with references to angels,"[95] and there are restrictions on membership in the community because of the presence of the angels.[96] A

---

93. So Mason, "What Josephus Says about Essenes" (Internet version), 7.

94. CD 15:1-2 is concerned that one not use the divine name in swearing.

95. Beall, *Josephus' Description*, 88. See Maxwell J. Davidson, *Angels at Qumran: A Comparative Study of 1 Enoch 1–36, 72–108 and Sectarian Writings from Qumran* (JSPSup 11; Sheffield: JSOT Press, 1992).

96. 1QSa 2:3-9. See J. A. Fitzmyer, "A Feature of Qumran Angelology and the Angels of 1 Cor 11:10," in Jerome Murphy-O'Connor and James H. Charlesworth, eds., *Paul and the Dead Sea Scrolls* (New York: Crossroad, 1990) 31-47, especially 42-43. Cf. CD 15:15-17.

restriction on divulging the names of the angels makes sense in the context of the *yaḥad*. It is not a typical feature of the apologetics of Josephus.

Offerings to the Temple

Josephus reports that the Essenes "send offerings to the temple, but perform their sacrifices using different customary purifications. For this reason, they are barred from entering into the common enclosure, but offer sacrifice among themselves." This statement is found in *Ant.* 18:18-19, which is closely related to Philo's account in *Quod Omnis* 75-91. Philo says: "they have shown themselves especially devout in the service of God, not by offering sacrifices of animals, but by resolving to sanctify their minds" (*Quod Omnis* 75). I have already suggested that the discrepancy between the two Greek accounts may be due to different interpretations of a common source, which said only that the Essenes were banned from the temple. Josephus's account is compatible with the ambiguous passage in the *Damascus Rule*: "all those who have been brought into the covenant shall not enter the temple to kindle his altar in vain" (CD 6:11), which leaves open the possibility that they make offerings according to their own rules. The *Damascus Rule* contains legislation pertaining to the temple cult. The *Community Rule,* in contrast, seems to envision the community as a replacement for the cult, and is perhaps comparable to Philo's emphasis on an alternative kind of offering. Even the *yaḥad* did not repudiate animal sacrifice as such, and it is arguable that Philo did not either.[97] Nor is there any evidence that the *yaḥad* continued to offer sacrifices, at a location other than the Jerusalem temple.[98] In view of the variation between Philo and Josephus on this matter it is difficult to be sure how the Essenes related to the temple cult. It is evident that they were at variance with the official

97. On the former see Jonathan Klawans, *Purity, Sacrifice and the Temple: Symbolism and Supersessionism in the Study of Ancient Judaism* (New York: Oxford University Press, 2006) 145-74. On the latter see Taylor, "Philo of Alexandria on the Essenes," 13.

98. There has been extensive debate about deposits of animal bones found at Qumran. The current consensus is that these were not the remains of animal sacrifices, since no altar was found at Qumran, but rather the remains of animals consumed at communal meals. See Magness, *Archaeology of Qumran*, 119; and eadem, "Communal Meals and Sacred Space at Qumran," in idem, *Debating Qumran: Collected Essays on Its Archaeology* (Leuven: Peeters, 2004) 81-112.

temple cult, and this was also true of the new covenant and the *yaḥad*. Whether they, or either branch of the movement known from the Scrolls, continued to send offerings to the temple is more difficult to say.[99] So while the issue of sacrifice is potentially important for the relation of the Scrolls to the Essenes, it is not decisive, because of the ambiguity of the evidence.

Celibacy

The main objection to the attribution of the Scrolls to the Essenes has always been that the Scrolls never require celibacy.[100] That the *Damascus Rule* clearly provides for marriage and families is not a problem: Josephus states explicitly that one order of the Essenes married, although the main Greek and Latin accounts were clearly based on a celibate order.[101] The issue is whether the *yaḥad*, as described in the *Community Rule,* was celibate. Several considerations suggest that it was. The absence of any reference to women and children is remarkable. That the community thought of itself as a replacement for the temple cult, and in communion with the angels, and that it was obsessed with issues of purity, all required a very restrictive approach to sex, if not outright abstinence. Against this, Regev argues that "it is inconceivable that a sect which went to such pains to scrupulously specify its social restrictions and organizational orders failed to address such a fundamental religious taboo and social boundary marker. How could the authors of the Community Rule fail to mention, even in passing, the renunciation of marriage life and the exclusion of women, when their celibacy was the main characteristic that set them apart from all other Jews?"[102] This argument has some force; the silence of the *Serek* on matters relating to marriage is extraordinary on either explanation. A decision on this matter depends on whether one is more impressed by the absence of an explicit rule of celibacy or by the absence of any reference to women and children. In my judgment the balance of evidence favors the view that

99. See Beall, *Josephus' Description,* 117-19.

100. For example, Baumgarten, "Who Cares?" 179.

101. Taylor, "Philo of Alexandria on Essenes," 23-25, argues that those who joined the Essenes would have been married earlier in life, but did not bring their wives into the community. This possibility is not excluded by the texts, but it is not explicitly affirmed either.

102. Regev, *Sectarianism,* 254.

the *yaḥad* was celibate, and that the sect was identical with the Essenes. But the evidence is not so clear-cut as to render dissent unreasonable.

Religious Beliefs

The evidence of the beliefs attributed to the Essenes is also ambiguous. Josephus's statement that the Essenes "make fate mistress of all and say that nothing comes to pass for humans unless fate has so voted" (*Ant.* 13.172) accords well with the deterministic theology of the *yaḥad*. The main doctrinal issue in the Greek sources concerns belief about the afterlife. Josephus says that "it is a firm belief among them that although bodies are corruptible, and their matter unstable, souls are immortal and endure for ever; that, come from subtlest ether, they are entwined with the bodies which serve them as prisons, drawn down as they are by some physical spell; but that when they are freed from the bonds of the flesh, liberated, so to speak, from long slavery, then they rejoice and rise up to the heavenly world" (*J. W.* 2.154-55).

He goes on to discuss their beliefs about reward and punishment after death. "An abode is reserved beyond the Ocean for the souls of the just," analogous to the Isles of the Blessed in Greek mythology, while "they relegate evil souls to a dark pit shaken by storms full of unending chastisement." The latter state is compared to the punishment of Sisyphus and other condemned figures in Hades. In *Antiquities* Josephus contents himself with a brief statement that "they also declare that souls are immortal" (*Ant.* 18.18). The Hellenistic coloring of the account, especially in *Jewish War*, is obvious.[103] The motif of death as the liberation of the soul from the body is one that occurs quite frequently in Josephus.[104] In *Jewish War* 3 he attributes to himself a speech attempting to dissuade the defenders of Jotapata from committing suicide. In the course of this speech he reiterates the view that we all have mortal bodies but immortal souls (*J. W.* 3.372). Yet the view that he expresses in his own name is not quite the same as what he attributes to the Essenes. In his speech at Jotapata he says that the righteous, "in the revolution of the ages, return to find in chaste bodies a new

103. Émile Puech, *La croyance des Esséniens en la vie future: Immortalité, résurrection, vie éternelle?* (2 vols.; EBib 21-22; Paris: Gabalda, 1993) 2.732.
104. Sievers, "Josephus and Afterlife," 20-34.

habitation." This must be understood as a reformulation of the belief in bodily resurrection. Compare his slightly different formulation of Pharisaic belief in terms of metempsychosis: "every soul, they maintain, is imperishable, but the soul of the good alone passes into another body, while the souls of the wicked suffer eternal punishment" (*J.W.* 2.163).[105]

Despite the Hellenistic coloring, Josephus's account of Essene eschatology has some notable similarity to what we find in the *Serek* from Qumran. In the *Instruction on the Two Spirits*, in 1QS 3–4, the visitation of those who walk in the spirit of light "will be for healing, plentiful peace in a long life, fruitful offspring with all everlasting blessings, eternal enjoyment with endless life, and a crown of glory with majestic raiment in eternal light" (1QS 4:6-8). The visitation of those who walk in the spirit of darkness

> will be for a glut of punishments at the hands of all the angels of destruction, for eternal damnation, for the scorching wrath of the God of revenge, for permanent error and shame without end with the humiliation of destruction by the fire of the dark regions. And all the ages of their generations they shall spend in bitter weeping and harsh evils in the abysses of darkness until their destruction, without there being a remnant or a survivor among them. (1QS 4:11-14)

Strikingly, there is no mention here of resurrection. The visitation of each spirit seems to follow automatically from their conduct. People seem to go directly to their reward or punishment. Some of the rewards of the righteous would seem to require a corporeal state, but the body in question may be a spiritual rather than an earthly one, to use the distinction drawn by Paul in 1 Corinthians 15. This conception is rather different from the Greek notion of immortality of the soul, and it is entirely in keeping with traditional Hebrew anthropology, whereby the *nephesh* survives the body in the netherworld. Insofar as there is no mention of bodily resurrection, however, it is not difficult to see how this conception could be identified with immortality of the soul by a hellenized observer. The punishment of the wicked in a place of darkness is quite reminiscent of Josephus's account of the eschatology of the Essenes, although he uses similar language elsewhere when the Essenes are not in view. There is nothing in the Hebrew

---

105. See further my essay, "Essenes and Afterlife."

sources, however, corresponding to the abode of the just beyond the Ocean, analogous to the Isles of the Blest.

The early Christian writer Hippolytus gives a different account of Essene eschatology, claiming that "the doctrine of the resurrection has also derived support among them, for they acknowledge both that the flesh will rise again, and that it will be immortal, in the same manner as the soul is already imperishable" (*Ref.* 9.27). Émile Puech has argued at length that Hippolytus's account is confirmed by the Dead Sea Scrolls.[106] The evidence of the sectarian scrolls is at best ambiguous. The crucial evidence is found in poetic passages in the *Hodayot,* notably 1QH^a 11:19-23; 14:29-33; 19:10-14.[107] However one adjudicates these passages, it is clear that resurrection language is not the primary mode for the expression of future hope in the sectarian scrolls.[108] Moreover, Hippolytus is an unreliable witness to the Essenes. He confuses them with the Zealots, and his account of their eschatology corresponds almost exactly to his summaries of Pharisaic eschatology and of general Jewish eschatology.[109]

Josephus's claim that the Essenes believed in immortality of the soul but not resurrection of the body is intriguing, in light of the reticence of the Scrolls on the subject of resurrection; and the description of the place of punishment is compatible with the Scrolls, although not distinctive. But the account of the abode of the blessed does not correspond to what we find in the Scrolls at all. Conversely, Josephus does not mention "majestic raiment in eternal light," or of life with the angels, such as we find in the *Hodayot.* It may be that he, or his source, adapted the Semitic beliefs to make them more intelligible to Hellenistic readers. But here again the correspondence between the *yaḥad* and the Essenes is incomplete, and admits of different interpretations.

---

106. Puech, *Croyance des Esséniens,* 2.703-69.

107. See John J. Collins, *Apocalypticism in the Dead Sea Scrolls* (London: Routledge, 1997) 110-29; idem, "Conceptions of Afterlife in the Dead Sea Scrolls," in Michael Labahn and Manfred Lang, eds., *Lebendige Hoffnung — ewiger Tod* (ABIG 24; Leipzig: Evangelische Verlagsanstalt, 2007) 103-25.

108. George J. Brooke, "The Structure of 1QHa XII 5-XIII 4 and the Meaning of Resurrection," in García Martínez et al., eds., *From 4QMMT to Resurrection,* 15-33, argues that resurrection is affirmed in the *Hodayot,* but that it is understood metaphorically.

109. Collins, "Essenes and Afterlife," 39-41.

Messianism and Apocalypticism

The major discrepancy between the accounts of the Essenes and what we find in the Scrolls, however, concerns a range of matters that are prominent in the latter but are not mentioned at all in the Greek and Latin authors. These include any reference to messiahs or to an apocalyptic war between sons of light and sons of darkness. Josephus gives little impression of the priestly character of the sect, or of the importance of calendrical issues. It is clear that the Essenes were concerned with the strict interpretation of the law, and with purity, but the Greek accounts scarcely convey the centrality of these concerns as they emerge in the Scrolls.

The omissions, however, must be seen in perspective. It was not only with respect to the Essenes that Josephus seemed to "miss" crucial aspects of the Judaism of his day, as Arnaldo Momigliano pointed out in a classic essay.[110] Josephus, wrote Momigliano, was "cut off from the two vital currents of Judaism of his time: the apocalypse and the synagogue."[111] He preserves the prophetic books but "deprives them of any subversive tendencies by showing that foreign rulers were satisfied with them."[112] In essence "Jewish prophets appear above all to be promising the empire to non-Jewish rulers."[113] He had no place for apocalypticism, as can be seen especially in his treatment of Daniel.[114] Tessa Rajak reformulates Momigliano's thesis, as "what Josephus did see but could not write about."[115] She finds it "somewhat more probable that Josephus perceived what was involved in Essene theology as wholly tainted by dangerously apocalyptic notions," but there were also constraints of genre. "The world of belief was less readily accommodated to the Greek model than the world of social organization and practice."[116]

Mason, in contrast, argues that

---

110. Arnaldo Momigliano, "What Josephus Did Not See," in idem, *Essays on Ancient and Modern Judaism* (Chicago: University of Chicago Press, 1994) 67-78.

111. Ibid., 77.

112. Ibid., 76.

113. Ibid.

114. On Josephus's nonapocalyptic reading of Daniel, see Steve Mason, "Josephus, Daniel and the Flavian House," in Parente and Sievers, eds., *Josephus and History,* 160-91.

115. Rajak, "Ciò que Flavio Giuseppe Vide," 158.

116. Ibid.

the people of the Scrolls were about as far as one could get from Josephus's view of the world. Their core beliefs involved rejection of the priestly establishment in Jerusalem and anticipation of a conflict that would destroy those sons of darkness along with the wicked foreign. They were a world-denying sect, in the language of William James, who espoused every kind of dualism: cosmic, anthropological, and temporal. The world-affirming Jerusalem aristocrat and statesman Josephus . . . embraced (as author) none of these perspectives.[117]

He could not, argues Mason, have presented the Essenes as shining examples if they were in fact such a world-denying sect.

Whether the Essenes as Josephus describes them were particularly world-affirming might be questioned. I am not persuaded, however, that Josephus had significant personal knowledge of, or interest in, the actual Essenes. Rather, as also in Philo's case, what he extolled was the literary portrayal of the Essenes, which was not necessarily an accurate representation of a group as it actually existed. It is certainly true that Josephus was very far from sharing the apocalyptic mind-set of the *yaḥad* described in the Dead Sea Scrolls, but I see little reason to think that he understood the actual mind-set of the people he described as Essenes, or that he would have made much effort to find out. The ethnographic idealization of the Essenes served his apologetic purposes. The realities of sectarian life did not.

I do not think, then, that the scholarly identification of the *yaḥad* with the Essenes is disproven by the fact that Josephus would not have approved of an apocalyptic group. At this point it is well to remember why scholars make the identification in the first place. One reason is the location. Qumran remains the only plausible site yet identified for the Essenes mentioned by Pliny. A second is that both the Essenes and the *yaḥad* were voluntary associations, with a lengthy process of admission over several years and a common life, to a degree otherwise unattested in Palestinian Judaism.[118] Mason claims that "the specific agreements between Essenes and Qumraners are not more extensive than those between Essenes and other utopian groups of the Greco-Roman world — Hyperboreans or Pythagoreans — and nowhere near as extensive as evocations of Sparta,

---

117. Mason, "Essenes and Lurking Spartans," 254.
118. For the case of the Therapeutae in Egypt, see appendix 2 below.

though no one would suggest that Essenes were Spartans."[119] But the Spartans were not a voluntary association at all, much less a religious one devoted to the study of the Jewish scriptures, and there is no evidence that the Pythagoreans or Hyperboreans had a settlement beside the Dead Sea. Location and lifestyle were more easily observable by outsiders than the religious beliefs of the sect, which were supposed to be kept secret in any case. The reasons for identifying the Essenes with the *yaḥad* remain substantial, and are in no way undermined by the use of common Hellenistic topoi in the Greek descriptions.

But if the *yaḥad* was indeed Essene, the Greek and Latin accounts do not give a very reliable picture of the sect, and have little value as independent witnesses to a movement that existed in Judea around the turn of the era. We cannot, for example, use these accounts to argue for a distinction between those who lived by the Dead Sea (Pliny) and the "urban Essenes" who lived in many towns and villages (Philo and Josephus).[120] They have some value as supporting witnesses, when we have independent confirmation of some of their details. But in themselves they are first of all, as Mason correctly argues, witnesses to the rhetoric of Philo and Josephus, and to the Greek tradition of ethnography of which they are part.

Appendix I: The Name *Essene*

The origin and etymology of the name "Essene" are enigmatic. Philo wrote that the members of this sect were called "Essaioi": "although this word is not, strictly speaking, Greek, I think it may be related to the word 'holiness'" (*hosiotēs; Quod Omnis* 75). But Philo seems to infer this etymology from their lifestyle. He does not appear to know how it was derived.

Most scholars assume that the name had a Semitic origin.[121] Josephus uses the word *essēn* as a transliteration of the Hebrew word for the breastplate worn by the high priest (*ḥōšen*) (*Ant.* 3.185, 218). He says that the Greeks call it "oracle" because of its oracular power. Josephus also credits some Essenes with the ability to predict, but he never suggests an

---

119. Mason, "Essenes and Lurking Spartans," 252-53.

120. *Pace* Boccaccini, *Beyond the Essene Hypothesis*, 21-49.

121. See the excellent overviews by Geza Vermes, "The Etymology of 'Essenes,'" *RevQ* 2 (1960): 427-43; and James VanderKam, "Identity and History of the Community," in Flint and VanderKam, eds., *Dead Sea Scrolls after Fifty Years*, 2.490-99.

association between the oracular *essēn* and the name of the sect. The usage is interesting mainly because it shows that the guttural *ḥ* could get lost in transliteration, and that the vowel *o* could be rendered as an *e*.

Long before the discovery of the Dead Sea Scrolls, Emil Schürer had proposed a derivation from the Aramaic *ḥsʾ* (absolute plural, *ḥsyn*, emphatic, *ḥsyʾ*), meaning "pious," although the term was not attested in Western Aramaic. This etymology received wide support after the discovery of the Dead Sea Scrolls, in part because of the assumption that the sect evolved from the Hasidim (the Hebrew equivalent of *ḥsyʾ*, "pious ones"), who are mentioned in the books of Maccabees.[122] The word *ḥsʾ* is now attested in the *Aramaic Levi Document* (4Q213a 3-4 6), but it is not a designation for a group. *Ḥsyʾ* is in fact the Semitic word that corresponds most closely to *Essaioi*, the form of the name given in our oldest source, Philo. When Philo tried to associate the name with the Greek *hosioi*, "holy ones," he may have been mistaking an explanation of its meaning for an etymology.[123]

Also in favor of this etymology is the fact that the Hebrew equivalent, *ḥsydym*, was used as the name of a party in the Maccabean era. The Hebrew word is transcribed as Asidaioi in 1 Macc 7:13. This derivation, however, lends only dubious support to the identification of the Essenes with the *yaḥad*. The word *ḥsydym* is not used as a self-designation for the group in the Scrolls. The view that the movement described in the *Damascus Document* evolved from the Hasidim of the Maccabean era now seems much less assured than it did forty years ago. Moreover, the sectarian rule books are in Hebrew, not Aramaic, and so it is difficult to see why the Aramaic form of the word should have been taken over by the Greek writers.

Vermes proposed the Aramaic *ʾsyʾ*, which he related to the Greek *Therapeutae*, the rather similar association described by Philo in his *Contemplative Life*. "The Essenes were θεραπευταί in both senses of this word: they were 'worshippers' because they were 'healers.'"[124] This suggestion, again, is etymologically possible, but we do not know that the Aramaic

---

122. This etymology was endorsed by Dupont-Sommer, *Dead Sea Scrolls*, 86-87; and F. M. Cross, *The Ancient Library of Qumran* (3rd ed.; BibSem 30; Sheffield: Sheffield Academic Press, 1995) 183, among many others.

123. As suggested by Joan Taylor, "Philo of Alexandria on Essenes," 11.

124. Vermes, "Etymology of 'Essenes,'" 437. This etymology is also endorsed by Étienne Nodet, "*Asidaioi* and Essenes," in Anthony Hilhorst, Émile Puech, and Eibert Tigchelaar, eds., *Flores Florentino: Dead Sea Scrolls and Other Early Jewish Studies in Honour of Florentino García Martínez* (JSJSup 122; Leiden: Brill, 2007) 87.

word was ever used as the name for a group, and it is not so used in the Scrolls. Despite the similarities between the Therapeutae and the Essenes, Philo describes them as separate groups.

The proposed etymology that finds most support in the Scrolls as a self-designation for the sect is the Hebrew phrase 'śy htwrh, "doers of the Law," proposed by Stephen Goranson.[125] This expression is used as a designation for the members of the sect in the *pesharim*. 1QpHab 7:10-12 reads: "Interpreted, this concerns the men of truth who keep the Law ('śy htwrh), whose hands shall not slacken in the service of truth when the final age is prolonged." Again in 1QpHab 8:1-3: "Interpreted, this concerns all those who observe the Law in the House of Judah, whom God will deliver from the house of judgment because of their suffering and because of their faith in the Teacher of Righteousness."[126] In this case, however, the etymology is difficult. If a participial form of the verb 'śh, "to do," lies behind the name, the forms *Ossaioi/Ossenoi*, which appear in Epiphanius, *Refutation of All Heresies* 19 and 20 (4th century CE), would be closest to the original, but this is probably mere coincidence. The transcription of the Hebrew *ḥōšen* (breastplate) as *essēn* by Josephus shows that a guttural plus *o* vowel could be rendered by *e* in Greek, but it is not a very close parallel. The main difficulty, however, is that the word 'śym, "doers," is never used alone as the designation for a group in Hebrew. It is always "doers of the law," or "doers of his will." Again, the phrase "doers of the law" occurs in Hebrew in the Scrolls, but the Greek forms of the name suggest Aramaic endings rather than Hebrew.[127]

---

125. Stephen Goranson, "Essenes: Etymology from עשה," *RevQ* 11 (1984): 483-98; idem, "Essenes," in E. M. Meyers, ed., *The Oxford Encyclopedia of Archaeology in the Near East* (5 vols.; New York: Oxford University Press, 1997) 2.268-69. This etymology was proposed as early as 1858 by Rabbi David Oppenheimer.

126. See further VanderKam, "Identity and History," 497. Cf. also 1QpHab 12:4-5; 4QpPsa 1-10 ii 15, 23; and the related phrase "doers of his will" in 4QpPsa 1-10 ii 5.

127. VanderKam, "Identity and History," 497-98, suggests that the etymology from 'śy htwrh provides the best explanation for the term *bytsyn* (= *byt 'syn* = *byt 'śyn*), usually read as "Boethusians," in rabbinic literature. He relies here on the arguments of Y. Sussmann that the Boethusians were none other than the Essenes (Sussmann, "Appendix 1: The History of the Halakha and the Dead Sea Scrolls," in Elisha Qimron and John Strugnell, eds., *Qumran Cave 4*, vol. V: *Miqṣat Maʿaśe Ha-Torah* [DJD 10; Oxford: Clarendon, 1994] 195-96). Sussmann has been refuted, however, by Adiel Schremer, "The Name of the Boethusians: A Reconsideration of Suggested Explanations and Another One," *JJS* 48 (1998): 290-99; and Eyal Regev, "Were the Priests All the Same? Qumranic Halakhah in Comparison with Sad-

The names "Essene/Essaioi" occur only in Greek and Latin sources. They are not attested in the Dead Sea Scrolls. We must consider the possibility that it was a name given to the sect by outsiders, not a self-designation, and not derived from any Semitic original.

The word *essēn* is attested in Greek, apart from its use in connection with the Jewish sect.[128] It occurs as a name for priests of Artemis of Ephesus. The Greek writer Pausanias, who wrote in the second century CE, says of the Mantineans: "For these not only in sexual matters but also in all other things live their lives in purity and neither baths nor other aspects of their way of life are done in the same manner as the common people. They do not enter the house of a private person."[129] He adds: "I know Ephesians who are members of a religious association dedicated to Artemis the Ephesian that practice a similar way of life for a year and no more who are called *essēnes* by the citizens." The name *essēnes*, referring to cultic officials of Artemis, is attested in inscriptions from 307/306 BCE to the third century CE.[130]

The idea that the name *Essene* was borrowed from this pagan group has been argued at length by John Kampen.[131] VanderKam dismisses this possibility with the question, "why should anyone associate these two groups?"[132] But Josephus says that the Essenes "live in no way different from, but as much as possible like, the so-called Dacians" (*Ant.* 18.22), surely a more far-fetched association.[133] The reason why someone might make an association with the *essēnai* of Ephesus was that both were known for their concern with purity (although the priests of Artemis observed this lifestyle only on a temporary basis). We read in an inscription from

---

ducean Halakhah," *DSD* 12 (2005): 158-88 (specifically 185-88). In rabbinic literature, when groups are identified as *byt* + a name (house of X), the name is always singular, never plural.

128. H. G. Liddell, R. Scott, and H. S. Jones, *A Greek-English Lexicon* (9th ed. with rev. supplement; Oxford: Clarendon, 1996) 697.

129. Pausanias 8.13.1. See John Kampen, *The Hasideans and the Origin of Pharisaism: A Study in 1 and 2 Maccabees* (SBLSCS 24; Atlanta: Scholars Press, 1988) 170-71.

130. H. Wankel et al., eds., *Die Inschriften von Ephesos*, vols. 1-7b (Bonn: Habelt, 1979–84) 1408, 1409, 1440, 1443, 1447, 1451, 1453, 1455, 1467, 1471, 2005. See Kampen, *Hasideans*, 161-69.

131. John Kampen, "A Reconsideration of the Name Essene," *HUCA* 57 (1986): 61-81; idem, *Hasideans*, 151-85. See also Allen H. Jones, *Essenes: The Elect of Israel and Priests of Artemis* (Lanham, MD: University Press of America, 1985).

132. VanderKam, "Identity and History," 492.

133. Dacia was situated in the loop of the lower Danube.

the late second century CE: "I Scaptius Frontinos, temple warden, senator, with also my wife Herennia Autronia, having held the office of *essēn* *(essēneusas)* in an undefiled and pious manner. . . ."[134]

It is unlikely that a Jewish author would have made this association. If, however, the accounts of the Essenes in Philo, Pliny, and Josephus depend on one or more accounts by a non-Jewish Hellenistic writer, then it is quite possible that the name was coined by an outsider, and does not reflect a Semitic self-designation at all. In this case we should not be surprised that the name is not attested at all in the Scrolls.

The correspondence between the name for the priests of Artemis and that of the Jewish sect is not exact, as they belong to different declensions. (The priests are *Essēnes* rather than *Essēnoi*.) A more significant problem is that the oldest attested form of the name for the sect is *Essaioi* rather than *Essēnoi*. The form *Essaioi* lends itself better to an Aramaic derivation. If *Essaioi* was the original Greek form, then the association with the *essēnai* would be at most secondary, suggested by the similarity of the names.

Obviously, any reconstruction of the etymology is hypothetical. But that the name "Essene" is not attested in the Hebrew scrolls is no objection to the Essene hypothesis.[135] *Essēnoi* and *Essaioi* were Greek names, for the convenience of Greek readers. The derivation from Aramaic *ḥsy'* is perhaps the most plausible of those that have been proposed, but it was not necessarily the self-designation of the sect. The arguments for (and against) the Essene identification are independent of the issue of the name.

Appendix II: The Therapeutae

The Therapeutae are known only from Philo's treatise *On the Contemplative Life*. These, we are told, are people who "desire the vision of the Existent and soar above the sun of our senses" (*Cont. Life* 11). To this end, they abandon their property to their relatives, and then leave brothers, children, parents, and kinsfolk, to devote themselves to the contemplative life. "This kind," says Philo, "exists in many places in the inhabited world . . . but it

---

134. Wankel et al., eds., *Inschriften von Ephesos*, 1578b: 3-10; Kampen, *Hasideans*, 166-67.

135. So also VanderKam, "Identity and History," 491.

abounds in Egypt . . . and especially around Alexandria" (*Cont. Life* 21).[136] The best of them avoid the city and go to a place near the Mareotic Lake. They live in houses close to one another, but not too close, so that they can enjoy both fellowship and privacy. In each house there is a sanctuary, into which they take only the holy books. They pray at sunrise and sunset, and spend the intervening hours entirely in spiritual exercises. They read the scriptures, and interpret them allegorically, and also have writings of the men of old. In addition to contemplation, they compose hymns and psalms. For six days they seek wisdom by themselves in solitude, but on the seventh they have a general assembly. They sit in order of their age, and the most senior among them gives a discourse. Their common sanctuary has separate areas for men and women, separated by a wall three or four cubits high, so that the women cannot be seen but can hear the discourse. They fast until sunset, but on the seventh day they have a common banquet of bread, flavored with salt and hyssop, and water. They partake of no wine or meat. Philo is at pains to contrast the sobriety of these banquets with the drunkenness typical of Greek symposia (*Cont. Life* 40), and he pointedly contrasts the meals of the Therapeutae with the symposia described by Plato and Xenophon (*Cont. Life* 57-63). The women are mostly "aged virgins" who have chosen to remain celibate. The Therapeutae have no slaves, and the younger members wait on the elders. After the meal, they stand and form two choirs, one of men and one of women, and they sing hymns to God. Then when each choir has done its part, they mix together and become a single choir, a copy of the choir set up of old beside the Red Sea (*Cont. Life* 85). Thus they continue until dawn.

Since the Therapeutae are otherwise unknown, and Philo depicts them rhetorically in idealizing terms, the suspicion has occasionally arisen that they were not a historical group at all but only "a philosopher's dream."[137] Against this, Joan Taylor has argued that "it is characteristic of

---

136. Quotations of Philo, *De Vita Contemplativa*, are from F. H. Colson in the Loeb edition, vol. 9. Presumably, Philo means that people devoted to contemplation are to be found in many places, not specifically Therapeutae. See the remarks of F. H. Colson, "Introduction to *De Vita Contemplativa*," in *Philo*, vol. IX (LCL; Cambridge: Harvard University Press, 1960) 104-11.

137. For a recent defense of this view see Troels Engberg-Pedersen, "Philo's *De Vita Contemplativa* as a Philosopher's Dream," *JSJ* 30 (1999): 40-64. For older scholarship on the Therapeutae see Jean Riaud, "Les Thérapeutes d'Alexandrie dans la tradition et dans la recherche critique jusqu'aux découvertes de Qumrân," *ANRW* 2.20.2.1189-1295.

the genre of utopian fantasies that the ideal society is found on a very far-off island, towards the edges of the world, as in Iambulus's idealizing account of the 'children of the sun.'"[138] Philo, in contrast, locates the Therapeutae just outside Alexandria. "No one," she concludes, "who wished to convince an audience of the truth of total fiction would make it so easy to be found out."[139] The Essenes, whom Philo also depicts in idealizing terms, were an actual group, and we should assume that the Therapeutae were also. Whether Philo's account is accurate or distorted is another matter, but since we have no other source, that is impossible to check.

The question of a relationship between the Therapeutae and the Essenes is raised directly at the beginning of *Contemplative Life*. Philo says that he has discussed the Essenes, who pursue the active life, presumably in a treatise that is now lost. He now turns to those who pursue the life of contemplation. Some scholars take this to mean that those who pursue the active life and the contemplatives are two branches of the Essenes.[140] In *Quod Omnis* 75, Philo calls the Essenes *therapeutai theou*, "servants of God." Yet there is no further indication in *Contemplative Life* that the Therapeutae are Essenes, and while they resemble the Essenes in many ways, there are also important differences. Geza Vermes and Martin Goodman conclude that "the available evidence does not justify a complete identification of the Therapeutae and the Essenes/Qumran sectaries. The most likely conclusion is that the former represented an Egyptian off-shoot of the Palestinian ascetic movement of the Essenes."[141] But even this conclusion goes beyond the evidence. Vermes suggested an etymological connection. He derived "Essaean" from Aramaic *ḥsy'*, "healers." This etymology of Essaean is not widely accepted, however. Philo offers two possible explanations of the name "Therapeutae": "either in the sense of 'cure' because they profess an art of healing better than that current in the cities,

---

138. Joan E. Taylor, *Jewish Women Philosophers of First-Century Alexandria: Philo's 'Therapeutae' Reconsidered* (Oxford: Oxford University Press, 2003) 8-9. Compare John Ferguson, *Utopias of the Classical World* (London: Thames and Hudson, 1975) 124-29; James S. Romm, *The Edges of the Earth in Ancient Thought: Geography, Exploration, and Fiction* (Princeton: Princeton University Press, 1992).

139. Taylor, *Jewish Women*, 10.

140. Bergmeier, *Essener-Berichte*, 42.

141. Vermes and Goodman, *Essenes*, 17. Nodet, "*Asidaioi* and Essenes," 86, also assumes that they had a common origin but regards the Therapeutae as the older form of the movement. His reconstruction is very speculative.

which cures only the bodies, while theirs treats also souls . . . or else in the sense of 'worship'" (*Cont. Life* 2). "Therapeutae" is most plausibly explained in Philo's second sense as "servants/attendants."[142]

The resemblances between the Therapeutae and the Essenes are summarized concisely by Vermes and Goodman:

> *Parallels with the accounts of the Essenes in both Philo and Josephus:*
> Communal meals, celibacy, frugality, extreme reverence for the Torah, and possibly the name.

> *Parallels with Philo's Essenes:*
> Avoidance of cities, allegorical Bible exegesis, summer and winter garments.

> *Parallels with Josephus's Essenes:*
> White robes, morning prayer toward the sun, the presence of young people, their own literary compositions, healing, prophetic gifts, self-defense against robbers.[143]

Parallels with Philo's account of the Essenes may reflect his own ideals, and it is also possible that his account of the Therapeutae was influenced by an account of the Essenes that was also known to Josephus.[144]

If we extend the comparison to the *yaḥad,* there is a general similarity with the communal meal, followed by extended study of the scriptures. Vermes argues that the most significant parallel was the common use of a solar calendar, and the importance attached to the Feast of Weeks or Pentecost.[145] The evidence for the calendar of the Therapeutae is sketchy, however. They are said to pray at sunrise and sunset, and they assemble after seven sets of seven days. The fiftieth day was a festival, but this was not necessarily Pentecost as Vermes and others have assumed, but rather a fes-

142. Taylor, *Jewish Women,* 55-68. She argues from Philo's own usage, from usage associated with the cult of Isis and Sarapis and from usage in currency from the time of Plato, which referred to those devoted to the service of the gods as *therapeutai.*

143. Vermes and Goodman, *Essenes,* 16.

144. So Bergmeier, *Essener-Berichte,* 48.

145. Geza Vermes, in Emil Schürer, *The History of the Jewish People in the Age of Jesus Christ (175 B.C.–A.D. 145)* (rev. and ed. Geza Vermes, Fergus Millar, and Martin Goodman; Edinburgh: T&T Clark, 1973–87) 2.595.

tival that recurred every fifty days.[146] Taylor supposes that this "pente-contad" reckoning was somehow reconciled with a 364-day solar calendar, such as we find in *Jubilees* and the *Temple Scroll*. She denies, however, that this calendar was exclusive to any one sect, and claims that a solar calendar was advocated by Alexandrian and other Egyptian Jews.[147] All this is very speculative, but the affinities between the Therapeutae and the Essenes/ *yaḥad* on the subject of the calendar are neither clear nor decisive.

In any case, there are several crucial differences between the Thera-peutae and the Essenes. Most obvious is the presence of celibate women among the Therapeutae. The degree of common life is different too. The Therapeutae assemble only once a week and abstain from wine and meat. They eat only one meal a day. They give away their property before join-ing the group, and do not merge it in a common fund. The feast on the fiftieth day is peculiar to them. They are located in Egypt, not in the land of Israel.

Beyond these differences, the Therapeutae, at least as Philo portrays them, reflect a different thought world from what we find in the Dead Sea Scrolls, and even differ from the classical accounts of the Essenes in their philosophical and contemplative focus. Taylor suggests that they belonged to the extreme allegorists, whom Philo condemned for their failure to keep the literal law (*Migration of Abraham* 86-93).[148] The Therapeutae observed the Sabbath, but do not seem to have observed the other Jewish festivals. They are not said to have practiced ritual washings. The obvious objection to this identification is that Philo would hardly have held the extreme allegorizers up as paragons of virtue, even if he is sympathetic to them in his criticism in *Migration of Abraham*. Taylor responds that the two trea-tises were written for different audiences, and that Philo suppressed his criticism when writing for outsiders (the Romans).[149] Be that as it may, the Therapeutae as described by Philo belong to the world of Alexandrian, philosophical Judaism. They resemble the Essenes insofar as both are vol-

146. Taylor, *Jewish Women*, 156-57.

147. Ibid., 154-70. On the possibility that the 364-day calendar was traditional before the persecution by Antiochus Epiphanes see James C. VanderKam, *Calendars in the Dead Sea Scrolls: Measuring Time* (London: Routledge, 1998), who is clear on the speculative char-acter of any reconstruction of the calendars in Second Temple Judaism.

148. Taylor, *Jewish Women*, 126-53. She does not claim that the Therapeutae were the only Alexandrian Jews who qualified as extreme allegorizers.

149. Ibid., 153.

untary associations dedicated to the pursuit of religious perfection, and the similarities may be exaggerated by Philo's idealizing rhetoric. But even similar practices, such as celibacy, may have had quite a different rationale in each case. It is quite unlikely that the Therapeutae were an Egyptian branch of the Essenes.

CHAPTER FIVE

The Site of Qumran

Khirbet Qumran is located about a mile to the west of the Dead Sea, three miles south of its northern end.[1] Jericho is about nine miles to the north, and Jerusalem some thirteen miles to the east. The ruins are located on a low marl plateau, between the rock cliffs and the plain. The plateau is bounded to the south by the Wadi Qumran, and by ravines to the north and west.

The site had been noted by visitors already in the nineteenth century.[2] In 1851 Ferdinand de Saulcy apparently noted the presence of burials near the site.[3] In 1873 two British surveyors, Claude Conder and Herbert Kitchener, noted an abandoned pool and a flight of steps leading down into it.[4] They also noted an "immense" number of graves, and excavated one of them. Shortly thereafter the French archaeologist Charles Clermont-Ganneau visited the site, and he too excavated one of the graves. He noted that the graves were oriented north-south instead of the usual east-west ori-

1. It has been suggested that the ancient name of the site was Secacah, one of six desert towns listed in Josh 15:61-62. See Hanan Eshel, "The Identification of the City of Salt," *IEJ* 45 (1995): 37-40; Jodi Magness, *The Archaeology of Qumran and the Dead Sea Scrolls* (SDSSRL; Grand Rapids: Eerdmans, 2002) 25. The suggestion was first made by John Allegro. Alternatively, it might be identified as the "City of Salt," as suggested by Martin Noth. Secacah is mentioned in the Copper Scroll.

2. Joan E. Taylor, "Khirbet Qumran in the Nineteenth Century and the Name of the Site," *PEQ* 134 (2002): 144-64; Magness, *Archaeology of Qumran,* 22-24.

3. Brian Schultz, "The Qumran Cemetery: 150 Years of Research," *DSD* 13 (2006): 194. De Saulcy did not mention the cemetery in his account of his trip, but appears to have communicated its existence to others.

4. See Yitzhar Hirschfeld, *Qumran in Context* (Peabody, MA: Hendrickson, 2004) 14.

entation of Muslim graves in Palestine. He inferred that the cemetery could not be Muslim, and suggested that it belonged to some pagan Arab tribe before the time of Muhammad.[5] A British explorer, Gurney Masterman, visited Qumran in 1900–1901. He was the first to describe the rock-cut aqueduct, and surmised that it filled the cisterns with winter rain.[6] He also inferred that the site may have been a small fortress. This was also the opinion of Gustaf Dalman, who visited the site in 1914.[7]

The first Dead Sea Scrolls were discovered by Bedouin in a cave a little more than half a mile north of the site, sometime in 1946–47. Shortly thereafter, war broke out in Palestine, and the cave was not identified until January 1949. Roland de Vaux, O.P., of the École Biblique in Jerusalem, and Lankaster Harding, chief inspector of antiquities in Jordan, excavated the cave, and also surveyed Qumran and excavated two graves in the cemetery.[8] At that time they found no evidence to connect the scrolls to the site, which they regarded as a Roman fort from the Christian era.

Harding and de Vaux returned to Qumran in November-December, 1951, and began to excavate the site. They noted the poor quality of the buildings, and concluded that it could not be a Roman fort as they had originally supposed. They also found a jar, identical to the ones in which the first scrolls were found, embedded in the floor of one of the rooms, and inferred that the scrolls were related to the site after all.[9] They found a coin dating to 10 BCE beside the jar, and noted that the same kinds of pottery and oil lamps that were found in the cave with the scrolls were also found in the site. In his account of this excavation, Harding concluded that

> it would appear, then, that the people who lived at Khirbet Qumran deposited the scrolls in the cave, probably about A.D. 70. The situation fits in well with Pliny the Elder's account of the Essenes who had a settlement 'above Engeddi,' and the ruin itself, with its peculiar cemetery

5. Charles Clermont-Ganneau, *Archaeological Researches in Palestine during the Years 1873–1874* (trans. Aubrey Stewart; 2 vols.; 1896–99; repr. Jerusalem: Raritas, 1971) 2.14-16.

6. E. W. G. Masterman, "Notes on Some Ruins and a Rock-Cut Aqueduct in the Wady Kumrân," *Palestine Exploration Fund Quarterly Statement* 28 (1903): 264-67.

7. G. Dalman, *Palästinajahrbuch des deutschen evangelischen Instituts für Altertums-wissenschaft des heiligen Landes zu Jerusalem* 10 (Berlin: Mittler, 1914) 9-11.

8. Magness, *Archaeology of Qumran*, 27.

9. G. Lankester Harding, "Khirbet Qumrân and Wady Murabba'at: Fresh Light on the Dead Sea Scrolls and New Manuscript Discoveries in Jordan," *PEQ* 84 (1952): 104-9.

which is without parallel in other sites in Jordan, is clearly not an ordinary defensive or agricultural post.[10]

Further reason to associate the scrolls with the site would soon emerge. In 1952 the cave known as Cave 4, containing fragments of more than five hundred scrolls, was discovered by the Bedouin. This cave was located at the edge of the marl plateau, literally a stone's throw from the ruins. Several other caves containing scroll fragments were found in the immediate vicinity: Cave 5 near Cave 4, Cave 6 in the limestone cliffs behind Qumran, and Caves 7, 8, and 9 at the southern end of the marl plateau. De Vaux went on to conduct large-scale excavations at Qumran for four more seasons from 1953 to 1956. During the last of these seasons he also excavated Ein Feshka, a site located some two miles south of Qumran, which he regarded as part of the sectarian complex.

There have been several excavations at Qumran since that of de Vaux.[11] The most extensive of these was conducted by Yizhak Magen and Yuval Peleg in the years 1996–2002.[12]

De Vaux's Stratigraphy of the Site

De Vaux distinguished four phases of settlement at the site.[13] The first phase dated from the Late Iron Age (8th-7th centuries BCE): "The foundations of some of the walls are on a lower level than others, being embedded in a layer of ash containing numerous sherds of Iron Age II."[14] He dated this stratum to the last century of the Judean monarchy. On the basis of the location of the sherds and the lowest levels of the walls he reconstructed

10. Ibid., 109; cf. Magness, *Archaeology of Qumran*, 28.

11. See Hirschfeld, *Qumran in Context*, 21.

12. Yizhak Magen and Yuval Peleg, "Back to Qumran: Ten Years of Excavation and Research, 1993–2004," in Katharina Galor, Jean-Baptiste Humbert, and Jürgen Zangenberg, eds., *Qumran: The Site of the Dead Sea Scrolls: Archaeological Interpretations and Debates. Proceedings of a Conference Held at Brown University, November 17-19, 2002* (STDJ 57; Leiden: Brill, 2006) 55-113.

13. Roland de Vaux, *Archaeology and the Dead Sea Scrolls* (Schweich Lectures 1959; London: Oxford University Press, for the British Academy, 1973) 1-44. Summaries of de Vaux's understanding of the site can be found in Philip R. Davies, *Qumran* (Cities of the Biblical World; Grand Rapids: Eerdmans, 1982); Magness, *Archaeology of Qumran*, 47-72.

14. De Vaux, *Archaeology and Dead Sea Scrolls*, 1.

the plan of the building: a rectangular building with a large courtyard and a row of rooms running along its eastern wall with one projecting outward at the northwest corner. This plan resembled that of other Judean fortresses. De Vaux assigned the large round cistern (locus 110) to this period, although it did not contain any Iron Age sherds. Fortresses that were not located near springs always included at least one cistern. This cistern is the only round one at Qumran. A final element assigned to this period is a long wall running from the southeast corner of the ruins to the Wadi Qumran. De Vaux's discussion of this period has not been especially controversial. Yitzhar Hirschfeld says that it is "entirely speculative," and yet offers a more specific dating to the reign of King Josiah (639–609 BCE).[15] It is agreed, in any case, that there was a fort at Qumran at the end of the Judean monarchy. It may have been located there to guard against the Edomites.

The site lay vacant for several centuries before it was reoccupied in the Hellenistic period. De Vaux distinguished three periods, of which the first was subdivided into two:

a brief initial settlement (Period Ia);
the period when the settlement got its definitive form (Period Ib), which ended in destruction;
Period II, when it was reoccupied in the Roman period, up to its destruction in 68 CE; and
Period III, a brief period of Roman occupation.

Coins from the Bar Kokhba revolt were also found on the site, indicating that the insurgents had used the abandoned buildings either as a hiding place or as a center of resistance.[16]

Period Ia

The first phase was modest in size. The remains of the Iron Age settlement served as a point of departure. A channel was built to collect the rain water. The round cistern was cleared and two new rectangular pools were dug

---

15. Hirschfeld, *Qumran in Context*, 57-59.
16. De Vaux, *Archaeology and Dead Sea Scrolls*, 45.

out. Some rooms were added in the vicinity of the round cistern, to the north. The plan of the eastern part of the building was unclear. De Vaux admitted that "only some sherds and a few pieces of pottery found beneath the later levels in the southern area of the main building" could be attributed to this phase.[17] This pottery was indistinguishable from that of Period Ib. The coins found on the site indicated that the buildings of Period Ib were certainly occupied under Alexander Jannaeus (103–76 BCE) and that they may have been constructed under John Hyrcanus. The more impressive buildings of Period Ib obliterated the earlier phases.

Jodi Magness, who generally agrees with de Vaux's interpretation of the site, finds "no clear or convincing evidence for de Vaux's Period Ia."[18] It is not identified by distinctive coins or pottery. Her critique at this point raises a question about de Vaux's stratigraphy. De Vaux "used the same locus numbers to designate a single room from the beginning to the end of the excavation, instead of changing the number as he dug through different levels or distinguished different features in the rooms."[19] In this respect, he was no different from other archeologists of his time, but the method makes it difficult to distinguish strata, and sometimes makes the basis for his stratigraphy difficult to discern. Consequently, Jean-Baptiste Humbert says that "despite the evidence of stratification that emerged in the course of excavation, de Vaux never produced a stratigraphic framework. His field notes mentioned time and again the superimposed traces of occupation and collapse, without providing stratigraphic cross-sections."[20] Hirschfeld claims that "the fact that the Qumran excavation was not conducted according to [what later became] the standard stratigraphic conventions . . . pulls the rug out from under most of the chronological conclusions that de Vaux set out

17. Ibid., 5.

18. Magness, *Archaeology of Qumran*, 63. The evidence for de Vaux's Period Ia was already questioned by Philip Davies, "How Not to Do Archaeology: The Story of Qumran," *BA* (1988): 203-7 (repr. in idem, *Sects and Scrolls: Essays on Qumran and Related Topics* [SFSHJ 134; Atlanta: Scholars Press, 1996] 79-86). E. M. Laperoussaz, *Qoumrân, l'établissement essénien des bords de la Mer Morte: Histoire et archéologie du site* (Paris: Picard, 1976), dated the beginning of the settlement to 104–103 BCE.

19. Magness, *Archaeology of Qumran*, 7.

20. Jean-Baptiste Humbert, "Reconsideration of the Archaeological Interpretation," in Jean-Baptiste Humbert and Jan Gunneweg, eds., *Khirbet Qumrân et ʿAïn Feshkha II: Études d'anthropologie, de physique et de chimie. Studies of Anthropology, Physics and Chemistry* (NTOA.SA 3; Fribourg: Academic Press, 2003) 421.

in successive publications."[21] Nonetheless, de Vaux did note different levels, and he evidently believed that there was a layer of occupation below the main buildings of Period Ib.

De Vaux's construction of the development of the site seems to have been guided by the assumption that the first settlers in the Hellenistic period would have used the older structure as a point of departure. This is not an unreasonable assumption in itself, but it lacks the support of a careful stratigraphic analysis, and opens the door for consideration of alternatives. Hirschfeld defends de Vaux's dating of the site to the time of John Hyrcanus, on the grounds that eleven Seleucid coins were found, in diverse locations. He argues that "because each ruler minted his own new coins, the coins found in excavations usually represent a level of occupation relating to the period of the rulers shown on the coin."[22] But this argument is undercut by his own admission that coins remained in circulation for long periods. The small number of Seleucid coins supports Magness's view that the reoccupation of the settlement dates from the time of Alexander Jannaeus. Rachel Bar-Nathan has argued independently that the similarity between the pottery of Hasmonean Jericho and that found at Qumran "seems to indicate that the settlement of these sites did not occur before the time of Alexander Jannaeus, probably around 100/90 B.C.E."[23]

More fundamentally, Hirschfeld and Humbert try to reconstruct the development of the site from its architecture, in the absence of clear stratigraphy. They regard the roughly square structure in the center of the complex, with the tower at its northwest corner, as the original nucleus. Hirschfeld writes: "Looking at the layout of the site, one is immediately struck by the square structure right in the center, that de Vaux called the 'main building.' The main building is notable for its straight walls forming a square built around an inner courtyard and for its corner tower surrounded by a massive stone revetment."[24] Humbert contends that "the archaeological plan of a site must follow a rational organization of coherent elements."[25]

---

21. Hirschfeld, *Qumran in Context,* 53.

22. Ibid., 55.

23. Rachel Bar-Nathan, "Qumran and the Hasmonaean and Herodian Winter Palaces of Jericho: The Implication of the Pottery Finds on the Interpretation of the Settlement at Qumran," in Galor et al., eds., *Qumran,* 277.

24. Hirschfeld, *Qumran in Context,* 60.

25. Humbert, "The Chronology During the First Century B.C.: De Vaux and His Method: A Debate," in Humbert and Gunneweg, eds., *Khirbet Qumrân II,* 432.

Construction evolved outwards from a well-constructed, self-contained core, which alone in the general design presupposes planning . . . its architectural coherence was sufficiently evident to excavators that they labeled it the central or main building. . . . This structure reflects a common architectural layout found throughout the empire, with a central courtyard surrounded by rooms placed at regular intervals.[26]

Magen and Peleg likewise begin their discussion of the Hasmonean settlement, which they, like Magness, date to the beginning of the first century BCE, as follows: "At this time, a solidly-constructed square building was erected around a central courtyard. A square tower was built on the building's northwest corner and, probably, a second smaller one on the northeast corner."[27] Humbert regards this structure as a residence; Hirschfeld and Magen and Peleg regard it as a fortress.

Whether the development of the site necessarily followed this "rational organization," however, may be disputed. De Vaux regarded the construction of this main building not as the original nucleus but as part of the development of the site in his Period Ib. While he may not have found compelling evidence that this structure was later than his supposed Period Ia, neither did he find stratigraphic evidence that the "main building" was earlier than the surrounding structures. Hanan Eshel, who accepts Magness's chronology of the site, grants that "since the pottery found in the foundation trenches of the building has not yet been published, we have no data on which to base a precise date for the construction."[28]

Period Ib

According to de Vaux, the site was greatly expanded in Period Ib, and attained its definitive shape at that time. The main entrance was in the center of the northern side, just north of a substantial tower, south of Locus 141.[29]

---

26. Humbert, "Reconsideration," 422.

27. Magen and Peleg, "Back to Qumran," 102.

28. Hanan Eshel, "Qumran Archaeology," *JAOS* 125 (2005): 389-94.

29. De Vaux, *Archaeology and Dead Sea Scrolls*, 5. De Vaux does not mention the tower in connection with Period Ia, but it appears in the plan of Period Ia in the synthesis of his notes by Jean-Baptiste Humbert, O.P., and Alain Chambon, *Fouilles de Khirbet Qumrân et de Aïn Feshkha*, vol. 1: *Album de photographies, Répertoire du fonds photographique, Synthèse des*

There was another, smaller gateway on the northwestern side (L138) and on the eastern side near a potter's workshop (L84). A passage or corridor divided the site into two parts. To the east was the main building, dominated by the tower in the northwest corner. The western part was centered around the Iron Age building. The main building consisted of rooms grouped around an open courtyard. The largest room (L77) is located south of the main building, and was identified as an assembly hall. Adjacent to this was a pantry (L86), which contained more than a thousand dishes. This suggested that Locus 77 also served as a dining room or refectory. It was designed so that the floor could be washed with water from a channel, draining through a doorway in the southeastern wall. Several stepped pools and an elaborate water system were also assigned to this period. Also noteworthy were several deposits of animal bones in the free spaces between the buildings. These were deposited between large sherds of pitchers or pots, or placed in jars. In one instance they were covered by a plate.[30]

De Vaux found two pieces of evidence relevant to the end of Period Ib: an earthquake and a fire.[31] The effects of an earthquake are clearly apparent in two cisterns at the eastern side of the main building. The steps and floor of the larger of these cisterns (L48, 49) are split, and the eastern part is sunk about 50 cm. lower than the western part. The crack was prolonged into the neighboring cistern (L50). The eastern wall of the tower was cracked. The pantry collapsed, burying the store of dishes mentioned above. De Vaux attributed this damage to a famous earthquake in the seventh year of Herod the Great, or 31 BCE, which is recorded by Josephus in *Ant.* 15.121-47 and *J.W.* 1.370-80. He also found evidence of destruction by fire, prior to the destruction by the Romans in 68 CE. De Vaux thought it the simplest solution to suppose that the earthquake had caused the fire, but admitted that the evidence was inconclusive. Other scholars supposed that Qumran had been burned by the Parthians and their Hasmonean ally Antigonus in 40–39 BCE.[32]

---

notes de chantier du Père Roland de Vaux OP (NTOA.SA 1; Fribourg: Éditions Universitaires, 1994) 15. This plan is not reproduced in the English translation and revision by Stephen J. Pfann, *The Excavations of Khirbet Qumran and Ain Feshkha: Synthesis of Roland de Vaux's Field Notes* (NTOA.SA 1B; Fribourg: University Press, 2003).

30. For a full account of Period Ib see de Vaux, *Archaeology and Dead Sea Scrolls*, 5-24; Magness, *Archaeology of Qumran*, 50-56.

31. De Vaux, *Archaeology and Dead Sea Scrolls*, 20.

32. So E. M. Laperrousaz, "Remarques sur les circonstances qui ont entouré la de-

After the destruction, the site lay vacant for a time. Sediment from the disrupted water system was found above the layer of ash from the fire. Only ten coins of Herod the Great were identified, and these were associated with coins from the first century CE.[33] (An eleventh Herodian coin was later discovered.)[34] De Vaux concluded that the site was not occupied for most of Herod's reign. Moreover, in Locus 120 a hoard of 561 silver pieces was found, in three pots.[35] Two of the pots were of types foreign to those found at Qumran. These pots were buried beneath the level of Period II and above Ib. The hoard consists mainly of Tyrian tetradrachmae, the coins used for the payment of the temple tax. Similar hoards consisting mostly of Tyrian tetradrachmae have been found at a number of sites in Palestine.[36] Some of the coins date from the last Seleucid kings, but most belong to the autonomous currency of Tyre. The latest coin in the hoard dates from 9/8 BCE. De Vaux concluded that the hoard was buried shortly after that date, either while the site was vacant or when it was reoccupied.[37] Further, coins found in rubble included coins from the Seleucid and Hasmonean periods, but none from the reign of Herod. There was one coin of Archelaus (4 BCE to 6 CE) in this lot, but de Vaux supposed that this had been lost during the work of clearing.

De Vaux believed that debris found in the excavation contained material cleared out when the site was reoccupied. Some of this debris was found north of the ruins. It contained only pottery of Period Ib and corresponding coins. Other debris formed a heap outside the walls.[38] Structures

---

struction des bâtiments de Qumrân à la fin de la Période Ib de leur occupation," *VT* 7 (1957): 337-49; J. T. Milik, *Ten Years of Discovery in the Wilderness of Judaea* (trans. J. Strugnell; SBT 1/26; London: SCM, 1959) 52.

33. De Vaux, *Archaeology and Dead Sea Scrolls*, 22-23.

34. Catherine M. Murphy, *Wealth in the Dead Sea Scrolls and in the Qumran Community* (STDJ 40; Leiden: Brill, 2002) 306-7. The coin was found by Magen Broshi and Hanan Eshel.

35. De Vaux, *Archaeology and Dead Sea Scrolls*, 34.

36. Donald T. Ariel, "A Survey of Coin Finds in Jerusalem (Until the End of the Byzantine Period)," *SBFLA* 32 (1982): 273-326; M. Thompson, O. Mørkholm, and C. M. Kraay, *An Inventory of Greek Coin Hoards* (New York: American Numismatic Society, 1973) 221-24.

37. When de Vaux wrote, Tyrian tetradrachmae were not attested for the period 8 BCE to 1 BCE, but examples were subsequently discovered. See Murphy, *Wealth in Dead Sea Scrolls*, 311.

38. De Vaux, *Archaeology and Dead Sea Scrolls*, 25.

that had been damaged were strengthened. The tower was consolidated by stones piled up against it, giving the appearance of a rampart. Some other walls were also buttressed in this way. The stepped pools damaged by the earthquake were not repaired, however, and the collapsed pantry was not cleared or restored.

The end of Period Ib has proven no less controversial than its beginning. Magness questions whether an earthquake would have caused the site to be abandoned for thirty years. She continues:

> In fact, scholars have wondered why the community at Qumran (assuming they were Essenes) would have felt it necessary to abandon the site, since Josephus indicates that Herod the Great held the Essenes in high regard. Also, how is it that after such a long period the site was reoccupied by the same population with the buildings being put to the same use? And where did the community go for 30 years?[39]

She finds a solution in the hoard of coins found in Locus 120, which de Vaux believed had been buried when the site was reoccupied. Magness argues that it is more likely to have been buried before the site was abandoned: "Hoards are often buried in times of trouble and can remain buried if the owner fails to return and retrieve the valuables. It is reasonable to assume that the hoard at Qumran was buried because of some impending danger or threat, and remained buried because the site was subsequently abandoned for some time. For whatever reason, the hoard was never retrieved even after the site was reoccupied."[40] She further reasons that "the fact that the hoard was buried, combined with the presence of a layer of ash, suggests that the fire which destroyed the settlement should be attributed to human agents instead of to natural causes. In other words, in 9/8 B.C.E. or some time thereafter, Qumran suffered a deliberate, violent destruction."[41] The exact occasion is unknown, but a possible context is provided by the turmoil that followed the death of Herod the Great (*J.W.* 2.1-79, especially 55-56).

That only eleven coins of Herod, all undated bronzes, were found at the site is still puzzling. Magness dismisses this concern by saying that Herod minted relatively few coins, and that coins of Alexander Jannaeus

---

39. Magness, *Archaeology of Qumran*, 66.
40. Ibid., 67.
41. Ibid.

were still in circulation. But Herod's coins were not so rare. In Jerusalem 462 coins from his reign were found. This number is modest, given the length of the reign (463 coins were found from the much shorter reign of Agrippa I). But the reign of Herod lasted as long at Qumran as it did at Jerusalem, and one would expect a greater cumulative total than what was found.[42] Tyrian coins from this period were found in the hoard. Ya'akov Meshorer has argued that Herod may have minted Tyrian coins himself,[43] and so the number of Herodian coins would be greater. The hoard was evidently related in some way to the temple tax; and as Magness herself has argued, it fits the profile of a savings hoard rather than an emergency one, since it is selective with respect to the kinds of coins it includes.[44] Such hoards typically represent the savings of the owners over a number of years. It was not necessarily buried in an emergency. Nonetheless, that it remained buried, and included no coins later than the reign of Herod, supports Magness's conclusion that the site was abandoned after it was buried rather than before.

Other scholars, including Hirschfeld and Humbert, have questioned de Vaux's identification of the earthquake as that of 31 BCE.[45] It would be surprising if the inhabitants had allowed the stepped pool in Locus 48/49 and the pantry to remain in disrepair while they continued to live at the site for most of a century. Moreover, de Vaux noted in his field notes for Locus 72 that "evidence was found that the main channel was cut by the

---

42. See Magen Broshi, "The Archaeology of Qumran," in Devorah Dimant and Uriel Rappaport, eds., *The Dead Sea Scrolls after Forty Years* (STDJ 10; Leiden: Brill, 1992) 107, following Ariel, "Survey of Coin Finds," especially 287 and 322. On Herod's coinage see more generally Ya'akov Meshorer, *Ancient Jewish Coinage*, vol. 2: *Herod the Great through Bar Cochba* (Dix Hills, NY: Amphora, 1982) 5-30; idem, *Jewish Coins of the Second Temple Period* (Tel Aviv: Am Hassefer, 1967) 64-68; Peter Richardson, *Herod: King of the Jews and Friend of the Romans* (Columbia, S.C.: University of South Carolina Press, 1996) 211-15.

43. Meshorer, *Ancient Jewish Coinage*, 2.6-9.

44. Jodi Magness, "Qumran Archaeology: Past Perspectives and Future Prospects," in Peter W. Flint and James C. VanderKam, eds., *The Dead Sea Scrolls after Fifty Years* (2 vols.; Leiden: Brill, 1998–99) 1.74.

45. Hirschfeld, *Qumran in Context*, 54; Humbert, "The Chronology of the First Century B.C.: De Vaux and His Method: A Debate," in Humbert and Gunneweg, eds., *Khirbet Qumrân II*, 436-37; idem, "Some Remarks on the Archaeology of Qumran," in Galor et al., eds., *Qumran*, 31. See also Yizhak Magen and Yuval Peleg, "Back to Qumran: Ten Years of Excavation and Research, 1993–2004," in Galor et al., eds., *Qumran*, 107. Magen and Peleg allow that the site was damaged by the earthquake of 31 BCE, but deny that the damage to the stepped pool and the pantry dates from that time.

earthquake."[46] This would have cut off the supply of water to several pools, including the large stepped pool in Locus 71.[47] Consequently, the possibility arises that the damage resulted from earthquakes long after the site had been abandoned. Earthquakes are known to have occurred in the area in 363 CE and 749 CE, and it is also possible that the damage was caused by a local tremor, not otherwise recorded. Hirschfeld and Humbert also deny that there was any level of violent destruction at the end of Period Ib.[48]

De Vaux, however, claimed that he found clear evidence of a fire, and this evidence cannot be simply "forgotten," as Humbert would have it.[49] Magen and Peleg suggest that the site may have been burned after the Roman invasion in 63 BCE.[50] Earlier scholars thought of the Parthian invasion of 40 BCE, as we have seen. Magness associates the fire with the burying of the hoard near the end of the first century BCE. But we must accept in any case that the site was destroyed by fire at the end of Period Ib. It also seems likely that the site sustained damage from the earthquake of 31 BCE. Magen and Peleg agree with de Vaux that several buildings were strengthened after the earthquake, including the tower, which "had to be supported by a surrounding stone glacis, at the expense of the room to the south of the tower (locus 12) and part of the hall to the east (loci 38 and 41)."[51] Hirschfeld claims that a probe on the western side of the tower showed that the wall behind the glacis or buttress was not finished like the other walls, and so that the buttress was part of the original construction.[52] This is disputed by Magness, who argues that the walls would have been covered with mud plaster anyway, and notes that the rampart blocked two windows in the tower.[53] The extension of the buttress into the surrounding rooms suggests that it was strengthened while the site was in use. This is not the only instance where walls were strengthened. Also, the pantry area was sealed off with a stone wall, and this too must have been done while the site was occupied.[54] If there is evidence of some earthquake damage in

46. Humbert and Chambon, *Excavations of Khirbet Qumran*, 37.

47. Humbert, "Chronology," 437.

48. Hirschfeld, *Qumran in Context*, 54; Humbert, "Chronology," 437.

49. Humbert, "Chronology," 437.

50. Magen and Peleg, "Back to Qumran," 106.

51. Ibid., 106.

52. Hirschfeld, *Qumran in Context*, 69.

53. Magness, review of Hirschfeld, *Qumran in Context, RBL* 08/27/2005.

54. Magness, *Archaeology of Qumran*, 57.

the first century BCE, it seems gratuitous to posit a second later earthquake, however surprising it may be that the damaged pools and pantry were not repaired.

In all, then, the evidence for the end of Period Ib is inconclusive. If we accept Magness's argument from the coin hoard, the period lasted until the end of Herod's reign. It is not impossible, however, that a transition occurred earlier, and that the hoard was buried by the people who reoccupied the site, as de Vaux had supposed. Hirschfeld distinguishes the Herodian period as Stratum III and attributes the expansion of the site beyond the main building to this period, but stratigraphic evidence is lacking.[55] There seems to be a consensus, however, in rejecting de Vaux's theory that the site was vacated for thirty years during Herod's reign. As Magen Broshi has argued, the accumulation of silt does not require such a long period.[56] At most, the site was vacated for only a few years.[57]

Period II

Even though de Vaux supposed that the site was vacant for thirty years, he still wrote,

> The period of abandonment was in fact of short duration, and the community which came to re-settle Khirbet Qumran was the same as that which had left it. The general plan remained, in effect, the same, and the principal elements were put to use once more for the purposes for which they had originally been intended. The necessary clearance and repairs were made, but only secondary modifications were introduced to the buildings.[58]

The settlement was destroyed again by fire at the end of this period. Arrowheads found in the debris are characteristic of those used by the Romans, and indicate that the destruction was caused by military action.

---

55. Hirschfeld, *Qumran in Context*, 87-88.

56. Broshi, "Archaeology of Qumran," 111. Broshi is also influenced by Josephus's report that Herod was favorable to the Essenes.

57. Broshi, writing in 1992, dated the interruption to 31–26 BCE. Magness, arguing on the basis of the coin hoard, puts it some thirty years later.

58. De Vaux, *Archaeology and Dead Sea Scrolls*, 24.

Ninety-four coins from the Jewish Revolt were associated with Period II. The latest dates to 68/69 CE, the third year of the revolt. The Romans occupied Jericho in the summer of 68 CE, and Vespasian advanced to the Dead Sea, where he had some bound men thrown into the water, to see whether they would float (they did).[59] De Vaux concluded reasonably that Qumran was destroyed by the Romans.

Two aspects of this period are controversial. One is the date of its beginning, which varies inevitably with the date assigned to the end of Period Ib. Humbert, for example, posits continuous occupation from 40/30 BCE to 68 CE.[60] The second controversial aspect is whether the occupants and function of the site were the same as in the previous period. Humbert accepts that the site was occupied by the Essenes in the first century CE but argues that "between the construction of the iron age fort and the Essene settlement there would have been time for a Hasmonean interlude."[61] Magen and Peleg, who hold that the site had been a fort in the Hasmonean period, claim that "the greatest change which the site underwent occurred following the Roman occupation of Palestine in the year 63 B.C.E. . . . . After the Roman conquest the site probably changed hands, perhaps more than once, and became a center for the production of clay vessels and perhaps also for trade with dates and date honey."[62] Hirschfeld also thinks that it was originally a fortress, but ceased to function as such in the Herodian period.[63] He argues that "it is reasonable to assume that the modification of the site took place at some time at the beginning of Herod's reign, which was a period of economic boom in Judea in general and in the Dead Sea Valley in particular."[64] All of these theories are based on the "architectural" view of the development of the site, according to which it was originally a square fort, and subsequently expanded, and also on inferences about what might have been expected to happen in light of the history of the period, especially the Roman conquest and the rise of Herod.

There is no dispute about the destruction of Qumran in 68 CE.

---

59. Josephus, *J.W.* 4.476; de Vaux, *Archaeology and Dead Sea Scrolls*, 38. De Vaux's arguments are summarized by Magness, *Archaeology of Qumran*, 62.

60. Humbert, "Chronology," 437.

61. Humbert, "Reconsideration," 422.

62. Magen and Peleg, "Back to Qumran," 106.

63. Hirschfeld, *Qumran in Context*, 60, 88.

64. Ibid., 54.

Period III

The site was occupied briefly by the Romans after its destruction, as shown by the presence of Roman coins, including four with the legend *Judaea Capta,* ascribed to Titus. Only part of the ruins was occupied. The tower was reutilized, and the wall extending eastward from it was doubled in thickness. De Vaux explained the occupation by "the continuing need for the Romans to keep watch on the shores of the Dead Sea. From the plateau of Qumran the view extends over the whole of the western shore from the mouth of the Jordan to Ras Feshka and over the whole southern half of the sea."[65] De Vaux suggested that this occupation would have lasted until the fall of Masada in 73 or 74 CE. There is also evidence of small-scale occupation by the insurgents during the Bar Kokhba revolt, fifty years later. Joan Taylor, however, followed by Hirschfeld, has argued on the basis of coin evidence that a small population continued to live at the site into the early decades of the second century and possibly through to 135 CE.[66] Magen and Peleg argue that all the post–68 coins may have been deposited during the Bar Kokhba rebellion. They argue that "it is highly unlikely that a Roman garrison would have been stationed at a burnt out, abandoned site whose water supply system was no longer operative."[67] It is clear enough that the full water system of the pre–68 CE period was not restored, but it was not needed. De Vaux reasonably supposed that the Romans kept only the large cistern (L71 in the southeast) and filled it by a new channel.[68]

Population and Living Quarters

De Vaux estimated that the site was occupied by a population of no more than 200 people.[69] This estimate was based on the assumption that the 1,200 people buried in the cemetery lived at the site over a period of nearly

65. De Vaux, *Archaeology and Dead Sea Scrolls,* 42.

66. Joan E. Taylor, "Khirbet Qumran in Period III," in Galor et al., eds., *Qumran,* 133-46; cf. Hirschfeld, *Qumran in Context,* 164.

67. Magen and Peleg, "Back to Qumran," 109.

68. De Vaux, *Archaeology and Dead Sea Scrolls,* 43; Magness, *Archaeology of Qumran,* 62-63.

69. De Vaux, *Archaeology and Dead Sea Scrolls,* 86.

two hundred years. They would have been supported by the nearby farm at Ein Feshka. J. T. Milik offered a slightly lower estimate of 150-200.[70] Magen Broshi estimates that the assembly hall (L77) could accommodate 120 to 150 men. He allows that there may have been some more people at the site who were not full members of the community, and so the whole community might have numbered 150-200.[71]

De Vaux believed that most of the buildings were used for community purposes, and included very few rooms suitable for living quarters. He noted, "There is a manifest disproportion between the number of the tombs and the number of inhabitants for whom there was room in the buildings." Some of the leaders of the group may have lived on the site, but the majority must have lived elsewhere. He distinguished between the manmade caves in the marl terrace and the natural caves in the cliffs. Objects found in the manmade caves included vases, scraps of leather and rope, and a mat, and these showed that these caves were in fact inhabited. Some of the natural caves may also have been habitable. He also suggested that some of the residents might have lived in tents or huts.[72]

A survey by Joseph Patrich in 1983, however, found no evidence of dwellings outside the site. He argued that "if the living quarters were really outside, one would expect to find a network of constructed paths to connect these quarters with the communal center."[73] He concluded that the inhabitants lived on the upper story of the buildings, and that they numbered only 50-70. (He later reduced this estimate to 30-50.)[74] Patrich, nonetheless, subscribes to the view that the site was a sectarian settlement, and offers an interesting explanation of the size of the cemetery: "The cemetery at Qumran may have served as a central burial ground for community members from Jerusalem and other mixed settlements in Judea."[75]

70. Milik, *Ten Years,* 97.

71. Broshi, "Archaeology of Qumran," 114.

72. De Vaux, *Archaeology and Dead Sea Scrolls,* 56-57.

73. Joseph Patrich, "Khirbet Qumran in Light of New Archaeological Explorations in the Qumran Caves," in Michael O. Wise et al., eds., *Methods of Investigation of the Dead Sea Scrolls and the Khirbet Qumran Site: Present Realities and Future Prospects* (ANYAS 722; New York: New York Academy of Sciences, 1994) 73-95.

74. Patrich, "Did Extra-mural Dwelling Quarters Exist at Qumran?" in Lawrence H. Schiffman, Emanuel Tov, and James C. VanderKam, eds., *The Dead Sea Scrolls: Fifty Years after Their Discovery* (Jerusalem: Israel Exploration Society, 2000) 720-27.

75. Ibid., 727.

The adjective "central," however, would seem to be poorly chosen, given the location of Qumran.

Broshi and Hanan Eshel explored the caves in the 1990s and confirmed evidence of occupation (pottery, food remains, mats, home utensils) in the manmade caves. Contrary to Patrich, they did find evidence for a network of paths. They also explored seven caves on the marl plateau that had not been excavated by de Vaux, and found fragments of jars and jugs. They concluded that most of the inhabitants lived in manmade caves.[76] Patrich responded by arguing that it is inherently unlikely that the members of the community lived permanently in caves. Consider the difficulty of returning to a cave after a late-night study session! He allows that the caves in the marl plateau south of Qumran were inhabited, but says that they would have added only an insignificant number of inhabitants. The new caves discovered by Eshel and Broshi are natural caves, in his view, and unsuitable for habitation. Evidence of habitation in caves shows only temporary lodging, perhaps on the part of postulants. In large part, Patrich's argument rests on the contrast between the meager evidence of cave dwelling at Qumran and the more substantial evidence found at later Christian monasteries in the Judean desert and in Egypt.

Hirschfeld, who rejects the sectarian hypothesis, claims that "there is no reason to assume that the inhabitants of Qumran did not lead a routine existence there, including sleeping, eating, and other mundane activities typical of humans."[77] He supposes that most people lived on the upper floor. Hirschfeld, however, estimates the population of the site in the Hasmonean period as only about 20 people.[78] (An even lower estimate, of 10-15 people, was offered by Humbert.)[79] Hirschfeld allows for a population of 72 in the Herodian period.[80] He bases his estimate on the area of the site, and assumes that the cemetery served a much larger area.

Obviously, a major consideration in this debate is whether one assumes that the people buried in the cemetery lived at the site. If they did,

76. Magen Broshi and Hanan Eshel, "How and Where Did the Qumranites Live?" in Donald W. Parry and Eugene Ulrich, eds., *The Provo International Conference on the Dead Sea Scrolls* (STDJ 30; Leiden: Brill, 1999) 266-73.

77. Hirschfeld, *Qumran in Context*, 88.

78. Ibid., 65.

79. J.-B. Humbert, "L'Espace sacré à Qumran: Propositions pour l'archéologie," *RB* 101 (1994): 175-77.

80. Hirschfeld, *Qumran in Context*, 90.

many must have lived in caves, even if the evidence for cave dwelling is less than conclusive. One's conclusion on this issue, however, will depend to a great degree on the general interpretation of the site.

The Interpretation of the Site

The different reconstructions of the chronology of the site are bound up with different interpretations of its function. De Vaux assumed that it was an Essene settlement from the time of reoccupation in the Hasmonean period to the Roman destruction. This interpretation was virtually unchallenged until the 1980s. In 1982 Philip Davies, a scholar distinguished for his skepticism and iconoclasm, wrote: "Roland de Vaux's work at Qumran was that of a brilliant scholar and a thoroughly competent archaeologist. He combined to an unusual degree the gifts of imagination and commonsense. In presenting the results of the excavations at Qumran, I make no apology for relying, in common with many other scholars, almost exclusively on de Vaux's reports."[81] A few years later, he declared that de Vaux's work was an example of "how not to do archaeology," because he used the scrolls to interpret the site instead of relying purely on archeological evidence.[82] This accusation became a refrain in the 1990s. Since de Vaux was a Dominican priest, his interpretation of the site as a kind of monastery was viewed with great suspicion. (For example, he identified rooms as a "refectory" and a "scriptorium.") But it was not de Vaux who first suggested that the sectarian scrolls were Essene, and he became convinced that the people who wrote these scrolls lived at the site only when he found the same kind of pottery on the site and in the caves. His interpretation of the site has been defended vigorously by such scholars as Magness, Broshi, and Eshel, all of whom are Jewish, with no particular attachment to monasticism. To be sure, de Vaux made heuristic use of monastic analogies in his interpretation of the site, but any other model (a fortress, a villa) is equally heuristic. The physical ruins do not interpret themselves.[83]

Indeed, it will make a crucial difference to the interpretation of the

81. Davies, *Qumran*, 35.

82. Davies, "How Not to Do Archaeology."

83. See the reflections of Edna Ullmann-Margalit, *Out of the Cave: A Philosophical Inquiry into the Dead Sea Scrolls Research* (Cambridge: Harvard University Press, 2006), especially chapter 2, "A Hard Look at 'Hard Facts': The Archaeology of Qumran."

site whether one takes the Scrolls into account. Cave 4 is literally a stone's throw from the settlement and could scarcely be reached without going through it. While no scrolls were found on the actual site (a fact that is hardly surprising since it was destroyed by fire), the caves are linked to the site by the common pottery.[84] Magness has argued forcefully and cogently that an archeologist must make use of all relevant evidence.[85] We will begin, however, by briefly considering the main alternative interpretations on their merits.

A Rustic Villa?

The idea that Qumran was *villa rustica* was put forward in the early 1990s by the Belgian archeologists Robert Donceel and Pauline Donceel-Voûte, who had been invited by Jean-Baptiste Humbert to help prepare material from de Vaux's excavations for publication.[86] They were impressed by the unexpected variety and richness of the objects, especially glass.[87] They argued that the furniture attributed by de Vaux to a scriptorium actually belonged to a *triclinium,* or dining room, on the upper floor. Subsequently, Jean-Baptiste Humbert found that the structure of the Qumran settlement was "reminiscent of the Pompeiian *villa* and, ironically, resembles more the urban *domus* than the *villa rustica* with its expansive distributions."[88] Hirschfeld, who held that the site was a fort in the early part of the first century BCE, thought that "the most striking feature of Herodian Qumran is the numerous industrial installations found in various parts of the site."[89] These included a potter's workshop, a winepress, and a mill for grinding grain. Hundreds of date pits suggest that dates were processed by removing their pits and drying them. Hirschfeld concludes that "it is most

---

84. See Magness, *Archaeology of Qumran,* 43-44.

85. See Magness, "Qumran: The Site of the Dead Sea Scrolls: A Review Article," *RevQ* 22 (2006): 641-64.

86. Robert Donceel and Pauline Donceel-Voûte, "The Archaeology of Khirbet Qumran," in Wise et al., eds., *Methods of Investigation,* 1-38; Pauline Donceel-Voûte, "Les ruines de Qumrân reinterprétées," *Archaeologia* 298 (1994) 24-35.

87. They found records of 150 fragments of glass vessels. See Donceel and Donceel-Voûte, "Archaeology of Khirbet Qumran," 7-9.

88. Humbert, "Reconsideration," 422.

89. Hirschfeld, *Qumran in Context,* 129.

likely that many of the installations at Qumran were connected with the processing of the unique resources of the region, the valuable perfumes and ointments from balsam."[90] But the specific evidence cited in support of this assertion is slight. For example, a "Herodian juglet found in one of the caves near the site and still containing remnants of oil — possibly balsam oil — hints at a perfume industry."[91] But it is not certain either that the juglet was related to the settlement or that it contained balsam.[92] Ancient sources associate the production of balsam with Jericho and Engedi, but not with Ein Feshka. Hirschfeld admits that the inhabitants seem to have subsisted mainly on agriculture.

Hirschfeld argued that Qumran was the center of a rural estate, a local version of the Roman *villa rustica*.[93] The presence of glass and lathe-turned stoneware, and also of coins found at the site, was taken to demonstrate the wealth of the inhabitants and their involvement in the regional economy. Some, admittedly few, imported vessels, such as fine tableware called eastern sigillata, were found among the pottery, and also some perfume bottles and miniature vessels and juglets. A rich collection of about two hundred fragments of stone vessels was found. Architectural remains included a number of column drums and bases. There was a related *villa rustica* and estate at Ein Feshka.[94] Hirschfeld argued that the roughly square shape of the building and the fortified tower resemble other manor houses in Herodian Palestine, including those at Hilkiah's Palace (a villa 9 miles west of Hebron), Horvat 'Eleq at Ramat Hanadiv (near Caesarea), Qasr el-Leja in Samaria, and Rujm el-Hamiri southeast of Hebron.[95] According to Hirschfeld and the Donceels, the main building at Qumran was the *pars urbana,* or residential part, and the surrounding areas and secondary buildings were the *pars rustica* or industrial area.

Even if the fragments of glass, fine ware, and columns are taken to reflect a measure of affluence and involvement in the local economy, this in

---

90. Ibid., 138.

91. Ibid.

92. See Magness's review in *RBL* 08/27/2005; and Joseph Patrich, "Khirbet Qumran in Light of New Archaeological Explorations in the Qumran Caves," in Wise et al., eds., *Methods of Investigation,* 73-95 (91).

93. Hirschfeld, *Qumran in Context,* 142.

94. Ibid., 183-209.

95. Hirschfeld, "Early Roman Manor Houses in Judea and the Site of Khirbet Qumran," *JNES* 57 (1998): 161-89.

itself is not incompatible with the view that Qumran was a religious settlement of the Essenes, or a kind of monastery. Christian monasteries in the Middle Ages and later were often quite wealthy, although individual monks lived under a vow of poverty. (The wealth of the monasteries was famously appreciated, and appropriated, by Henry VIII in the course of the English Reformation.) Members of the *yaḥad* described in the Scrolls brought their "wealth" or possessions into the community. Monks also have to support themselves, and have typically engaged in agriculture and crafts. Josephus says that after morning prayers the Essenes each went to the craft with which he was familiar (*J.W.* 2.129). Josephus also says that "they regard oil as a defilement, and should any of them be involuntarily anointed, he wipes his body clean" (*J.W.* 2.123), but this does not necessarily mean that they had no use for oil at all.[96]

Other scholars, however, have been impressed rather with the poverty of the site.[97] Magness, like de Vaux, finds that "the repertoire of [pottery] types represented at Qumran is limited and repetitive," and that the various types of fine ware found throughout Judea in this period "are either rare or unattested at Qumran."[98] Catherine Murphy concludes her discussion of archaeological evidence for wealth at Qumran as follows: "The relatively low number of coins, ostraca and documentary texts compared to other Judean desert sites indicates that this economic network was largely characterized by barter between members rather than by purchase and sale with outsiders."[99] She finds only limited evidence of cultural and/or economic connections with Jerusalem on the one side, and Nabatea on the other. In short, signs of affluence are not entirely lacking at Qumran, but the evidence is very limited. The Donceels and Hirschfeld take the presence of any such evidence as decisive; Magness and Murphy emphasize rather its scarcity. Moreover, even Hirschfeld agrees that fine wares and pottery are rare throughout the Dead Sea region:

96. Steve Mason, "Essenes and Lurking Spartans in Josephus' *Judean War:* From Story to History," in Zuleika Rodgers, ed., *Making History: Josephus and Historical Method* (JSJSup 110; Leiden: Brill, 2007) 255, points out the avoidance of oil is a common topos also in accounts of the Spartans.

97. See the comments of James H. Charlesworth in the discussion of the Donceels' paper in Wise et al., eds., *Methods of Investigation,* 36.

98. Jodi Magness, "The Community at Qumran in Light of Its Pottery," in Wise et al., eds., *Methods of Investigation,* 45, and the following discussion, especially p. 50.

99. Murphy, *Wealth in the Dead Sea Scrolls,* 359.

I agree with Magness that this is a regional phenomenon. In the Dead Sea region, eastern terra sigillata and imported amphorae seem to be restricted almost entirely to royal palatial sites such as Jericho and Masada. Because of the high cost of overland transport, only residents of the region's palaces could afford to purchase fine red-slipped dining services or expensive wines and luxury foods.[100]

But while this observation allows Hirschfeld to claim that Qumran is no different from other sites in the Dead Sea region, it undercuts to a great degree his argument about the signs of wealth at the site.

Magness has offered a thorough comparison of Qumran with Judean villas, noting especially the relative lack of decoration and luxury items at Qumran.[101] She considers (1) royal Hasmonean and Herodian palaces at Masada, Herodium, and Herodian Jericho; (2) the private, upper-class urban Jewish mansions of the Herodian period in Jerusalem; (3) Hilkiah's palace; and (4) recently published early Roman villas at Ramat Hanadiv and Ein ez-Zara (ancient Callirhoe) on the eastern shore of the Dead Sea. The relevance of the first two categories might be questioned: one would expect royal palaces to be more luxurious and there was naturally a difference between urban houses and rural estates. The comparison with the manor houses adduced by Hirschfeld, however, is especially helpful.[102] Horvat 'Eleq at Ramat Hanadiv had a tower similar to that at Qumran, but also has a surrounding wall that forms a fortified enclosure. Finds there include imported amphoras and significant amounts of fine ware. It also has a Roman style bath house with a heating system. Another fortified farmhouse at Ramat Hanadiv called Horvat 'Aqav shows a high standard of construction and at least some of its floors had mosaics. At Callirhoe about twenty column drums were found, reflecting a colonnaded courtyard, and some finely molded stucco fragments were discovered. While the difference in luxury between Qumran and these sites is not as great as in a comparison with Herodian palaces, we are left with the impression that if Qumran was a villa it was an exceptionally poor one.

---

100. Hirschfeld, *Qumran in Context*, 147. Cf. Magness, *Archaeology of Qumran*, 78.

101. Magness, "A Villa at Khirbet Qumran?" in eadem, *Debating Qumran: Collected Essays on Archaeology* (Interdisciplinary Studies in Ancient Culture and Religion 4; Leuven: Peeters, 2004) 17-39; eadem, *Archaeology of Qumran*, 90-100.

102. Magness, "Villa at Khirbet Qumran?" 33-39.

One might also wonder about the location of Qumran as a site for a villa. Hirschfeld claims that in antiquity this was a busy intersection:

> In the Second Temple period, three ancient roads converged at Qumran. The main road ran from Jericho in the north, running along the marl plateau at the foot of the cliff and ending at Wadi Qumran. The second road arrived from En-Gedi and Masada in the south. It took a straight course along the Dead Sea shore to 'Ein Feshkha and then mounted the plateau on which Qumran is situated. This was the main artery connecting the Dead Sea sites of the period with Jericho, and from there with Jerusalem. . . . The third route reached Qumran directly from Jerusalem to the west.[103]

In contrast, Broshi argues that no major road passed by Qumran, only narrow trails.[104] He denies that there could have been a road from Masada in antiquity because the level of the Dead Sea was higher, as can be seen from the harbor at Rujm el-Bahr (Maaganit ha-Melaḥ) and the dry dock at Khirbet Mazin. The main east-west road at the northern end of the Dead Sea always ran between Jerusalem and Jericho.[105] Magness argues that the location of Qumran would be anomalous: "Contemporary villas in Judaea are located in urban settlements like the Jewish Quarter in Jerusalem, by the fresh-water springs at Ein Gedi and Jericho, or by the thermal springs at Ein ez-Zara. Hilkiah's palace sits atop a hill in Idumaea, at an important crossroads."[106] This is not necessarily to say that Qumran was either inaccessible or isolated. The pottery and other objects found at the site show that there was some commerce between Qumran and Jerusalem, Jericho, and other sites in the region.[107] Nonetheless, Qumran would seem to be an unpromising site for a villa.

The greatest difficulty for the villa hypothesis, however, is presented by the presence of at least ten stepped pools (*mikvehs* or *miqva'ot*) and a cemetery with more than a thousand graves. On any interpretation, a cem-

103. Hirschfeld, *Qumran in Context,* 3-4.

104. Magen Broshi, "Was Qumran a Crossroads?" *RevQ* 19 (1999): 273-75.

105. Magness, "Villa at Khirbet Qumran?" 38.

106. Ibid., 37-38.

107. Jürgen Zangenberg, "Opening Up Our View: Khirbet Qumran in a Regional Perspective," in Douglas R. Edwards, ed., *Religion and Society in Roman Palestine: Old Questions, New Approaches* (London: Routledge, 2004) 170-87.

etery of this size presents a problem for the thesis that the site was a villa. Hirschfeld can only suggest that "the cemetery served a far larger population than those living at the site."[108] But this proposal does not account for the peculiar character of this cemetery, with a preponderance of male burials, a point to which we will return below.

For most observers, the aqueduct and pools constitute the most striking feature of the Qumran site. There are three large pools without steps: the round cistern in Locus 110, Locus 91, and Locus 58, which is thought to have been created after the earthquake, when the stepped pool in Locus 56 was divided in two. According to Bryant Wood, Loci 110 and 91 would have provided enough water for two hundred people and their animals during the dry season (mid-March to mid-November).[109] Ronny Reich identified ten of the sixteen pools as *miqva'ot*, pools for ritual immersion, of a type that became common in the last century before the turn of the era.[110] Some of these have small partitions on the upper part of their stairs, presumably to separate the pure from the impure. The Qumran pools are considerably larger than most contemporary *miqva'ot*, a fact that may have been necessitated by the desert location and by the size of the community using them.

A few scholars have disputed the identification of these pools as *miqva'ot*.[111] Hirschfeld accepts the identification in most cases, but he claims that "it is now clear that the number of *mikvehs* at Qumran is not exceptional but is close to the norm in houses owned by affluent Judean Jews of the period."[112] These pools occupy approximately 17 percent of the site of Qumran, and similar *miqva'ot* occupy about 15 percent of the space in private houses in Jerusalem in the Upper City and near the gates of the Temple Mount. Reich suggests that the abundance of these in Jerusalem was due to the high proportion of priests in the vicinity of the temple. The priests would have used these pools to purify themselves from consuming their shares of the priestly offerings. Reich suggests that the abundance of pools at Qumran served a similar purpose, in connection with the communal

---

108. *Qumran in Context*, 162.

109. Bryant G. Wood, "To Dip or Sprinkle? The Qumran Cisterns in Perspective," *BASOR* 256 (1984): 45-60; Magness, *Archaeology of Qumran*, 147.

110. Ronny Reich, "Miqwa'ot at Khirbet Qumran and the Jerusalem Connection," in Schiffman et al., eds., *Dead Sea Scrolls: Fifty Years After*, 728-31.

111. For example, Magen and Peleg, whose theory is discussed below.

112. Hirschfeld, *Qumran in Context*, 128.

meal.[113] The analogy supports the view that the inhabitants of Qumran were priestly, and greatly concerned with purity. None of the manor houses discussed by Hirschfeld has a similar multiplicity of *miqva'ot*.[114]

The stepped pools and the cemetery pose a greater problem for Hirschfeld's formulation of the villa hypothesis than for that of Humbert, who believes that the site became an Essene settlement at the beginning of the Herodian period. Humbert's hypothesis would require that most of the pools were added at that time.[115]

A Pottery Factory?

Magen and Peleg have proposed a novel interpretation of the stepped pools at Qumran.[116] They allow that two or three of these pools (Loci 68, 138, and 118) may have been ritual baths, but they contend that the others were not, since the water was collected by a channel and passed through sedimentation basins.[117] Rather, they propose that "the main purpose of the entire complex water system, with its channels and pools, was to provide potter's clay."[118] Their basis for this assertion is that when they excavated the largest reservoir (L71) they found a thick layer of clay, which they describe as "high-quality potter's clay."

This rather astounding claim cries out for parallels: is there any other known case where stepped pools were constructed for this purpose? Magen and Peleg do not cite any. Neither do they cite any evidence that the

---

113. Reich, "Miqwa'ot at Khirbet Qumran," 731.

114. Magness, "Villa at Khirbet Qumran?" 35. Hirschfeld, *Qumran in Context,* 128, refers to sites with two or three *miqva'ot,* and one with four.

115. On the difficulty of dating the pools, see Katharina Galor, "Plastered Pools: A New Perspective," in Humbert and Gunneweg, eds., *Khirbet Qumrân II,* 291-320, especially 308.

116. Magen and Peleg, "Back to Qumran." See also their preliminary excavation report, *The Qumran Excavations 1993-2004: Preliminary Report* (Jerusalem: Israel Antiquities Authority, 2007).

117. "Back to Qumran," 89. Their interpretation does not seem to be supported by the Mishnaic texts that they cite, *m. Miqva'ot* 1:4, 7. Magness claims that decantation basins or small pools are sometimes found in association with contemporary *miqva'ot* elsewhere in Judea, including the Hasmonean palaces at Jericho (review of *Qumran: Site of the Dead Sea Scrolls, RevQ* 22 [2006]: 654).

118. "Back to Qumran," 68.

pottery found at the site was made from clay collected in the pools. Some pottery was certainly made at Qumran, but about half the vessels analyzed were made from Jerusalem clay.[119] The pottery found at Qumran is closely related to that found in Jericho. Rachel Bar-Nathan suggests that "the similarity between the two sites may hint to a common workshop," wherever that was located.[120] Magness has argued that it would be difficult to transport pottery from Qumran to other locations, because of the problem of breakages.[121] Without some supporting evidence, the theory that the stepped pools were designed to collect clay for pottery must be dismissed as unfounded speculation.[122]

A Military Fort?

The idea that Qumran was a military fort has at least some initial plausibility. It is agreed that there was a fort there in the preexilic period. It was evidently destroyed by military assault in 68 CE. De Vaux believed that the Romans maintained a small garrison there after the site was destroyed. He noted that "from the plateau of Qumran the view extends over the whole of the western shore from the mouth of the Jordan to Ras Feshka and over the whole southern half of the sea."[123] The question then arises whether it may not also have been a fort for part or all of its history, from Hasmonean times to its destruction by the Romans.

119. Joseph Yellin, Magen Broshi, and Hanan Eshel, "Pottery of Qumran and Ein Ghuweir: The First Chemical Exploration of Provenience," *BASOR* 321 (2001): 65-78; Magness, *Archaeology of Qumran*, 74. Frederick E. Zeuner, "Notes on Qumran," *PEQ* 92 (1960): 27-36, concluded that the sediment that washed into Qumran's pools was not conducive to the manufacture of ceramic vessels.

120. Rachel Bar-Nathan, "Qumran and the Hasmonaean and Herodian Winter Palaces of Jericho: The Implication of the Pottery Finds on the Interpretation of the Settlement at Qumran," in Galor et al., eds., *Qumran*, 277. She also suggests that "ceramics produced at the site were distributed to other sites in the region," but does not cite specific evidence that pottery found in Jericho was produced at Qumran.

121. Review of *Qumran: Site of the Dead Sea Scrolls*, 656. Cf. *Archaeology of Qumran*, 74.

122. See further the review by Kenneth Atkinson of Galor et al., eds., *Qumran: Site of the Dead Sea Scrolls*, RBL 3/8/2008: "Magen and Peleg make a claim that not only goes beyond the evidence but enters the realm of speculation."

123. De Vaux, *Archaeology and Dead Sea Scrolls*, 42.

In the Hasmonean era there was a chain of fortresses in the general area of the Dead Sea. Most of these were built in the wake of the expansion of the Hasmonean state under John Hyrcanus, Aristobulus, and Alexander Jannaeus. The northern end of this chain was Alexandrion-Sartaba and Dok, near Jericho.[124] The fortress of Kypros protected the main road to Jerusalem. There were fortified docks at Rujm al-Bahr and Khirbet Mazin, south of Qumran. Inland from Qumran was Hyrcania. Far to the south stood Masada. On the Jordanian side of the Dead Sea was the fortress of Machaerus, built by Alexander Jannaeus as a bulwark against the Nabateans. Norman Golb suggested that Qumran, with its tower on the west side of the Dead Sea, could receive communications from Machaerus, either by fire signals or carrier pigeon.[125] Another tower, at Ein el-Turabeh, south of Qumran, directly across the Dead Sea from Machaerus, would seem to be located more suitably for this purpose.

Magen and Peleg argue that "Qumran was, thus, an integral element in the chain of fortifications and early warning stations along the Dead Sea."[126] They recognize that "this was not a fortress capable of withstanding the assault of an attacking enemy, but rather a forward observation and supervision point which controlled land and sea traffic along the Dead Sea coast." They suggest that it was the headquarters of the commander of the Dead Sea coast, subordinate to the main headquarters at Hyrcania.[127] The site lacks the monumental architecture of the Hasmonean fortresses.[128] If the sect described in the Scrolls was hostile to the Hasmoneans, as is generally assumed, it is difficult to imagine that it would have been allowed to occupy a site that is encircled by Hasmonean fortresses, or indeed that the members would choose such a site. Even if, as I have argued, the conflict between the Teacher and the Wicked Priest occurred after the death of Alexander Jannaeus, when Salome Alexandra and Hyrcanus II endorsed the

---

124. The fortress of Dok was in existence before the Hasmoneans rose to power. See 1 Macc 9:50; 16:11-17; Josephus, *Ant.* 13.230-34. This is where Simon Maccabee was murdered by Ptolemy, son of Abubus.

125. Norman Golb, *Who Wrote the Dead Sea Scrolls? The Search for the Secret of Qumran* (New York: Scribner, 1995) 39.

126. Magen and Peleg, "Back to Qumran," 82.

127. Ibid.

128. Golb claims that the tower and surrounding walls were originally covered with slabs of thick limestone, but that these were removed over the centuries (*Who Wrote the Dead Sea Scrolls?* 38).

teachings of the Pharisees, the problem is not resolved, since the site evidently flourished down to the end of the Hasmonean period. The hypothesis that the site was a fortress or observation point, at least in the Hasmonean period, is therefore attractive.

The main objections to the view that Qumran was a fortress arise from the great number of stepped pools and the cemetery. It is difficult to see why a small garrison would have required so many *miqva'ot*. Magen and Peleg avoid this difficulty, since they believe that it ceased to be a fortress when the Romans conquered Judea, and suppose that most of the pools were introduced after this time.[129] The viability of this proposal, then, depends on their view of the development of the site, based on architecture rather than stratigraphy.

Golb argues that the graves in the cemetery "are obviously better interpreted as the graves of the warriors who fought at Qumran," and claims that the regular rows and style of burial suggest that all the graves were dug at once.[130] But it would be surprising if Josephus made no mention of a battle in which 1,200 people were killed, and who should we suppose performed such orderly burials in the wake of a military disaster?[131] No cemetery has been found beside any other fortress in Judea.

Magen and Peleg, in contrast, argue that the number of graves is reasonable in view of the length of the occupation of the site.[132] (They suppose that it had been occupied for some 130 years in the First Temple period and again for about 170 years in the Second Temple period.) The scarcity of female skeletons would not be surprising if this were a military garrison. But this would require that the same style of burial persisted from the seventh century BCE to the Common Era. If all or most of the graves are assigned to a period of about 150 years around the turn of the era, then the rate of burials would be approximately eight per year, which is high for a troop of young men in what was mostly peacetime.

129. Magen and Peleg, "Back to Qumran," 88.

130. Golb, *Who Wrote the Dead Sea Scrolls?* 34.

131. John R. Bartlett, "The Archaeology of Qumran," in J. R. Bartlett, ed., *Archaeology and Biblical Interpretation* (London: Routledge, 1997) 87: "a carefully dug and well laid out cemetery seems unlikely for the losers."

132. Magen and Peleg, "Back to Qumran," 97.

A Religious, Sectarian Settlement?

Most scholars have assumed that the site was occupied by the community that preserved the Scrolls, which is called the *yaḥad* in the *Community Rule*. Frank Cross and Esther Eshel have claimed actually to find mention of the *yaḥad* on an ostracon found at the site.[133] (An ostracon is a piece of broken pottery used for writing.)

The So-called Yaḥad Ostracon

This Hebrew ostracon was found by James F. Strange in the winter of 1996 while investigating the marl terrace at Qumran. It was found at the base of the wall separating the settlement from the cemetery, on the east side, apparently in a dump.[134] Cross and Eshel read the first half of the inscription as follows:

> In year two of the [ ]
> in Jericho, Ḥōnî so[n of] gave
> to 'El'azar son of Naḥămanî[ ]
> Ḥisdai from Ḥōlôn[ ]
> from this day to perpetui[ty]
> the boundaries of the house and[ ]
> and the figs, the ol[ives(?)]
> when he fulfills (his oath) to the community [ ][135]

They relate this document to the requirement that new members hand over their property to the community: "we are dealing here with a deed of gift written in Qumran Hebrew, addressed to a man, which is a rare occurrence in the Second Temple period. Its subject matter is of great importance. The deed is not a grant to a family member, but, we believe, to a

---

133. F. M. Cross and E. Eshel, "Ostraca from Khirbet Qumrân," *IEJ* 47 (1997): 17-28; idem, "The Missing Link: Does a New Inscription Establish a Connection between Qumran and the Dead Sea Scrolls?" *BAR* 24/2 (1998): 48-53, 69; idem, "1. Khirbet Qumran Ostracon," in Stephen J. Pfann et al., *Qumran Cave 4*, vol. XXVI: *Cryptic Texts and Miscellanea, Part 1* (DJD 36; Oxford: Clarendon, 2000) 497-507 and plate XXXIII.

134. Cross and Eshel, "Ostraca from Khirbet Qumrân," 26, say that it "ended up in a dump outside the perimeter wall of the site."

135. Cross and Eshel, "1. Khirbet Qumrân Ostracon," 500.

member of the community living where the ostracon was found, namely the bursar of the sectarian community."[136]

But this reading of the ostracon has been challenged. The Israeli epigrapher Ada Yardeni reads the same lines as follows:

> On the second year of [. . .]
> in Jericho, Ḥny s[on of . . .](?) gave
> To 'El'azar son of N . . .[. . .]
> The . . . [. . .] sacks/sackcloths [. . .]
> . . . . . .[. . .]
> and the walls(?)/coverings(?) of the house(?) of . . .[. . .]
> and the fig-(tree)s, the p[alms (?), . . .(?)]
> and every oth[er(?)] tree[. . .][137]

The crucial eighth line, where Cross and Eshel read *yaḥad* (community), is difficult on either reading. Yardeni's reading is accepted by Elisha Qimron and Émile Puech.[138] Puech also recognizes that the ostracon was not necessarily written at Qumran, since it refers to a transaction in Jericho. But nonetheless he interprets the transaction in a manner similar to Cross and Eshel, as relating to the transfer of property to the community at Qumran, and as confirming definitively the interpretation of the site as a sectarian settlement.[139] He deciphers a few more lines of the inscription than did the editors or Yardeni, and finds a reference to a *mebaqqer,* the term used for the superintendent especially in the *Damascus Rule.* But he admits that this reading is "difficile et désespérée," although he asserts that it is not surprising and rather to be expected.[140] But it is only to be ex-

---

136. Ibid., 505.

137. Ada Yardeni, "A Draft of a Deed on an Ostracon from Khirbet Qumrân," *IEJ* 47 (1997): 233-37; idem, "Breaking the Missing Link: Cross and Eshel Misread the Qumran Ostracon Relating the Settlement to the Dead Sea Scrolls," *BAR* 24/3 (1998): 44-47.

138. Elisha Qimron, "Improving the Editions of the Dead Sea Scrolls" (Hebrew), in Moshe Bar-Asher and Devorah Dimant, eds., *Meghillot: Studies in the Dead Sea Scrolls I* (Hebrew) (Jerusalem: Bialik Institute, 2003) 144-45; Émile Puech, "L'Ostracon de Khirbet Qumrân (KHQ1996/1) et une vente de terrain à Jéricho, témoin de l'occupation Essénienne à Qumran," in Anthony Hilhorst, Émile Puech, and Eibert Tigchelaar, eds., *Flores Florentino: Dead Sea Scrolls and Other Early Jewish Studies in Honour of Florentino García Martínez* (JSJSup 122; Leiden: Brill, 2007) 10.

139. Puech, "L'Ostracon," 25.

140. Ibid., 17.

pected if we are already convinced that the ostracon is related to the community described in the Scrolls. The only basis for this conviction, if the reading *yaḥad* is rejected, is simply the fact that the ostracon was found at Qumran. But this is a very shaky basis, especially since the ostracon was found in a dump, without a clear stratigraphic context. We do not know how this ostracon came to Qumran. The ostracon, as read by Yardeni and Puech, does not speak at all of a donation to a community, and would rather seem to describe a routine sale of property. It lends no support to the interpretation of the site as a religious settlement.

The argument that Qumran was a religious, sectarian settlement is based especially on three features: the burial of animal bones, the cemetery, and the number of *miqva'ot*.

The Burial of Animal Bones

Among the more puzzling discoveries at Qumran were deposits of animal bones in pitchers or pots that were found between or around the buildings. There is no doubt that these bones were the remains of animals used for food. The flesh had been boiled, or less often roasted. De Vaux thought that they indicated "a religious preoccupation."[141] In an early publication he declared that they were "certainly the remains of the sacred banquets of the community,"[142] but he stopped short of associating them with sacrifices. Cross tentatively took them as evidence for a sacrificial cult.[143] Most scholars do not think that sacrifices were offered at Qumran, because there are no remains of an altar.[144] Magness suggests that "since meat was rarely consumed by most people in antiquity, the animal bones at Qumran might therefore represent the remains of occasional sacral or ritual meals that were nonsacrificial."[145] She further suggests that "just as the sectarians considered their communal meals to be a substitute for participation in

---

141. De Vaux, *Archaeology and Dead Sea Scrolls*, 14.

142. In *RB* 63 (1956): 74. See Johannes van der Ploeg, "The Meals of the Essenes," *JSS* 2 (1957): 172.

143. F. M. Cross, *The Ancient Library of Qumran* (3rd ed.; BibSem 30; Sheffield: Sheffield Academic Press, 1995) 86.

144. Jodi Magness, "Communal Meals and Sacred Space at Qumran," in eadem, *Debating Qumran*, 93; contra Jean-Baptiste Humbert, "L'Espace sacré a Qumrân," *RB* 101-2 (1994): 199-203.

145. Magness, "Communal Meals," 94.

the Temple cult, they treated the animals consumed at these meals in a manner analogous to the Temple sacrifices, although they were not technically sacrifices."[146] But it is far from certain that the sectarians considered their meals specifically as a substitute for participation in the cult. Lawrence Schiffman suggests that the bones were buried to keep dogs from eating them. 4QMMT says that dogs "are not to be brought to the sacred camp for they may eat some of the bones from the Sanctuary to which meat is still attached. For Jerusalem is [the sacred camp]."[147] Magness questions this explanation, pointing out that they could have disposed of the bones in the wilderness or buried them in deeper pits.[148] Nonetheless, Schiffman's suggestion seems to me to have merit. The animal bone deposits do not require that the communal meals were substitutes for the temple cult. A concern to prevent scavenging, for reasons of purity, does not require that the site have a religious character.

The Cemetery

As noted at the beginning of this chapter, the cemetery at Qumran was noticed by travelers already in the mid-nineteenth century. De Vaux identified about 1,100 tombs.[149] These were distributed in three cemeteries. The main cemetery was just east of the ruins, one was south of Wadi Qumran, and another lay to the north, about a ten-minute walk away. De Vaux further divided the main cemetery into five sections. The main part lay to the west, and four extensions extended eastward like fingers. He excavated 43 graves in all, 28 in the main cemetery, 9 in the eastern extensions, 2 in the northern cemetery, and 4 in the southern.[150] Ten more graves were excavated by Solomon Steckoll in 1967.[151] All of these were

146. Ibid., 95.

147. Geza Vermes's translation, *The Complete Dead Sea Scrolls in English* (rev. ed.; London: Penguin, 2004) 225. See Lawrence H. Schiffman, *Reclaiming the Dead Sea Scrolls* (Philadelphia: Jewish Publication Society, 1994) 338. Van der Ploeg, "Meals of the Essenes," 173, had already suggested that the bones were buried for reasons of purity.

148. Magness, *Debating Qumran*, 96-97.

149. De Vaux, *Archaeology and Dead Sea Scrolls*, 46.

150. Brian Schultz, "The Qumran Cemetery: 150 Years of Research," *DSD* 13 (2006): 196.

151. S. H. Steckoll, "Preliminary Excavation Report on the Qumran Cemetery," *RevQ* 6 (1968): 323-36.

simple shaft tombs, from 0.8 to 2.5 meters deep, covered by an oval pile of fieldstones. For the most part, they were without grave goods, except for a few that had fragments of pottery or remains of wooden coffins or jewelry. Most were oriented north-south, but ten of the excavated graves had an east-west orientation. Only one male skeleton from Steckoll's excavation was analyzed by anthropologists. The material from his excavation is no longer available.

Similar cemeteries were found at Ein el-Ghuweir, on the western shore of the Dead Sea, south of Qumran and Ein Feshka, and Hiam el-Sagha, south of Ein el-Ghuweir in the Judean desert.[152] Qumran-type graves (shaft tombs with a north-south orientation) have also been found in Jerusalem.[153]

Much of the controversy about the Qumran cemetery has concerned the presence, or scarcity, of female skeletons. Since Pliny had said that the Essenes near the Dead Sea lived "without women," the presence of female skeletons was regarded as a problem for the Essene hypothesis. The excavations of de Vaux and Steckoll yielded 58 skeletons. Initial studies claimed that these included eight to eleven women and six infants. New studies in the 1990s came to slightly different conclusions.[154] Two skeletons that had originally been identified as male and two others that had been undetermined were now classified as female. One skeleton initially identified as female was now tentatively classified as male.[155] Consequently, the number of female skeletons increased to 13 or 14. (It is evidently difficult to distin-

152. For the former see Pesach Bar-Adon, "Another Settlement of the Judean Desert Sect at 'En el-Ghuweir on the Shores of the Dead Sea," *BASOR* 225 (1977): 2-25; for the latter, Magness, *Archaeology of Qumran*, 174; Hanan Eshel and Zvi Greenhut, "Ḥiam el-Sagha, a Cemetery of the Qumran Type, Judaean Desert," *RB* 100 (1993): 252-59.

153. Boaz Zissu, "'Qumran Type' Graves in Jerusalem: Archaeological Evidence of an Essene Community?" *DSD* 5 (1998): 158-71; idem, "Odd Tomb Out: Has Jerusalem's Essene Cemetery Been Found?" *BAR* 25/2 (1999): 50-55, 62.

154. Olav Röhrer-Ertl, Ferdinand Rohrhirsch, and Dietbert Hahn, "Über die Gräbenfelder von Khirbet Qumran insbesondere die Funde der Campagne 1956, I: Anthropologische Datenvorlage und Erstauswertung aufgrund der Collectio Kurth," *RevQ* 19 (1999): 3-47; Röhrer-Ertl, "Facts and Results Based on Skeletal Remains from Qumran Found in the *Collectio Kurth:* A Study in Methodology," in Galor et al., eds., *Site of Dead Sea Scrolls*, 181-93. See now also Susan Guise Sheridan and Jaime Ullinger, "A Reconsideration of the Human Remains in the French Collection from Qumran," in Galor et al., eds., *Site of Dead Sea Scrolls*, 195-212.

155. Schultz, "Qumran Cemetery," 199.

guish the gender of skeletons that are two thousand years old and only partially preserved.)

A new consideration was injected into the discussion in 2000, when Joe Zias argued that the graves that are oriented east-west were not Jewish graves from antiquity, but Bedouin graves that are no more than two hundred years old.[156] His argument rested in part on the presence of jewelry datable to much later periods in three graves that contained female skeletons.[157] Five other female skeletons and four children were also from east-west tombs. Zias argued that all the women and children in the cemetery were intrusive, that is, Bedouin, burials. His arguments were generally welcomed by defenders of the hypothesis that Qumran was an Essene site, and greeted with skepticism by others.[158]

Magen and Peleg report that they excavated nine graves at the southern end of the cemetery. Four of these contained no bones. Four others contained the bones of adults (gender unspecified), and one contained a wooden coffin. Two of the graves without bones contained jars with residue of an organic material, probably date honey.[159]

In 2001 a new survey of the cemetery was conducted by Hanan Eshel and Magen Broshi.[160] They located 1,054 graves, and also detected 124 potential graves by Ground Penetrating Radar. Of these, 999 are oriented north-south and 55 are east-west. They discovered that in addition to the graves that had been excavated officially, 31 others had been robbed. One of these robbed tombs yielded fragments of a zinc coffin. A small square structure, thought to be a mourning enclosure (Tomb 1000), was found to contain the partial remains of two women in secondary burial in a shallow grave. These were dated to the Second Temple period by Carbon-14 tests. Below these bones there was a primary burial, 1.10 meters below the surface, oriented east-west, with a cooking pot from the first half of the first

156. Joseph E. Zias, "The Cemeteries of Qumran and Celibacy: Confusion Laid to Rest?" *DSD* 7 (2000): 220-53.

157. See C. Clamer, "Jewellery Finds from the Cemetery," in Humbert and Gunneweg, eds., *Khirbet Qumrân II*, 173, 176; Schultz, "Qumran Cemetery," 199.

158. Jürgen Zangenberg, "Bones of Contention: 'New' Bones from Qumran Help Settle Old Questions (and Raise New Ones): Remarks on Two Recent Conferences," *QC* 9 (2000): 51-76; Röhrer-Ertl, "Skeletal Remains," 192.

159. Magen and Peleg, "Back to Qumran," 98.

160. Hanan Eshel, Magen Broshi, Richard Freund, and Brian Schultz, "New Data on the Cemetery East of Qumran," *DSD* 9 (2001): 155-63.

century BCE near the legs of the deceased. In the words of Brian Schultz: "As fate would have it, Tomb 1000 has complicated an otherwise orderly picture of the cemetery. At least two women dating to the Second Temple period were buried in the cemetery, as proven by the Carbon-14 tests done on the teeth from the secondary burial, and at least one primary burial from the Second Temple period was buried east-west."[161] Schultz emphasizes the exceptional character of Tomb 1000 and cautions against basing conclusions on it.

Female skeletons have also been found in the other "Qumran-type" burials in Judea. In Ein el-Ghuweir seventeen tombs were excavated, oriented north-south. These yielded thirteen male skeletons, seven female, and one child. At Hiam el-Sagha only two (of twenty) graves were opened. One contained a male skeleton. The other had a 3-4-year-old child, with a necklace of glass beads.[162] In Jerusalem fifty graves were discovered at Beit Safafa (in southern Jerusalem). Only half of these graves had a north-south orientation. Fifteen men, ten women, and five children were identified.[163] Because of the similarity to Qumran, there has been a tendency to assume that all such burials are sectarian. In the words of Boaz Zissu: "The method of burial in Qumran and the Dead Sea sites is essentially different from the 'normative' method of the second temple period at Jerusalem, Jericho, 'Ein Gedi and many other sites."[164] Not only are there no family tombs, but very few articles (grave goods) accompany the burials, and we do not find secondary burials in ossuaries or bone repositories.

The picture has been complicated, however, by the discovery in 1996–1997 of a Nabatean cemetery south of the Dead Sea at Khirbet Qazone.[165] This cemetery contained over 3,500 burials in single, shaft graves, most more than 1.5 meters deep, with a north-south orientation. The Nabatean character of these graves is shown by the grave goods, all of

---

161. Schultz, "Qumran Cemetery," 201.

162. Rachel Hachlili, "The Qumran Cemetery: A Reconsideration," in Schiffman et al., eds., *Dead Sea Scrolls: Fifty Years After*, 665.

163. Zissu, "'Qumran Type' Graves in Jerusalem," 160.

164. Ibid., 169; cf. Rachel Hachlili, "Burial Practices at Qumran," *RevQ* 62 (1993): 247-64; eadem, *Jewish Funerary Customs, Practices and Rites in the Second Temple Period* (JSJSup 94; Leiden: Brill, 2005) 450-79.

165. Konstantinos D. Politis, "The Discovery and Excavation of the Khirbet Qazone Cemetery and Its Significance Relative to Qumran," in Galor et al., eds., *Site of Dead Sea Scrolls*, 213-19.

which date to the late Roman period. The cemetery shows, however, that burial in single graves with a north-south orientation was not peculiar to Qumran, and it raises the possibility that this style of burial may have been characteristic of the Dead Sea region. The majority of the Khirbet Qazone graves belong to women and children.

This evidence is interpreted by scholars in widely different ways. J. T. Milik had proposed that the north-south orientation of the graves was due to the fact that Paradise was located in the north. The Essenes were buried in this way so that they would rise facing north and march directly to Paradise. This position was later endorsed by Puech.[166] That the cemetery at Khirbet Qazone has a similar orientation, however, shows that this was not a peculiarity of Essene belief. Hirschfeld suggested that it was a regional phenomenon, inspired by the geography of the Dead Sea valley.[167] Similar burials are found in Jerusalem, but they are exceptional there.

Golb dismissed the distinction between different parts of the cemetery as a tendentious attempt to salvage the Essene hypothesis, but his own refusal to recognize such distinctions is clearly tendentious too.[168] Hirschfeld, who found only 823 graves at Qumran, likewise makes no distinction between the different areas in the cemetery. He summarizes the findings as 33 men and 23 women and children, and finds the ratio similar to what was found at Ein el-Ghuweir and Beit Safafa. For him, this ratio rules out the Essene hypothesis. Joan Taylor is also skeptical of the distinction between a "main" cemetery and extensions, and she notes that the relative absence of women and children could be explained in various ways: they may, for example, have fled before an impending battle.[169] She argues that the presence of gendered objects such as spindle whorls are *prima facie* evidence of the presence of women at the site.

But differences between different parts of the cemetery are at least potentially significant. Magness finds it significant that "no more than two

---

166. J. T. Milik, "Hénoch au pays des aromates (chap XXVII à XXXII): Fragments araméens de la grotte 4 de Qumrân," *RB* 65 (1958): 77; cf. Émile Puech, *La croyance des Esséniens en la vie future: Immortalité, résurrection, vie éternelle* (2 vols.; EBib 21-22; Paris: Gabalda, 1993) 2.700-701; idem, "The Necropolis of Khirbet Qumran and 'Ain el-Ghuweir and the Essene Belief in the Afterlife," *BASOR* 312 (1998): 21-36.

167. Hirschfeld, *Qumran in Context*, 157.

168. Golb, *Who Wrote the Dead Sea Scrolls?* 16-18.

169. Joan E. Taylor, "The Cemeteries of Khirbet Qumran and Women's Presence at the Site," *DSD* 6 (1999): 285-323.

adult females are known to be represented in the western sector of the cemetery at Qumran," with one more apparently sectarian adult female in the northern cemetery.[170] She believes that Zias is correct in identifying the women and children in the southern extension and in the southern cemetery as recent Bedouin burials. She sums up:

> Thus, the evidence from the western sector of the cemetery suggests that women were present at Qumran but represented a disproportionately small part of the population. The complete absence of infants and children among the excavated burials in the western sector is striking given the high rate of infant and child mortality in antiquity. Despite the small size of the sample, this evidence suggests that the community at Qumran did not include families. If we reject Zias's suggestion regarding the identification of the burials in the extensions as bedouins, then women and children were present in larger numbers among the sectarians (although still in a minority), but their graves were marginalized.[171]

I may add that it is not unusual to find some women buried in the graveyards of Catholic monasteries, whose inhabitants undoubtedly professed celibacy. These women may have been responsible for cooking and cleaning. (In Catholic monasteries they were often nuns.) In some cases they may have been relatives of the monks.

Eshel and Broshi also accepted Zias's view that the east-west burials are Bedouin. In light of this, "there is now little difference between the western section and the eastern extensions of the cemetery."[172]

Zias's thesis has been severely criticized, however, by Jürgen Zangenberg and Jonathan Norton.[173] There are at least some ancient graves that are oriented east-west, and the dating of the jewelry is uncertain. Norton does not deny that there are some Bedouin graves. He figures that the proportion of females among the ancient burials may have been as high as 23 percent, but regards this as still exceptionally low, and he does

---

170. Magness, *Archaeology of Qumran*, 172.

171. Ibid., 173.

172. Eshel et al., "New Data," 153.

173. Zangenberg, "Bones of Contention," 65-72; Jonathan Norton, "A Reassessment of Controversial Studies on the Cemetery," in Humbert and Gunneweg, eds., *Khirbet Qumrân II*, 107-27, especially 118-19.

not regard it as invalidating the Essene hypothesis. He also notes that the samples for the individual parts of the cemetery are too small to permit conclusions about the relation of that part to the rest.

Brian Schultz has responded to Norton by a more careful study of Muslim burials. He finds significant differences between Bedouin burial practices and the majority of the graves at Qumran, although they admit of exceptions. Muslim burials are most often east-west, although there are exceptions. Besides the oval heap of stones typical of Qumran, graves may be marked by a circle of stones or be unmarked. Muslim graves are generally shallower than those at Qumran. Bodies are often buried lying on the side, while this is exceptional at Qumran. Side loculi dug at the bottom of a shaft are unusual in Muslim burials, but the norm at Qumran.[174] He argues that it is inherently likely that there would be some Bedouin intrusions in the Qumran cemetery, and argues that as many as fourteen of the excavated tombs may be identified as such. Six of these, almost half, are oriented north-south. He finds a maximum total of five women, but one of these is tentative and another is debated. The only female skeleton in primary burial over which there is no controversy is in a separate cemetery some distance away. The two women buried in Tomb 1000 are also exceptional, since they are secondary burials. He concludes, "whatever the case may be, the cemetery unequivocally points to a special treatment of women in an otherwise male-oriented community."[175] Schultz does not recognize any burials of children under 15 as part of the ancient cemetery.

In light of all this, it is apparent that the cemetery will remain controversial, unless and until it can be more fully excavated. From the evidence now available it is apparent that there were some women buried at Qumran in antiquity, but that they were very much a minority, and marginal. If this were a regional cemetery, like the one in Khirbet Qazone, we should expect a greater proportion of women and children. In view of the gender imbalance, it would seem that the cemetery served a community that was preponderantly male. A religious community or a military settlement would seem to be the main options. As already noted, no such cemetery is found near any other military fort. There is nothing inherently religious about the cemetery, but such a community might account for the gender imbalance. On the question of celibacy, the evidence is inconclu-

174. Schultz, "Qumran Cemetery," 214.
175. Ibid., 219.

sive. Many of the female burials are controversial in one way or another, and the practice of celibacy does not require that no females whatsoever be present. In this regard, both the defenders of the Essene hypothesis and their critics have been prone to overstate their case.

One other possible objection to the view that Qumran was a religious settlement should be considered. Is it conceivable that a community that was obsessed with purity would have placed a cemetery so close to its settlement?[176] According to the *Temple Scroll*: "You shall not do as the Gentiles do: they bury their dead in every place, they even bury them in the middle of their houses; instead you shall keep places apart within your land where you shall bury your dead. Among four cities you shall establish a place in which to bury" (48:11-14). It goes on to dwell on the gravity of corpse impurity (49:5–50:19).[177] The Mishnah (*m. Baba Batra* 2:9) requires that a burial site be separated from a town. This requirement is satisfied, rather minimally, by the Qumran cemetery as identified by de Vaux.[178] The survey by Eshel and Broshi, however, detected several graves closer to the settlement, by Ground-Penetrating Radar, some as close as 10 meters.[179] (These graves, however, have not been excavated, and they are only *potential* burials.) Jonathan Klawans suggests that the sectarians may have regarded corpse impurity as an irresolvable problem, as it required purification with special water containing the ashes of a red heifer. There is no evidence that this ritual was performed by the sectarians, who generally boycotted the temple cult.[180] If corpse impurity was an irresolvable problem, it need not be avoided. This was the approach taken by traditional Judaism after the destruction of the temple. Alternatively, the sectarians may have believed that their righteous dead were not defiling at all, but this is purely speculative. The proximity of the cemetery is a problem for the Essene hypothesis, but it is not necessarily a decisive one.

176. Golb, *Who Wrote the Dead Sea Scrolls?* 34.

177. On corpse impurity in the Scrolls, see Hannah K. Harrington, *The Purity Texts* (CQS 5; London: T&T Clark, 2004) 71-85.

178. Hachlili, "Qumran Cemetery," 661.

179. Eshel et al., "New Data," 139.

180. Jonathan Klawans, "Purity in the Dead Sea Scrolls," in Timothy Lim and John J. Collins, eds., *The Oxford Handbook of the Dead Sea Scrolls* (New York: Oxford University Press, forthcoming). Compare Harrington, *Purity Texts*, 83.

The *Miqva'ot*

As Broshi has argued, the existence of ten *miqva'ot* in an area no larger than an acre is the strongest archeological reason for defining Qumran as a religious site.[181] Even allowing for the fact that all ten may not have been in use at the same time (one was not repaired after the earthquake, another is thought to have been built later), the concentration is unparalleled outside Jerusalem. The importance of ritual washing is amply attested in the Scrolls.[182] At the very least, the abundance of *miqva'ot* is highly compatible with the view that the site was inhabited by a religious sect. At the same time, it is difficult to see why a villa or a military garrison should require so many pools, and the alternative use suggested by Magen and Peleg (collecting clay for pottery) lacks support and plausibility.

A Possible Problem

A possible problem for the sectarian interpretation of the site is presented by the presence of a toilet in Locus 51. This toilet was identified by de Vaux and has been defended especially by Magness.[183] If Qumran was an Essene settlement, this installation is surprising. The *Temple Scroll* (46:13-16) requires that latrines be located 3,000 cubits outside the city. According to the *War Scroll*, the required distance was 2,000 cubits outside the camp. Yigael Yadin noted that this was more than the limit that one could walk on the Sabbath, and correlated it with the testimony of Josephus that Essenes did not relieve themselves on the Sabbath.[184] Neither the *Temple Scroll*, a utopian document that is probably presectarian, nor the *War*

181. Magen Broshi, "Was Qumran Indeed a Monastery? The Consensus and Its Challengers: An Archaeologist's View," in James H. Charlesworth, ed., *Caves of Enlightenment* (North Richland Hills, TX: Bibal, 1997) 19-37 (24).

182. Jonathan D. Lawrence, *Washing in Water: Trajectories of Ritual Bathing in the Hebrew Bible and Second Temple Literature* (SBLAB 23; Leiden: Brill, 2006) 81-154.

183. *Archaeology of Qumran*, 105-13. Hirschfeld, *Qumran in Context*, 100, regards the identification as "intrinsically implausible."

184. Yigael Yadin, *The Temple Scroll* (3 vols. in 4; Jerusalem: Israel Exploration Society, 1977–83) 1.294-304. Cf. Harrington, *Purity Texts*, 106-7. Albert Baumgarten, "The Temple Scroll, Toilet Practices, and the Essenes," *Jewish History* 10 (1996): 9-20, argues that the toilet practices described by Josephus (*J.W.* 2.147) are incompatible with those described in the Scrolls, since the latter require a roofed enclosure.

Scroll, which is intended for the eschatological age, necessarily reflected the practice of the sect. It is clear, however, that the sectarians regarded defecation as a polluting activity, and that they differed from contemporary Jews in this respect.

Magness concludes only that "the sectarians attended to their bodily needs in various ways depending on the available facilities."[185] She also notes that the toilet would satisfy one major concern, both in the Scrolls and in the account of Josephus, that the excrement be covered, a concern deriving from Deut 23:12-14. Deuteronomy, however, not only requires the Israelites to cover their excrement, but also specifies that they must have "a place outside the camp." Hence the placement of the toilet at Qumran is surprising.

It is possible that the sect, for all its idealism, made provision for an emergency, in which case the toilet might be preferable to the alternatives. It should be noted, however, that the toilet, like the adjacent ritual bath, was not repaired for use after the earthquake. The problem would be removed if we were to suppose, with Humbert, Hirschfeld, and Magen and Peleg, that the character of the site changed in the Herodian period, and that it was not originally a sectarian settlement. Positive evidence for such a change, however, is difficult to find.

The Site and the Scrolls

In view of the proximity of the caves to the site, and the fact that similar pottery was found in both, it is counterintuitive to deny that the scrolls are related to the site. Even Hirschfeld admits that there was "a close connection between those who deposited the scrolls and the inhabitants of Qumran, at least at the time of concealment."[186] Humbert also acknowledges that "the theory of the Essene settlement is more than probable" for the post-Hasmonean phase of occupation.[187]

It has usually been assumed that the time of concealment was 68 CE. It has recently been suggested that some of the scrolls were deposited in the caves already at the turn of the era. The average age of the scrolls in

185. *Archaeology of Qumran*, 111.
186. Hirschfeld, *Qumran in Context*, 43.
187. Humbert, "Some Remarks," 36.

Caves 1 and 4 is considerably older than that of the scrolls in the other caves. (The age of the scrolls is based on the dates assigned to the various scrolls by the editors in the DJD series, which are not necessarily beyond dispute.) In one hypothetical scenario, Cave 4 may have been used as a depository at that time, although some scrolls were added later.[188] The scrolls in Cave 1 may also have been hidden at that time, or may represent a special selection that was moved to a safer hiding place in 68. This scenario is by no means certain, but if it should prove correct, and the scrolls were deposited in caves on at least two occasions, this would strengthen the argument that the scrolls belonged to people who lived at the site. It would not necessarily rule out the possibility that the site had served another purpose in the Hasmonean period. The community could conceivably have occupied the site in the Herodian period, and brought a collection of manuscripts with it. The community could have been established for some time before the first scrolls were deposited in the caves.

Conclusion

The hypothesis that the site was occupied by a different group (most probably a military garrison) in the Hasmonean period is attractive in some respects.[189] The proximity of the site to Hasmonean fortresses is a problem for the sectarian settlement, in view of the conflict between the Teacher and the Wicked Priest. Also, the presence of a toilet would not be anomalous in a presectarian phase. Neither of these considerations is necessarily decisive. The Hasmoneans may not have been as concerned about the sect as the sectarian literature would suggest, and the conflict with the Wicked

---

188. Daniel Stökl Ben Ezra, "Old Caves and Young Caves: A Statistical Reevaluation of a Qumran Consensus," *DSD* 14 (2007): 316. Gregory L. Doudna has argued more sweepingly that "the complete absence of even one allusion to a figure, circumstance, or event in the first century C.E. in a corpus of texts on the scale of the finds at Qumran — compared to dozens of such allusions from the first century B.C.E. — is well explained if the text deposits themselves ended in the first century BCE" ("The Legacy of an Error in Archaeological Interpretation: The Dating of the Qumran Cave Scroll Deposits," in Galor et al., eds., *Qumran*, 155). Doudna questions the basis of the paleographical dating of some scrolls to the first century CE.

189. The view that Qumran was a fortress in the Hasmonean period is now defended by Robert R. Cargill, *Qumran Through Real Time: A Virtual Reconstruction of Qumran and the Dead Sea Scrolls* (Piscataway, NJ: Gorgias, 2009) 210-12.

Priest may have been short-lived. The toilet may conceivably have been an emergency provision. The hypothesis that the site was originally a military fort would require that most of the stepped pools were constructed late, when the site was adapted for sectarian use. The only archeological evidence that has been adduced for such adaptation is the argument from architecture that supposes that the square building with the tower must have been the original settlement. It is not necessarily the case, however, that the site developed in such a logical way, especially since an older, Iron Age structure was being adapted. De Vaux associated two stepped pools with his Period Ia. Without clear stratigraphic evidence of the date of the pools, this argument will remain inconclusive.

If the site was a military outpost, or served some other nonreligious function in the Hasmonean era, then the famous passage in 1QS 8:13-14, about going to the wilderness to prepare the way of the Lord, could not be a reference to the settlement at Qumran. But in any case the interpretation of the Scrolls should not be tied too closely to that of the site. At most, Qumran was one settlement of the *yahad*. It was never the *yahad* in its entirety. Even the *Community Rule (Serek ha-Yahad)* was not written specifically for a community at Qumran, although it may have applied to that community among others. The *yahad,* and still more the new covenant of the *Damascus Rule,* was not an isolated monastic community, as has sometimes been imagined, but was part of a religious association spread widely throughout the land.

Epilogue

The scholarly consensus that identifies the sectarian movement known from the Scrolls with the Essenes is most probably correct, even if not indisputable. The site of Qumran was most probably a sectarian settlement, at least from the mid-first century BCE until its destruction by the Romans, although there is some reason to question whether it was already occupied by sectarians in the Hasmonean period, in view of its proximity to several Hasmonean fortresses. But the sect was never confined to Qumran. Both the Greek accounts of the Essenes, by Philo and Josephus, and the Scrolls testify to a movement that had multiple settlements. The *yahad* described in the *Serek ha-Yahad* and the "new covenant" of the *Damascus Rule* correspond substantially to the two orders of the Essenes (celibate and marrying) according to Josephus. These movements described by these Rules should be viewed as complementary, in a harmonious relationship, not the result of a schism in the Essene movement.

The movement probably had its beginnings late in the second century BCE, and flourished in the later Hasmonean era. According to the recent summary of the data by Brian Webster, "As reflected by the dates of the surviving documents from Qumran, the greatest amount of scribal activity occurred during the late Hasmonaean and early Herodian periods, from 75-1 BCE."[1] The great majority of the distinctively sectarian writings were composed during this period.

---

1. Brian Webster, "Chronological Index of the Texts from the Judaean Desert," in Emanuel Tov, ed., *The Texts from the Judaean Desert: Indices and an Introduction to the Discoveries in the Judaean Desert Series* (DJD 39; Oxford: Clarendon, 2002) 375.

It seems to me unlikely that all the scrolls found at Qumran were composed or copied at the site. Rather, I would suggest that scrolls were brought to Qumran for safekeeping from various Essene settlements. The most obvious occasion for such an operation was the Jewish war and Roman conquest of 66–68 CE. It may be that this was not the first occasion on which scrolls were hidden, at least in Cave 4, since a disproportionately high number of the scrolls found there date to the first century BCE or earlier.[2] It is also possible that scrolls copied at various locations were brought to Qumran by sectarians who moved there at various times. Much remains uncertain about the provenance and use of the scrolls found in the caves. It seems clear, however, that the sect continued down to the time of the Jewish war against Rome, even if its literary creativity declined in the first century CE.[3]

It is commonly assumed that the Essene sect did not survive the destruction of Qumran. In the words of Geza Vermes: "the sect's disappearance from history may well have been brought about in the lethal blow suffered by its central establishment during the fateful summer of 68 CE. The fact that no attempt was made to recover nearly 800 manuscripts from the caves confirms, it would seem, such a reconstruction of the end of Qumran and, with the annihilation of its central establishment, of the whole Essene movement."[4] We cannot, however, think of Qumran as an Alamo, where the Essenes made their last stand and were wiped out. According to Philo and Josephus, the Essenes at one time numbered more than four thousand. Josephus presumably took over this number either from Philo or from a common source, and so it probably reflects an estimate of their number around the turn of the era. He puts the number of Pharisees at the end of Herod's reign at six thousand (*Ant.* 17.43). These figures are not necessarily reliable, and the number did not necessarily stay the same up to the time of the war. But if the numbers are even approxi-

2. Daniel Stökl Ben Ezra, "Old Caves and Young Caves: A Statistical Reevaluation of a Qumran Consensus," *DSD* 14 (2007): 313-33. He notes, however, that about 97 texts found in Cave 4 were written in the first century CE (p. 318).

3. Stökl Ben Ezra, ibid., 333, questions whether the extant fragments are necessarily representative of the entire collection. It is conceivable that more recent scrolls were kept above ground at the site, and consequently destroyed. The available evidence, however, suggests a decline in literary output in the first century CE.

4. Geza Vermes, *The Complete Dead Sea Scrolls in English* (rev. ed.; London: Penguin, 2004) 66.

mately correct, the great majority of Essenes must have lived at places other than Qumran. (The highest estimate of the number of residents at any point is about two hundred.) Even if we suppose that many Essenes had fled to the settlement in the wilderness before the advancing Romans, taking their scrolls with them, only a fraction of the sect could have been killed at the site. The Essenes may have suffered heavy casualties during the war, but there is no reason to think that they were heavier than those suffered by the Pharisees.

Accordingly, scholars have occasionally looked for evidence of Essene survival after 70 CE, but they have not found much.[5] It is true that both Pliny and Josephus speak of the Essenes in the present tense, but they were using sources from a time before the war. The same is true of Christian writers, such as Hippolytus and Epiphanius. No source says that these sects came to an end. James Charlesworth tried to argue for Essene survival on the basis of parallels between the Scrolls and late New Testament writings such as Ephesians, and also from parallels in later Syriac literature.[6] But while individual Essenes must surely have survived, and some of their ideas continued to circulate, none of this requires the continued existence of Essene communities. More recently, Joshua Burns has tried to find evidence of Essene survival in rabbinic criticisms of *minim,* or heretics.[7] The charges concern such issues as maintaining separate houses of worship, calendrical deviation, or excessive concern with ritual purification. But while these charges would be relevant to Essenes, it is not clear that they could apply *only* to Essenes. It is possible, of course, that Essene communities continued to exist, but they have left no clearly discernible historical traces.

In fact, the rise and fall of the Essenes, or of the "new covenant" and *yaḥad,* parallels to a great degree that of the Sadducees and Pharisees.[8] All

---

5. See, e.g., Martin Goodman, "Sadducees and Essenes after 70 C.E.," in idem, *Judaism in the Roman World: Collected Essays* (AGJU 66; Leiden: Brill, 2007) 153-62.

6. James H. Charlesworth, "The Origin and Subsequent History of the Authors of the Dead Sea Scrolls: Four Transitional Phases among the Qumran Essenes," *RevQ* 10 (1979–81): 228-32.

7. Joshua E. Burns, "Essene Sectarianism and Social Differentiation in Judaea after 70 C.E.," *HTR* 99 (2006): 247-74. On the *minim* see also Martin Goodman, "The Function of *Minim* in Early Rabbinic Judaism," in idem, *Judaism in the Roman World,* 163-73.

8. Compare Seth Schwartz, *Imperialism and Jewish Society, 200 B.C.E. to 640 C.E.* (Princeton: Princeton University Press, 2001) 96.

first appear on the scene in the late second or early first century BCE. All were concerned with the correct interpretation of the Torah and with the correct observance of the temple cult. The Pharisees and Sadducees enjoyed fluctuating influence over the later Hasmonean kings, who sometimes deferred to the halakic rulings of one or the other party. The sectarian Scrolls also show their greatest interest in political affairs in that period. From the reign of Herod on, the political influence of the sects diminished. The Scrolls do not even mention any historical figures later than the early Herodian period, and the Essenes receive no notice in the Gospels. It seems likely then that they withdrew from public debate for the later part of their existence, and indeed there are intimations of this already in the *Serek*.[9]

It is commonly assumed that after 70 CE the Pharisees became the dominant party. Yet as Shaye Cohen has argued, they no longer functioned as a sect.[10] The rabbinic literature attests to a form of discourse where disagreement, and difference of interpretation, is tolerated and even encouraged. To be sure there were still *minim*, whose views were not tolerated, but they appear to be marginal figures (at least from the rabbinic point of view).[11] Cohen further argues that "with the destruction of the temple the primary focal point of Jewish sectarianism disappeared. . . . For most Jews . . . sectarian self-definition ceased to make sense after 70."[12]

Albert Baumgarten has argued that while sectarianism may be present at any time, it flourishes more in some circumstances than in others.[13] The rise of sectarianism in the Hasmonean period was due in some part to the impact of Hellenism, which presented a challenge to traditional ways and prompted different groups to set boundaries over against the encroaching culture. That they did so in different ways led to the multiplication of sects. Since sectarian disputation centered on the interpretation of

9. For example, 1QS 10:19, where the Maskil promises to refrain from disputation with the men of the pit.

10. Shaye J. D. Cohen, "The Significance of Yavneh: Pharisees, Rabbis, and the End of Jewish Sectarianism," *HUCA* 55 (1984): 27-53.

11. Note the caution of Goodman, *Judaism in the Roman World*, 159, that the lack of reference to Sadducees and Essenes in rabbinic literature may not indicate that these sects disappeared but that the rabbis were not interested in them.

12. Ibid., 45.

13. Albert I. Baumgarten, *The Flourishing of Jewish Sects in the Maccabean Era: An Interpretation* (JSJSup 55; Leiden: Brill, 1997) 15-23.

the Torah, it presupposed a relatively high degree of literacy.[14] This in turn was related to increased urbanization, even if this led some to flee from the city in pursuit of a purer life.

Regardless of how many Essenes died in the war against Rome, the sect was sure to be affected by the huge disruption of Judean society. Josephus estimated the number of people killed in the siege of Jerusalem at 1,100,000, and the number of prisoners at 97,000.[15] While these numbers are not necessarily reliable, the carnage must have been vast. Urban life in Judea was destroyed. The temple was no more. Moreover, the divine aid anticipated in the Qumran *War Scroll* for the final battle against the Kittim (Romans) had not materialized, and this must have led to some disillusionment. In all, it is hardly surprising that the flow of recruits to the demanding life of the sect should have dried up.

The surprise is rather that the sect endured as long as it did, especially if a significant segment of it was celibate and so reliant on new recruits in every generation. In its earliest phase the sect was fueled by outrage against those who interpreted the law differently. It is clear from the *pesharim* that the sectarians expected divine retribution on their enemies around the time of the Roman conquest, even though they wisely refrained from setting a specific date for the "end."[16] They could, perhaps, claim a measure of fulfillment in the downfall of the Hasmoneans, but there was no corresponding conversion of Israel to their own interpretation of the law. No doubt Herod and the procurators provided plenty of new occasions for outrage, but nonetheless the shrill antagonism of the sectarian writings would have been difficult to maintain indefinitely. It may be that already in its later phase the *raison d'être* of the sect became less polemical and focused more positively on the pursuit of purity and holiness. We can see some evidence of a move in that direction in the ideal proposed for the *yaḥad* in 1QS 8–9, already in the Hasmonean period.

But in any case, the rejectionist, world-denying stance of the sect was no longer able to sustain an ongoing community after the disaster of the

---

14. Baumgarten, ibid., 124 n. 32, cites an analogy from the rise of Puritanism: "In the sixteenth century newly literate people were reading it for the first time, with no historical sense and believing all its texts to be divinely inspired" (Christopher Hill, *Society and Puritanism in Pre-Revolutionary England* [New York: Schocken, 1964] 146).

15. *J.W.* 6.420. See Schwartz, *Imperialism and Jewish Society,* 108 n. 12.

16. See John J. Collins, *Apocalypticism in the Dead Sea Scrolls* (London: Routledge, 1997) 64-68.

Jewish War. The future of Judaism lay rather with the rabbis, who accepted that more than one interpretation of the Torah could be accepted as words of the living God.[17]

17. *b. 'Erubin* 13b; *b. Gittin* 6b. A. Sagi, "'Both Are the Words of the Living God': A Typological Analysis of Halakhic Pluralism," *HUCA* 65 (1995): 105-36.

Bibliography

Abegg, Martin. *The Dead Sea Scrolls Concordance.* 2 vols. Leiden: Brill, 2003.

Alexander, Loveday, ed. *Images of Empire.* JSOTSup 122. Sheffield: Sheffield Academic Press, 1991.

Alexander, Philip. "The Redaction-History of *Serek ha-Yahad*: A Proposal." *RevQ* 17 (Milik Festschrift) (1996): 437-53.

Alexander, Philip, and Geza Vermes. *Qumran Cave 4.* Vol. XIX: *Serekh ha-Yahad and Two Related Texts.* DJD 26. Oxford: Clarendon, 1998.

Amit, David, and Jodi Magness. "Not a Settlement of Hermits or Essenes: A Response to Y. Hirschfeld, 'A Settlement of Hermits above En Gedi.'" *TA* 27 (2000): 273-85.

Amitai, Janet, ed. *Biblical Archaeology Today: Proceedings of the International Congress on Biblical Archaeology, Jerusalem, April 1984.* Jerusalem: Israel Exploration Society, 1985.

Argall, Randal A. "A Hellenistic Jewish Source on the Essenes in Philo, *Every Good Man Is Free* 75-91, and Josephus, *Antiquities* 18.18-22." Pages 13-24 in *For a Later Generation: The Transformation of Tradition in Israel, Early Judaism and Early Christianity.* Edited by Randal A. Argall, Beverly A. Bow, and Rodney A. Werline. Harrisburg: Trinity Press International, 2000.

Ariel, Donald T. "A Survey of Coin Finds in Jerusalem (Until the End of the Byzantine Period)." *SBFLA* 32 (1982): 273-326.

Arnold, Russell C. D. *The Social Role of Liturgy in the Religion of the Qumran Community.* STDJ 60. Leiden: Brill, 2006.

Atkinson, Kenneth. "Josephus the Essene on the Qumran Essenes and Related Jewish Sectarians along the Dead Sea." Paper presented at the SBL annual meeting in San Diego, November 18, 2007.

———. Review of Katharina Galor, Jean-Baptiste Humbert, and Jürgen Zangenberg, eds., *Qumran: The Site of the Dead Sea Scrolls. RBL* 3/8/2008.

Atwill, Joseph, and Steve Braunheim. "Redating the Radiocarbon Dating of the Dead Sea Scrolls." *DSD* 11 (2004): 143-57.

Avemarie, Friedrich. " *'Tohorat ha-Rabbim'* and *'Mashqeh ha-Rabbim'*: Jacob Licht Reconsidered." Pages 215-29 in *Legal Texts and Legal Issues: Proceedings of the Second Meeting of the International Organization for Qumran Studies, Cambridge 1995. Published in Honour of Joseph M. Baumgarten.* Edited by Moshe J. Bernstein, Florentino García Martínez, and John Kampen. STDJ 23. Leiden: Brill, 1997.

Avery-Peck, Alan J., Jacob Neusner, and Bruce Chilton, eds. *Judaism in Late Antiquity.* Part 5: *The Judaism of Qumran: A Systemic Reading of the Dead Sea Scrolls.* Vol. 1: *Theory of Israel.* Handbuch der Orientalstik 1/56. Leiden: Brill, 2001.

Bar-Adon, Pesach. "Another Settlement of the Judean Desert Sect at 'En el-Ghuweir on the Shores of the Dead Sea." *BASOR* 225 (1977): 2-25.

Bar-Asher, Moshe, and Emanuel Tov, eds. *Meghillot: Studies in the Dead Sea Scrolls V-VI: A Festschrift for Devorah Dimant* (Hebrew). Jerusalem: Bialik Institute, 2007.

Bar-Nathan, Rachel. "Qumran and the Hasmonaean and Herodian Winter Palaces of Jericho: The Implication of the Pottery Finds on the Interpretation of the Settlement at Qumran." Pages 263-77 in *Qumran: The Site of the Dead Sea Scrolls: Archaeological Interpretations and Debates. Proceedings of a Conference Held at Brown University, November 17-19, 2002.* Edited by Katharina Galor, Jean-Baptiste Humbert, and Jürgen Zangenberg. STDJ 57. Leiden: Brill, 2006.

Barag, Dan. "A Silver Coin of Yohanan the High Priest and the Coinage of Judea in the Fourth Century B.C." *Israel Numismatic Journal* 9 (1986–87): 4-21.

Bardtke, Hans. "Die Rechtsstellung der Qumran-Gemeinde." *TLZ* 86 (1961): 93-104.

Barrera, Julio Trebolle, and Luis Vegas Montaner, eds. *The Madrid Qumran Congress: Proceedings of the International Congress on the Dead Sea Scrolls, Madrid, 18-21 March 1991.* 2 vols. STDJ 11. Leiden: Brill, 1992.

Bartlett, John R. "The Archaeology of Qumran." Pages 67-94 in *Archaeology and Biblical Interpretation.* Edited by John R. Bartlett. London: Routledge, 1997.

———, ed. *Archaeology and Biblical Interpretation.* London: Routledge, 1997.

Bauer, Walter. "Essener." Pages 386-430 in vol. 4 of PWSup. Stuttgart: Metzler, 1924. Repr. in pages 1-59 of *Aufsätze und kleine Schriften.* Edited by Georg Strecker. Tübingen: Mohr Siebeck, 1967.

Baumgarten, Albert I. "The Temple Scroll, Toilet Practices, and the Essenes." *Jewish History* 10 (1996): 9-20.

———. *The Flourishing of Jewish Sects in the Maccabean Era: An Interpretation.* JSJSup 55. Leiden: Brill, 1997.

―――. "Graeco-Roman Voluntary Associations and Ancient Jewish Sects." Pages 93-111 in *Jews in a Greco-Roman World*. Edited by Martin Goodman. Oxford: Clarendon, 1998.

―――. "Pharisees." Pages 657-63 in vol. 1 of *Encyclopedia of the Dead Sea Scrolls*. Edited by Lawrence H. Schiffman and James C. VanderKam. 2 vols. New York: Oxford University Press, 2000.

―――. "Seekers after Smooth Things." Pages 857-58 in vol. 2 of *Encyclopedia of the Dead Sea Scrolls*. Edited by Lawrence H. Schiffman and James C. VanderKam. 2 vols. New York: Oxford University Press, 2000.

―――. "Who Cares and Why Does It Matter? Qumran and the Essenes, Once Again." *DSD* 11 (2004): 174-90.

Baumgarten, Joseph M. "The Heavenly Tribunal and the Personification of Sedeq in Jewish Apocalyptic." Pages 219-39 in *ANRW* 2.19.1. Berlin: de Gruyter, 1979.

―――. "The Pharisaic-Sadducean Controversies about Purity and the Qumran Texts." *JJS* 31 (1980): 157-70.

―――. "Qumran-Essene Restraints on Marriage." Pages 13-24 in *Archaeology and History in the Dead Sea Scrolls: The New York University Conference in Memory of Yigael Yadin*. Edited by Lawrence H. Schiffman. JSPSup 8. Sheffield: JSOT Press, 1990.

―――. "The Cave 4 Versions of the Qumran Penal Code." *JJS* 43 (1992): 268-76.

―――. *Qumran Cave 4*. Vol. XIII: *The Damascus Document (4Q266-273)*. DJD 18. Oxford: Clarendon, 1996.

Baumgarten, Joseph M., with Michael T. Davis. "Cave IV, V, VI Fragments Related to the Damascus Document (4Q266-273 = 4QDa-h, 5Q12 = 5QD, 6Q15 = 6QD)." Pages 59-79 in *Damascus Document, War Scroll, and Related Documents*. Vol. 2 of *The Dead Sea Scrolls: Hebrew, Aramaic, and Greek Texts with English Translations*. Edited by James H. Charlesworth. PTSDSSP. Louisville: Westminster John Knox, 1995.

Baumgarten, Joseph M., with James H. Charlesworth, Lidija Novakovic, and Henry W. M. Rietz. "Damascus Document: 4Q266-273 (4QD a-h)." Pages 1-185 in *Damascus Document II, Some Works of the Torah and Related Documents*. Vol. 3 of *The Dead Sea Scrolls: Hebrew, Aramaic, and Greek Texts with English Translations*. Edited by James H. Charlesworth. PTSDSSP. Louisville: Westminster John Knox, 1995.

Baumgarten, Joseph M., Esther G. Chazon, and Avital Pinnick. *The Damascus Document: A Centennial of Discovery. Proceedings of the Third International Symposium of the Orion Center for the Study of the Dead Sea Scrolls and Associated Literature, 4-8 February, 1998*. STDJ 34. Leiden: Brill, 2000.

Beall, Todd S. *Josephus' Description of the Essenes Illustrated by the Dead Sea Scrolls*. SNTSMS 58. Cambridge: Cambridge University Press, 1988.

Bedenbender, Andreas. *Der Gott der Welt tritt auf den Sinai*. Arbeiten zur neutestamentlichen Theologie und Zeitgeschichte 8. Berlin: Institut Kirche und Judentum, 2000.

Bengtsson, Håkan. *What's in a Name? A Study of the Sobriquets in the Pesharim*. Uppsala: Uppsala University Press, 2000.

Berg, Shane A. "An Elite Group within the *Yaḥad*: Revisiting 1QS 8-9." Pages 161-77 in *Qumran Studies: New Approaches, New Questions*. Edited by Michael Thomas Davis and Brent A. Strawn. Grand Rapids: Eerdmans, 2007.

Bergmeier, Roland. *Die Essener-Berichte des Flavius Josephus*. Kampen: Kok Pharos, 1993.

———. "Die drei jüdischen Schulrichtungen nach Josephus und Hippolyt von Rom." *JSJ* 34 (2003): 443-70.

———. "Zum historischen Wert der Essenerberichte von Philo und Josephus." Pages 11-22 in *Qumran Kontrovers: Beiträge zu den Textfunden vom Toten Meer*. Edited by Jörg Frey and Hartmut Stegemann. Paderborn: Bonifatius, 2003.

Bernstein, Moshe J., Florentino García Martínez, and John Kampen, eds. *Legal Texts and Legal Issues: Proceedings of the Second Meeting of the International Organization for Qumran Studies, Cambridge 1995. Published in Honour of Joseph M. Baumgarten*. STDJ 23. Leiden: Brill, 1997.

Berrin, Shani. *The Pesher Nahum Scroll from Qumran: An Exegetical Study of 4Q169*. STDJ 53. Leiden: Brill, 2004.

Betz, Otto. *Offenbarung und Schriftforschung in der Qumransekte*. Tübingen: Mohr, 1960.

Betz, Otto, Klaus Haacker, and Martin Hengel, eds. *Josephus-Studien: Untersuchungen zu Josephus, dem antiken Judentum und dem Neuen Testament. Otto Michel z. 70. Geburtstag*. Göttingen: Vandenhoeck & Ruprecht, 1974.

Bickerman, Elias. "The Jewish Historian Demetrios." Pages 72-84 in vol. 3 of *Christianity, Judaism, and Other Greco-Roman Cults*. Edited by Jacob Neusner. 5 vols. SJLA 12. Leiden: Brill, 1975.

Bilde, Per. "The Essenes in Philo and Josephus." Pages 32-68 in *Qumran Between the Old and New Testaments*. Edited by Frederick Cryer and Thomas L. Thompson. JSOTSup 290. Sheffield: Sheffield Academic Press, 1998.

Black, Matthew. "The Account of the Essenes in Hippolytus and Josephus." Pages 172-82 in *The Background of the New Testament and Its Eschatology*. Edited by William D. Davies and David Daube. Cambridge: Cambridge University Press, 1956.

———. *The Scrolls and Christian Origins*. New York: Scribner, 1961. Repr., BJS 48. Atlanta: Scholars Press, 1983.

Blanton, Thomas R., IV. *Constructing a New Covenant*. WUNT 2/233. Tübingen: Mohr, 2007.

Boccaccini, Gabriele. *Beyond the Essene Hypothesis.* Grand Rapids: Eerdmans, 1998.

———. "Enochians, Urban Essenes, Qumranites: Three Social Groups, One Intellectual Movement." Pages 301-27 in *The Early Enoch Literature.* Edited by John J. Collins and Gabriele Boccaccini. JSJSup 121. Leiden: Brill, 2007.

———, ed. *Enoch and Qumran Origins: New Light on a Forgotten Connection.* Grand Rapids: Eerdmans, 2005.

Brettler, Marc, and Michael Fishbane, eds. *Minḥah le-Naḥum: Biblical and Other Studies Presented to Nahum M. Sarna in Honour of His 70th Birthday.* JSOTSup 154. Sheffield: Sheffield Academic Press, 1993.

Brooke, George J., ed. *Temple Scroll Studies: Papers Presented at the International Symposium on the Temple Scroll, Manchester, December 1987.* JSPSup 7. Sheffield: Sheffield Academic Press, 1989.

———. "The Kittim in the Qumran Pesharim." Pages 135-59 in *Images of Empire.* Edited by Loveday Alexander. JSOTSup 122. Sheffield: Sheffield Academic Press, 1991.

———. "Isaiah 40:3 and the Wilderness Community." Pages 117-32 in *New Qumran Texts and Studies: Proceedings of the First Meeting of the International Organization for Qumran Studies, Paris 1992.* Edited by George J. Brooke with Florentino García Martínez. STJD 15. Leiden: Brill, 1994.

———. "The Pesharim and the Origins of the Dead Sea Scrolls." Pages 339-52 in *Methods of Investigation of the Dead Sea Scrolls and the Khirbet Qumran Site: Present Realities and Future Prospects.* Edited by Michael O. Wise, Norman Golb, John J. Collins, and Dennis G. Pardee. ANYAS 722. New York: New York Academy of Sciences, 1994.

———. "The Structure of 1QH^a XII 5–XIII 4 and the Meaning of Resurrection." Pages 15-33 in *From 4QMMT to Resurrection: Mélanges qumraniens en hommage à Émile Puech.* Edited by Florentino García Martínez, Annette Steudel, and Eibert Tigchelaar. STDJ 61. Leiden: Brill, 2006.

Brooke, George J., and Florentino García Martínez, eds. *New Qumran Texts and Studies.* STDJ 15. Leiden: Brill, 1994.

Broshi, Magen. "The Archaeology of Qumran." Pages 103-15 in *The Dead Sea Scrolls after Forty Years.* Edited by Devorah Dimant and Uriel Rappaport. STDJ 10. Leiden: Brill, 1992.

———. "Was Qumran Indeed a Monastery? The Consensus and Its Challengers: An Archaeologist's View." Pages 19-37 in *Caves of Enlightenment.* Edited by James H. Charlesworth. North Richland Hills, TX: Bibal, 1997.

———. "Was Qumran a Crossroads?" *RevQ* 19 (1999): 273-75.

———. "Essenes at Qumran? A Rejoinder to Albert Baumgarten." *DSD* 14 (2007): 24-33.

Broshi, Magen, and Hanan Eshel. "How and Where Did the Qumranites Live?" Pages 266-73 in *The Provo International Conference on the Dead Sea Scrolls:*

Technological Innovations, New Texts and Reformulated Issues. Edited by Donald W. Parry and Eugene Ulrich. STDJ 30. Leiden: Brill, 1999.

————. "Qumran and the Dead Sea Scrolls: The Contention of Twelve Theories." Pages 162-69 in *Religion and Society in Roman Palestine: Old Questions and New Approaches.* Edited by Douglas R. Edwards. London: Routledge, 2004.

Brownlee, William H. *The Midrash Pesher of Habakkuk.* SBLMS 24. Missoula, MT: Scholars Press for SBL, 1979.

Bruce, Frederick F. *Biblical Exegesis in the Qumran Texts.* Grand Rapids: Eerdmans, 1959.

Brutti, Maria. *The Development of the High Priesthood during the Pre-Hasmonean Period.* JSJSup 108. Leiden: Brill, 2006.

Burchard, Christoph. "Zur Nebenüberlieferung von Josephus' Bericht über die Essener Bell 2,119-61 bei Hippolyt, Porphyrius, Josippus, Niketas Choniates und anderen." Pages 77-96 in *Josephus-Studien: Untersuchungen zu Josephus, dem antiken Judentum und dem Neuen Testament: Otto Michel z. 70. Geburtstag gewidmet.* Edited by Otto Betz, Klaus Haacker, and Martin Hengel. Göttingen: Vandenhoeck & Ruprecht, 1974.

————. "Die Essener bei Hippolyt: Hippolyt, *Ref.* IX 18, 2-28,2 und Josephus, *Bell.* 2,119-61." *JSJ* 8 (1977): 1-41.

Burkert, Walter. "Hellenistische Pseudopythagorica." *Philologus* 105 (1961): 16-43, 226-46.

Burns, Joshua E. "Essene Sectarianism and Social Differentiation in Judaea after 70 C.E." *HTR* 99 (2006): 247-74.

Burrows, Millar. *The Dead Sea Scrolls.* New York: Viking, 1955.

Callaway, Philip R. *The History of the Qumran Community: An Investigation.* JSPSup 3. Sheffield: Sheffield Academic Press, 1988.

Campbell, Jonathan G., William John Lyons, and Lloyd K. Pietersen, eds. *New Directions in Qumran Studies: Proceedings of the Bristol Colloquium on the Dead Sea Scrolls.* London: T&T Clark, 2005.

Cancik, Hubert, Hermann Lichtenberger, and Peter Schaefer, eds. *Geschichte-Tradition-Reflexion: Festschrift für Martin Hengel zum 70. Geburtstag.* 3 vols. Tübingen: Mohr Siebeck, 1996.

Cargill, Robert R. *Qumran Through Real Time: A Virtual Reconstruction of Qumran and the Dead Sea Scrolls.* Piscataway, NJ: Gorgias, 2009.

Carmignac, Jean. "Le retour du Docteur de Justice à la fin des jours?" *RevQ* 1 (1958-59): 235-48.

Chalcraft, David J. "The Development of Weber's Sociology of Sects: Encouraging a New Fascination." Pages 26-51 in *Sectarianism in Early Judaism: Sociological Advances.* Edited by David J. Chalcraft. London: Equinox, 2007.

Chalcraft, David J., ed. *Sectarianism in Early Judaism: Sociological Advances.* London: Equinox, 2007.

Bibliography

Charlesworth, James H. "The Origin and Subsequent History of the Authors of the Dead Sea Scrolls: Four Transitional Phases among the Qumran Essenes." *RevQ* 10 (1979–81): 213-33.

——. "Community Organization in the Rule of the Community." Pages 133-36 in vol. 1 of *The Encyclopedia of the Dead Sea Scrolls*. Edited by Lawrence H. Schiffman and James C. VanderKam. 2 vols. New York: Oxford University Press, 2000.

——. *The Pesharim and Qumran History: Chaos or Consensus?* Grand Rapids: Eerdmans, 2002.

——, ed. *Rule of the Community and Related Documents*. Vol. 1 of *The Dead Sea Scrolls: Hebrew, Aramaic, and Greek Texts with English Translations*. PTSDSSP. Louisville: Westminster John Knox, 1994.

——, ed. *Damascus Document, War Scroll, and Related Documents*. Vol. 2 of *The Dead Sea Scrolls: Hebrew, Aramaic, and Greek Texts with English Translations*. PTSDSSP. Louisville: Westminster John Knox, 1995.

——, ed. *Damascus Document II, Some Works of the Torah, and Related Documents*. Vol. 3 of *The Dead Sea Scrolls: Hebrew, Aramaic, and Greek Texts with English Translations*. PTSDSSP. Louisville: Westminster John Knox, 1995.

——, ed. *Caves of Enlightenment*. North Richland Hills, TX: Bibal, 1997.

Chazon, Esther G., and Michael E. Stone, eds. *Pseudepigraphic Perspectives: The Apocrypha and Pseudepigrapha in Light of the Dead Sea Scrolls*. STDJ 31. Leiden: Brill, 1999.

Clamer, Christa. "Jewellery Finds from the Cemetery." Pages 171-83 in *Khirbet Qumrân et 'Aïn Feshkha II: Études d'anthropologie, de physique et de chimie. Studies of Anthropology, Physics and Chemistry*. Edited by Jean-Baptiste Humbert and Jan Gunneweg. NTOA.SA 3. Fribourg: Academic Press, 2003.

Clermont-Ganneau, Charles. *Archaeological Researches in Palestine during the Years 1873–1874*. Translated by Aubrey Stewart. 2 vols. 1896–99. Repr. Jerusalem: Raritas, 1971.

Cohen, Shaye J. D. *Josephus in Galilee and Rome: His Vita and Development as a Historian*. Leiden: Brill, 1979.

——. "The Significance of Yavneh: Pharisees, Rabbis, and the End of Jewish Sectarianism." *HUCA* 55 (1984): 27-53.

Collins, John J. "The Origin of the Qumran Community: A Review of the Evidence." Pages 159-78 in *To Touch the Text: Biblical and Related Studies in Honor of Joseph A. Fitzmyer, S.J.* Edited by Maurya P. Horgan and Paul J. Kobelski. New York: Crossroad, 1989. Repr. in pages 239-60 of idem, *Seers, Sibyls, and Sages in Hellenistic-Roman Judaism*. JSJSup 54. Leiden: Brill, 1997.

——. "Essenes." Pages 619-26 in vol. 2 of *The Anchor Bible Dictionary*. Edited by David Noel Freedman. 6 vols. New York: Doubleday, 1992.

——. *Daniel*. Hermeneia. Minneapolis: Fortress, 1993.

———. "Teacher and Messiah?" Pages 193-210 in *The Community of the Renewed Covenant: The Notre Dame Symposium on the Dead Sea Scrolls*. Edited by Eugene Ulrich and James VanderKam. CJA 10. Notre Dame, IN: University of Notre Dame Press, 1994.

———. "'He Shall Not Judge by What His Eyes See': Messianic Authority in the Dead Sea Scrolls." *DSD* 2 (1995): 145-64.

———. *The Scepter and the Star: The Messiahs of the Dead Sea Scrolls and Other Ancient Literature*. Anchor Bible Reference Library. New York: Doubleday, 1995.

———. *Apocalypticism in the Dead Sea Scrolls*. London: Routledge, 1997.

———. *Seers, Sibyls, and Sages in Hellenistic-Roman Judaism*. JSJSup 54. Leiden: Brill, 1997.

———. "Pseudepigraphy and Group Formation in Second Temple Judaism." Pages 43-58 in *Pseudepigraphic Perspectives: The Apocrypha and Pseudepigrapha in Light of the Dead Sea Scrolls*. Edited by Esther G. Chazon and Michael E. Stone. STDJ 31. Leiden: Brill, 1999.

———. *Between Athens and Jerusalem: Jewish Identity in the Hellenistic Diaspora*. Rev. ed. Grand Rapids: Eerdmans, 2000.

———. "The Construction of Israel in the Sectarian Rule Books." Pages 25-42 in *Theory of Israel*. Vol. 1 of *The Judaism of Qumran: A Systemic Reading of the Dead Sea Scrolls*. Part 5 of *Judaism in Late Antiquity*. Edited by Alan J. Avery-Peck, Jacob Neusner, and Bruce Chilton. Handbuch der Orientalstik 1/56. Leiden: Brill, 2001.

———. "Forms of Community in the Dead Sea Scrolls." Pages 97-111 in *Emanuel: Studies in Hebrew Bible, Septuagint, and Dead Sea Scrolls in Honor of Emanuel Tov*. Edited by Shalom M. Paul, Robert A. Kraft, Lawrence H. Schiffman, and Weston W. Fields. VTSup 94. Leiden: Brill, 2003.

———. "The *Yaḥad* and 'the Qumran Community.'" Pages 81-96 in *Biblical Traditions in Transmission: Essays in Honour of Michael A. Knibb*. Edited by Charlotte Hempel and Judith M. Lieu. JSJSup 111. Leiden: Brill, 2005.

———. "Enoch, the Dead Sea Scrolls, and the Essenes: Groups and Movements in Judaism in the Early Second Century B.C.E." Pages 345-50 in *Enoch and Qumran Origins: New Light on a Forgotten Connection*. Edited by Gabriele Boccaccini. Grand Rapids: Eerdmans, 2005.

———. "The Essenes and the Afterlife." Pages 35-53 in *From 4QMMT to Resurrection: Mélanges qumraniens en hommage à Émile Puech*. Edited by Florentino García Martínez, Annette Steudel, and Eibert Tigchelaar. STDJ 61. Leiden: Brill, 2006.

———. "The Time of the Teacher: An Old Debate Renewed." Pages 212-29 in *Studies in the Hebrew Bible, Qumran, and the Septuagint Presented to Eugene*

Ulrich. Edited by Peter W. Flint, Emanuel Tov, and James C. VanderKam. VTSup 101. Leiden: Brill, 2006.

———. "Conceptions of Afterlife in the Dead Sea Scrolls." Pages 103-25 in *Lebendige Hoffnung — ewiger Tod.* Edited by Michael Labahn and Manfred Lang. ABIG 24. Leipzig: Evangelische Verlagsanstalt, 2007.

———. "Enochic Judaism and the Sect of the Dead Sea Scrolls." Pages 283-99 in *The Early Enoch Literature.* Edited by John J. Collins and Gabriele Boccaccini. JSJSup 121. Leiden: Brill, 2007.

———. "The Angelic Life." Pages 291-310 in *Metamorphoses: Resurrection, Body and Transformative Practices in Early Christianity.* Edited by Turid Karlsen Seim and Jorunn Økland. Berlin: de Gruyter, 2009.

———. "Josephus on the Essenes: The Sources of His Evidence." In *A Wandering Galilean: Essays in Honour of Sean Freyne.* Edited by Zuleika Rodgers with Margaret Daly-Denton and Anne Fitzpatrick McKinley. JSJSup 132. Leiden: Brill, 2009.

Collins, John J., and Gabriele Boccaccini, eds. *The Early Enoch Literature.* JSJSup 121. Leiden: Brill, 2007.

Collins, John J., and Robert A. Kugler, eds. *Religion in the Dead Sea Scrolls.* SDSSRL. Grand Rapids: Eerdmans, 2000.

Cross, Frank Moore. "The Development of the Jewish Scripts." Pages 169-71 in *The Bible and the Ancient Near East: Essays in Honor of William Foxwell Albright.* Edited by George Ernest Wright. Garden City, NY: Doubleday, 1965.

———. *Canaanite Myth and Hebrew Epic.* Cambridge: Harvard University Press, 1973.

———. "Appendix: Paleographical Dates of the Manuscripts." Page 57 in *Rule of the Community and Related Documents.* Vol. 1 of *The Dead Sea Scrolls: Hebrew, Aramaic, and Greek Texts with English Translations.* Edited by James H. Charlesworth. PTSDSSP. Louisville: Westminster John Knox, 1994.

———. *The Ancient Library of Qumran.* 3rd ed. BibSem 30. Sheffield: Sheffield Academic Press, 1995. (1st ed. 1958.)

Cross, Frank Moore, and Esther Eshel. "Ostraca from Khirbet Qumrân." *IEJ* 47 (1997): 17-28.

———. "The Missing Link: Does a New Inscription Establish a Connection Between Qumran and the Dead Sea Scrolls?" *BAR* 24/2 (1998): 48-53, 69.

———. "1. Khirbet Qumran Ostracon." Pages 497-507 and Plate XXXIII in Stephen J. Pfann et al. *Qumran Cave 4.* Vol. XXVI: *Cryptic Texts and Miscellanea, Part 1.* DJD 36. Oxford: Clarendon, 2000.

Dalman, Gustaf. *Palästinajahrbuch des deutschen evangelischen Instituts für Altertumswissenschaft des heiligen Landes zu Jerusalem.* Vol. 10. Berlin: Mittler, 1914.

Davidson, Maxwell J. *Angels at Qumran: A Comparative Study of 1 Enoch 1–36, 72–*

108 and Sectarian Writings from Qumran. JSPSup 11. Sheffield: JSOT Press, 1992.

Davies, Philip R. "Hasidim in the Maccabean Period." *JJS* 28 (1977): 127-40.

―――. *Qumran*. Cities of the Biblical World. Grand Rapids: Eerdmans, 1982.

―――. *The Damascus Covenant: An Interpretation of the "Damascus Document."* JSOTSup 25. Sheffield: JSOT Press, 1983.

―――. *Behind the Essenes: History and Ideology in the Dead Sea Scrolls*. BJS 84. Atlanta: Scholars Press, 1987.

―――. "The Teacher of Righteousness at the End of Days." *RevQ* 13 (1988): 313-17.

―――. "How Not to Do Archaeology: The Story of Qumran." *BA* 51 (1988): 203-7. Repr. in pages 79-86 of *Sects and Scrolls: Essays on Qumran and Related Topics*. SFSHJ 134. Atlanta: Scholars Press, 1996.

―――. "The 'Damascus Sect' and Judaism." Pages 70-84 in *Pursuing the Text: Studies in Honor of Ben Zion Wacholder on the Occasion of His Seventieth Birthday*. Edited by John C. Reeves and John Kampen. JSOTSup 184. Sheffield: Sheffield Academic Press, 1994.

―――. *Sects and Scrolls: Essays on Qumran and Related Topics*. SFSHJ 134. Atlanta: Scholars Press, 1996.

―――. "Sects from Texts: On the Problems of Doing a Sociology of the Qumran Literature." Pages 69-82 in *New Directions in Qumran Studies: Proceedings of the Bristol Colloquium on the Dead Sea Scrolls*. Edited by Jonathan G. Campbell, William John Lyons, and Lloyd K. Pietersen. London: T&T Clark, 2005.

―――. "What History Can We Get from the Scrolls, and How?" In *Proceedings of the Birmingham Dead Sea Scrolls Conference, October 2007*. Edited by Charlotte Hempel, forthcoming.

Davies, Philip R., and Joan Taylor. "On the Testimony of Women in 1QSa." *DSD* 3 (1996): 223-35.

Davies, Philip R., and Richard T. White. *A Tribute to Geza Vermes: Essays on Jewish and Christian Literature and History*. JSOTSup 100. Sheffield: JSOT Press, 1990.

Davies, William D., and David Daube, eds. *The Background of the New Testament and Its Eschatology*. Cambridge: Cambridge University Press, 1956.

Davis, Michael Thomas, and Brent A. Strawn, eds. *Qumran Studies: New Approaches, New Questions*. Grand Rapids: Eerdmans, 2007.

De Troyer, Kristin, and Armin Lange, eds. *Reading the Present in the Qumran Library: The Perception of the Contemporary by Means of Scriptural Interpretations*. SBLSymS 30. Atlanta: SBL, 2005.

Dillon, John, and Jackson Hershbell. *Iamblichus on the Pythagorean Way of Life*. SBL Texts and Translations 29, Graeco-Roman Religion Series 11. Atlanta: Scholars Press, 1991.

Dimant, Devorah. "Qumran Sectarian Literature." Pages 483-550 in *Jewish Writ-*

ings of the Second Temple Period: Apocrypha, Pseudepigrapha, Qumran Sectarian Writings, Philo, Josephus. Edited by Michael E. Stone. CRINT 2/2. Philadelphia: Fortress, 1984.

Dimant, Devorah, and Uriel Rappaport, eds. *The Dead Sea Scrolls: Forty Years of Research.* STDJ 10. Leiden: Brill, 1992.

Dittenberger, Wilhelm. *Sylloge Inscriptionum Graecarum.* 3rd ed. 4 vols. Leipzig: Hirzelium, 1916–24.

Donceel, Robert, and Pauline Donceel-Voûte. "The Archaeology of Khirbet Qumran." Pages 1-38 in *Methods of Investigation of the Dead Sea Scrolls and the Khirbet Qumran Site: Present Realities and Future Prospects.* Edited by Michael O. Wise, Norman Golb, John J. Collins, and Dennis G. Pardee. ANYAS 722. New York: New York Academy of Sciences, 1994.

Donceel-Voûte, Pauline. "Les ruines de Qumrân reinterprétées." *Archaeologia* 298 (1994): 24-35.

Doudna, Gregory L. "Dating the Scrolls on the Basis of Radiocarbon Analysis." Pages 430-71 in vol. 1 of *The Dead Sea Scrolls after Fifty Years: A Comprehensive Assessment.* Edited by Peter W. Flint and James C. VanderKam. 2 vols. Leiden: Brill, 1998–99.

———. *4Q Pesher Nahum: A Critical Edition.* JSPSup 35. London: Sheffield Academic Press, 2001.

———. "The Legacy of an Error in Archaeological Interpretation: The Dating of the Qumran Cave Scroll Deposits." Pages 147-57 in *Qumran: The Site of the Dead Sea Scrolls: Archaeological Interpretations and Debates. Proceedings of a Conference Held at Brown University, November 17-19, 2002.* Edited by Katharina Galor, Jean-Baptiste Humbert, and Jürgen Zangenberg. STDJ 57. Leiden: Brill, 2006.

Driver, Godfrey Rolles. *The Judaean Scrolls: The Problem and a Solution.* Oxford: Blackwell, 1965.

Duggan, Michael. *Covenant Renewal in Ezra-Nehemiah (Neh 7:72b–10:40): An Exegetical, Literary, and Theological Study.* SBL Dissertation Series 164. Atlanta: SBL, 2001.

Dupont-Sommer, André. *Observations sur le Manuel de Discipline découvert près de la Mer Morte.* Paris: Maisonneuve, 1951.

———. *The Dead Sea Scrolls: A Preliminary Survey.* Translated by E. Margaret Rowley. Oxford: Blackwell, 1952.

———. "Le problème des influences étrangères sur la secte juive de qoumrân." *Revue d'histoire et de philosophie religieuses* 35 (1955): 75-92.

———. *The Essene Writings from Qumran.* Translated by Geza Vermes. Gloucester, MA: Peter Smith, 1973.

Edwards, Douglas R., ed. *Religion and Society in Roman Palestine: Old Questions and New Approaches.* London: Routledge, 2004.

Eisenman, Robert E. *Maccabees, Zadokites, Christians and Qumran: A New Hypothesis of Qumran Origins.* Leiden: Brill, 1983.

Elgvin, Torleif. "The *Yaḥad* Is More than Qumran." Pages 273-79 in *Enoch and Qumran Origins: New Light on a Forgotten Connection.* Edited by Gabriele Boccaccini. Grand Rapids: Eerdmans, 2005.

Elledge, Casey D. *Life after Death in Early Judaism: The Evidence of Josephus.* WUNT 2/208. Tübingen: Mohr Siebeck, 2006.

Elliger, Karl. *Studien zum Habakuk-Kommentar vom Toten Meer.* Beiträge zur historischen Theologie 15. Tübingen: Mohr Siebeck, 1953.

Engberg-Pedersen, Troels. "Philo's *De Vita Contemplativa* as a Philosopher's Dream." *JSJ* 30 (1999): 40-64.

Eshel, Esther, Hanan Eshel, and Ada Yardeni. "A Qumran Scroll Containing Part of Psalm 154 and a Prayer for the Welfare of King Jonathan and His Kingdom." *IEJ* 42 (1992): 199-229.

———. "448: 4QApocryphal Psalm and Prayer." Pages 403-35 in Esther Eshel et al., *Qumran Cave 4.* Vol. VI: *Poetical and Liturgical Texts, Part 1.* DJD 11. Oxford: Clarendon, 1998.

Eshel, Esther, et al. *Qumran Cave 4.* Vol. VI: *Poetical and Liturgical Texts, Part 1.* DJD 11. Oxford: Clarendon, 1998.

Eshel, Hanan. "The Identification of the City of Salt." *IEJ* 45 (1995): 37-40.

———. "4QMMT and the History of the Hasmonean Period." Pages 53-65 in *Reading 4QMMT: New Perspectives on Qumran Law and History.* Edited by John Kampen and Moshe J. Bernstein. SBLSymS 2. Atlanta: SBL, 1996.

———. "The Meaning and Significance of CD 20:13-15." Pages 330-36 in *The Provo International Conference on the Dead Sea Scrolls: Technological Innovations, New Texts and Reformulated Issues.* Edited by Donald W. Parry and Eugene Ulrich. STDJ 30. Leiden: Brill, 1999.

———. "Qumran Archaeology." *JAOS* 125 (2005): 389-94.

———. *The Dead Sea Scrolls and the Hasmonean State.* SDSSRL. Grand Rapids: Eerdmans, 2008.

Eshel, Hanan, and Zvi Greenhut. "Ḥiam el-Sagha, a Cemetery of the Qumran Type, Judaean Desert." *RB* 100 (1993): 252-59.

Eshel, Hanan, Magen Broshi, Richard Freund, and Brian Schultz. "New Data on the Cemetery East of Qumran." *DSD* 9 (2001): 155-63.

Fabry, Heinz-Josef. "Zadokiden und Aaroniden in Qumran." Pages 201-17 in *Das Manna fällt auch heute noch: Beiträge zur Geschichte und Theologie des Alten, Ersten Testaments: Festschrift für Erich Zenger.* Edited by Frank-Lothar Hossfeld and Ludger Schwienhorst-Schönberger. Herders biblische Studien 44. Freiburg: Herder, 2004.

Ferguson, John. *Utopias of the Classical World.* London: Thames and Hudson, 1975.

Fields, Weston W. "Discovery and Purchase." Pages 208-12 in vol. 1 of *Encyclopedia of the Dead Sea Scrolls.* Edited by Lawrence H. Schiffman and James C. VanderKam. 2 vols. New York: Oxford University Press, 2000.

———. *The Dead Sea Scrolls: A Short History.* Leiden: Brill, 2006.

Fitzmyer, Joseph A. "Divorce among First-Century Palestinian Jews." *ErIsr* 14 (H. L. Ginsberg Volume) (1978): 106*-10*.

———. "A Feature of Qumran Angelology and the Angels of 1 Cor 11:10." Pages 31-47 in *Paul and the Dead Sea Scrolls.* Edited by Jerome Murphy-O'Connor and James H. Charlesworth. New York: Crossroad, 1990.

———. "The Gathering In of the Community's Teacher." *Maarav* 8 (1992): 223-28.

Flint, Peter W., and James C. VanderKam, eds. *The Dead Sea Scrolls after Fifty Years: A Comprehensive Assessment.* 2 vols. Leiden: Brill, 1998–99.

Flint, Peter W., Emanuel Tov, and James C. VanderKam, eds. *Studies in the Hebrew Bible, Qumran, and the Septuagint Presented to Eugene Ulrich.* VTSup 101. Leiden: Brill, 2006.

Fraade, Steven D. "To Whom It May Concern: 4QMMT and Its Addressee(s)." *RevQ* 19 (2000): 507-26.

———. "Law, History, and Narrative in the Damascus Document." Pages *35-*55 in *Meghillot: Studies in the Dead Sea Scrolls V-VI: A Festschrift for Devorah Dimant* (Hebrew). Edited by Moshe Bar-Asher and Emanuel Tov. Jerusalem: Bialik Institute, 2007.

Frey, Jörg. "Zur historischen Auswertung der antiken Essenerberichte. Ein Beitrag zum Gespräch mit Roland Bergmeier." Pages 23-57 in *Qumran Kontrovers: Beiträge zu den Textfunden vom Toten Meer.* Edited by Jörg Frey and Hartmut Stegemann. Paderborn: Bonifatius, 2003.

Frey, Jörg, and Hartmut Stegemann, eds. *Qumran Kontrovers: Beiträge zu den Textfunden vom Toten Meer.* Paderborn: Bonifatius, 2003.

Galor, Katharina. "Plastered Pools: A New Perspective." Pages 291-320 in *Khirbet Qumrân et ʿAïn Feshkha II: Études d'anthropologie, de physique et de chimie. Studies of Anthropology, Physics and Chemistry.* Edited by Jean-Baptiste Humbert and Jan Gunneweg. NTOA.SA 3. Fribourg: Academic Press, 2003.

Galor, Katharina, Jean-Baptiste Humbert, and Jürgen Zangenberg, eds. *Qumran: The Site of the Dead Sea Scrolls: Archaeological Interpretations and Debates. Proceedings of a Conference Held at Brown University, November 17-19, 2002.* STDJ 57. Leiden: Brill, 2006.

Gammie, John G., and Leo G. Perdue, eds. *The Sage in Israel and the Ancient Near East.* Winona Lake, IN: Eisenbrauns, 1990.

García Martínez, Florentino. "Qumran Origins and Early History: A Groningen Hypothesis." *Folia orientalia* 25 (1988): 113-26.

———. *The Dead Sea Scrolls Translated.* Translated by Wilfred G. E. Watson. Grand Rapids: Eerdmans, 1994.

———. *Qumranica Minora.* STDJ 63. Leiden: Brill, 2007.

García Martínez, Florentino, and Adam S. van der Woude. "A Groningen Hypothesis of Qumran Origins and Early History." *RevQ* 14 (1990): 521-41.

García Martínez, Florentino, and Eibert J. Tigchelaar. *The Dead Sea Scrolls Study Edition.* 2 vols. Leiden: Brill, 1997.

García Martínez, Florentino, and Gerard P. Luttikhuizen, eds. *Jerusalem, Alexandria, Rome: Studies in Honour of A. Hilhorst.* JSJSup 82. Leiden: Brill, 2003.

García Martínez, Florentino, Annette Steudel, and Eibert Tigchelaar, eds. *From 4QMMT to Resurrection: Mélanges qumraniens en homage à Émile Puech.* STDJ 61. Leiden: Brill, 2006.

Gärtner, Bertil. *The Temple and the Community in Qumran and the New Testament.* Cambridge: Cambridge University Press, 1965.

Gillihan, Yonder M. "Civic Ideology among the Covenanters of the Dead Sea Scrolls and Other Greco-Roman Voluntary Associations." Ph.D diss., University of Chicago, 2007.

Ginzberg, Louis. *An Unknown Jewish Sect.* New York: Ktav, 1976. Translation of *Eine unbekannte jüdische Sekte.* Published privately in 1922, and repr., Hildesheim: Olms, 1972.

Golb, Norman. *Who Wrote the Dead Sea Scrolls? The Search for the Secret of Qumran.* New York: Scribner, 1995.

Goodman, Martin, "Sadducees and Essenes after 70 CE." Pages 153-62 in idem, *Judaism in the Roman World: Collected Essays.* AGJU 66. Leiden: Brill, 2007.

———. "The Function of Minim in Early Rabbinic Judaism." Pages 163-74 in idem, *Judaism in the Roman World: Collected Essays.* AGJU 66. Leiden: Brill, 2007.

Goranson, Stephen. "Posidonius, Strabo and Marcus Vipsanius Agrippa as Sources on Essenes." *JJS* 45 (1994): 295-98.

———. "Essenes: Etymology from עשה." *RevQ* 11 (1984): 483-98.

———. "Essenes." Pages 268-69 in vol. 2 of *The Oxford Encyclopedia of Archaeology in the Near East.* Edited by Eric M. Meyers. 5 vols. New York: Oxford University Press, 1997.

———. "Others and Intra-Jewish Polemic as Reflected in Qumran Texts." Pages 534-51 in vol. 2 of *The Dead Sea Scrolls after Fifty Years: A Comprehensive Assessment.* Edited by Peter W. Flint and James C. VanderKam. 2 vols. Leiden: Brill, 1998–99.

———. "Rereading Pliny on the Essenes: Some Bibliographic Notes." Online: http://orion.mscc.huji.ac.il/symposiums/programs/Goranson98.shtml.

Grabbe, Lester L. "When Is a Sect a Sect — or Not? Groups and Movements in the Second Temple Period." Pages 114-32 in *Sectarianism in Early Judaism: Sociological Advances.* Edited by D. J. Chalcraft. London: Equinox, 2007.

Graf, Fritz. "Pythagoras, Pythagoreanism." Pages 1283-85 in *The Oxford Classical*

Dictionary. Edited by Simon Hornblower and Anthony Spawforth. 3rd ed. Oxford: Oxford University Press, 1999.

Grossman, Maxine L. *Reading for History in the Damascus Document: A Methodological Study.* STDJ 45. Leiden: Brill, 2002.

Hachlili, Rachel. "Burial Practices at Qumran." *RevQ* 62 (1993): 247-64.

———. "The Qumran Cemetery: A Reconsideration." Pages 661-67 in *The Dead Sea Scrolls: Fifty Years after Their Discovery: Proceedings of the Jerusalem Congress, July 20-25, 1997.* Edited by Lawrence H. Schiffman, Emanuel Tov, and James C. VanderKam. Jerusalem: Israel Exploration Society, 2000.

———. *Jewish Funerary Customs, Practices and Rites in the Second Temple Period.* JSJSup 94. Leiden: Brill, 2005.

Hadas, Moses. *Hellenistic Culture: Fusion and Diffusion.* New York: Columbia University Press, 1959.

Halpern, Baruch. *The First Historians: The Hebrew Bible and History.* San Francisco: Harper & Row, 1988.

Harding, G. Lankester. "Khirbet Qumrân and Wady Murabba'at: Fresh Light on the Dead Sea Scrolls and New Manuscript Discoveries in Jordan." *PEQ* 84 (1952): 104-9.

Harrington, Hannah K. *The Purity Texts.* CQS 5. London: T&T Clark, 2004.

Heger, Paul. *Cult as the Catalyst for Division: Cult Disputes as the Motive for Schism in the Pre–70 Pluralistic Environment.* STDJ 65. Leiden: Brill, 2007.

Hempel, Charlotte. "The Earthly Essene Nucleus of 1QSa." *DSD* 3 (1996): 253-69.

———. "The Penal Code Reconsidered." Pages 337-48 in *Legal Texts and Legal Issues: Proceedings of the Second Meeting of the International Organization for Qumran Studies, Cambridge 1995. Published in Honour of Joseph M. Baumgarten.* Edited by Moshe J. Bernstein, Florentino García Martínez, and John Kampen. STDJ 23. Leiden: Brill, 1997.

———. "Community Structures in the Dead Sea Scrolls: Admission, Organization, Disciplinary Procedures." Pages 67-97 in vol. 2 of *The Dead Sea Scrolls after Fifty Years: A Comprehensive Assessment.* Edited by Peter W. Flint and James C. VanderKam. 2 vols. Leiden: Brill, 1998–99.

———. *The Laws of the Damascus Document: Sources, Traditions and Redaction.* STDJ 29. Leiden: Brill, 1998.

———. "Community Origins in the Damascus Document in the Light of Recent Scholarship." Pages 316-29 in *The Provo International Conference on the Dead Sea Scrolls: Technological Innovations, New Texts and Reformulated Issues.* Edited by Donald W. Parry and Eugene Ulrich. STDJ 30. Leiden: Brill, 1999.

———. *The Damascus Texts.* CQS 1. Sheffield: Sheffield Academic Press, 2000.

———. "Interpretative Authority in the Community Rule Tradition." *DSD* 10 (2003): 59-80.

———. "The Sons of Aaron in the Dead Sea Scrolls." Pages 207-24 in *Flores*

Florentino: Dead Sea Scrolls and Other Early Jewish Studies in Honour of Florentino García Martínez. Edited by Anthony Hilhorst, Émile Puech, and Eibert Tigchelaar. JSJSup 122. Leiden: Brill, 2007.

————, ed. *Proceedings of the Birmingham Dead Sea Scrolls Conference, October 2007*, forthcoming.

Hempel, Charlotte, and Judith M. Lieu, eds. *Biblical Traditions in Transmission: Essays in Honour of Michael A. Knibb.* JSJSup 111. Leiden: Brill, 2006.

Hengel, Martin. *Judaism and Hellenism: Studies in Their Encounter in Palestine during the Early Hellenistic Period.* Translated by John Bowden. 2 vols. Philadelphia: Fortress, 1974.

Hilhorst, Anthony, Émile Puech, and Eibert Tigchelaar, eds. *Flores Florentino: Dead Sea Scrolls and Other Early Jewish Studies in Honour of Florentino García Martínez.* JSJSup 122. Leiden: Brill, 2007.

Hill, Christopher. *Society and Puritanism in Pre-Revolutionary England.* New York: Schocken, 1964.

Himmelfarb, Martha. *A Kingdom of Priests: Ancestry and Merit in Ancient Judaism.* Philadelphia: University of Pennsylvania Press, 2006.

Hirschfeld, Yizhar. "Early Roman Manor Houses in Judea and the Site of Khirbet Qumran." *JNES* 57 (1998): 161-89.

————. "A Settlement of Hermits above Engedi." *TA* 27 (2000): 103-55.

————. *Qumran in Context.* Peabody, MA: Hendrickson, 2004.

Hölscher, Gustav. "Josephus." Pages 1934-2000 in PW 9/2. Stuttgart: Metzler, 1916.

Hopkins, Jamal-Dominique. "Sacrifice in the Dead Sea Scrolls: Khirbet Qumran, the Essenes and Cultic Spiritualization." Ph.D. diss., Manchester, 2005.

————. "Josephus, the Dead Sea Scrolls, and the Qumran Essenes: Examining a Jewish Sectarian Movement." Paper presented at the SBL annual meeting in San Diego, November 14, 2007.

Horgan, Maurya P. *Pesharim: Qumran Interpretations of Biblical Books.* Catholic Biblical Quarterly Monograph Series B. Washington, DC: Catholic Biblical Association, 1979.

————. "Habakkuk Pesher (1QpHab)." Pages 157-85 in *Pesharim, Other Commentaries, and Related Documents.* Vol. 6B of *The Dead Sea Scrolls: Hebrew, Aramaic, and Greek Texts with English Translations.* Edited by James H. Charlesworth. PTSDSSP. Louisville: Westminster John Knox, 2002.

Horgan, Maurya P., and Paul J. Kobelski, eds. *To Touch the Text: Biblical and Related Studies in Honor of Joseph A. Fitzmyer, S.J.* New York: Crossroad, 1989.

Hornblower, Simon, and Anthony Spawforth, eds. *The Oxford Classical Dictionary.* 3rd ed. Oxford: Oxford University Press, 1999.

Hossfeld, Frank-Lothar, and Ludger Schwienhorst-Schönberger, eds. *Das Manna fällt auch heute noch: Beiträge zur Geschichte und Theologie des Alten, Ersten Testaments: Festschrift für Erich Zenger.* Freiburg: Herder, 2004.

Hultgren, Stephen. *From the Damascus Covenant to the Covenant of the Community: Literary, Historical, and Theological Studies in the Dead Sea Scrolls.* STDJ 66. Leiden: Brill, 2007.

Humbert, Jean-Baptiste. "L'Espace sacré à Qumran: Propositions pour l'archéologie." *RB* 101 (1994): 161-214.

―――. "Reconsideration of the Archaeological Interpretation." Pages 419-25 in *Khirbet Qumrân et 'Aïn Feshkha II: Études d'anthropologie, de physique et de chimie. Studies of Anthropology, Physics and Chemistry.* Edited by Jean-Baptiste Humbert and Jan Gunneweg. NTOA.SA 3. Fribourg: Academic Press, 2003.

―――. "The Chronology During the First Century B.C.: De Vaux and His Method: A Debate." Pages 425-37 in *Khirbet Qumrân et 'Aïn Feshkha II: Études d'anthropologie, de physique et de chimie. Studies of Anthropology, Physics and Chemistry.* Edited by Jean-Baptiste Humbert and Jan Gunneweg. NTOA.SA 3. Fribourg: Academic Press, 2003.

―――. "Some Remarks on the Archaeology of Qumran." Pages 19-39 in *Qumran: The Site of the Dead Sea Scrolls: Archaeological Interpretations and Debates. Proceedings of a Conference Held at Brown University, November 17-19, 2002.* Edited by Katharina Galor, Jean-Baptiste Humbert, and Jürgen Zangenberg. STDJ 57. Leiden: Brill, 2006.

Humbert, Jean-Baptiste, and Alain Chambon. *Fouilles de Khirbet Qumrân et de Aïn Feshkha: Album de photographies, Répertoire du fonds photographique, Synthèse des notes de chantier du Père Roland de Vaux OP.* NTOA.SA 1. Fribourg: Éditions Universitaires, 1994.

Humbert, Jean-Baptiste, and Jan Gunneweg, eds. *Khirbet Qumrân et 'Aïn Feshkha II: Études d'anthropologie, de physique et de chimie. Studies of Anthropology, Physics and Chemistry.* NTOA.SA 3. Fribourg: Academic Press, 2003.

Hunt, Alice. *Missing Priests. The Zadokites in Tradition and History.* Library of Hebrew Bible/Old Testament Studies [= JSOTSup] 452; New York: T&T Clark, 2006.

Iwry, Samuel. "Was There a Migration to Damascus? The Problem of שבי ישראל." *ErIsr* 9 (Albright Festschrift) (1969): 80-88.

Jastram, Nathan. "Hierarchy at Qumran." Pages 349-76 in *Legal Texts and Legal Issues: Proceedings of the Second Meeting of the International Organization for Qumran Studies, Cambridge 1995. Published in Honour of Joseph M. Baumgarten.* Edited by Moshe J. Bernstein, Florentino García Martínez, and John Kampen. STDJ 23. Leiden: Brill, 1997.

Jeremias, Gert. *Der Lehrer der Gerechtigkeit.* SUNT 2. Göttingen: Vandenhoeck & Ruprecht, 1963.

Jokiranta, Jutta. "'Sectarianism' of the Qumran 'Sect': Sociological Notes." *RevQ* 20 (2001): 223-39.

————. "Identity on a Continuum: Constructing and Expressing Sectarian Social Identity in Qumran *Serakhim* and *Pesharim.*" Ph.D. diss., Helsinki, 2005.

————. "Pesharim: A Mirror of Self-Understanding." Pages 23-34 in *Reading the Present in the Qumran Library: The Perception of the Contemporary by Means of Scriptural Interpretations.* Edited by Kristin De Troyer and Armin Lange. SBLSymS 30. Atlanta: SBL, 2005.

Jones, Allen H. *Essenes: The Elect of Israel and Priests of Artemis.* Lanham, MD: University Press of America, 1985.

Kahn, Charles. *Pythagoras and the Pythagoreans: A Brief History.* Indianapolis: Hackett, 2001.

Kampen, John. "A Reconsideration of the Name 'Essene' in Greco-Jewish Literature in Light of Recent Perceptions of the Qumran Sect." *HUCA* 57 (1986): 61-81.

————. *The Hasideans and the Origin of Pharisaism: A Study in 1 and 2 Maccabees.* SBLSCS 24. Atlanta: Scholars Press, 1988.

Kampen, John, and Moshe J. Bernstein. *Reading 4QMMT: New Perspectives on Qumran Law and History.* SBLSymS 2. Atlanta: SBL, 1996.

Kapera, Zdzislaw Jan, ed. *Mogilany 1989: Papers on the Dead Sea Scrolls Offered in Memory of Jean Carmignac. Part II: The Teacher of Righteousness: Literary Studies.* Kraków: Enigma, 1991.

Kapfer, Hillary Evans. "The Relationship between the Damascus Document and the Community Rule: Attitudes toward the Temple as a Test Case." *DSD* 14 (2007): 152-77.

Kingsley, Peter. *Ancient Philosophy, Mystery, and Magic: Empedocles and Pythagorean Tradition.* Oxford: Oxford University Press, 1995.

Klauck, Hans-Josef. "Gütergemeinschaft in der klassischen Antike, in Qumran und im Neuen Testament." *RevQ* 11 (1982): 47-79.

Klawans, Jonathan. *Purity, Sacrifice, and the Temple: Symbolism and Supersessionism in the Study of Ancient Judaism.* New York: Oxford University Press, 2006.

————. "Purity in the Dead Sea Scrolls." In *The Oxford Handbook of the Dead Sea Scrolls.* Edited by Timothy Lim and John J. Collins, forthcoming.

Klinghardt, Matthias. "The Manual of Discipline in the Light of Statutes of Hellenistic Associations." Pages 251-79 in *Methods of Investigation of the Dead Sea Scrolls and the Khirbet Qumran Site: Present Realities and Future Prospects.* Edited by Michael O. Wise, Norman Golb, John J. Collins, and Dennis G. Pardee. ANYAS 722. New York: New York Academy of Sciences, 1994.

Klinzing, Georg. *Die Umdeutung des Kultus in der Qumrangemeinde und im Neuen Testament.* SUNT 7. Göttingen: Vandenhoeck & Ruprecht, 1971.

Kloppenborg, John S., and Stephen G. Wilson, eds. *Voluntary Associations in the Graeco-Roman World.* London: Routledge, 1996.

Knibb, Michael A. "The Exile in the Literature of the Intertestamental Period." *HeyJ* 17 (1976): 249-72.

———. "Exile in the Damascus Document." *JSOT* 25 (1983): 99-117.

———. *The Qumran Community.* Cambridge Commentaries on Jewish Writings of the Jewish and Christian World 200 BC to AD 200, 2. Cambridge: Cambridge University Press, 1988.

———. "The Teacher of Righteousness — A Messianic Title?" Pages 51-65 in *A Tribute to Geza Vermes: Essays on Jewish and Christian Literature and History.* Edited by Philip R. Davies and Richard T. White. JSOTSup 100. Sheffield: JSOT Press, 1990.

———. "The Place of the Damascus Document." Pages 153-60 in *Methods of Investigation of the Dead Sea Scrolls and the Khirbet Qumran Site: Present Realities and Future Prospects.* Edited by Michael O. Wise, Norman Golb, John J. Collins, and Dennis G. Pardee. ANYAS 722. New York: New York Academy of Sciences, 1994.

König, Roderich, and Gerhard Winkler. *Plinius der ältere: Leben und Werk eines antiken Naturforschers.* Munich: Heimeran, 1979.

Kraft, Robert A. "Pliny on Essenes, Pliny on Jews." *DSD* 8 (2001): 255-61.

Kugler, Robert. "A Note on 1QS 9:14: The Sons of Righteousness or the Sons of Zadok." *DSD* 3 (1996): 315-20.

———. "Priesthood at Qumran." Pages 93-116 in vol. 2 of *The Dead Sea Scrolls after Fifty Years: A Comprehensive Assessment.* Edited by Peter W. Flint and James C. VanderKam. 2 vols. Leiden: Brill, 1998–99.

Laato, Antti. "The Chronology of the Damascus Document of Qumran." *RevQ* 60 (1992): 605-7.

———. *A Star Is Rising: The Historical Development of the Old Testament Royal Ideology and the Rise of the Jewish Messianic Expectations.* University of South Florida International Studies in Formative Christianity and Judaism 5. Atlanta: Scholars Press, 1997.

Labahn, Michael, and Manfred Lang, eds. *Lebendige Hoffnung — ewiger Tod.* ABIG 24. Leipzig: Evangelische Verlagsanstalt, 2007.

Lacocque, André. "The Socio-Spiritual Formative Milieu of the Daniel Apocalypse." Pages 315-43 in *The Book of Daniel in the Light of New Findings.* Edited by Adam S. van der Woude. BETL 106. Leuven: Peeters, 1993.

Lambert, David. "Did Israel Believe That Redemption Awaited Its Repentance? The Case of *Jubilees* 1." *CBQ* 68 (2006): 631-50.

Lange, Armin. *Weisheit und Prädestination in den Textfunden von Qumran.* STDJ 18. Leiden: Brill, 1995.

Laperrousaz, Ernest-Marie. "Remarques sur les circonstances qui ont entouré la destruction des bâtiments de Qumrân à la fin de la Période Ib de leur occupation." *VT* 7 (1957): 337-49.

————. *Qoumrân, l'établissement essénien des bords de la Mer Morte: Histoire et archéologie du site*. Paris: Picard, 1976.

————, ed. *Qoumrân et les manuscrits de la mer morte: Un cinquantenaire*. Paris: Cerf, 1997.

Lawrence, Jonathan D. *Washing in Water: Trajectories of Ritual Bathing in the Hebrew Bible and Second Temple Literature*. SBLAB 23. Leiden: Brill, 2006.

Leaney, Alfred Robert Clare. *The Rule of Qumran and Its Meaning*. London: SCM, 1966.

Lemaire, André. "Le roi Jonathan à Qoumrân (4Q448 B-C)." Pages 57-70 in *Qoumrân et les manuscrits de la mer morte: Un cinquantenaire*. Edited by Ernest-Marie Laperrousaz. Paris: Cerf, 1997.

Lévy, Isidore. *La légende de Pythagore de Grèce en Palestine*. Paris: Champion, 1927.

Lieberman, Saul. "The Discipline in the So-Called Dead Sea Manual of Discipline." *JBL* 71 (1952): 199-206.

Lied, Liv Ingeborg. "Another Look at the Land of Damascus: The Spaces of the *Damascus Document* in the Light of Edward W. Soja's Thirdspace Approach." Pages 101-25 in *New Directions in Qumran Studies: Proceedings of the Bristol Colloquium on the Dead Sea Scrolls, 8-10 September 2003*. Edited by Jonathan G. Campbell, William John Lyons, and Lloyd K. Pietersen. Library of Second Temple Studies [= JSPSup] 52. London: T&T Clark, 2005.

Lim, Timothy. "The Wicked Priests of the Groningen Hypothesis." *JBL* 112 (1993): 415-25.

————. *Pesharim*. CQS 3. New York: Continuum, 2002.

Lim, Timothy, and John J. Collins, eds. *The Oxford Handbook of the Dead Sea Scrolls*. New York: Oxford University Press, forthcoming.

Liver, Jacob. "The 'Sons of Zadok the Priests' in the Dead Sea Sect." *RevQ* 6 (1967): 3-32.

Magen, Yizhak, and Yuval Peleg. "Back to Qumran: Ten Years of Excavation and Research, 1993–2004." Pages 55-113 in *Qumran: The Site of the Dead Sea Scrolls: Archaeological Interpretations and Debates. Proceedings of a Conference Held at Brown University, November 17-19, 2002*. Edited by Katharina Galor, Jean-Baptiste Humbert, and Jürgen Zangenberg. STDJ 57. Leiden: Brill, 2006.

Magness, Jodi. "The Community at Qumran in Light of Its Pottery." Pages 39-47 in *Methods of Investigation of the Dead Sea Scrolls and the Khirbet Qumran Site: Present Realities and Future Prospects*. Edited by Michael O. Wise, Norman Golb, John J. Collins, and Dennis G. Pardee. ANYAS 722. New York: New York Academy of Sciences, 1994.

————. "Qumran Archaeology: Past Perspectives and Future Prospects." Pages 47-77 in vol. 1 of *The Dead Sea Scrolls after Fifty Years: A Comprehensive Assess-*

ment. Edited by Peter W. Flint and James C. VanderKam. 2 vols. Leiden: Brill, 1998–99.

————. *The Archaeology of Qumran and the Dead Sea Scrolls*. SDSSRL. Grand Rapids: Eerdmans, 2002.

————. *Debating Qumran: Collected Essays on Archaeology*. Interdisciplinary Studies in Ancient Culture and Religion 4. Leuven: Peeters, 2004.

————. Review of Yizhar Hirschfeld, *Qumran in Context*. *RBL* 08/27/2005.

————. "Qumran: The Site of the Dead Sea Scrolls: A Review Article." *RevQ* 22 (2006): 641-64.

Main, Emmanuelle. "For King Jonathan or Against? The Use of the Bible in 4Q448." Pages 113-35 in *Biblical Perspectives: Early Use and Interpretation of the Bible in Light of the Dead Sea Scrolls*. Edited by Michael E. Stone and Esther G. Chazon. STDJ 28. Leiden: Brill, 1998.

Mason, Steve. "What Josephus Says about the Essenes in His Judean War." Online: http://orion.mscc.huji.ac.il/orion/programs/Mason00-1.shtml.

————. "Was Josephus a Pharisee? A Reexamination of Life 10–12." *JJS* 40 (1989): 31-46.

————. *Flavius Josephus on the Pharisees: A Composition-Critical Study*. SPB 39. Leiden: Brill, 1991.

————. "Josephus, Daniel and the Flavian House." Pages 160-91 in *Josephus and the History of the Greco-Roman Period: Essays in Memory of Morton Smith*. Edited by Fausto Parente and Joseph Sievers. SPB 41. Leiden: Brill, 1994.

————, ed. *Understanding Josephus: Seven Perspectives*. JSPSup 32. Sheffield: Sheffield Academic Press, 1998.

————. "What Josephus Says about the Essenes in His *Judean War*." Pages 423-55 in *Text and Artifact in the Religions of Mediterranean Antiquity: Essays in Honour of Peter Richardson*. Edited by Stephen G. Wilson and Michel Desjardins. Studies in Christianity and Judaism 9. Waterloo: Wilfrid Laurier University Press, 2000.

————. *Life of Josephus. Translation and Commentary*. Flavius Josephus Translation and Commentary 9. Leiden: Brill, 2001.

————. *Josephus and the New Testament*. 2nd ed. Peabody, MA: Hendrickson, 2003.

————. "Essenes and Lurking Spartans in Josephus' *Judean War*: From Story to History." Pages 219-61 in *Making History: Josephus and Historical Method*. Edited by Zuleika Rodgers. JSJSup 110. Leiden: Brill, 2007.

Masterman, Ernest William Gurney. "Notes on Some Ruins and a Rock-Cut Aqueduct in the Wady Kumrân." *Palestine Exploration Fund Quarterly Statement* 28 (1903): 264-67.

Mendels, Doron. "Hellenistic Utopia and the Essenes." *HTR* 72 (1979): 207-22.

Meshorer, Ya'akov. *Jewish Coins of the Second Temple Period.* Translated by I. H. Levine. Tel Aviv: Am Hassefer, 1967.

―――. *Ancient Jewish Coinage.* Vol. 2: *Herod the Great through Bar Cochba.* Dix Hills, NY: Amphora, 1982.

Metso, Sarianna. *The Textual Development of the Qumran Community Rule.* STDJ 21. Leiden: Brill, 1997.

―――. "In Search of the Sitz im Leben of the Qumran Community Rule." Pages 306-15 in *The Provo International Conference on the Dead Sea Scrolls: Technological Innovations, New Texts and Reformulated Issues.* Edited by Donald W. Parry and Eugene Ulrich. STDJ 30. Leiden: Brill, 1999.

―――. "Qumran Community Structure and Terminology as Theological Statement." *RevQ* 20 (2002): 429-44.

―――. "Whom Does the Term Yaḥad Identify?" Pages 213-35 in *Biblical Traditions in Transmission: Essays in Honour of Michael A. Knibb.* Edited by Charlotte Hempel and Judith M. Lieu. JSJSup 111. Leiden: Brill, 2006.

―――. *The Serekh Texts.* CQS 9. London: T&T Clark, 2007.

Meyers, Eric M., ed. *The Oxford Encyclopedia of Archaeology in the Near East.* 5 vols. New York: Oxford University Press, 1997.

Milik, Józef T. "Hénoch au pays des aromates (ch. XXVII à XXXII): Fragments araméens de la grotte 4 de Qumrân." *RB* 65 (1958): 70-77.

―――. *Ten Tears of Discovery in the Wilderness of Judaea.* Translated by J. Strugnell. SBT 1/26. London: SCM, 1959.

Momigliano, Arnaldo. "What Josephus Did Not See." Pages 67-78 in idem, *Essays on Ancient and Modern Judaism.* Chicago: University of Chicago Press, 1994.

―――. *Essays on Ancient and Modern Judaism.* Chicago: University of Chicago Press, 1994.

Murphy, Catherine M. *Wealth in the Dead Sea Scrolls and in the Qumran Community.* STDJ 40. Leiden: Brill, 2002.

Murphy-O'Connor, Jerome. "La genèse littéraire de la *Règle de la Communauté.*" *RB* 76 (1969): 528-49.

―――. "A Literary Analysis of the Damascus Document VI, 2–VIII, 3." *RB* 78 (1971): 210-32.

―――. "The Essenes and Their History." *RB* 81 (1974): 215-44.

―――. "Judah the Essene and the Teacher of Righteousness." *RevQ* 10 (1981): 579-86.

―――. "The Damascus Document Revisited." *RB* 92 (1985): 224-30.

Murphy-O'Connor, Jerome, and James H. Charlesworth, eds. *Paul and the Dead Sea Scrolls.* New York: Crossroad, 1990.

Musial, Danuta. "'*Sodalicium Nigidiani*': Les pythagoriciens à Rome à la fin de la République." *Revue de l'histoire des religions* 218 (2001): 339-67.

Najman, Hindy. "Philosophical Contemplation and Revelatory Inspiration in Ancient Judean Traditions." *SPA* 19 (2007): 101-11.

Neusner, Jacob. "The Fellowship (חבורה) in the Second Jewish Commonwealth." *HTR* 53 (1960): 125-42.

———. *Fellowship in Judaism: The First Century and Today.* London: Vallentine, Mitchell, 1963.

———, ed. *Christianity, Judaism, and Other Greco-Roman Cults.* 5 vols. SJLA 12. Leiden: Brill, 1975.

Newsom, Carol A. "The Sage in the Literature of Qumran: The Functions of the *Maśkîl.*" Pages 373-82 in *The Sage in Israel and the Ancient Near East.* Edited by John G. Gammie and Leo G. Perdue. Winona Lake, IN: Eisenbrauns, 1990.

———. *The Self as Symbolic Space: Constructing Identity and Community at Qumran.* STDJ 54. Leiden: Brill, 2004.

Nickelsburg, George W. E. *Resurrection, Immortality, and Eternal Life in Intertestamental Judaism.* Harvard Theological Studies 26. Cambridge: Harvard University Press, 1972. Revised ed., 2006.

———. "Enochic Wisdom: An Alternative to Mosaic Torah?" Pages 123-32 in *Hesed ve-Emet: Studies in Honor of Ernest S. Frerichs.* Edited by Jodi Magness and Seymour Gitin. BJS 320. Atlanta: Scholars Press, 1998.

———. *1 Enoch 1.* Hermeneia. Minneapolis: Fortress, 2001.

Nitzan, Bilhah. *Pesher Habakkuk: A Scroll from the Wilderness of Judaea (1QpHab): Text, Introduction, and Commentary* (Hebrew). Jerusalem: Bialik Institute, 1986.

———. "The *Pesher* and Other Methods of Instruction." Pages 209-20 in *Mogilany 1989: Papers on the Dead Sea Scrolls Offered in Memory of Jean Carmignac.* Part II: *The Teacher of Righteousness: Literary Studies.* Edited by Zdzislaw Jan Kapera. Kraków: Enigma, 1991.

Nodet, Étienne. "*Asidaioi* and Essenes." Pages 63-87 in *Flores Florentino: Dead Sea Scrolls and Other Early Jewish Studies in Honour of Florentino García Martínez.* Edited by Anthony Hilhorst, Émile Puech, and Eibert Tigchelaar. JSJSup 122. Leiden: Brill, 2007.

Norton, Jonathan. "Reassessment of Controversial Studies on the Cemetery." Pages 107-27 in *Khirbet Qumrân et 'Aïn Feshkha II: Études d'anthropologie, de physique et de chimie. Studies of Anthropology, Physics and Chemistry.* Edited by Jean-Baptiste Humbert and Jan Gunneweg. NTOA.SA 3. Fribourg: Academic Press, 2003.

Olyan, Saul. "Ben Sira's Relationship to the Priesthood." *HTR* 80 (1987): 261-86.

Oppenheimer, Aharon. "Haverim." Pages 333-36 in vol. 1 of *Encyclopedia of the Dead Sea Scrolls.* Edited by Lawrence H. Schiffman and James C. VanderKam. 2 vols. New York: Oxford University Press, 2000.

Ory, Georges. *A la recherche des Esséniens: Essai critique.* Paris: Cercle Ernest-Renan, 1975.

Parente, Fausto, and Joseph Sievers, eds. *Josephus and the History of the Greco-Roman Period: Essays in Memory of Morton Smith.* SPB 41. Leiden: Brill, 1994.

Parry, Donald W., and Eugene Ulrich, eds. *The Provo International Conference on the Dead Sea Scrolls: Technological Innovations, New Texts and Reformulated Issues.* STDJ 30. Leiden: Brill, 1999.

Patrich, Joseph. "Khirbet Qumran in Light of New Archaeological Explorations in the Qumran Caves." Pages 73-95 in *Methods of Investigation of the Dead Sea Scrolls and the Khirbet Qumran Site: Present Realities and Future Prospects.* Edited by Michael O. Wise, Norman Golb, John J. Collins, and Dennis G. Pardee. ANYAS 722. New York: New York Academy of Sciences, 1994.

———. "Did Extra-mural Dwelling Quarters Exist at Qumran?" Pages 720-27 in *The Dead Sea Scrolls: Fifty Years after Their Discovery: Proceedings of the Jerusalem Congress, July 20-25, 1997.* Edited by Lawrence H. Schiffman, Emanuel Tov, and James C. VanderKam. Jerusalem: Israel Exploration Society, 2000.

Paul, André. "Flavius Josèphe et les Esséniens." Pages 126-38 in *The Dead Sea Scrolls: Forty Years of Research.* Edited by Devorah Dimant and Uriel Rappaport. STDJ 10. Leiden: Brill, 1992.

Paul, Shalom M., Robert A. Kraft, Lawrence H. Schiffman, and Weston W. Fields, eds. *Emanuel: Studies in the Hebrew Bible, Septuagint, and Dead Sea Scrolls in Honor of Emanuel Tov.* VTSup 94. Leiden: Brill, 2003.

Petit, Madeleine. "Les Esséens de Philon d'Alexandrie." Pages 139-55 in *The Dead Sea Scrolls: Forty Years of Research.* Edited by Devorah Dimant and Uriel Rappaport. STDJ 10. Leiden: Brill, 1992.

Pfann, Stephen J. "Cryptic Texts." Pages 515-74 in Pfann et al. *Qumran Cave 4. Vol. XXVI: Cryptic Texts and Miscellanea, Part 1.* DJD 36. Oxford: Clarendon, 2000.

———. *The Excavations of Khirbet Qumran and Ain Feshkha: Synthesis of Roland de Vaux's Field Notes.* NTOA 1B. Fribourg: University Press, 2003.

Pfann, Stephen J., et al. *Qumran Cave 4. Vol. XXVI: Cryptic Texts and Miscellanea, Part 1.* DJD 36. Oxford: Clarendon, 2000.

Philip, James A. *Pythagoras and Early Pythagoreanism.* Toronto: University of Toronto Press, 1966.

Plicht, Johannes van der. "Radiocarbon Dating and the Dead Sea Scrolls: A Comment on 'Redating.'" *DSD* 14 (2007): 77-89.

Ploeg, Johannes van der. "The Meals of the Essenes." *JSS* 2 (1957): 163-75.

Politis, Konstantinos D. "The Discovery and Excavation of the Khirbet Qazone Cemetery and Its Significance Relative to Qumran." Pages 213-19 in *Qumran: The Site of the Dead Sea Scrolls: Archaeological Interpretations and Debates.*

Proceedings of a Conference Held at Brown University, November 17-19, 2002. Edited by Katharina Galor, Jean-Baptiste Humbert, and Jürgen Zangenberg. STDJ 57. Leiden: Brill, 2006.

Puech, Émile. *La croyance des Esséniens en la vie future: Immortalité, résurrection, vie éternelle? Histoire d'une croyance dans le Judaïsme ancien.* 2 vols. EBib 21-22. Paris: Gabalda, 1993.

———. "The Necropolis of Khirbet Qumran and ʿAin el-Ghuweir and the Essene Belief in the Afterlife." *BASOR* 312 (1998): 21-36.

———. "L'Ostracon de Khirbet Qumrân (KHQ1996/1) et une vente de terrain à Jéricho, témoin de l'occupation Essénienne à Qumran." Pages 1-29 in *Flores Florentino: Dead Sea Scrolls and Other Early Jewish Studies in Honour of Florentino García Martínez.* Edited by Anthony Hilhorst, Émile Puech, and Eibert Tigchelaar. JSJSup 122. Leiden: Brill, 2007.

Qimron, Elisha. "Celibacy in the Dead Sea Scrolls and the Two Kinds of Sectarians." Pages 287-94 in vol. 1 of *The Madrid Qumran Congress: Proceedings of the International Congress on the Dead Sea Scrolls, Madrid, 18-21 March 1991.* Edited by Julio Trebolle Barrera and Luis Vegas Montaner. 2 vols. STDJ 11. Leiden: Brill, 1992.

———. *The Temple Scroll: A Critical Edition with Extensive Restorations.* Jerusalem: Israel Exploration Society, 1996.

———. "Improving the Editions of the Dead Sea Scrolls" (Hebrew). Pages 135-45 in *Meghillot: Studies in the Dead Sea Scrolls I* (Hebrew). Edited by Moshe Bar-Asher and Devorah Dimant. Jerusalem: Bialik Institute, 2003.

Qimron, Elisha, and John Strugnell. "An Unpublished Halakhic Letter from Qumran." Pages 400-407 in *Biblical Archaeology Today: Proceedings of the International Congress on Biblical Archaeology, Jerusalem, April 1984.* Edited by Janet Amitai. Jerusalem: Israel Exploration Society, 1985.

———. *Qumran Cave 4. Vol. V: Miqṣat Maʿaśe Ha-Torah.* DJD 10. Oxford: Clarendon, 1994.

Rabin, Chaim. *Qumran Studies.* Oxford: Oxford University Press, 1957.

Rajak, Tessa. *Josephus the Historian and His Society.* London: Duckworth, 1983.

———. *The Jewish Dialogue with Greece and Rome: Studies in Cultural and Social Interaction.* AGJU 48. Leiden: Brill, 2002.

———. "Ciò che Flavio Giuseppe Vide: Josephus and the Essenes." Pages 141-60 in *Josephus and the History of the Greco-Roman Period. Essays in Memory of Morton Smith.* Edited by Fausto Parente and Joseph Sievers. SPB 41. Leiden: Brill, 1994. Repr. in pages 219-40 of *The Jewish Dialogue with Greece and Rome: Studies in Cultural and Social Interaction.* AGJU 48. Leiden: Brill, 2002.

Reeves, John C., and John Kampen, eds. *Pursuing the Text: Studies in Honor of Ben*

Zion Wacholder on the Occasion of His Seventieth Birthday. JSOTSup 184. Sheffield: Sheffield Academic Press, 1994.

Regev, Eyal. "The *Yaḥad* and the *Damascus Covenant*: Structure, Organization and Relationship." *RevQ* 21 (2003): 233-62.

―――. "Were the Priests All the Same? Qumranic Halakhah in Comparison with Sadducean Halakhah." *DSD* 12 (2005): 158-88.

―――. *Sectarianism in Qumran: A Cross-Cultural Perspective.* RelSoc 45. Berlin: de Gruyter, 2007.

Reich, Ronny. "Miqwa'ot at Khirbet Qumran and the Jerusalem Connection." Pages 728-31 in *The Dead Sea Scrolls: Fifty Years after Their Discovery: Proceedings of the Jerusalem Congress, July 20-25, 1997.* Edited by Lawrence H. Schiffman, Emanuel Tov, and James C. VanderKam. Jerusalem: Israel Exploration Society, 2000.

Reif, Stefan C. "The Damascus Document from the Cairo Genizah: Its Discovery, Early Study and Historical Significance." Pages 109-31 in *The Damascus Document: A Centennial of Discovery. Proceedings of the Third International Symposium of the Orion Center for the Study of the Dead Sea Scrolls and Associated Literature, 4-8 February, 1998.* Edited by Joseph M. Baumgarten, Esther G. Chazon, and Avital Pinnick. STDJ 34. Leiden: Brill, 2000.

Riaud, Jean. "Les Thérapeutes d'Alexandrie dans la tradition et dans la recherche critique jusqu'aux découvertes de Qumrân." Pages 1189-1295 in *ANRW* 2.20.2. Berlin: de Gruyter, 1987.

Richardson, Peter. *Herod: King of the Jews and Friend of the Romans.* Columbia, SC: University of South Carolina Press, 1996.

Rodgers, Zuleika, ed. *Making History: Josephus and Historical Method.* JSJSup 110. Leiden: Brill, 2007.

Röhrer-Ertl, Olav. "Facts and Results Based on Skeletal Remains from Qumran Found in the *Collectio Kurth*: A Study in Methodology." Pages 181-93 in *Qumran: The Site of the Dead Sea Scrolls: Archaeological Interpretations and Debates. Proceedings of a Conference Held at Brown University, November 17-19, 2002.* Edited by Katharina Galor, Jean-Baptiste Humbert, and Jürgen Zangenberg. STDJ 57. Leiden: Brill, 2006.

Röhrer-Ertl, Olav, Ferdinand Rohrhirsch, and Dietbert Hahn. "Über die Gräbenfelder von Khirbet Qumran insbesondere die Funde der Campagne 1956." *RevQ* 19 (1999): 3-47.

Romm, James S. *The Edges of the Earth in Ancient Thought: Geography, Exploration, and Fiction.* Princeton: Princeton University Press, 1992.

Rooke, Deborah W. *Zadok's Heirs: The Role and Development of the High Priesthood in Ancient Israel.* Oxford: Oxford University Press, 2000.

Roth, Cecil. *The Historical Background of the Dead Sea Scrolls.* Oxford: Blackwell, 1958.

Bibliography

Rowley, Harold Henry. *The Zadokite Fragments and the Dead Sea Scrolls.* Oxford: Alden, 1952.

Sagi, Avi. "'Both Are the Words of the Living God': A Typological Analysis of Halakhic Pluralism." *HUCA* 65 (1995): 105-36.

Sanders, E. P. *Judaism: Practice and Belief 63 BCE–66 CE.* Philadelphia: Trinity Press International, 1992.

Schalit, Abraham. *Namenwörterbuch zu Flavius Josephus.* Leiden: Brill, 1968.

Schechter, Solomon. *Fragments of a Zadokite work edited from Hebrew manuscripts in the Cairo Genizah collection now in the possession of the University Library, Cambridge and provided with an English translation, introduction and notes.* Cambridge: Cambridge University Press, 1910. Repr., with a prolegomenon by Joseph A. Fitzmyer, as *Documents of Jewish Sectaries.* Vol. 1: *Fragments of a Zadokite Work.* New York: Ktav, 1970.

Schiffman, Lawrence H. "Legislation Concerning Relations with Non-Jews in the Zadokite Fragments and in Tannaitic Literature." *RevQ* 11 (1989): 379-89.

———. "The Temple Scroll and the Systems of Jewish Law of the Second Temple Period." Pages 239-55 in *Temple Scroll Studies: Papers Presented at the International Symposium on the Temple Scroll, Manchester, December 1987.* Edited by George J. Brooke. JSPSup 7. Sheffield: Sheffield Academic Press, 1989.

———. *The Eschatological Community of the Dead Sea Scrolls: A Study of the Rule of the Congregation.* SBLMS 38. Atlanta: Scholars Press, 1989.

———. "The Law of Vows and Oaths (Num. 30. 3-15) in the Zadokite Fragments and the Temple Scroll." *RevQ* 15 (1991): 199-214.

———. "The Sadducean Origins of the Dead Sea Scrolls." Pages 35-49 in *Understanding the Dead Sea Scrolls: A Reader from the* Biblical Archaeology Review. Edited by Hershel Shanks. New York: Random House, 1992.

———. "Pharisees and Sadducees in *Pesher Nahum.*" Pages 272-90 in *Minhah leNahum: Biblical and Other Studies Presented to Nahum M. Sarna in Honour of His 70th Birthday.* Edited by Marc Brettler and Michael Fishbane. JSOTSup 154. Sheffield: Sheffield Academic Press, 1993.

———. *Reclaiming the Dead Sea Scrolls.* Philadelphia: Jewish Publication Society, 1994.

———. "The Place of 4QMMT in the Corpus of Qumran Manuscripts." Pages 90-94 in *Reading 4QMMT: New Perspectives on Qumran Law and History.* Edited by John Kampen and Moshe J. Bernstein. SBLSymS 2. Atlanta: Scholars Press, 1996.

———. "Community Without Temple: The Qumran Community's Withdrawal from the Jerusalem Temple." Pages 267-84 in *Gemeinde ohne Tempel/Community without Temple: Zur Substituierung und Transformation des Jerusalemer Tempels und seines Kults im Alten Testament, antiken Judentum und frühen Christentum.* Edited by Beate Ego, Armin Lange, and Peter Pilhofer. Tübingen: Mohr Siebeck, 1999.

———. "The Zadokite Fragments and the Temple Scroll." Pages 133-45 in *The Damascus Document: A Centennial of Discovery. Proceedings of the Third International Symposium of the Orion Center for the Study of the Dead Sea Scrolls and Associated Literature, 4-8 February, 1998.* Edited by Joseph M. Baumgarten, Esther G. Chazon, and Avital Pinnick. STDJ 34. Leiden: Brill, 2000.

———, ed. *Archaeology and History in the Dead Sea Scrolls: The New York University Conference in Memory of Yigael Yadin.* JSPSup 8. Sheffield: JSOT Press, 1989.

Schiffman, Lawrence H., and James C. VanderKam, eds. *Encyclopedia of the Dead Sea Scrolls.* 2 vols. New York: Oxford University Press, 2000.

Schiffman, Lawrence H., Emanuel Tov, and James C. VanderKam, eds. *The Dead Sea Scrolls: Fifty Years after Their Discovery: Proceedings of the Jerusalem Congress, July 20-25, 1997.* Jerusalem: Israel Exploration Society, 2000.

Schneider, Carl. "Zur Problematik des Hellenistischen in den Qumrāntexten." Pages 299-314 in *Qumran-Probleme.* Edited by Hans Bardtke. Berlin: Akademie, 1963.

Schofield, Alison. "Rereading S: A New Model of Textual Development in Light of the Cave 4 *Serekh* Copies." *DSD* 15 (2008): 96-120.

———. *From Qumran to the Yaḥad: A New Paradigm of Textual Development for The Community Rule.* STDJ 77. Leiden: Brill, 2009.

Schofield, Alison, and James C. VanderKam. "Were the Hasmoneans Zadokites?" *JBL* 124 (2005): 73-87.

Schremer, Adiel. "The Name of the Boethusians: A Reconsideration of Suggested Explanations and Another One." *JJS* 48 (1998): 290-99.

———. "Qumran Polemic on Marital Law: CD 4:20–5:11 and Its Social Background." Pages 147-60 in *The Damascus Document: A Centennial of Discovery. Proceedings of the Third International Symposium of the Orion Center for the Study of the Dead Sea Scrolls and Associated Literature, 4-8 February, 1998.* Edited by J. M. Baumgarten, Esther G. Chazon, and Avital Pinnick. STDJ 34. Leiden: Brill, 2000.

Schultz, Brian. "The Qumran Cemetery: 150 Years of Research." *DSD* 13 (2006): 194-228.

Schürer, Emil. *The History of the Jewish People in the Age of Jesus Christ (175 B.C.– A.D. 135).* Revised and edited by Geza Vermes, Fergus Millar, and Martin Goodman. 3 vols. in 4. Edinburgh: T&T Clark, 1973–87.

Schwartz, Daniel R. "Josephus and Nicolaus on the Pharisees." *JSJ* 13 (1983): 157-71.

———. "On Two Aspects of a Priestly View of Descent at Qumran." Pages 157-79 in *Archaeology and History in the Dead Sea Scrolls: The New York University*

Conference in Memory of Yigael Yadin. Edited by Lawrence H. Schiffman. JSPSup 8. Sheffield: JSOT Press, 1990.

Schwartz, Seth. *Imperialism and Jewish Society, 200 B.C.E. to 640 C.E.* Princeton: Princeton University Press, 2001.

Segal, Michael. *The Book of Jubilees: Rewritten Bible, Redaction, Ideology and Theology.* JSJSup 117. Leiden: Brill, 2007.

Seim, Turid Karlsen, and Jarunn Økland, eds. *Metamorphoses: Resurrection, Body and Transformative Practices in Early Christianity.* Berlin: de Gruyter, 2009.

Shanks, Hershel, ed. *Understanding the Dead Sea Scrolls.* New York: Random House, 1992.

Sheridan, Susan Guise, and Jaime Ullinger. "A Reconsideration of the Human Remains in the French Collection from Qumran." Pages 195-212 in *Qumran: The Site of the Dead Sea Scrolls: Archaeological Interpretations and Debates. Proceedings of a Conference Held at Brown University, November 17-19, 2002.* Edited by Katharina Galor, Jean-Baptiste Humbert, and Jürgen Zangenberg. STDJ 57. Leiden: Brill, 2006.

Sievers, Joseph. "Josephus and the Afterlife." Pages 20-34 in *Understanding Josephus: Seven Perspectives.* Edited by Steve Mason. JSPSup 32. Sheffield: Sheffield Academic Press, 1998.

————. "Josephus, First Maccabees, Sparta, the Three Haireseis — and Cicero." *JSJ* 32 (2001): 24-51.

Sivertsev, Alexei. "Sects and Households: Social Structure of the Proto-Sectarian Movement of Nehemiah 10 and the Dead Sea Sect." *CBQ* 67 (2005): 59-78.

————. *Households, Sects, and the Origins of Rabbinic Judaism.* JSJSup 102. Leiden: Brill, 2005.

Smith, Morton. "The Description of the Essenes in Josephus and the Philosophumena." *HUCA* 29 (1958): 273-313.

————. "The Dead Sea Sect in Relation to Ancient Judaism." *New Testament Studies* 7 (1961): 347-60.

————. "Helios in Palestine." *ErIsr* 16 (1982): 199*-214*.

Stark, Rodney, and William Sims Bainbridge. *The Future of Religion: Secularization, Revival and Cult Formation.* Berkeley: University of California Press, 1985.

————. *A Theory of Religion.* Toronto Studies in Religion 2. New York: Lang, 1987.

————. *Religion, Deviance and Social Control.* London: Routledge, 1996.

Steckoll, Solomon H. "Preliminary Excavation Report on the Qumran Cemetery." *RevQ* 6 (1968): 323-36.

Stegemann, Hartmut. *Die Entstehung der Qumran Gemeinde.* Bonn: published privately, 1971.

————. "The Qumran Essenes — Local Members of the Main Jewish Union in Late Second Temple Times." Pages 83-166 in vol. 1 of *The Madrid Qumran*

Congress: Proceedings of the International Congress on the Dead Sea Scrolls, Madrid, 18-21 March 1991. Edited by Julio Trebolle Barrera and Luis Vegas Montanerin. 2 vols. STDJ 11. Leiden: Brill, 1992.

———. "Some Remarks to 1QSa, 1QSb, and Qumran Messianism." *RevQ* 17 (1996): 479-505.

———. *The Library of Qumran: On the Essenes, Qumran, John the Baptist, and Jesus.* Grand Rapids: Eerdmans, 1998.

———. "Towards Physical Reconstructions of the Qumran Damascus Document Scrolls." Pages 177-200 in *The Damascus Document: A Centennial of Discovery. Proceedings of the Third International Symposium of the Orion Center for the Study of the Dead Sea Scrolls and Associated Literature, 4-8 February, 1998).* Edited by Joseph M. Baumgarten, Esther G. Chazon, and Avital Pinnick. STDJ 34. Leiden: Brill, 2000.

Sterling, Gregory E. *Historiography and Self-Definition: Josephos, Luke-Acts and Apologetic Historiography.* Novum Testamentum Supplement 64. Leiden: Brill, 1992.

———. "'Athletes of Virtue': An Analysis of the Summaries in Acts (2:41-47; 4:32-35; 5:12-16)." *JBL* 113 (1994): 679-96.

Stern, Menahem. *Greek and Latin Authors on Jews and Judaism.* 3 vols. Jerusalem: Israel Academy of Sciences and Humanities, 1974–84.

Steudel, Annette. "אחרית הימים in the Texts from Qumran." *RevQ* 16 (1993): 225-46.

———. *Der Midrasch zur Eschatologie aus der Qumrangemeinde (4QMidr-Eschat[a,b]).* STDJ 13. Leiden: Brill, 1994.

Stökl Ben Ezra, Daniel. "Old Caves and Young Caves: A Statistical Reevaluation of a Qumran Consensus." *DSD* 14 (2007): 313-33.

Stone, Michael E., ed. *Jewish Writings of the Second Temple Period: Apocrypha, Pseudepigrapha, Qumran Sectarian Writings, Philo, Josephus.* CRINT 2/2. Philadelphia: Fortress, 1984.

Stone, Michael E., and Esther G. Chazon, eds. *Biblical Perspectives: Early Use and Interpretation of the Bible in Light of the Dead Sea Scrolls.* STDJ 28. Leiden: Brill, 1998.

Strecker, Georg, ed. *Aufsätze und kleine Schriften.* Tübingen: Mohr Siebeck, 1967.

Strugnell, John. "MMT: Second Thoughts on a Forthcoming Edition." Pages 57-73 in *The Community of the Renewed Covenant: The Notre Dame Symposium on the Dead Sea Scrolls.* Edited by Eugene Ulrich and James VanderKam. CJA 9. Notre Dame, IN: University of Notre Dame Press, 1994.

Strugnell, John, and Daniel J. Harrington. "Qumran Cave 4 Texts: A New Publication." *JBL* 112 (1993): 491-99.

Stuckenbruck, Loren T. "Temporal Shifts from Text to Interpretation: Concerning the Use of the Perfect and Imperfect in the *Habakkuk Pesher* (1QpHab)."

Pages 124-49 in *Qumran Studies: New Approaches, New Questions*. Edited by Michael Thomas Davis and Brent A. Strawn. Grand Rapids: Eerdmans, 2007.

Sukenik, Eleazar L. *Megillot Genuzot mi-Tokh Genizah Qedumah she-Nimṣe'ah be-Midbar Yehudah: Seqirah Rishonah.* Jerusalem: Bialik Institute, 1948.

Sussmann, Ya'akov. "Appendix 1: The History of the Halakha and the Dead Sea Scrolls." Pages 179-200 in Elisha Qimron and John Strugnell, *Qumran Cave 4.* Vol. V: *Miqṣat Ma'aśe Ha-Torah.* DJD 10. Oxford: Clarendon, 1994.

Sutcliffe, Edmund F. "The First Fifteen Members of the Qumran Community." *JSS* 4 (1959): 134-38.

Talmon, Shemaryahu. "Yom hakippurim in the Habakkuk Scroll." *Biblica* 32 (1951): 549-63.

————. *The World of Qumran from Within: Collected Studies.* Jerusalem: Magnes, 1989.

————. "The Community of the Renewed Covenant." Pages 3-24 in *The Community of the Renewed Covenant: The Notre Dame Symposium on the Dead Sea Scrolls.* Edited by Eugene Ulrich and James VanderKam. CJA 10. Notre Dame, IN: University of Notre Dame Press, 1994.

————. "Calendars and Mishmarot." Pages 108-17 in vol. 1 of *Encyclopedia of the Dead Sea Scrolls.* Edited by Lawrence H. Schiffman and James C. VanderKam. 2 vols. New York: Oxford, 2000.

Tantlevskij, Igor R. *The Two Wicked Priests in the Qumran Commentary on Habakkuk.* QC Appendix C. Kraków: Enigma, 1995.

Taylor, Joan E. "The Cemeteries of Khirbet Qumran and Women's Presence at the Site." *DSD* 6 (1999): 285-323.

————. "Khirbet Qumran in the Nineteenth Century and the Name of the Site." *PEQ* 134 (2002): 144-64.

————. *Jewish Women Philosophers of First-Century Alexandria: Philo's 'Therapeutae' Reconsidered.* Oxford: Oxford University Press, 2003.

————. "Khirbet Qumran in Period III." Pages 133-46 in *Qumran: The Site of the Dead Sea Scrolls: Archaeological Interpretations and Debates. Proceedings of a Conference Held at Brown University, November 17-19, 2002.* Edited by Katharina Galor, Jean-Baptiste Humbert, and Jürgen Zangenberg. STDJ 57. Leiden: Brill, 2006.

————. "Philo of Alexandria on the Essenes: A Case Study of the Use of Classical Sources in Discussions of the Qumran-Essene Hypothesis." *SPA* 19 (2007): 1-28.

Taylor, Justin. *Pythagoreans and Essenes: Structural Parallels.* Collection de la Revue des Études Juives 32. Leuven: Peeters, 2004.

Testuz, Michel. *Les idées religieuses du livre des Jubilés.* Geneva: Minard, 1960.

Thiering, Barbara E. *Redating the Teacher of Righteousness*. Sydney: Theological Explorations, 1979.

⸻. *The Qumran Origins of the Christian Church*. Sydney: Theological Explorations, 1983.

Thompson, Margaret, Otto Mørkholm, and Colin M. Kraay. *An Inventory of Greek Coin Hoards*. New York: American Numismatic Society, 1973.

Tierney, John J. "The Map of Agrippa." *Proceedings of the Royal Irish Academy* 63-C no. 4 (1963): 151-66.

Tigchelaar, Eibert. "The White Dress of the Essenes and Pythagoreans." Pages 301-21 in *Jerusalem, Alexandria, Rome: Studies in Honour of A. Hilhorst*. Edited by Florentino García Martínez and Gerard P. Luttikhuizen. JSJSup 82. Leiden: Brill, 2003.

Tov, Emanuel, ed. *The Texts from the Judaean Desert: Indices and an Introduction to the Discoveries in the Judaean Desert Series*. DJD 39. Oxford: Clarendon, 2002.

Ullmann-Margalit, Edna. *Out of the Cave: A Philosophical Inquiry into the Dead Sea Scrolls Research*. Cambridge: Harvard University Press, 2006.

Ulrich, Eugene, and James VanderKam, eds. *The Community of the Renewed Covenant: The Notre Dame Symposium on the Dead Sea Scrolls*. CJA 10. Notre Dame, IN: University of Notre Dame Press, 1994.

VanderKam, James C. "The Temple Scroll and the Book of Jubilees." Pages 211-36 in *Temple Scroll Studies*. Edited by George J. Brooke. JSPSup 7. Sheffield: Sheffield Academic Press, 1989.

⸻. *The Book of Jubilees*. Leuven: Peeters, 1989.

⸻. "The People of the Dead Sea Scrolls: Essenes or Sadducees?" Pages 50-62 in *Understanding the Dead Sea Scrolls*. Edited by Hershel Shanks. New York: Random House, 1992.

⸻. *The Dead Sea Scrolls Today*. Grand Rapids: Eerdmans, 1994.

⸻. "Identity and History of the Community." Pages 487-533 in vol. 2 of *The Dead Sea Scrolls after Fifty Years: A Comprehensive Assessment*. Edited by Peter W. Flint and James C. VanderKam. 2 vols. Leiden: Brill, 1998–99.

⸻. *Calendars in the Dead Sea Scrolls: Measuring Time*. London: Routledge, 1998.

⸻. "Those Who Look for Smooth Things, Pharisees, and Oral Law." Pages 465-77 in *Emanuel: Studies in Hebrew Bible, Septuagint, and Dead Sea Scrolls in Honor of Emanuel Tov*. Edited by Shalom M. Paul, Robert A. Kraft, Lawrence H. Schiffman, and Weston W. Fields. VTSup 94. Leiden: Brill, 2003.

⸻. *From Joshua to Caiaphas: High Priests after the Exile*. Minneapolis: Fortress, 2004.

VanderKam, James C., and Peter Flint. *The Meaning of the Dead Sea Scrolls*. San Francisco: HarperSanFrancisco, 2002.

Vaux, Roland de. *Archaeology and the Dead Sea Scrolls.* Translated by David Bourke. Schweich Lectures on Biblical Archaeology. Oxford: Oxford University Press, 1973.

Vermes, Geza. *Les manuscrits du désert de Juda.* 2nd ed. Paris: Desclée, 1954. (1st ed. 1953.)

———. "The Etymology of 'Essenes.'" *RevQ* 2 (1960): 427-43.

———. *Scripture and Tradition in Judaism: Haggadic Studies.* SPB 4. Leiden: Brill, 1973.

———. "Preliminary Remarks on Unpublished Fragments of the Community Rule from Qumran Cave 4." *JJS* 42 (1991): 250-55.

———. "The Leadership of the Qumran Community: Sons of Zadok — Priests — Congregation." Pages 375-84 in vol. 1 of *Geschichte-Tradition-Reflexion: Festschrift für Martin Hengel zum 70. Geburtstag.* Edited by Hubert Cancik, Hermann Lichtenberger, and Peter Schaefer. 3 vols. Tübingen: Mohr Siebeck, 1996.

———. "Eschatological Worldview in the Dead Sea Scrolls and in the New Testament." Pages 479-94 in *Emanuel: Studies in the Hebrew Bible, Septuagint, and Dead Sea Scrolls in Honor of Emanuel Tov.* Edited by Shalom M. Paul, Robert A. Kraft, Lawrence H. Schiffman, and Weston W. Fields. VTSup 94. Leiden: Brill, 2003.

———. *The Complete Dead Sea Scrolls in English.* Rev. ed. London: Penguin, 2004.

Vermes, Geza, and Martin Goodman, eds. *The Essenes According to the Classical Sources.* Sheffield: Sheffield Academic Press, 1989.

Wacholder, Ben Zion. *Nicolaus of Damascus.* University of California Publications in History 75. Berkeley: University of California Press, 1962.

———. *The Dawn of Qumran: The Sectarian Torah and the Teacher of Righteousness.* Monographs of Hebrew Union College 8. Cincinnati: Hebrew Union College, 1983.

———. "Does Qumran Record the Death of the *Moreh?* The Meaning of *he'aseph* in *Damascus Covenant* XIX,35, XX,14." *RevQ* 13 (Carmignac Memorial) (1988): 323-30.

———. *The New Damascus Document: The Midrash on the Eschatological Torah of the Dead Sea Scrolls: Reconstruction, Translation and Commentary.* STDJ 56. Leiden: Brill, 2007.

Wagner, Siegfried. *Die Essener in der wissenschaftlichen Diskussion vom Ausgang des 18. bis zum Beginn des 20. Jahrhunderts.* BZAW 79. Berlin: de Gruyter, 1960.

Walker-Ramisch, Sandra. "Graeco-Roman Voluntary Associations and the Damascus Document." Pages 128-45 in *Voluntary Associations in the Graeco-Roman World.* Edited by John S. Kloppenborg and Stephen G. Wilson. London: Routledge, 1996.

Wankel, Hermann, et al., eds., *Die Inschriften von Ephesos*. Bonn: Rudolf Habelt, 1979–84.

Wassen, Cecilia. *Women in the Damascus Document*. SBLAB 21. Leiden: Brill, 2005.

Wassen, Cecilia, and Jutta Jokiranta. "Groups in Tension: Sectarianism in the Damascus Document and the Community Rule." Pages 205-45 in *Sectarianism in Early Judaism: Sociological Advances*. Edited by David J. Chalcraft. London: Equinox, 2007.

Webster, Brian. "Chronological Index of the Texts from the Judaean Desert." Pages 351-446 in *The Texts from the Judaean Desert: Indices and an Introduction to the Discoveries in the Judaean Desert Series*. Edited by Emanuel Tov. DJD 39. Oxford: Clarendon, 2002.

Weinfeld, Moshe. *The Organizational Pattern and the Penal Code of the Qumran Sect: A Comparison with the Guilds and Religious Associations of the Hellenistic Period*. NTOA 2. Fribourg: Éditions Universitaires, 1986.

Weissenberg, Hanne von. "4QMMT: The Problem of the Epilogue." Ph.D. diss., Helsinki, 2006.

Wernberg-Møeller, Preben. *The Manual of Discipline: Translated and Annotated with an Introduction*. STDJ 1. Leiden: Brill, 1957.

White, Hayden. *Metahistory: The Historical Imagination in Nineteenth-Century Europe*. Baltimore: Johns Hopkins University Press, 1973.

———. *Tropics of Discourse*. Baltimore: Johns Hopkins University Press, 1978.

Williams, David S. *Stylometric Studies in Flavius Josephus and Related Literature*. Jewish Studies 12. Lewiston, NY: Edwin Mellen, 1992.

———. "Josephus and the Authorship of *War* 2.119-61 (on the Essenes)." *JSJ* 25 (1994): 207-21.

Wilson, Stephen G., and Michel Desjardins, eds. *Text and Artifact in the Religions of Mediterranean Antiquity: Essays in Honour of Peter Richardson*. Waterloo: Wilfrid Laurier University Press, 2000.

Wise, Michael O. *A Critical Study of the Temple Scroll from Qumran Cave 11*. Studies in Ancient Oriental Civilization 49. Chicago: Oriental Institute of the University of Chicago, 1990.

———. "The Teacher of Righteousness and the High Priest of the Intersacerdotium: Two Approaches." *RevQ* 14 (1990): 587-614.

———. *The First Messiah: Investigating the Savior before Jesus*. San Francisco: HarperSanFrancisco, 1999.

———. "Dating the Teacher of Righteousness and the *Floruit* of His Movement." *JBL* 122 (2003): 53-87.

Wise, Michael O., Norman Golb, John J. Collins, and Dennis G. Pardee, eds. *Methods of Investigation of the Dead Sea Scrolls and the Khirbet Qumran Site: Present Realities and Future Prospects*. ANYAS 722. New York: New York Academy of Sciences, 1994.

Wise, Michael O., Martin Abegg, and Ed Cook. *The Dead Sea Scrolls: A New Translation.* San Francisco: HarperSanFrancisco, 1996.

Wood, Bryant G. "To Dip or Sprinkle? The Qumran Cisterns in Perspective." *BASOR* 256 (1984): 45-60.

Woude, Adam S van der. "Wicked Priest or Wicked Priests? Reflections on the Identification of the Wicked Priest in the Habakkuk Commentary." *JJS* 33 (Yadin Festschrift) (1982): 349-59.

————. "Once Again: The Wicked Priests in the *Habakkuk Pesher* from Cave 1 of Qumran." *RevQ* 17 (1996): 375-84.

————, ed. *The Book of Daniel in the Light of New Findings.* BETL 106. Leuven: Peeters, 1993.

Wright, George Ernest, ed. *The Bible and the Ancient Near East: Essays in Honor of William Foxwell Albright.* Garden City, NY: Doubleday, 1961.

Yadin, Yigael. *The Temple Scroll.* 3 vols. in 4. Jerusalem: Israel Exploration Society, 1977-83.

Yardeni, Ada. "A Draft of a Deed on an Ostracon from Khirbet Qumrân." *IEJ* 47 (1997): 233-37.

————. "Breaking the Missing Link: Cross and Eshel Misread the Qumran Ostracon Relating the Settlement to the Dead Sea Scrolls." *BAR* 24/3 (1998): 44-47.

Yellin, Joseph, Magen Broshi, and Hanan Eshel. "Pottery of Qumran and Ein Ghuweir: The First Chemical Exploration of Provenience." *BASOR* 321 (2001): 65-78.

Zangenberg, Jürgen. "Bones of Contention: 'New' Bones from Qumran Help Settle Old Questions (and Raise New Ones): Remarks on Two Recent Conferences." *QC* 9 (2000): 51-76.

————. "Opening Up Our View: Khirbet Qumran in a Regional Perspective." Pages 170-87 in *Religion and Society in Roman Palestine: Old Questions, New Approaches.* Edited by Douglas R. Edwards. London: Routledge, 2004.

Zeller, Eduard. *Philosophie der Griechen in ihrer geschichtlichen Entwicklung,* vol. 2. Leipzig: Riesland, 1923.

Zeuner, Frederick E. "Notes on Qumran." *PEQ* 92 (1960): 27-36.

Zias, Joseph E. "The Cemeteries of Qumran and Celibacy: Confusion Laid to Rest?" *DSD* 7 (2000): 220-53.

Zissu, Boaz. "'Qumran Type' Graves in Jerusalem: Archaeological Evidence of an Essene Community?" *DSD* 5 (1998): 158-71.

————. "Odd Tomb Out: Has Jerusalem's Essene Cemetery Been Found?" *BAR* 25/2 (1999): 50-55, 62.

Index of Modern Authors

Index of Ancient Names and Sobriquets

Index of Scripture and Other Ancient Sources

7648